Workshop on Deep Linguistic Processing 2007

Held in conjunction with ACL 2007

Prague, Czech Republic
28 June 2007

ISBN: 978-1-61738-519-3

Printed from e-media with permission by:

Curran Associates, Inc.
57 Morehouse Lane
Red Hook, NY 12571
www.proceedings.com

Some format issues inherent in the e-media version may also appear in this print version.

Printed by Curran Associates, Inc. (2010)

Association for Computational Linguistics
209 N. Eighth Street
Stroudsburg, Pennsylvania 18360

Phone: 1-570-476-8006
Fax: 1-570-476-0860

acl@aclweb.org

Preface

This workshop was conceived with the aim of bringing together the different computational linguistic sub-communities which model language predominantly by way of theoretical syntax, either in the form of a particular theory (e.g. CCG, HPSG, LFG, TAG or the Prague School) or a more general framework which draws on theoretical and descriptive linguistics. We characterise this style of computational linguistic research as deep linguistic processing, due to it aspiring to model the complexity of natural language in rich linguistic representations. Aspects of this research have in the past had their own separate fora, such as the ACL 2005 workshop on deep lexical acquisition, as well as TAG+, Alpino, ParGram and DELPH-IN meetings. However, since the fundamental approach of building a linguistically-founded system, as well as many of the techniques used to engineer efficient systems, are common across these projects and independent of the specific grammar formalism chosen, we felt the need for a common meeting in which experiences could be shared among a wider community.

Deep linguistic processing has traditionally been concerned with grammar development for parsing and generation, with many deep processing systems using the same grammar for both directions. The linguistic precision and complexity of the grammars meant that they had to be manually developed and maintained, and were computationally expensive to run. With recent developments in computer hardware, parsing and generation algorithms and statistical learning theory, the way has been opened for deep linguistic processing to be successfully applied to an ever-growing range of languages, domains and applications.

The same trends that have made broad-coverage deep linguistic processing feasible have occurred at the same time as the rise of machine learning and statistical approaches to natural language processing. For a time, these two approaches were pursued separately, often without reference to advances in the other approach, even when the same problems were being addressed. In the past couple of years, this divide has begun to close from both sides. As witnessed by many of the papers in this workshop, many deep systems have statistical components to them (e.g., as pre- or post-processing to control ambiguity, as means of acquiring and extending lexical resources) or even use machine learning techniques to acquire deep grammars (semi-)automatically. From the other side of the divide, many of the largely statistical approaches are using progressively richer linguistic based features and are taking advantage of these deeper features to tackle problems traditionally reserved for deep systems, such as thematic role labelling.

The workshop has indeed brought together a range of theoretical perspectives, not just those originally foreseen. The papers presented cover current approaches to grammar development and issues of theoretical properties, as well as the application of deep linguistic techniques to large-scale applications such as question answering and dialogue systems. Having industrial-scale, efficient parsers and generators opens up new application domains for natural language processing, as well as interesting new ways in which to approach existing applications, e.g., by combining statistical and deep processing techniques in a triage process to process massive data quickly and accurately at a fine level of detail. Notably, several of the papers addressed the relationship of deep linguistic processing to topical statistical approaches, in particular in the area of parsing.

There were 45 submissions to the workshop, each of which was peer reviewed by three members of the international programme committee; at the end of the process 10 were accepted as papers to be presented orally and 10 as posters. We feel that such a large number of submissions for a one-day workshop reflects an increasing interest in deep linguistic processing, an interest which is buoyed by the realization that new, often hybrid, techniques combined with highly engineered parsers and generators and state-of-the-art machines open the way towards practical, real-world application of this research. We look forward to further opportunities for the different computational linguistic sub-communities who took part in this workshop, and others, to come together in the future.

We would like to thank all the authors who submitted papers, as well as the members of the programme committee for the time and effort they contributed in reviewing the papers, in some cases at very short notice. We should also like to thank Anette Frank for providing the perfect complement to the workshop with her invited talk.

The workshop received sponsorship from the Large Scale Syntactic Annotation of written Dutch (Lassy) project. The Lassy project is carried out within the STEVIN programme, which is funded by the Dutch and Flemish governments (`http://taalunieversum.org/taal/technologie/stevin/`).

Timothy Baldwin
Mark Dras
Julia Hockenmaier
Tracy Holloway King
Gertjan van Noord

Organizers

Chairs:

Timothy Baldwin (University of Melbourne)
Mark Dras (Macquarie University)
Julia Hockenmaier (University of Pennsylvania)
Tracy Holloway King (PARC)
Gertjan van Noord (University of Groningen)

Program Committee:

Jason Baldridge (University of Texas at Austin)
Emily Bender (University of Washington)
Raffaella Bernardi (University of Bolzano)
Francis Bond (NICT)
Gosse Bouma (University of Groningen)
Ted Briscoe (University of Cambridge)
Miriam Butt (University of Konstanz)
Aoife Cahill (Stuttgart University)
David Chiang (ISI)
Stephen Clark (Oxford University)
Ann Copestake (University of Cambridge)
James Curran (University of Sydney)
Stefanie Dipper (Potsdam University)
Katrin Erk (University of Texas at Austin)
Dominique Estival (Appen Pty Ltd)
Dan Flickinger (Stanford University)
Anette Frank (University of Heidelberg)
Josef van Genabith (Dublin City University)
John Hale (Michigan State University)
Ben Hutchinson (Google)
Mark Johnson (Brown University)
Aravind Joshi (University of Pennsylvania)
Laura Kallmeyer (Tübingen University)
Ron Kaplan (Powerset)
Martin Kay (Stanford University/Saarland University)
Valia Kordoni (Saarland University)
Anna Korhonen (University of Cambridge)
Jonas Kuhn (Potsdam University)
Rob Malouf (San Diego State University)
Ryan McDonald (Google)
Yusuke Miyao (University of Tokyo)
Diego Molla (Macquarie University)

Stefan Müller (Bremen University)
Joakim Nivre (Växjö University)
Stephan Oepen (University of Oslo and Stanford University)
Anoop Sarkar (Simon Fraser University)
David Schlangen (Potsdam University)
Mark Steedman (University of Edinburgh)
Beata Trawinski (Tübingen University)
Aline Villavicencio (Federal University of Rio Grande do Sul)
Tom Wasow (Stanford University)
Michael White (Ohio State University)
Shuly Wintner (University of Haifa)
Fei Xia (University of Washington)

Invited Speaker:

Anette Frank (University of Heidelberg)

Table of Contents

Conference Program

08:35–08:45 Opening Remarks

Session 1: Parsing

08:45–09:15 *Multi-Component Tree Adjoining Grammars, Dependency Graph Models, and Linguistic Analyses*
Joan Chen-Main and Aravind Joshi

09:15–09:45 *Perceptron Training for a Wide-Coverage Lexicalized-Grammar Parser*
Stephen Clark and James Curran

09:45–10:15 *Filling Statistics with Linguistics – Property Design for the Disambiguation of German LFG Parses*
Martin Forst

10:15–10:45 *Exploiting Semantic Information for HPSG Parse Selection*
Sanae Fujita, Francis Bond, Stephan Oepen and Takaaki Tanaka

10:45–11:15 Coffee Break

Session 2: Applications of Deep Linguistic Processing

11:15–11:45 *Deep Grammars in a Tree Labeling Approach to Syntax-based Statistical Machine Translation*
Mark Hopkins and Jonas Kuhn

11:45–12:15 *Question Answering based on Semantic Roles*
Michael Kaisser and Bonnie Webber

12:15–13:45 Lunch

13:45–14:45 Invited Talk

Across Languages and Grammar Paradigms – New Perspectives on Resource Acquisition, Grammar Engineering and Application
Anette Frank

SESSION 3: POSTERS

14:45–15:45 *Deep Linguistic Processing for Spoken Dialogue Systems*
James Allen, Myroslava Dzikovska, Mehdi Manshadi and Mary Swift

Self- or Pre-Tuning? Deep Linguistic Processing of Language Variants
Branco António and Costa Francisco

Pruning the Search Space of a Hand-Crafted Parsing System with a Probabilistic Parser
Aoife Cahill, Tracy Holloway King and John T. Maxwell III

Semantic Composition with (Robust) Minimal Recursion Semantics
Ann Copestake

A Task-based Comparison of Information Extraction Pattern Models
Mark Greenwood and Mark Stevenson

Creating a Systemic Functional Grammar Corpus from the Penn Treebank
Matthew Honnibal and James R. Curran

Verb Valency Semantic Representation for Deep Linguistic Processing
Aleš Horák, Karel Pala, Marie Duží and Pavel Materna

The Spanish Resource Grammar: Pre-processing Strategy and Lexical Acquisition
Montserrat Marimon, Nria Bel, Sergio Espeja and Natalia Seghezzi

Extracting a Verb Lexicon for Deep Parsing from FrameNet
Mark McConville and Myroslava O. Dzikovska

Fips, A "Deep" Linguistic Multilingual Parser
Eric Wehrli

Partial Parse Selection for Robust Deep Processing
Yi Zhang, Valia Kordoni and Erin Fitzgerald

15:45–16:15 COFFEE BREAK

Session 4: Grammar Engineering

Multi-Component Tree Adjoining Grammars, Dependency Graph Models, and Linguistic Analyses

Joan Chen-Main* and Aravind K. Joshi*⁺
*Institute for Research in Cognitive Science, and
⁺Dept of Computer and Information Science
University of Pennsylvania
Philadelphia, PA 19104-6228
{chenmain,joshi}@seas.upenn.edu

Abstract

Recent work identifies two properties that appear particularly relevant to the characterization of graph-based dependency models of syntactic structure[1]: the absence of interleaving substructures (*well-nestedness*) and a bound on a type of discontinuity (*gap-degree* ≤ 1) successfully describe more than 99% of the structures in two dependency treebanks (Kuhlmann and Nivre 2006).[2] Bodirsky et al. (2005) establish that every dependency structure with these two properties can be recast as a lexicalized Tree Adjoining Grammar (LTAG) derivation and vice versa. However, multi-component extensions of TAG (MC-TAG), argued to be necessary on linguistic grounds, induce dependency structures that do not conform to these two properties (Kuhlmann and Möhl 2006). In this paper, we observe that several types of MC-TAG as used for linguistic analysis are more restrictive than the formal system is in principle. In particular, tree-local MC-TAG, tree-local MC-TAG with *flexible composition* (Kallmeyer and Joshi 2003), and special cases of set-local TAG as used to describe certain linguistic phenomena satisfy the well-nested and gap degree ≤ 1 criteria. We also observe that gap degree can distinguish between prohibited and allowed *wh*-extractions in English, and report some preliminary work comparing the predictions of the graph approach and the MC-TAG approach to scrambling.

1 Introduction

Bodirsky et al. (2005) introduce a class of graphical dependency models, called *graph drawings* (which differ from standard dependency structures), that are equivalent to lexicalized Tree Adjoining Grammar (LTAG) derivations (Joshi and Schabes 1997). Whereas TAG is a generative framework in which each well-formed expression corresponds with a legitimate derivation in that system, the graph drawing approach provides a set of structures and a set of constraints on well-formedness. Bodirsky et al. offer the class of graph drawings that satisfy these constraints as a model-based perspective on TAG. Section 2 summarizes this relationship between TAG derivations and these graph drawings.

In related work, Kuhlmann and Nivre (2006) evaluate a number of constraints that have been proposed to restrict the class of dependency structures characterizing natural language with respect to two dependency treebanks: the Prague Dependency Treebank (PDT) (Hajič et al., 2001) and the Danish Dependency Treebank (DDT) (Kromann, 2003). The results indicate that two properties provide good coverage of the structures in both

[1] Whereas weak equivalence of grammar classes is only concerned with string sets and fails to shed light on equivalence at the structural level, our work involves the equivalence of derivations and graph based models of dependencies. Thus, our work is relevant to certain aspects of grammar engineering that weak equivalence does not speak to.

[2] These properties hold for many of the so-called non-projective dependency structures and the corresponding non-context free structures associated with TAG, further allowing CKY type dynamic programming approaches to parsing to these dependency graphs.

Proceedings of the 5th Workshop on Important Unresolved Matters, pages 1–8,
Ann Arbor, June 2005.

treebanks.[3] The first is a binary *well-nestedness* constraint.[4] The other is a bound on *gap degree*, a graded measure of discontinuity. These results are given in Table 1. What is noteworthy is that the graph drawings which correspond to LTAG derivations share these two properties: LTAG induced graph drawings are both well-nested and have gap degree ≤ 1, and for every graph drawing that is both well-nested and gap degree ≤ 1, there exists a corresponding LTAG derivation (Möhl 2006). In section 3, these two properties are defined.

property	Danish Dep. Treebank	Prague Dep. Tree-bank
all structures	n = 4393	n = 73088
well-nested	99.89%	99.89%
gap degree 0	84.95%	76.85%
gap degree 1	14.89%	22.72%
gap degree ≤ 1	99.84%	99.57%

Table 1. Relevant results from Kuhlmann and Nivre (2006).

In section 4, we show that gap degree can be used to distinguish between strong island violations and weak island violations in English. This supports the notion that gap-degree is a linguistically relevant measure.

Although TAG is a linguistically expressive formalism, a closer look at the linguistic data has motivated extensions of TAG.[5] One of the most widely used extensions for handling cases that are difficult for classic TAG is Multi-Component TAG (Weir 1988). Like basic TAG, MC-TAG is a formalism for rewriting nodes of a tree as other trees. The set of underived trees are called *elementary trees*. The rewriting is accomplished via two operations: *substitution*, which rewrites a leaf node labeled X with a tree rooted in a node labeled X, and *adjoining*, which rewrites a node X with a tree that labels both its root and a distinguished leaf node, the *foot*, with X. The observation that linguistic dependencies typically occur within some sort of local domain is expressed in the TAG hypothesis that all such dependencies occur within the basic building blocks of the grammar. Recursive structure is "factored out," which allows apparent non-local dependencies to be recast as local ones. Whereas basic TAG takes the basic unit to be a single elementary tree, MC-TAG extends the domain of locality to encompass a set of elementary trees. That is, these sets are the objects over which the combinatory operations apply. The MC-extension allows for linguistically satisfying accounts for a number of attested phenomena, such as: English extraposition (Kroch and Joshi 1986), subj-aux inversion in combination with raising verbs (Frank 1992), anaphoric binding (Ryant and Scheffler 2006), quantifier scope ambiguity (Joshi et al. 2003), clitic climbing in Romance (Bleam 1994), and Japanese causatives (Heycock 1986).

The primary concern of this paper is the reconciliation of the observation noted above, that MC-TAG appears to be on the right track for a good generative characterization of natural language, with a second observation: The graph drawings that correspond to MC-TAG derivations, are not guaranteed to retain the properties of basic-TAG induced graph drawings. Kuhlmann and Möhl (2006) report that if an entire MC set is anchored by a single lexical element (the natural extension of "lexicalization" of TAGs to MC-TAGs), then the class of dependency structures is expanded with respect to both conditions that characterized the TAG-induced graph drawings: MC-TAG induced graph drawings include structures that are not well-nested, have gap degree > 1, or both. As Kuhlmann and Möhl point out, the gap degree increases with the number of components, which we will elaborate in section 6. This is true even if we require that all components of a set combine with a single elementary tree (i.e. tree-local MC-TAG, which is known to allow more derivation structures (i.e. derivation trees) than TAG, although they generate the same set of derived trees). If we suppose that the characterization of dependency structures as reported by Kuhlmann and Nivre (2006) for Czech and Danish extends cross-linguistically, i.e. the dependency structures for natural language falls within the class of well-nested and gap degree ≤ 1 dependency structures, then MC-TAG appears to correspond to the wrong class of model-theoretic dependency structures. It is desirable to account for the apparent mismatch.

One possibility is that the linguistic analyses that depend on a multi-component approach are ex-

[3] A third property based on *edge degree* also characterizes the structures, but has no clear relationship to TAG-derivations. Thus, reference to it is omitted in the remaining text. See Kuhlmann and Nivre (2006) for the definition of edge degree.
[4] Well-nestedness differs from *projectivity*. (See section 3.)
[5] For a readable introduction, see Chapter 1 of Frank (2002).

tremely infrequent, and that this is reflected in the small proportion (< 1%) of data in the PDT and DDT that are not both well-nested and gap degree ≤ 1. A second possibility is that the structures in the PDT and DDT are actually not good representatives of the structures needed to characterize natural languages in general. However, a look at the cases in which MC-TAG is employed reveals that these particular analyses yield derivations that correspond to graph drawings that do satisfy well-nestedness and have gap degree ≤ 1. In practice, MC-TAG seems to be used more restrictively than what the formal system allows in principle. This keeps the corresponding graph drawings within the class of structures identified by Bodirsky et al. (2005) as a model of TAG derivations, and by Kuhlmann and Nivre (2006) as empirically relevant. Lastly, we compare the scrambling patterns that are possible in an MC-TAG extension with those that conform to the well-nestedness and gap degree ≤ 1 properties of the graph approach.

2 TAG-induced Graph Dependencies

The next two sections are intended to provide an intuition for the terms defined more formally in Bodirsky et al. (2005) and Kuhlmann and Nivre (2006). In the former, the authors define their dependency structures of interest, called *graph drawings*, as a three-tuple: a set of nodes, a dominance relation, and a (total) precedence relation. These dependency structures are based on information from both a TAG-derivation and that derivation's final phrase structure. The anchor of each elementary tree of a strictly lexicalized TAG (LTAG) is used as a node label in the induced dependency structure. E.g. suppose tree A is anchored by lexical item *a* in the LTAG grammar. Then *a* will be a node label in any dependency structure induced by an LTAG derivation involving tree A.

To see how the dominance relation and precedence relation mirror the derivation and the final derived phrase structure, let us further suppose that LTAG tree B is anchored by lexical item *b*. Node *a* dominates node *b* in the dependency structure iff Tree A dominates tree B in the derivation structure. (I.e. tree B must substitute or adjoin into tree A during the TAG-derivation.[6]) Node *a* precedes node *b* in the dependency structure iff *a* linearly precedes *b* in the derived phrase structure tree.

An example based on the cross-serial dependencies seen in Dutch subordinate clauses is given in Figure 1. In the graph drawing in (4), the four nodes names, {*Jan, de kinderen, zag, zwemmen*}, are the same set as the anchors of the elementary trees in (1), which is the same as the set of terminals in (3), the derived phrase structure. The ordering of these nodes is exactly the ordering of the terminals in (3). The directed edges between the nodes mirrors the immediate dominance relation represented in (2), the derivation structure showing how the trees in (1) combine. E.g. Just as the *zwemmen* node has the *zag* and *de kinderen* nodes as its two children in (2), so does the *zwemmen* node dominate *zag* and *de kinderen* in (4).

Möhl (2006) provides the formal details showing that such LTAG-induced dependency structures have the properties of being 1) well-nested and 2) gap degree ≤ 1, and, conversely, that any structures with these properties have a corresponding LTAG derivation.[7] These properties are defined in the next section.

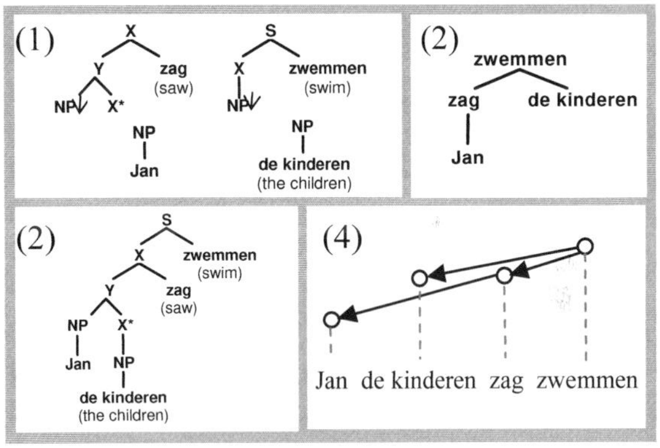

Figure 1. Derivation for *Jan de kinderen zag zwemmen* and corresponding graph drawing

3 Properties of Dependency Graphs

3.1 Gap-Degree

It will be useful to first define the term *projection*.

Definition: The projection of a node x is the set of nodes dominated by x (including x). (E.g. in (4), the projection of *zag* = {*Jan, zag*}.)

[6] Whereas in standard dependency graphs, adjunction of t2 to t1 generally corresponds to a dependency directed from t2 to t1, in a TAG-induced dependency graph, adjoining t2 to t1 corresponds to the reverse dependency.

[7] This result refers to single graph drawings and particular LTAG derivation. See Kuhlmann and Möhl (2007) on the relationship between sets of graph drawings and LTAGs.

Recall that the nodes of a graph drawing are in a precedence relation, and that this precedence relation is total.

Definition: A gap is a discontinuity with respect to precedence in the projection of a node in the drawing. (E.g. in (4), *de kinderen* is the gap preventing *Jan* and *zag* from forming a contiguous interval.)

Definition: The gap degree of a node is the number of gaps in its projection. (E.g. the gap degree of node *zag* = 1.)

Definition: The gap degree of a drawing is the maximum among the gap degrees of its nodes. (E.g. in (4), only the projection of *zag* is interrupted by a gap. Thus, the gap degree of the graph drawing in (4) = 1.)

In TAG drawings, a gap arises from an interruption of the dependencies in an auxiliary tree. If B is adjoined into A, the gap is the material in A that is below the foot node of B. E.g. in figure 1, *De kinderen* is substituted into the *zwemmen* tree below the node into which the *zag* tree adjoins into the *zwemmen* tree. Thus, *de kinderen* interrupts the pronounced material on the left of the *zag* tree's foot node, *Jan*, from the pronounced material on the right of the foot node, *zag*.

3.2 Well-Nestedness

Definition: If the roots of two subtrees in the drawing are not in a dominance relation, then the trees are *disjoint*. (E.g. in (5), the subtrees rooted in *b* and *c* are disjoint, while the subtrees rooted in *a* and *b* are not.)

Definition: If nodes x_1, x_2 belong to tree X, nodes y_1, y_2 belong to tree Y, precedence orders these nodes: $x_1 > y_1 > x_2 > y_2$, and X and Y are disjoint, then trees X and Y *interleave*. (E.g. in (5), *b* and *d* belong to the subtree rooted in *b*, while *c* and *e* belong to the subtree rooted in *c*. These two subtrees are disjoint. Since the nodes are ordered *b* > *c* > *d* > *e*, the two trees interleave.)

Definition: If there is no interleaving between disjoint subtrees, then a graph drawing is *well-nested*. (e.g. (4) is well-nested, but (5) is not)

(5)

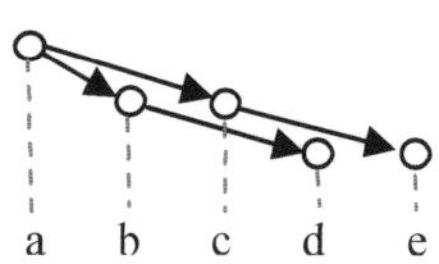

Non-well nested graph drawing

4 Island Effects and Gap-Degree

When standard TAG analyses of island effects are adopted (see Frank 2002), we observe that differences in gap degree align with the division between *wh*-extractions that are attested in natural language (grammatical *wh*-movement and weak island effects) and those claimed to be prohibited (strong island effects). Specifically, four strong island violations, extraction from an adverbial modifier, relative clause, complex NP, or subject, correspond to structures of gap degree 1, while cyclic *wh*-movement and a weak island violation (extraction from a *wh*-island) are gap degree 0 in English. Interestingly, while it is clear that weak islands vary in their island status from language to language, strong islands have been claimed to block extraction cross-linguistically. We tentatively postulate that gap degree is useful for characterizing strong islands cross-linguistically.

An example is given in (6), a standard TAG derivation for adverbial modification: the *after*-tree adjoins into the *buy*-tree (the matrix clause), the *got*-tree substitutes into the *after*-tree, and the two arguments *who* and *a-raise* substitute into the *got*-tree. In (7), the corresponding dependency structure, the projection of *got* includes *who*, which is separated from *got* by the string comprising the matrix clause and adverbial. Clearly, we do not want to claim that any gap degree of 1 is a sure source of ungrammaticality. However, it is possible that a gap degree of 1 in conjunction with a *wh*-element yields ungrammaticality. For the particular set of islands we examined, we postulate that the projection of the node immediately dominating the *wh*-element is prohibited from containing gaps.

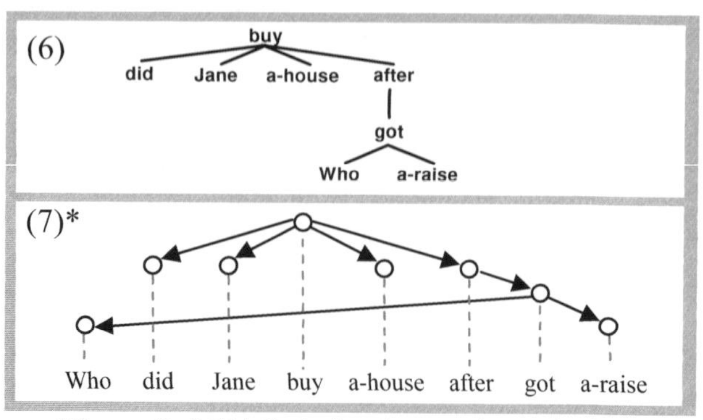

Figure 2. LTAG derivation and graph drawing for **Who did Jane buy a house after got a raise?*

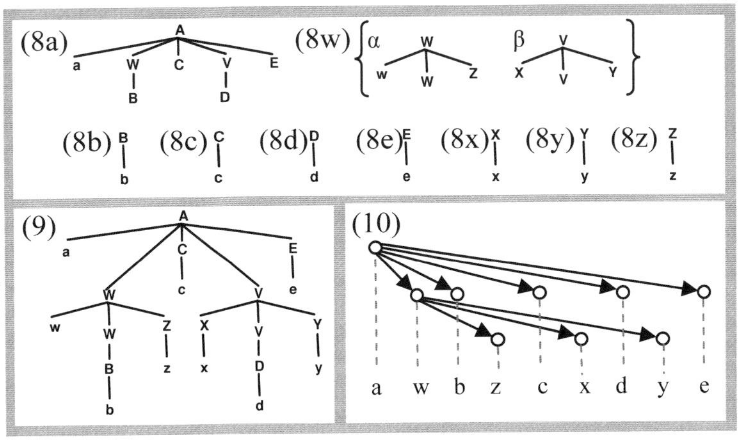

Figure 3. MC-TAG induced graph drawing of gap degree 3

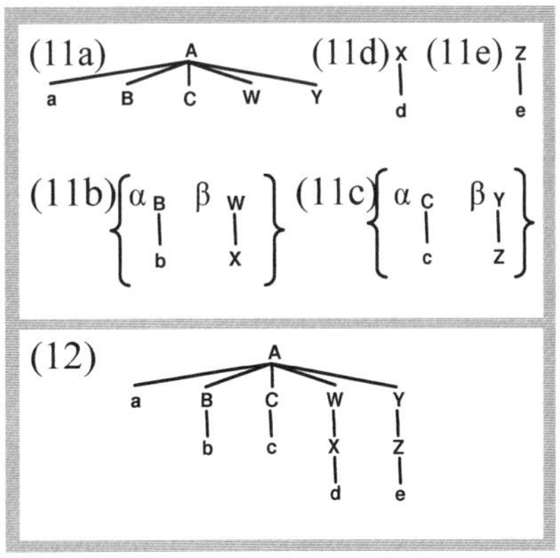

Figure 4. Non-well-nested MC-TAG induced graph drawing

5 MC-TAG-induced Dependency Graphs

5.1 Gap-Degree Beyond 1

As reviewed in section 3, the source of every gap in a TAG drawing comes from an interruption of the dependencies in an auxiliary tree. Since the auxiliary tree only has one foot, it only has a slot for a single gap. A MC-set, however, could be comprised of two auxiliary trees. This means there are slots for two gaps, one associated with each foot. Furthermore, a gap may arise as a result of any pronounced material between the two components. Thus, when we already have at least one foot, adding an additional foot increases the maximum gap degree by 2. The maximum gap degree $= 1 + 2(n - 1) = 2n - 1$, where n is the max # of foot nodes in any elementary tree set.

As an example, consider the composition of the trees in (8), Figure 3 (Kuhlmann, p.c.) The tree set in (8w) is comprised of two auxiliary trees. One tree, (8wα), adjoins into (8a), and a gap is created by the material in (8a) that falls below the foot node of (8wα), namely *b*. When (8wβ) is adjoined into (8α) at node V, a second gap is created below (8wβ) by *d*. A third gap is created by the material between the two components. (9) shows the derived phrase structure, and (10), the corresponding graph drawing. The projection of node *w*, {*w*, *x*, *y*, *z*} has three discontinuities, nodes *b*, *c*, and *d*.

5.2 Non-Well-Nestedness

Kuhlmann and Möhl (2006) show that even a tree-local MC-TAG that allows only substitution can induce a non-well-nested graph drawing. Figure 4 replicates their example. This derivation involves two MC-sets, (11b) and (11c). The tree anchored by d, (11d), substitutes into the second component of the set anchored by b, (11b). Similarly, the tree anchored by e, (11e), substitutes into the second component of the set anchored by c, (11c). Both MC-sets compose into the tree anchored by a, yielding the derived phrase structure in (12). The corresponding graph drawing is exactly our earlier example of non-well-nestedness in (5).

6 MC-TAG in Practice

We now turn to cases in which linguists have used MC-TAGs to account for cases argued to have no satisfying solution in basic TAG. Unlike the examples in 5.1 and 5.2, these particular MC-derivations correspond to dependency structures that are well-nested and have gap degree ≤ 1. Table 2 summarizes these cases. The last column indicates the type of MC-extension assumed by the analysis: tree-local MC-TAGs, tree-local MC-TAGs with *flexible composition*, the mirror operation to adjoining; if tree α adjoins into tree β, the combination can be alternatively viewed as tree β "flexibly" composing with tree α (Joshi et al. 2003, Kallmeyer and Joshi 2003)[8], and set-local MC-TAGs. Set-local MC-TAGs are generally more powerful than TAGs, but since these particular cases induce well-nested graph drawings of gap degree ≤ 1, we can conclude that set-local MC-TAG as used in

[8] I.e. When composing A and B, we can take A as the function and B as the argument or vice versa. For CFGs, such flexibility has no added benefit. For categorical type grammars, this kind of flexibility is accomplished via type raising, which allows for some new types of constituents but does not give rise to any new word orders. For tree local MC-TAGs, such flexibility does allow more word orders (permutations) to be generated than are possible without flexible composition.

analysis source	phenomenon	first component	second component	MC-type
Kroch and Joshi 1986	English extraposition *A man arrived who knew Mary.*	Auxiliary 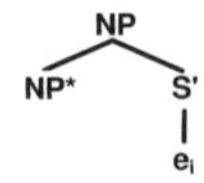	Auxiliary 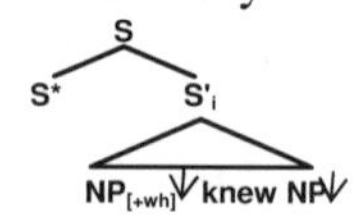	Tree-local
Frank 1992	subj-aux inversion with raising verb constructions *Does Gabriel seem to like gnocchi?*	Non-auxiliary 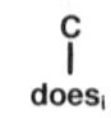	Auxiliary 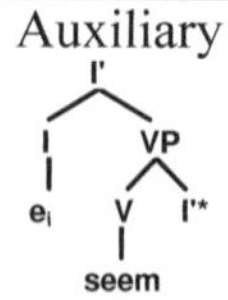	Tree-local
Ryant and Scheffler 2006	anaphoric binding *John$_i$ likes himself$_i$.*	Auxiliary 	Non-auxiliary 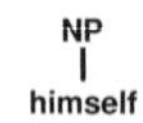	Tree-local + flexible composition
Joshi, Kallmeyer, & Romero 2003	quantifier scope ambiguity *An FBI agent is spying on every professor.* ($\forall y$ [prof(y) $\rightarrow \exists x$ [agent(x) $\wedge$ spy (x, y)]]) OR ($\exists x$ [agent(x) $\wedge \forall y$ [prof(y)$\rightarrow$ spy (x, y)]])	Auxiliary 	Non-auxiliary 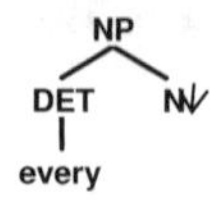	Tree-local + flexible composition
Bleam 1994	clitic climbing in Romance *Mari telo quiere permitir ver.* Mari you-it wants to permit to see "Mari wants to permit you to see it."	Auxiliary 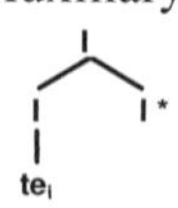	Non-auxiliary 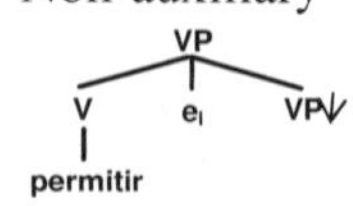	Set-local
Heycock 1986	Japanese causatives *Watasi-wa Mitiko-ni Taroo-o ik –ase (–sase) –ta.* I TOP DAT ACC go –CS –CS –PST "I made Mitiko make Taroo go."	Auxiliary 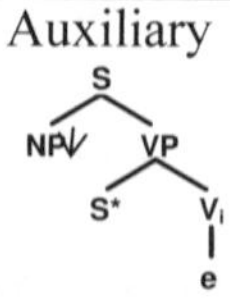	Auxiliary 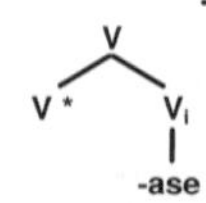	Set-local

Table 2. Canonical tree sets used in MC-TAG analyses of several phenomena

these cases is weakly equivalent to TAG.

From Table 2, we can draw two generalizations. First, in an MC-TAG analysis, a two-component set is typically used. One of the trees is often a very small piece of structure that corresponds to the "base position," surface position, or scope position of a single element. Second, the auxiliary tree components typically have elements with phonological content only on one side of the foot.

At this point, we make explicit an assumption that we believe aligns with Bodirsky et al. (2005). Since silent elements, such as traces, do not anchor an elementary tree, they do not correspond to a node in the dependency structure.

6.1 Why the Gap-Degree Remains ≤ 1

Recall that in example (8), each of the two components in the example MC-TAG has a foot with phonological material on both sides, giving rise to two gaps, and a third gap is created via the material between the two components. In contrast, in the MC-TAG sets shown in Table 2, the auxiliary trees have pronounced material only on one side of the foot node. This eliminates the gap that would have arisen due to the interruption of material on the left side of the foot from the right side of the foot as a result of the pronounced material beneath the foot. The only way to obtain pronounced material on both sides of the foot node is to adjoin a component into one of these auxiliary trees. Interestingly, the set-local analyses (in which all components of a set must combine with components of a single set vs. tree-local MC-TAG) for clitic climbing and Japanese causatives do posit recursive components adjoining into other recursive components, but only while maintaining all pronounced material on one side of the foot. In the absence of a derivational step resulting in pronounced material on both sides of a foot, the only remaining possible gap is that which arises from pronounced material that appears between the two components.

Note that the observation about the position of pronounced material applies only to auxiliary trees in sets with multiple components. That is, auxiliary trees that comprise a singleton set may still have pronounced material on both sides of the foot.

6.2 Why the Structures Remain Well-Nested

Since Kuhlmann and Möhl (2006) show that even a MC-TAG that allows only non-auxiliary trees in MC-sets will expand the drawings to include non-well-nested drawings, there is no way to pare back the MC-TAG via restrictions on the types of trees allowed in MC-sets so as to avoid interleaving.

Recall that to satisfy the definition of interleaving, it is necessary that the two MC-sets are not in any dominance relation in the derivation structure. In Kuhlmann and Möhl's example, this is satisfied because the two MC-sets are sisters in the derivation; they combine into the same tree. In the linguistic analyses considered here, no more than one MC-set combines into the same tree. For tree-local MC-TAG, it appears to be sufficient to bar more than one MC-set from combining into a single tree.

7 MC-TAG and Scrambling

In subordinate clauses in Standard German, the canonical order of verbs and their subject arguments is a nested dependency order. However, other orderings are also possible. For example, in the case of a clause-final cluster of three verbs, the canonical order is as given in (13), $NP_1NP_2NP_3$ $V_3V_2V_1$, but all the other permutations of the NP arguments are also possible orderings. All six permutations of the NPs can be derived via tree-local MC-TAG. From the graph-model perspective adopted here, this is unsurprising: All the sequences are well-nested and have gap degree ≤ 1.

(13)	NP_1	NP_2	NP_3	V_3	V_2	V_1
	. . . Hans	Peter	Marie	schwimmen	lassen	sah
	. . . Hans	Peter	Marie	swim	make	saw

"... Hans saw Peter make Marie swim."

However, with an additional level of embedding, i.e. four NPs and four verbs, the situation is different, both linguistically and formally. Our focus is on making the formal predictions of a linguistically informed system precise. We start with a tree-local MC-TAG that is restricted to linguistically motivated tree-sets and to semantically coherent derivations. The former linguistic restriction is illustrated in (14), the possible tree-sets anchored by a verb that takes a VP argument. The latter linguistic restriction is that there is no semantic feature clash at any stages of the derivation: the VP argument of V_i must be associated with V_{i+1}.

(14)
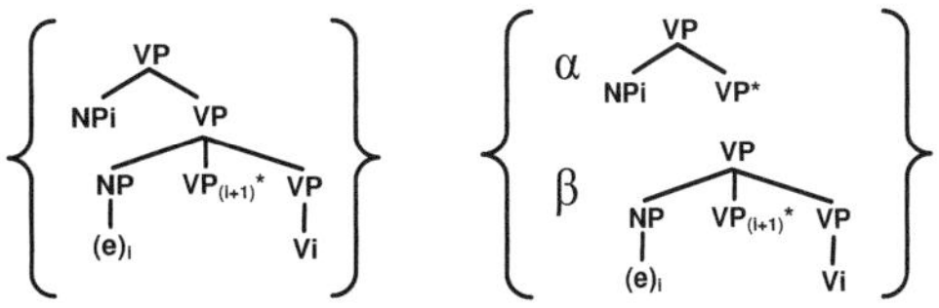

Single and two-component sets for V_i

As MC-TAG is enriched in various ways (by allowing flexible composition, multiple adjoining at the same node, and/or components from the same MC-set to target the same node), all 24 orderings where the nouns permute while the verbs remain fixed can be derived. (We are aware that German also allows verbs to scramble.) Taking the dependency structures of these sequences to consist of an edge from each verb V_i to its subject NP and to the head of its argument VP, V_{i+1}, we can compare the predictions of the graph drawing approach and the MC-TAG approach. It turns out that the permutations of gap degree ≤ 1 and those of gap-degree 2 do not align in an obvious way with particular enrichments. For example, $NP_4NP_2NP_3NP_1V_4V_3V_2V_1$ (gap degree 2) is derivable via basic tree-local MC-TAG, but $NP_3NP_1NP_4NP_2V_4V_3V_2V_1$ and $NP_3NP_2NP_4NP_1V_4V_3V_2V_1$ (also gap degree 2) appear to require both flexible composition and allowing components from the same MC-set to target the same node.

8 Conclusion and Future Work

This paper reviews the connection established in previous work between TAG derivations and model-theoretic graph drawings, i.e. well-nested dependency structures of gap degree ≤ 1, and reports several observations that build on this work. First, additional evidence of the linguistic relevance of the gap degree measure is given. The gap degree measure can distinguish *wh*-movement that is assumed to be generally disallowed from *wh*-movement that is permitted in natural language. Second, we observe that the graph drawings induced by MC-TAGs used in linguistic analyses continue to fall within the class of well-nested, gap degree $\leq$ 1 dependency structures. While Kuhlmann and Möhl (2006) show that MC-TAGs in which each set has a single lexical anchor induce graph drawings that are outside this class, this extra complexity in the dependency structures does not appear to be utilized. Even for the crucial cases used to argue for MC-extensions, MC-TAG is used in a manner requiring less complexity than the formal system allows. Examining these particular grammars lays the groundwork for identifying a natural class of MC-TAG grammars whose derivations correspond to well-nested graph drawings of gap degree $\leq$ 1. Specifically, the observations suggest the class to be MC-TAGs in which 1) component sets have up to two members, 2) auxiliary trees that are members of non-singleton MC-sets have pronounced material on only one side of the foot, whether the auxiliary member is derived or not, and 3) up to one MC-set may combine into each tree. Though these constraints appears stipulative from a formal perspective, a preliminary look suggests that natural language will not require their violation. That is, we may find linguistic justification for these constraints. Lastly, in ongoing work, we explore how allowing flexible composition and multiple adjoining enables MC-TAGs to derive a range of scrambling patterns.

References

Tonia Bleam. 2000. Clitic climbing and the power of Tree Adjoining Grammar. In A. Abeillé and O. Rambow (eds.), *Tree Adjoining Grammars: formalisms, linguistic analysis and processing*. Stanford: CSLI Publications, 193-220. (written in 1994).

Manuel Bodirsky, Marco Kuhlmann, and Mathias Möhl. 2005. Well-nested drawings as models of syntactic structure. In *10th Conference of Formal Grammar and 9th Meeting on Mathematics of Language (FG-MoL)*, Edinburgh, UK.

Robert Frank. 1992. *Syntactic Locality and Tree Adjoining Grammar: grammatical, acquisition, and processing perspectives*. PhD dissertation, University of Pennsylvania, Philadelphia, USA.

Robert Frank. 2002. *Phrase Structure Composition and Syntactic Dependencies*. MIT Press.

Jan Hajič, Barbora Vidova Hladka, Jarmila Panevová, Eva Hajičová, Petr Sgall, and Petr Pajas. 2001. Prague Dependency Treebank 1.0. LDC, 2001T10.

Caroline Heycock. 1986. The structure of the Japanese causative. Technical Report MS-CIS-87-55, University of Pennsylvania.

Aravind K. Joshi, Laura Kallmeyer, and Maribel Romero. 2003. Flexible composition in LTAG: quantifier scope and inverse linking. In H. Bunt and R. Muskens (eds.), *Computing Meaning* 3. Dordrecht: Kluwer.

Aravind K. Joshi and Y. Schabes. 1997. Tree-Adjoining Grammars. In G. Rozenberg and A. Salomaa (eds.): *Handbook of Formal Languages*. Berlin: Springer, 69–123.

Laura Kallmeyer and Aravind K. Joshi. 2003. Factoring predicate argument and scope semantics: underspecified semantics with LTAG. *Research on Language and Computation* 1(1-2), 3-58.

Anthony Kroch and Aravind K. Joshi. 1990. Extraposition in a Tree Adjoining Grammar. In G. Huck and A. Ojeda, eds., *Syntax and Semantics: Discontinuous Constituents*, 107-149.

Matthias Trautner Kromann. 2003. The Danish Dependency Treebank and the DTAG treebank tool. In *2nd Workshop on Treebanks and Linguistic Theories (TLT)*, 217-220.

Marco Kuhlmann and Mathias Möhl. 2006. Extended cross-serial dependencies in Tree Adjoining Grammars. In *Proceedings of the 8th International Workshop on Tree Adjoining Grammar and Related Formalisms*, Sydney, Australia, 121-126.

Marco Kuhlmann and Mathias Möhl. 2007. Mildly context-sensitive dependency languages. In *45th Annual Meeting of the Association for Computational Linguistics (ACL)*, Prague, Czech Republic.

Marco Kuhlmann and Joakim Nivre. 2006. Mildly non-projective dependency structures. In *21st International Conference on Computational Linguistics and 44th Annual Meeting of the Association for Computational Linguistics (COLING-ACL), Companion Volume*, Sydney, Australia.

Mathias Möhl. 2006. *Drawings as Models of Syntactic Structure: Theory and Algorithms*, Masters thesis, Saarland University, Saarbrücken, Germany.

Neville Ryant and Tatjana Scheffler. 2006. Binding of anaphors in LTAG. In *Proceedings of the 8th International Workshop on Tree Adjoining Grammar and Related Formalisms*, Sydney, Australia, 65-72.

David Weir. 1988. *Characterizing mildly context-sensitive grammar formalisms*. PhD dissertation, University of Pennsylvania, Philadelphia, USA.

Perceptron Training for a Wide-Coverage Lexicalized-Grammar Parser

Stephen Clark
Oxford University Computing Laboratory
Wolfson Building, Parks Road
Oxford, OX1 3QD, UK
stephen.clark@comlab.ox.ac.uk

James R. Curran
School of Information Technologies
University of Sydney
NSW 2006, Australia
james@it.usyd.edu.au

Abstract

This paper investigates perceptron training for a wide-coverage CCG parser and compares the perceptron with a log-linear model. The CCG parser uses a phrase-structure parsing model and dynamic programming in the form of the Viterbi algorithm to find the highest scoring derivation. The difficulty in using the perceptron for a phrase-structure parsing model is the need for an efficient decoder. We exploit the lexicalized nature of CCG by using a finite-state supertagger to do much of the parsing work, resulting in a highly efficient decoder. The perceptron performs as well as the log-linear model; it trains in a few hours on a single machine; and it requires only a few hundred MB of RAM for practical training compared to 20 GB for the log-linear model. We also investigate the order in which the training examples are presented to the online perceptron learner, and find that order does not significantly affect the results.

1 Introduction

A recent development in data-driven parsing is the use of discriminative training methods (Riezler et al., 2002; Taskar et al., 2004; Collins and Roark, 2004; Turian and Melamed, 2006). One popular approach is to use a log-linear parsing model and maximise the *conditional* likelihood function (Johnson et al., 1999; Riezler et al., 2002; Clark and Curran, 2004b; Malouf and van Noord, 2004; Miyao and Tsujii, 2005). Maximising the likelihood involves calculating feature expectations, which is computationally expensive. Dynamic programming (DP) in the form of the inside-outside algorithm can be used to calculate the expectations, if the features are sufficiently local (Miyao and Tsujii, 2002); however, the memory requirements can be prohibitive, especially for automatically extracted, wide-coverage grammars. In Clark and Curran (2004b) we use cluster computing resources to solve this problem.

Parsing research has also begun to adopt discriminative methods from the Machine Learning literature, such as the perceptron (Freund and Schapire, 1999; Collins and Roark, 2004) and the large-margin methods underlying Support Vector Machines (Taskar et al., 2004; McDonald, 2006). Parser training involves decoding in an iterative process, updating the model parameters so that the decoder performs better on the training data, according to some training criterion. Hence, for efficient training, these methods require an efficient decoder; in fact, for methods like the perceptron, the update procedure is so trivial that the training algorithm essentially is decoding.

This paper describes a decoder for a lexicalized-grammar parser which is efficient enough for practical discriminative training. We use a lexicalized phrase-structure parser, the CCG parser of Clark and Curran (2004b), together with a DP-based decoder. The key idea is to exploit the properties of lexicalized grammars by using a finite-state supertagger prior to parsing (Bangalore and Joshi, 1999; Clark and Curran, 2004a). The decoder still uses the CKY algorithm, so the worst case complexity of

Proceedings of the 5th Workshop on Important Unresolved Matters, pages 9–16,
Ann Arbor, June 2005. ©2005 Association for Computational Linguistics

the parsing is unchanged; however, by allowing the supertagger to do much of the parsing work, the efficiency of the decoder is greatly increased in practice.

We chose the perceptron for the training algorithm because it has shown good performance on other NLP tasks; in particular, Collins (2002) reported good performance for a perceptron tagger compared to a Maximum Entropy tagger. Like Collins (2002), the decoder is the same for both the perceptron and the log-linear parsing models; the only change is the method for setting the weights. The perceptron model performs as well as the log-linear model, but is considerably easier to train.

Another contribution of this paper is to advance wide-coverage CCG parsing. Previous discriminative models for CCG (Clark and Curran, 2004b) required cluster computing resources to train. In this paper we reduce the memory requirements from 20 GB of RAM to only a few hundred MB, but without greatly increasing the training time or reducing parsing accuracy. This provides state-of-the-art CCG parsing with a practical development environment.

More generally, this work provides a practical environment for experimenting with discriminative models for phrase-structure parsing; because the training time for the CCG parser is relatively short (a few hours), experiments such as comparing alternative feature sets can be performed. As an example, we investigate the order in which the training examples are presented to the perceptron learner. Since the perceptron training is an online algorithm — updating the weights one training sentence at a time — the order in which the data is processed affects the resulting model. We consider random ordering; presenting the shortest sentences first; and presenting the longest sentences first; and find that the order does not significantly affect the final results.

We also use the random orderings to investigate model averaging. We produced 10 different models, by randomly permuting the data, and averaged the weights. Again the averaging was found to have no impact on the results, showing that the perceptron learner — at least for this parsing task — is robust to the order of the training examples.

The contributions of this paper are as follows. First, we compare perceptron and log-linear parsing models for a wide-coverage phrase-structure parser, the first work we are aware of to do so. Second, we provide a practical framework for developing discriminative models for CCG, reducing the memory requirements from over 20 GB to a few hundred MB. And third, given the significantly shorter training time compared to other discriminative parsing models (Taskar et al., 2004), we provide a practical framework for investigating discriminative training methods more generally.

2 The CCG Parser

Clark and Curran (2004b) describes the CCG parser. The grammar used by the parser is extracted from CCGbank, a CCG version of the Penn Treebank (Hockenmaier, 2003). The grammar consists of 425 lexical categories, expressing subcategorisation information, plus a small number of combinatory rules which combine the categories (Steedman, 2000). A Maximum Entropy supertagger first assigns lexical categories to the words in a sentence, which are then combined by the parser using the combinatory rules and the CKY algorithm. A log-linear model scores the alternative parses. We use the normal-form model, which assigns probabilities to single derivations based on the normal-form derivations in CCGbank. The features in the model are defined over local parts of the derivation and include word-word dependencies. A packed chart representation allows efficient decoding, with the Viterbi algorithm finding the most probable derivation.

The supertagger is a key part of the system. It uses a log-linear model to define a distribution over the lexical category set for each word and the previous two categories (Ratnaparkhi, 1996) and the forward backward algorithm efficiently sums over all histories to give a distibution for each word. These distributions are then used to assign a set of lexical categories to each word (Curran et al., 2006).

Supertagging was first defined for LTAG (Bangalore and Joshi, 1999), and was designed to increase parsing speed for lexicalized grammars by allowing a finite-state tagger to do some of the parsing work. Since the elementary syntactic units in a lexicalized grammar — in LTAG's case elementary trees and in CCG's case lexical categories – contain a significant amount of grammatical information, combining them together is easier than the parsing typically performed by phrase-structure parsers. Hence

Bangalore and Joshi (1999) refer to supertagging as *almost parsing*.

Supertagging has been especially successful for CCG: Clark and Curran (2004a) demonstrates the considerable increases in speed that can be obtained through use of a supertagger. The supertagger interacts with the parser in an adaptive fashion. Initially the supertagger assigns a small number of categories, on average, to each word in the sentence, and the parser attempts to create a spanning analysis. If this is not possible, the supertagger assigns more categories, and this process continues until a spanning analysis is found. The number of categories assigned to each word is determined by a parameter β in the supertagger: all categories are assigned whose forward-backward probabilities are within β of the highest probability category (Curran et al., 2006).

Clark and Curran (2004a) also shows how the supertagger can reduce the size of the packed charts to allow discriminative log-linear training. However, even with the use of a supertagger, the packed charts for the complete CCGbank require over 20 GB of RAM. Reading the training instances into memory one at a time and keeping a record of the relevant feature counts would be too slow for practical development, since the log-linear model requires hundreds of iterations to converge. Hence the packed charts need to be stored in memory. In Clark and Curran (2004b) we use a cluster of 45 machines, together with a parallel implementation of the BFGS training algorithm, to solve this problem.

The need for cluster computing resources presents a barrier to the development of further CCG parsing models. Hockenmaier and Steedman (2002) describe a generative model for CCG, which only requires a non-iterative counting process for training, but it is generally acknowledged that discriminative models provide greater flexibility and typically higher performance. In this paper we propose the perceptron algorithm as a solution. The perceptron is an online learning algorithm, and so the parameters are updated one training instance at a time. However, the key difference compared with the log-linear training is that the perceptron converges in many fewer iterations, and so it is practical to read the training instances into memory one at a time.

The difficulty in using the perceptron for training phrase-structure parsing models is the need for an efficient decoder (since perceptron training essentially is decoding). Here we exploit the lexicalized nature of CCG by using the supertagger to restrict the size of the charts over which Viterbi decoding is performed, resulting in an extremely effcient decoder. In fact, the decoding is so fast that we can estimate a state-of-the-art discriminative parsing model in only a few hours on a single machine.

3 Perceptron Training

The parsing problem is to find a mapping from a set of sentences $x \in X$ to a set of parses $y \in Y$. We assume that the mapping F is represented through a feature vector $\Phi(x, y) \in \mathcal{R}^d$ and a parameter vector $\overline{\alpha} \in \mathcal{R}^d$ in the following way (Collins, 2002):

$$F(x) = \underset{y \in \text{GEN}(x)}{\text{argmax}} \; \Phi(x, y) \cdot \overline{\alpha} \tag{1}$$

where $\text{GEN}(x)$ denotes the set of possible parses for sentence x and $\Phi(x, y) \cdot \overline{\alpha} = \sum_i \alpha_i \Phi_i(x, y)$ is the inner product. The learning task is to set the parameter values (the feature weights) using the training set as evidence, where the training set consists of examples (x_i, y_i) for $1 \leq i \leq N$. The decoder is an algorithm which finds the argmax in (1).

In this paper, Y is the set of possible CCG derivations and $\text{GEN}(x)$ enumerates the set of derivations for sentence x. We use the same feature representation $\Phi(x, y)$ as in Clark and Curran (2004b), to allow comparison with the log-linear model. The features are defined in terms of local subtrees in the derivation, consisting of a parent category plus one or two children. Some features are lexicalized, encoding word-word dependencies. Features are integer-valued, counting the number of times some configuration occurs in a derivation.

$\text{GEN}(x)$ is defined by the CCG grammar, plus the supertagger, since the supertagger determines how many lexical categories are assigned to each word in x (through the β parameter). Rather than try to recreate the adaptive supertagging described in Section 2 for training, we simply fix the the value of β so that $\text{GEN}(x)$ is the set of derivations licenced by the grammar for sentence x, given that value. β is now a parameter of the training process which we determine experimentally using development data. The β parameter can be thought of as determining the set of incorrect derivations which the training algorithm uses to "discriminate against", with a smaller value of β resulting in more derivations.

3.1 Feature Forests

The same decoder is used for both training and testing: the Viterbi algorithm. However, the packed representation of GEN(x) in each case is different. When running the parser, a lot of grammatical information is stored in order to produce linguistically meaningful output. For training, all that is required is a packed representation of the features on each derivation in GEN(x) for each sentence in the training data. The *feature forests* described in Miyao and Tsujii (2002) provide such a representation.

Clark and Curran (2004b) describe how a set of CCG derivations can be represented as a feature forest. The feature forests are created by first building packed charts for the training sentences, and then extracting the feature information. Packed charts group together equivalent chart entries. Entries are equivalent when they interact in the same manner with both the generation of subsequent parse structure and the numerical parse selection. In practice, this means that equivalent entries have the same span, and form the same structures and generate the same features in any further parsing of the sentence. Back pointers to the daughters indicate how an individual entry was created, so that any derivation can be recovered from the chart.

A feature forest is essentially a packed chart with only the feature information retained (see Miyao and Tsujii (2002) and Clark and Curran (2004b) for the details). Dynamic programming algorithms can be used with the feature forests for efficient estimation. For the log-linear parsing model in Clark and Curran (2004b), the inside-outside algorithm is used to calculate feature expectations, which are then used by the BFGS algorithm to optimise the likelihood function. For the perceptron, the Viterbi algorithm finds the features corresponding to the highest scoring derivation, which are then used in a simple additive update process.

3.2 The Perceptron Algorithm

The training algorithm initializes the parameter vector as all zeros, and updates the vector by decoding the examples. Each feature forest is decoded with the current parameter vector. If the output is incorrect, the parameter vector is updated by adding the feature vector of the correct derivation and subtracting the feature vector of the decoder output. Training typically involves multiple passes over the data. Figure 1 gives the algorithm, where N is the number of training sentences and T is the number of iterations over the data.

Inputs: training examples (x_i, y_i)
Initialisation: set $\overline{\alpha} = 0$
Algorithm:
  for $t = 1..T$, $i = 1..N$
    calculate $z_i = \arg\max_{y \in \text{GEN}(x_i)} \Phi(x_i, y) \cdot \overline{\alpha}$
    if $z_i \neq y_i$
      $\overline{\alpha} = \overline{\alpha} + \Phi(x_i, y_i) - \Phi(x_i, z_i)$
Outputs: $\overline{\alpha}$

Figure 1: The perceptron training algorithm

For all the experiments in this paper, we used the averaged version of the perceptron. Collins (2002) introduced the averaged perceptron, as a way of reducing overfitting, and it has been shown to perform better than the non-averaged version on a number of tasks. The averaged parameters are defined as follows: $\gamma_s = \sum_{t=1...T,i=1...N} \alpha_s^{t,i}/NT$ where $\alpha_s^{t,i}$ is the value of the sth feature weight after the tth sentence has been processed in the ith iteration.

A naive implementation of the averaged perceptron updates the accumulated weight for each feature after each example. However, the number of features whose values change for each example is a small proportion of the total. Hence we use the algorithm described in Daume III (2006) which avoids unnecessary calculations by only updating the accumulated weight for a feature f_s when α_s changes.

4 Experiments

The feature forests were created as follows. First, the value of the β parameter for the supertagger was fixed (for the first set of experiments at 0.004). The supertagger was then run over the sentences in Sections 2-21 of CCGbank. We made sure that every word was assigned the correct lexical category among its set (we did not do this for testing). Then the parser was run on the supertagged sentences, using the CKY algorithm and the CCG combinatory rules. We applied the same normal-form restrictions used in Clark and Curran (2004b): categories can only combine if they have been seen to combine in Sections 2-21 of CCGbank, and only if they do not violate the Eisner (1996a) normal-form constraints. This part of the process requires a few hundred MB of RAM to run the parser, and takes a few hours for Sections 2-21 of CCGbank. Any further training times or memory requirements reported do not include the resources needed to create the forests.

The feature forests are extracted from the packed chart representation used in the parser. We only use a feature forest for training if it contains the correct derivation (according to CCGbank). Some forests do not have the correct derivation, even though we ensure the correct lexical categories are present, because the grammar used by the parser is missing some low-frequency rules in CCGbank. The total number of forests used for the experiments was 35,370 (89% of Sections 2-21) . Only features which occur at least twice in the training data were used, of which there are 477,848. The complete set of forests used to obtain the final perceptron results in Section 4.1 require 21 GB of disk space.

The perceptron is an online algorithm, updating the weights after each forest is processed. Each forest is read into memory one at a time, decoding is performed, and the weight values are updated. Each forest is discarded from memory after it has been used. Constantly reading forests off disk is expensive, but since the perceptron converges in so few iterations the training times are reasonable.

In contrast, log-linear training takes hundreds of iterations to converge, and so it would be impractical to keep reading the forests off disk. Also, since log-linear training uses a batch algorithm, it is more convenient to keep the forests in memory at all times. In Clark and Curran (2004b) we use a cluster of 45 machines, together with a parallel implementation of BFGS, to solve this problem, but need up to 20 GB of RAM.

The feature forest representation, and our implementation of it, is so compact that the perceptron training requires only 20 MB of RAM. Since the supertagger has already removed much of the practical parsing complexity, decoding one of the forests is extremely quick, and much of the training time is taken with continually reading the forests off disk. However, the training time for the perceptron is still only around 5 hours for 10 iterations.

model	RAM	iterations	time (mins)
perceptron	20 MB	10	312
log-linear	19 GB	475	91

Table 1: Training requirements for the perceptron and log-linear models

Table 1 compares the training for the perceptron and log-linear models. The perceptron was run for 10 iterations and the log-linear training was run to convergence. The training time for 10 iterations of the perceptron is longer than the log-linear training, although the results in Section 4.1 show that the perceptron typically converges in around 4 iterations. The striking result in the table is the significantly smaller memory requirement for the perceptron.

4.1 Results

Table 2 gives the first set of results for the averaged perceptron model. These were obtained using Section 00 of CCGbank as development data. Gold-standard POS tags from CCGbank were used for all the experiments. The parser provides an analysis for 99.37% of the sentences in Section 00. The F-scores are based only on the sentences for which there is an analysis. Following Clark and Curran (2004b), accuracy is measured using F-score over the gold-standard predicate-argument dependencies in CCGbank. The table shows that the accuracy increases initially with the number of iterations, but converges quickly after only 4 iterations. The accuracy after only one iteration is also surprisingly high.

Table 3 compares the accuracy of the perceptron and log-linear models on the development data. LP is labelled precision, LR is labelled recall, and CAT is the lexical category accuracy. The same feature forests were used for training the perceptron and log-linear models, and the same parser and decoding algorithm were used for testing, so the results for the two models are directly comparable. The only difference in each case was the weights file used.[1]

The table also gives the accuracy for the perceptron model (after 6 iterations) when a smaller value of the supertagger β parameter is used during the

[1] Both of these models have parameters which have been optimised on the development data, in the log-linear case the Gaussian smoothing parameter and in the perceptron case the number of training iterations.

iteration	1	2	3	4	5	6	7	8	9	10
F-score	85.87	86.28	86.33	86.49	86.46	86.51	86.47	86.52	86.53	86.54

Table 2: Accuracy on the development data for the averaged perceptron ($\beta = 0.004$)

model	LP	LR	F	CAT
log-linear$_{\beta=0.004}$	87.02	86.07	86.54	93.99
perceptron$_{\beta=0.004}$	87.11	85.98	86.54	94.03
perceptron$_{\beta=0.002}$	87.25	86.20	86.72	94.08

Table 3: Comparison of the perceptron and log-linear models on the development data

forest creation (with the number of training iterations again optimised on the development data). A smaller β value results in larger forests, giving more incorrect derivations for the training algorithm to "discriminate against". Increasing the size of the forests is no problem for the perceptron, since the memory requirements are so modest, but this would cause problems for the log-linear training which is already highly memory intensive. The table shows that increasing the number of incorrect derivations gives a small improvement in performance for the perceptron.

Table 4 gives the accuracies for the two models on the test data, Section 23 of CCGbank. Here the coverage of the parser is 99.63%, and again the accuracies are computed only for the sentences with an analysis. The figures for the averaged perceptron were obtained using 6 iterations, with $\beta = 0.002$. The perceptron slightly outperforms the log-linear model (although we have not carried out significance tests). We justify the use of different β values for the two models by arguing that the perceptron is much more flexible in terms of the size of the training forests it can handle.

Note that the important result here is that the perceptron model performs *at least as well as* the log-linear model. Since the perceptron is considerably easier to train, this is a useful finding. Also, since the log-linear parsing model is a Conditional Random Field (CRF), the results suggest that the perceptron should be compared with a CRF for other tasks for which the CRF is considered to give state-of-the-art results.

model	LP	LR	F	CAT
log-linear$_{\beta=0.004}$	87.39	86.51	86.95	94.07
perceptron$_{\beta=0.002}$	87.50	86.62	87.06	94.08

Table 4: Comparison of the perceptron and log-linear models on the test data

5 Order of Training Examples

As an example of the flexibility of our discriminative training framework, we investigated the order in which the training examples are presented to the online perceptron learner. These experiments were particularly easy to carry out in our framework, since the 21 GB file containing the complete set of training forests can be sampled from directly. We stored the position on disk of each of the forests, and selected the forests one by one, according to some order.

The first set of experiments investigated ordering the training examples by sentence length. Buttery (2006) found that a psychologically motivated Categorial Grammar learning system learned faster when the simplest linguistic examples were presented first. Table 5 shows the results both when the shortest sentences are presented first and when the longest sentences are presented first. Training on the longest sentences first provides the best performance, but is no better than the standard ordering.

For the random ordering experiments, forests were randomly sampled from the complete 21 GB training file on disk, without replacement. The new forests file was then used for the averaged-perceptron training, and this process was repeated 9 times.

The number of iterations for each training run was optimised in terms of the accuracy of the resulting model on the development data. There was little variation among the models, with the best model scoring 86.84% F-score on the development data and the worst scoring 86.63%. Table 6 shows that the performance of this best model on the test data is only slightly better than the model trained using the CCGbank ordering.

iteration	1	2	3	4	5	6
Standard order	86.14	86.30	86.53	86.61	86.69	86.72
Shortest first	85.98	86.41	86.57	86.56	86.54	86.53
Longest first	86.25	86.48	86.66	86.72	86.74	86.75

Table 5: F-score of the averaged perceptron on the development data for different data orderings ($\beta = 0.002$)

perceptron model	LP	LR	F	CAT
standard order	87.50	86.62	87.06	94.08
best random order	87.52	86.72	87.12	94.12
averaged	87.53	86.67	87.10	94.09

Table 6: Comparison of various perceptron models on the test data

Finally, we used the 10 models (including the model from the original training set) to investigate model averaging. Corston-Oliver et al. (2006) motivate model averaging for the perceptron in terms of Bayes Point Machines. The averaged perceptron weights resulting from each permutation of the training data were simply averaged to produce a new model. Table 6 shows that the averaged model again performs only marginally better than the original model, and not as well as the best-performing "random" model, which is perhaps not surprising given the small variation among the performances of the component models.

In summary, the perceptron learner appears highly robust to the order of the training examples, at least for this parsing task.

6 Comparison with Other Work

Taskar et al. (2004) investigate discriminative training methods for a phrase-structure parser, and also use dynamic programming for the decoder. The key difference between our work and theirs is that they are only able to train on sentences of 15 words or less, because of the expense of the decoding.

There is work on discriminative models for dependency parsing (McDonald, 2006); since there are efficient decoding algorithms available (Eisner, 1996b), complete resources such as the Penn Treebank can used for estimation, leading to accurate parsers. There is also work on discriminative models for parse reranking (Collins and Koo, 2005). The main drawback with this approach is that the correct parse may get lost in the first phase.

The existing work most similar to ours is Collins and Roark (2004). They use a beam-search decoder as part of a phrase-structure parser to allow practical estimation. The main difference is that we are able to store the complete forests for training, and can guarantee that the forest contains the correct derivation (assuming the grammar is able to generate it given the correct lexical categories). The downside of our approach is the restriction on the locality of the features, to allow dynamic programming. One possible direction for future work is to compare the search-based approach of Collins and Roark with our DP-based approach.

In the tagging domain, Collins (2002) compared log-linear and perceptron training for HMM-style tagging based on dynamic programming. Our work could be seen as extending that of Collins since we compare log-linear and perceptron training for a DP-based wide-coverage parser.

7 Conclusion

Investigation of discriminative training methods is one of the most promising avenues for breaking the current bottleneck in parsing performance. The drawback of these methods is the need for an efficient decoder. In this paper we have demonstrated how the lexicalized nature of CCG can be used to develop a very efficient decoder, which leads to a practical development environment for discriminative training.

We have also provided the first comparison of a perceptron and log-linear model for a wide-coverage phrase-structure parser. An advantage of the perceptron over the log-linear model is that it is considerably easier to train, requiring 1/1000th of the memory requirements and converging in only 4 iterations.

Given that the global log-linear model used here (CRF) is thought to provide state-of-the-art performance for many NLP tasks, it is perhaps surprising that the perceptron performs as well. The evaluation in this paper was based solely on CCGbank, but we have shown in Clark and Curran (2007) that the CCG parser gives state-of-the-art performance, outperforming the RASP parser (Briscoe et al., 2006) by over 5% on DepBank. This suggests the need for more comparisons of CRFs and discriminative methods such as the perceptron for other NLP tasks.

Acknowledgements

James Curran was funded under ARC Discovery grants DP0453131 and DP0665973.

References

Srinivas Bangalore and Aravind Joshi. 1999. Supertagging: An approach to almost parsing. *Computational Linguistics*, 25(2):237–265.

Ted Briscoe, John Carroll, and Rebecca Watson. 2006. The second release of the RASP system. In *Proceedings of the Interactive Demo Session of COLING/ACL-06*, Sydney, Austrailia.

Paula Buttery. 2006. Computational models for first language acquisition. Technical Report UCAM-CL-TR-675, University of Cambridge Computer Laboratory.

Stephen Clark and James R. Curran. 2004a. The importance of supertagging for wide-coverage CCG parsing. In *Proceedings of COLING-04*, pages 282–288, Geneva, Switzerland.

Stephen Clark and James R. Curran. 2004b. Parsing the WSJ using CCG and log-linear models. In *Proceedings of the 42nd Meeting of the ACL*, pages 104–111, Barcelona, Spain.

Stephen Clark and James R. Curran. 2007. Formalism-independent parser evaluation with CCG and DepBank. In *Proceedings of the 45th Annual Meeting of the ACL*, Prague, Czech Republic.

Michael Collins and Terry Koo. 2005. Discriminative reranking for natural language parsing. *Computational Linguistics*, 31(1):25–69.

Michael Collins and Brian Roark. 2004. Incremental parsing with the perceptron algorithm. In *Proceedings of the 42nd Meeting of the ACL*, pages 111–118, Barcelona, Spain.

Michael Collins. 2002. Discriminative training methods for hidden markov models: Theory and experiments with perceptron algorithms. In *Proceedings of the 40th Meeting of the ACL*, Philadelphia, PA.

S. Corston-Oliver, A. Aue, K. Duh, and E. Ringger. 2006. Multilingual dependency parsing using bayes point machines. In *Proceedings of HLT/NAACL-06*, New York.

James R. Curran, Stephen Clark, and David Vadas. 2006. Multi-tagging for lexicalized-grammar parsing. In *Proceedings of COLING/ACL-06*, pages 697–704, Sydney, Austrailia.

Jason Eisner. 1996a. Efficient normal-form parsing for Combinatory Categorial Grammar. In *Proceedings of the 34th Meeting of the ACL*, pages 79–86, Santa Cruz, CA.

Jason Eisner. 1996b. Three new probabilistic models for dependency parsing: An exploration. In *Proceedings of the 16th COLING Conference*, pages 340–345, Copenhagen, Denmark.

Yoav Freund and Robert E. Schapire. 1999. Large margin classification using the perceptron algorithm. *Machine Learning*, 37(3):277–296.

Julia Hockenmaier and Mark Steedman. 2002. Generative models for statistical parsing with Combinatory Categorial Grammar. In *Proceedings of the 40th Meeting of the ACL*, pages 335–342, Philadelphia, PA.

Julia Hockenmaier. 2003. *Data and Models for Statistical Parsing with Combinatory Categorial Grammar*. Ph.D. thesis, University of Edinburgh.

Mark Johnson, Stuart Geman, Stephen Canon, Zhiyi Chi, and Stefan Riezler. 1999. Estimators for stochastic 'unification-based' grammars. In *Proceedings of the 37th Meeting of the ACL*, pages 535–541, University of Maryland, MD.

Robert Malouf and Gertjan van Noord. 2004. Wide coverage parsing with stochastic attribute value grammars. In *Proceedings of the IJCNLP-04 Workshop: Beyond shallow analyses - Formalisms and statistical modeling for deep analyses*, Hainan Island, China.

Ryan McDonald. 2006. *Discriminative Training and Spanning Tree Algorithms for Dependency Parsing*. Ph.D. thesis, University of Pennsylvania.

Yusuke Miyao and Jun'ichi Tsujii. 2002. Maximum entropy estimation for feature forests. In *Proceedings of the Human Language Technology Conference*, San Diego, CA.

Yusuke Miyao and Jun'ichi Tsujii. 2005. Probabilistic disambiguation models for wide-coverage HPSG parsing. In *Proceedings of the 43rd meeting of the ACL*, pages 83–90, University of Michigan, Ann Arbor.

Adwait Ratnaparkhi. 1996. A maximum entropy part-of-speech tagger. In *Proceedings of the EMNLP Conference*, pages 133–142, Philadelphia, PA.

Stefan Riezler, Tracy H. King, Ronald M. Kaplan, Richard Crouch, John T. Maxwell III, and Mark Johnson. 2002. Parsing the Wall Street Journal using a Lexical-Functional Grammar and discriminative estimation techniques. In *Proceedings of the 40th Meeting of the ACL*, pages 271–278, Philadelphia, PA.

Mark Steedman. 2000. *The Syntactic Process*. The MIT Press, Cambridge, MA.

B. Taskar, D. Klein, M. Collins, D. Koller, and C. Manning. 2004. Max-margin parsing. In *Proceedings of the EMNLP conference*, pages 1–8, Barcelona, Spain.

Joseph Turian and I. Dan Melamed. 2006. Advances in discriminative parsing. In *Proceedings of COLING/ACL-06*, pages 873–880, Sydney, Australia.

Filling Statistics with Linguistics – Property Design for the Disambiguation of German LFG Parses

Martin Forst
Institute of Natural Language Processing
University of Stuttgart, Germany
forst@ims.uni-stuttgart.de

Abstract

We present a log-linear model for the disambiguation of the analyses produced by a German broad-coverage LFG, focussing on the properties (or features) this model is based on. We compare this model to an initial model based only on a part of the properties provided to the final model and observe that the performance of a log-linear model for parse selection depends heavily on the types of properties that it is based on. In our case, the error reduction achieved with the log-linear model based on the extended set of properties is 51.0% and thus compares very favorably to the error reduction of 34.5% achieved with the initial model.

1 Introduction

In the development of stochastic disambiguation modules for 'deep' grammars, relatively much work has gone into the definition of suitable probability models and the corresponding learning algorithms. Property design, on the contrary, has rather been underemphasized, and the properties used in stochastic disambiguation modules are most often presented only superficially. This paper's aim is to draw more attention to property design by presenting linguistically motivated properties that are used for the disambiguation of the analyses produced by a German broad-coverage LFG and by showing that property design is of crucial importance for the quality of stochastic models for parse selection.

We present, in Section 2, the system that the disambiguation module was developed for as well as the initially used properties. In Section 3, we then present a selection of the properties that were expressly designed for the resolution of frequent ambiguities in German LFG parses. Section 4 describes experiments that we carried out with log-linear models based on the initial set of properties and on an extended one. Section 5 concludes.

2 Background

2.1 The German ParGram LFG

The grammar for which the log-linear model for parse selection described in this paper was developed is the German ParGram LFG (Dipper, 2003; Rohrer and Forst, 2006). It has been developed with and for the grammar development and processing platform XLE (Crouch et al., 2006) and consists of a symbolic LFG, which can be employed both for parsing and generation, and a two-stage disambiguation module, the log-linear model being the component that carries out the final selection among the parses that have been retained by an Optimality-Theoretically inspired prefilter (Frank et al., 2001; Forst et al., 2005).

The grammar has a coverage in terms of full parses that exceeds 80% on newspaper corpora. For sentences out of coverage, it employs the robustness techniques (fragment parsing, 'skimming') implemented in XLE and described in Riezler et al. (2002), so that 100% of our corpus sentences receive at least some sort of analysis. A dependency-based evaluation of the analyses produced by the grammar on the TiGer Dependency Bank (Forst et al., 2004) results in an F-score between 80.42% on all gram-

Proceedings of the 5th Workshop on Important Unresolved Matters, pages 17–24,
Ann Arbor, June 2005.

matical relations and morphosyntactic features (or 72.59% on grammatical relations only) and 85.50% (or 79.36%). The lower bound is based on an arbitrary selection among the parses built up by the symbolic grammar; the upper bound is determined by the best possible selection.

2.2 Log-linear models for disambiguation

Since Johnson et al. (1999), log-linear models of the following form have become standard as disambiguation devices for precision grammars:

$$P_\lambda(x|y) = \frac{e^{\sum_{j=1}^{m} \lambda_j \cdot f_j(x,y)}}{\sum_{x' \in X(y)} e^{\sum_{j=1}^{m} \lambda_j \cdot f_j(x',y)}}$$

They are used for parse selection in the English Resource Grammar (Toutanova et al., 2002), the English ParGram LFG (Riezler et al., 2002), the English Enju HPSG (Miyao and Tsujii, 2002), the HPSG-inspired Alpino parser for Dutch (Malouf and van Noord, 2004; van Noord, 2006) and the English CCG from Edinburgh (Clark and Curran, 2004).

While relatively much work has gone into the question of how to estimate the property weights $\lambda_1 \ldots \lambda_m$ efficiently and accurately on the basis of (annotated) corpus data, the question of how to define suitable and informative property functions $f_1 \ldots f_m$ has received relatively little attention. However, we are convinced that property design is *the* possibility of improving log-linear models for parse selection now that the machine learning machinery is relatively well established.

2.3 Initially used properties for disambiguation

The first set of properties with which we conducted experiments was built on the model of the property set used for the disambiguation of English ParGram LFG parses (Riezler et al., 2002; Riezler and Vasserman, 2004). These properties are defined with the help of thirteen property templates, which are parameterized for c-structure categories, f-structure attributes and/or their possible values. The templates are hardwired in XLE, which allows for a very efficient extraction of properties based on them from packed c-/f-structure representations. The downside of the templates being hardwired, however, is that, at least at first sight, the property developer is confined to what the developers of the property templates anticipated as potentially relevant for disambiguation or, more precisely, for the disambiguation of English LFG analyses.

The thirteen property templates can be subdivided into c-structure-based property templates and f-structure-based ones. The c-structure-based property templates are:

- cs_label <XP>: counts the number of XP nodes in the c-structure of an analysis.
- cs_num_children <XP>: counts the number of children of all XP nodes in a c-structure.
- cs_adjacent_label <XP> <YP>: counts the number of XP nodes that immediately dominate a YP node.
- cs_sub_label <XP> <YP>: counts the number of XP nodes that dominate a YP node (at arbitrary depth).
- cs_embedded <XP> <n>: counts the number of XP nodes that dominate n other distinct XP nodes (at arbitrary depth).
- cs_conj_nonpar <n>: counts the number of coordinated constituents that are not parallel at the nth level of embedding.
- cs_right_branch: counts the number of right children in the c-structure of an analysis.

The f-structure-based property templates are:

- fs_attrs <Attr$_1$ ... Attr$_n$>: counts the number of times that attributes *Attr*$_1$ ... *Attr*$_n$ occur in the f-structure of an analysis.
- fs_attr_val <Attr> <Val>: counts the number of times that the atomic attribute *Attr* has the value Val.
- fs_adj_attrs <Attr$_1$> <Attr$_2$>: counts the number of times that the complex attribute *Attr*$_1$ immediately embeds the attribute *Attr*$_2$.
- fs_subattr <Attr$_1$> <Attr$_2$> counts the number of times that the complex attribute *Attr*$_1$ embeds the attribute *Attr*$_2$ (at arbitrary depth).
- lex_subcat <Lemma> <SCF$_1$ ... SCF$_n$>: counts the number of times that the subcategorizing element $Lemma$ occurs with one of the subcategorization frames $SCF_1 \ldots SCF_n$.

- verb_arg <Lemma> <GF>: counts the number of times that the element *Lemma* subcategorizes for the argument *GF*.

Automatically instantiating these templates for all c-structure categories, f-structure attributes and values used in the German ParGram LFG as well as for all lexical elements present in its lexicon results in 460,424 properties.

3 Property design for the disambiguation of German LFG parses

Despite the very large number of properties that can be directly constructed on the basis of the thirteen property templates provided by XLE, many common ambiguities in German LFG parses cannot be captured by any of these.

3.1 Properties that record the relative linear order of functions

Consider, e.g., the SUBJ-OBJ ambiguity in (1).

(1) [...] peilt [$_{S/O}$ das Management] [$_{O/S}$ ein
[...] aims the management a
"sichtbar verbessertes" Ergebnis] an.
"visibly improved" result at.

'[...] the management aims at a "visibly improved" result.' (TIGER Corpus s20834)

The c-structure is shared by the two readings of the sentence, so that c-structure-based properties cannot contribute to the selection of the correct reading; the only f-structure-based properties that differ between the two analyses are of the kinds fs_adj_attrs SUBJ ADJUNCT and fs_subattr OBJ ADJUNCT, which are only remotely, if at all, related to the observed SUBJ-OBJ ambiguity. The crucial information from the intended reading, namely that the SUBJ precedes the OBJ, is not captured directly by any of the initial properties. We therefore introduce a new property template that records the linear order of two grammatical functions and instantiate it for all relevant combinations. The new properties created this way make it possible to capture the default order of nominal arguments, which according to Lenerz (1977) and Uszkoreit (1987) (among others), is SUBJ, OBJ-TH, OBJ.

Similarly to the SUBJ-OBJ ambiguity just considered, the ADJUNCT-OBL ambiguity in (2) cannot at all be resolved on the basis of c-structure-based properties, and the f-structure-based properties whose values differ among the two readings seem only remotely related to the observed ambiguity.

(2) [$_{A/O}$ Dagegen] sprach sich
Against that/In contrast spoke himself
[...] Micha Guttmann [$_{O/A}$ für getrennte
[...] Micha Guttmann for separate
Gedenkstätten] aus.
memorials out.

'In contrast, [...] Michael Guttmann argued for separate memorials.' (s2090)

However, the literature on constituent order in German, e.g. Helbig and Buscha (2001), documents the tendency of ADJUNCT PPs to precede OBL PPs, which also holds in (2). We therefore introduced properties that record the relative linear order of ADJUNCT PPs and OBL PPs.

3.2 Properties that consider the nature of a constituent wrt. its function

Although linear order plays a major role in the functional interpretation of case-ambiguous DPs in German, it is only one among several 'soft' constraints involved. The nature of such a DP may actually also give hints to its grammatical function.

The tendency of SUBJs to be high on the definiteness scale and the animacy scale as well as the tendency of OBJs to be low on these scales has mainly been observed in studies on differential object/subject marking (see, e.g., Aissen (2003)). Nevertheless, these tendencies also seem to hold in languages like German, which does not exhibit differential object/subject marking. In (3), the indefinite inanimate DP is to be interpreted as the OBJ of the sentence and the definite human DP, as its SUBJ although the former precedes the latter.

(3) [$_{O/S}$ Nahezu stabile Preise] prognostizieren
Nearly stable prices forecast
[$_{S/O}$ die bayerischen Experten] [...]
the Bavarian experts [...].

'The Bavarian experts forecast nearly stable prices [...].' (s7357)

In order to allow these regularities to be learned from corpus data, we defined additional property templates like `isDef_<GF>` and `isHuman_<GF>`,[1] which are instantiated for all relevant grammatical functions.

3.3 Properties for the resolution of attachment ambiguities concerning extraposed constituents

A further common ambiguity in German concerns the functional attachment of extraposed constituents, such as relative clauses, *dass* clauses and infinitival VPs. In (4), e.g., there is no hard constraint that would allow us to determine whether the relative clause modifies *Rolle* or *Autoversicherung*.

(4) Eine zentrale Rolle [...] kommt der
A central role [...] comes the
Autoversicherung zu, die ein Fünftel
car insurance to, which a fifth
[...] vereinnahmt.
[...] receives.

'There is a central role for the car insurance, which receives a fifth [...].' (s27539)

In order to allow for an improved resolution of this kind of attachment ambiguity, we introduced properties that extract the surface distance of an extraposed constituent to its functional head as well as properties that record how the functional uncertainty paths involved in these attachments were instantiated. This way, we hope to extract the information necessary to model the tendencies observed, e.g., in Uszkoreit et al. (1998).

3.4 Lexicalized properties capturing dependencies

Inspired by Malouf and van Noord (2004), we finally also introduced lexicalized properties capturing dependencies. These are built on the following property templates: `DEP12_<PoS1>_<Dep>_<PoS2>_<Lemma2>`, `DEP21_<PoS1>_<Lemma1>_<Dep>_<PoS2>` and `DEP22_<PoS1>_<Lemma1>_<Dep>_<PoS2>_<Lemma2>`. These are intended to capture information on the subcategorization behavior of lexical elements and on typical collocations.

[1] Humanness information is imported from *GermaNet*.

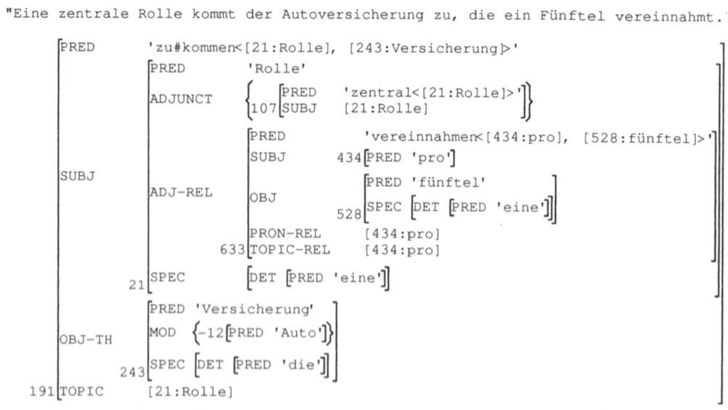

(a) evaluated as relatively improbable due to negative weight of `DISTANCE-TO-ANTECEDENT %X`

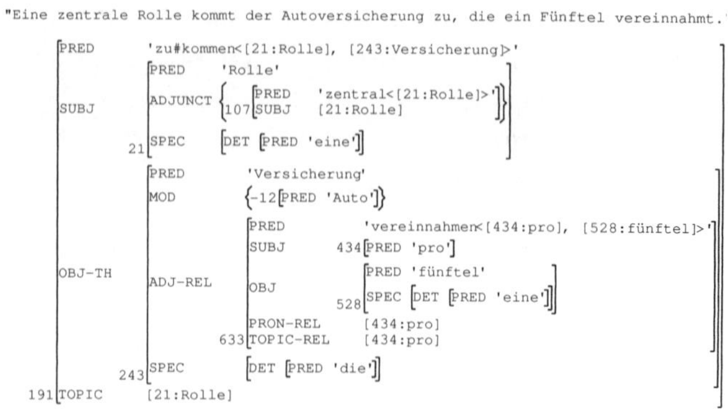

(b) evaluated as more probable

Figure 1: Competing f-structures for (4)

In the case of (5), the property `DEP21_common_Anwalt_APP_proper`, which counts the number of occurrences of the common noun *Anwalt* ('lawyer') that govern a proper name via the dependency `APP` (close apposition), contributes to the correct selection among the analyses illustrated in Figure 2 by capturing the fact that *Anwalt* is a prototypical head of a close apposition.[2]

(5) [...], das den Anwalt Klaus Bollig zum
[...] which the lawyer Klaus Bollig to the
vorläufigen Verwalter bestellte.
interim administrator appointed.

'[...] which appointed lawyer Klaus Bollig as interim administrator.' (s37596)

[2] Since we have a list of title nouns available, we might also introduce a more general property that would count the number of occurrences of title nouns in general that govern a proper name via the dependency `APP`. Note, however, that the nouns that be heads of `APP`s comprise not only title nouns, but also nouns like *Abteilung* 'department', *Buch* 'book', etc.

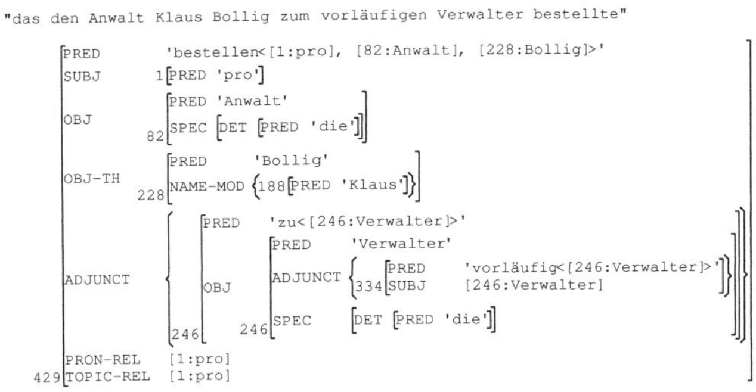

(a) evaluated as less probable

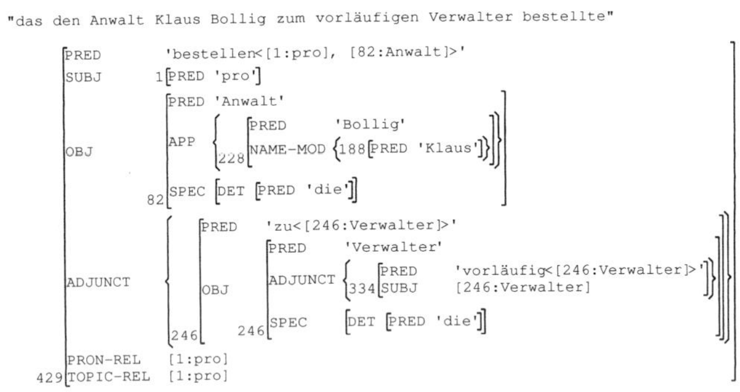

(b) evaluated as relatively probable due to highly positive weight of DEP21_common_Anwalt_APP_proper

Figure 2: Competing f-structures for (5)

4 Experiments

4.1 Data

All the data we use are from the TIGER Corpus (Brants et al., 2002), a treebank of German newspaper texts comprising about 50,000 sentences. The 1,868 dependency annotations of the TiGer Dependency Bank, which have been semi-automatically derived from the corresponding treebank graphs, are used for evaluation purposes; we split these into a held-out set of 371 sentences (and corresponding dependency annotations) and a test set of 1,497 sentences. For training, we use packed, i.e. ambiguous, c/f-structure representations where a proper subset of the f-structures can be determined as compatible with the TIGER graph annotations. Currently, these are 8,881 pairs of labelled and unlabelled packed c/f-structure reprentations.

From these 8,881 pairs of c/f-structure reprentations, we extract two sets of property forests, one containing only the initially used properties, which are based on the hardwired templates, and one containing all properties, i.e. both the initially used and the newly introduced ones.

4.2 Training

For training, we use the *cometc* software by Stefan Riezler, which is part of XLE. Prior to training, however, we apply a frequency-based cutoff c to the data that ensures that a property is discriminative between the intended reading(s) and the unintended reading(s) in at least c sentences; c is set to 4 on the basis of the evaluation results achieved on our held-out set and following a policy of a 'conservative' cutoff whose only purpose is to prevent that weights be learned for sparse properties. (For a longer discussion of frequency-based cutoffs, see Forst (2007).) For the actual estimation of property weights, we then apply the combined method of incremental property selection and l_1 regularization proposed in Riezler and Vasserman (2004), adjusting the hyperparameters on our held-out set for each of the two sets of properties. In order to comparatively evaluate the importance of property selection and regularization, we also train models based on each of the two sets of properties without applying any kind of these techniques.

4.3 Evaluation

The overall results in terms of F-score and error reduction, defined as $F_\kappa = \frac{F_{actual}-F_{lower}}{F_{upper}-F_{lower}}$, that the four resulting systems achieve on our test set of 1,497 TiGer DB structures are shown in Table 1. In order to give the reader an idea of the size of the different models, we also indicate the number of properties that they are based on. All of the F-scores were calculated by means of the evaluation software by Crouch et al. (2002).

We observe that the models obtained using property selection and regularization, in addition to being much more compact than their unregularized counterparts, perform significantly better than these. More importantly though, we can see that the most important improvement, namely from an error reduction of 32.5% to one of 42.0% or from 34.8% to 51.0% respectively, is achieved by adding more informative properties to the model.

Table 2 then shows results broken down according to individual dependencies that are achieved with, on the one hand, the best-performing model based on both the XLE template-based and the newly in-

	# prop.	F-sc.	err. red.
XLE template-based properties, unregularized MLE	14,263	82.07	32.5%
XLE templ.-based pr. that survive a freq.-b. cutoff of 4, n-best grafting with l_1 regularization	3,400	82.19	34.8%
all properties, unregularized MLE	57,934	82.55	42.0%
all properties that survive a freq.-b. cutoff of 4, n-best grafting with l_1 regularization	4,340	83.01	51.0%

Table 1: Overall F-score and corresponding error reduction achieved by the four different systems on the 1,497 TiGer DB structures of our test set

troduced properties and, on the other hand, the best-performing model based on XLE template-based properties only. Furthermore, we indicate the respective upper and lower bound F-scores, determined by the best possible parse selection and by an arbitrary selection respectively.

We observe that the overall F-score is significantly better with a selection based on the model that includes the newly introduced properties than with a selection based on the model that relies on the XLE template-based properties only; overall error reduction increases from 34.5% to 51.0%. What is particularly interesting is the considerably better error reduction for the core grammatical functions `sb` (subject) and `oa` (accusative object). But also for `rcs` (relative clauses) and `mos` (modifiers or adjuncts), which are notoriously difficult for disambiguation due to PP and ADVP attachment ambiguities, we observe an improvement in F-score.

Our error reduction of 51.0% also compares favorably to the 36% error reduction on English LFG parses reported in Riezler et al. (2002). However, it is considerably lower than the error reduction of 78% reported for the Dutch Alpino parser (Malouf and van Noord, 2004), but this may be due to the fact that our lower bound is calculated on the basis of analyses that have already passed a prefilter and is thus relatively high.

5 Conclusions

Our results show that property design is of crucial importance in the development of a disambiguation module for a 'deep' parser. They also indicate that it is a good idea to carry out property design in a linguistically inspired fashion, i.e. by referring to the theoretical literature that deals with soft constraints that are active in the language for which the system is developed. Property design thus requires a profound knowledge of the language under consideration (and the theoretical literature that deals with its syntax), and since the disambiguation module operates on the output of the symbolic grammar, a good knowledge of the grammar is necessary as well.

Weighting against each other the contributions of different measures taken for improving log-linear models for parse selection, we can conclude that property design is at least as important as property selection and/or regularization, since even a completely unregularized model based on all properties performs significantly better than the best-adjusted model among the ones that are based on the template-based properties only. Moreover, property design can be carried out in a targeted way, i.e. properties can be designed in order to improve the disambiguation of grammatical relations that, so far, are disambiguated particularly poorly or that are of special interest for the task that the system's output is used for. By demonstrating that property design is the key to good log-linear models for 'deep' syntactic disambiguation, our work confirms that "specifying the features of a SUBG [stochastic unification-based grammar] is as much an empirical matter as specifying the grammar itself" (Johnson et al., 1999).

Acknowledgements

The work described in this paper has been carried out in the DLFG project, which was funded by the German Research Foundation (DFG).

Furthermore, I thank the audiences at several ParGram meetings, at the Research Workshop of the Israel Science Foundation on Large-scale Grammar Development and Grammar Engineering at the University of Haifa and at the SFB 732 Opening Colloquium in Stuttgart for their important feedback on earlier versions of this work.

References

Judith Aissen. 2003. Differential Object Marking: Iconicity vs. Economy. *Natural Language and Linguistic Theory*, 21:435–483.

gramm. relation/morphosynt. feature	upper bound F-sc.	stoch. select. all properties F-sc.	stoch. select. all properties err. red.	stoch. select. templ.-based pr. F-sc.	stoch. select. templ.-based pr. err. red.	lower bound F-sc.
all	85.50	83.01	51.0	82.17	34.5	80.42
PREDs only	79.36	75.74	46.5	74.69	31.0	72.59
app (close apposition)	63	60	63	61	75	55
app_cl (appositive clause)	53	53	100	52	86	46
cc (comparative complement)	28	19	-29	19	-29	21
cj (conjunct of coord.)	70	68	50	67	25	66
da (dative object)	67	63	67	62	58	55
det (determiner)	92	91	50	91	50	90
gl (genitive in spec. pos.)	89	88	75	88	75	85
gr (genitive attribute)	88	84	56	84	56	79
mo (modifier)	70	63	36	62	27	59
mod (non-head in compound)	94	89	29	89	29	87
name_mod (non-head in compl. name)	82	80	33	81	67	79
number (number as determiner)	83	81	33	81	33	80
oa (accusative object)	78	75	77	69	31	65
obj (arg. of prep. or conj.)	90	88	50	87	25	86
oc_fin (finite cl. obj.)	67	64	0	64	0	64
oc_inf (infinite cl. obj.)	83	82	0	82	0	82
op (prepositional obj.)	57	54	40	54	40	52
op_dir (directional argument)	30	23	13	23	13	22
op_loc (local argument)	59	49	29	49	29	45
pd (predicative argument)	62	60	50	59	25	58
pred_restr	92	87	62	84	38	79
quant (quantifying determiner)	70	68	33	68	33	67
rc (relative clause)	74	62	20	59	0	59
sb (subject)	76	73	63	71	38	68
sbp (logical subj. in pass. constr.)	68	63	62	61	46	55
case	87	85	75	83	50	79
comp_form (complementizer form)	74	72	0	74	100	72
coord_form (coordinating conj.)	86	86	100	86	100	85
degree	89	88	50	87	0	87
det_type (determiner type)	95	95	–	95	–	95
fut (future)	86	86	–	86	–	86
gend (gender)	92	90	60	89	40	87
mood	90	90	–	90	–	90
num (number)	91	89	50	89	50	87
pass_asp (passive aspect)	80	80	100	79	0	79
perf (perfect)	86	85	0	86	100	85
pers (person)	85	84	83	82	50	79
pron_form (pronoun form)	73	73	–	73	–	73
pron_type (pronoun type)	71	70	0	71	100	70
tense	92	91	0	91	0	91

Table 2: F-scores (in %) in the 1,497 TiGer DB examples of our test set

Sabine Brants, Stefanie Dipper, Silvia Hansen, Wolfgang Lezius, and George Smith. 2002. The TIGER treebank. In *Proceedings of the Workshop on Treebanks and Linguistic Theories*, Sozopol, Bulgaria.

Stephen Clark and James R. Curran. 2004. Parsing the WSJ using CCJ and Log-Linear Models. In *Proceedings of the 42nd Annual Meeting of the Association for Computational Linguistics (ACL '04)*, Barcelona, Spain.

Richard Crouch, Ronald M. Kaplan, Tracy H. King, and Stefan Riezler. 2002. A comparison of evaluation metrics for a broad-coverage parser. In *Proceedings of the LREC Workshop 'Beyond PARSEVAL—Towards improved evaluation mesures for parsing systems'*, pages 67–74, Las Palmas, Spain.

Dick Crouch, Mary Dalrymple, Ron Kaplan, Tracy King, John Maxwell, and Paula Newman. 2006. XLE documentation. Technical report, Palo Alto Research Center, Palo Alto, CA.

Stefanie Dipper. 2003. *Implementing and Documenting Large-scale Grammars – German LFG*. Ph.D. thesis, IMS, University of Stuttgart. Arbeitspapiere des Instituts für Maschinelle Sprachverarbeitung (AIMS), Volume 9, Number 1.

Martin Forst, Núria Bertomeu, Berthold Crysmann, Frederik Fouvry, Silvia Hansen-Schirra, and Valia Kordoni. 2004. Towards a dependency-based gold standard for German parsers – The TiGer Dependency Bank. In *Proceedings of the COLING Workshop on Linguistically Interpreted Corpora (LINC '04)*, Geneva, Switzerland.

Martin Forst, Jonas Kuhn, and Christian Rohrer. 2005. Corpus-based learning of OT constraint rankings for large-scale LFG grammars. In *Proceedings of the 10th International LFG Conference (LFG'05)*, Bergen, Norway. CSLI Publications.

Martin Forst. 2007. *Disambiguation for a Linguistically Precise German Parser*. Ph.D. thesis, University of Stuttgart.

Anette Frank, Tracy Holloway King, Jonas Kuhn, and John T. Maxwell. 2001. Optimality Theory Style Constraint Ranking in Large-Scale LFG Grammars. In Peter Sells, editor, *Formal and Empirical Issues in Optimality Theoretic Syntax*, pages 367–397. CSLI Publications, Stanford, CA.

Gerhard Helbig and Joachim Buscha. 2001. *Deutsche Grammatik – Ein Handbuch für den Ausländerunterricht*. Langenscheidt, Berlin and Munich, Germany.

Mark Johnson, Stuart Geman, Stephen Canon, Zhiyi Chi, and Stefan Riezler. 1999. Estimators for stochastic "unification-based" grammars. In *Proceedings of the 37th Annual Meeting of the Association for Computational Linguistics 1999*, College Park, MD.

Jürgen Lenerz. 1977. *Zur Abfolge nominaler Satzglieder im Deutschen*. Number 5 in Studien zur deutschen Grammatik. Narr, Tübingen, Germany.

Robert Malouf and Gertjan van Noord. 2004. Wide Coverage Parsing with Stochastic Attribute Value Grammars. In *Proceedings of the IJCNLP-04 Workshop "Beyond Shallow Analyses - Formalisms and statistical modeling for deep analyses"*.

Yusuke Miyao and Jun'ichi Tsujii. 2002. Maximum entropy estimation for feature forests. In *Proceedings of the Human Language Technology Conference*, San Diego, CA.

Stefan Riezler and Alexander Vasserman. 2004. Gradient feature testing and l_1 regularization for maximum entropy parsing. In *Proceedings of the 2004 Conference on Empirical Methods in Natural Language Processing (EMNLP'04)*, Barcelona, Spain.

Stefan Riezler, Tracy Holloway King, Ronald M. Kaplan, Richard Crouch, John T. Maxwell, and Mark Johnson. 2002. Parsing the Wall Street Journal using a Lexical-Functional Grammar and Discriminative Estimation Techniques. In *Proceedings of the 40th Annual Meeting of the Association for Computational Linguistics 2002*, Philadelphia, PA.

Christian Rohrer and Martin Forst. 2006. Improving coverage and parsing quality of a large-scale LFG for German. In *Proceedings of the Language Resources and Evaluation Conference (LREC-2006)*, Genoa, Italy.

Kristina Toutanova, Christopher D. Manning, Stuart M. Shieber, Dan Flickinger, and Stephan Oepen. 2002. Parse disambiguation for a rich HPSG grammar. In *First Workshop on Treebanks and Linguistic Theories (TLT2002)*, pages 253–263.

Hans Uszkoreit, Thorsten Brants, Brigitte Krenn, Lars Konieczny, Stephan Oepen, and Wojciech Skut. 1998. Relative Clause Extraposition in German – Evidence from Corpus Studies and Acceptability Ratings. In *Proceedings of AMLaP-98*, Freiburg, Germany.

Hans Uszkoreit. 1987. *Word Order and Constituent Structure in German*. CSLI Publications, Stanford, CA.

Gertjan van Noord. 2006. At Last Parsing Is Now Operational. In Piet Mertens, Cedrick Fairon, Anne Dister, and Patrick Watrin, editors, *TALN06. Verbum Ex Machina. Actes de la 13e conférence sur le traitement automatique des langues naturelles*, pages 20–42, Leuven, Belgium.

Exploiting Semantic Information for HPSG Parse Selection

Sanae Fujita,♡ Francis Bond,♠ Stephan Oepen,♣ Takaaki Tanaka♡
♡ {sanae,takaaki}@cslab.kecl.ntt.co.jp, ♠ bond@ieee.org, ♣ oe@ifi.uio.no
♡ NTT Communication Science Laboratories, Nippon Telegraph and Telephone Corporation
♠ National Institute of Information and Communications Technology (Japan)
♣ University of Oslo, Department of Informatics (Norway)

Abstract

In this paper we present a framework for experimentation on parse selection using syntactic and semantic features. Results are given for syntactic features, dependency relations and the use of semantic classes.

1 Introduction

In this paper we investigate the use of semantic information in parse selection.

Recently, significant improvements have been made in combining symbolic and statistical approaches to various natural language processing tasks. In parsing, for example, symbolic grammars are combined with stochastic models (Oepen et al., 2004; Malouf and van Noord, 2004). Much of the gain in statistical parsing using lexicalized models comes from the use of a small set of function words (Klein and Manning, 2003). Features based on general relations provide little improvement, presumably because the data is too sparse: in the Penn treebank standardly used to train and test statistical parsers *stocks* and *skyrocket* never appear together. However, the superordinate concepts *capital* ($\supset$ *stocks*) and *move upward* ($\supset$ *sky rocket*) frequently appear together, which suggests that using word senses and their hypernyms as features may be useful

However, to date, there have been few combinations of sense information together with symbolic grammars and statistical models. We hypothesize that one of the reasons for the lack of success is that there has been no resource annotated with both syntactic and semantic information. In this paper, we use a treebank with both syntactic information (HPSG parses) and semantic information (sense tags from a lexicon) (Bond et al., 2007). We use this to train parse selection models using both syntactic and semantic features. A model trained using syntactic features combined with semantic information outperforms a model using purely syntactic information by a wide margin (69.4% sentence parse accuracy vs. 63.8% on definition sentences).

2 The Hinoki Corpus

There are now some corpora being built with the syntactic and semantic information necessary to investigate the use of semantic information in parse selection. In English, the OntoNotes project (Hovy et al., 2006) is combining sense tags with the Penn treebank. We are using Japanese data from the Hinoki Corpus consisting of around 95,000 dictionary definition and example sentences (Bond et al., 2007) annotated with both syntactic parses and senses from the same dictionary.

2.1 Syntactic Annotation

Syntactic annotation in Hinoki is *grammar based corpus annotation* done by selecting the best parse (or parses) from the full analyses derived by a broad-coverage precision grammar. The grammar is an HPSG implementation (JACY: Siegel and Bender, 2002), which provides a high level of detail, marking not only dependency and constituent structure but also detailed semantic relations. As the grammar is based on a monostratal theory of grammar (HPSG: Pollard and Sag, 1994), annotation by manual disambiguation determines syntactic and semantic structure at the same time. Using a grammar

Proceedings of the 5th Workshop on Important Unresolved Matters, pages 25–32,
Ann Arbor, June 2005. ©2005 Association for Computational Linguistics

helps treebank consistency — all sentences annotated are guaranteed to have well-formed parses. The flip side to this is that any sentences which the parser cannot parse remain unannotated, at least unless we were to fall back on full manual mark-up of their analyses. The actual annotation process uses the same tools as the Redwoods treebank of English (Oepen et al., 2004).

A (simplified) example of an entry is given in Figure 1. Each entry contains the word itself, its part of speech, and its lexical type(s) in the grammar. Each sense then contains definition and example sentences, links to other senses in the lexicon (such as hypernym), and links to other resources, such as the Goi-Taikei Japanese Lexicon (Ikehara et al., 1997) and WordNet (Fellbaum, 1998). Each content word of the definition and example sentences is annotated with sense tags from the same lexicon.

There were 4 parses for the definition sentence. The correct parse, shown as a phrase structure tree, is shown in Figure 2. The two sources of ambiguity are the conjunction and the relative clause. The parser also allows the conjunction to combine 電車 *densha* and 人 *hito*. In Japanese, relative clauses can have gapped and non-gapped readings. In the gapped reading (selected here), 人 *hito* is the subject of 運転 *unten* "drive". In the non-gapped reading there is some underspecified relation between the modifee and the verb phrase. This is similar to the difference in the two readings of *the day he knew* in English: "the day that he knew about" (gapped) vs "the day on which he knew (something)" (non-gapped). Such semantic ambiguity is resolved by selecting the correct derivation tree that includes the applied rules in building the tree (Fig 3).

The semantic representation is Minimal Recursion Semantics (Copestake et al., 2005). We simplify this into a dependency representation, further abstracting away from quantification, as shown in Figure 4. One of the advantages of the HPSG sign is that it contains all this information, making it possible to extract the particular view needed. In order to make linking to other resources, such as the sense annotation, easier predicates are labeled with pointers back to their position in the original surface string. For example, the predicate densha_n_1 links to the surface characters between positions 0 and 3:電車.

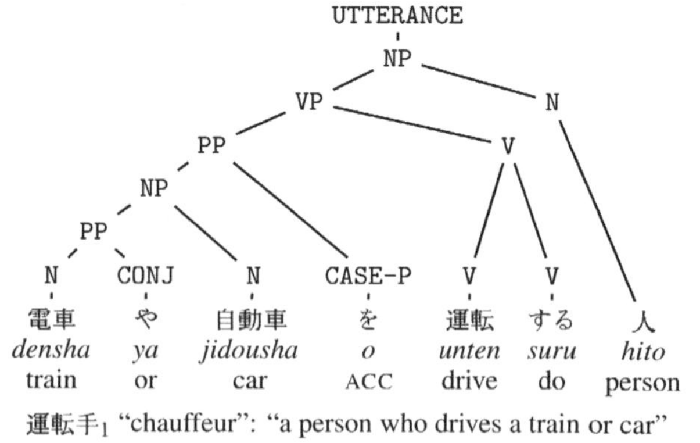

Figure 2: Syntactic View of the Definition of 運転手$_1$ *untenshu* "chauffeur"

```
e2:unknown<0:13>[ARG x5:_hito_n]
x7:densha_n_1<0:3>[]
x12:_jidousha_n<4:7>[]
x13:_ya_p_conj<0:4>[LIDX x7:_densha_n_1,
                    RIDX x12:_jidousha_n]
e23:_unten_s_2<8:10>[ARG1 x5:_hito_n]
e23:_unten_s_2<8:10>[ARG2 x13:_ya_p_conj]
```

Figure 4: Simplified Dependency View of the Definition of 運転手$_1$ *untenshu* "chauffeur"

2.2 Semantic Annotation

The lexical semantic annotation uses the sense inventory from Lexeed (Kasahara et al., 2004). All words in the fundamental vocabulary are tagged with their sense. For example, the word 大きい *ookii* "big" (of example sentence in Figure 1) is tagged as sense 5 in the example sentence, with the meaning "elder, older".

The word senses are further linked to semantic classes in a Japanese ontology. The ontology, Goi-Taikei, consists of a hierarchy of 2,710 semantic classes, defined for over 264,312 nouns, with a maximum depth of 12 (Ikehara et al., 1997). We show the top 3 levels of the Goi-Taikei common noun ontology in Figure 5. The semantic classes are principally defined for nouns (including verbal nouns), although there is some information for verbs and adjectives.

3 Parse Selection

Combining the broad-coverage JACY grammar and the Hinoki corpus, we build a parse selection model on top of the symbolic grammar. Given a set of can-

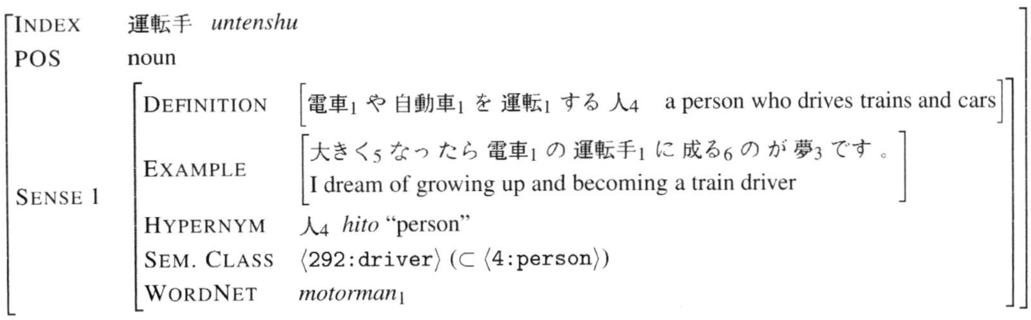

Figure 1: Dictionary Entry for 運転手$_1$ *untenshu* "chauffeur"

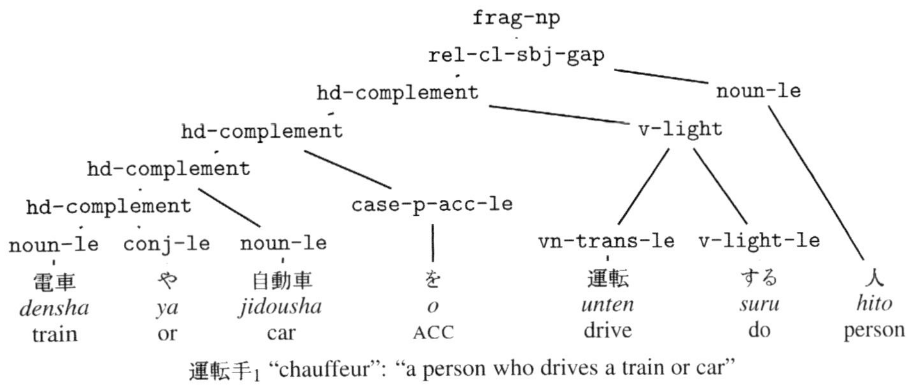

Figure 3: Derivation Tree of the Definition of 運転手$_1$ *untenshu* "chauffeur"
Phrasal nodes are labeled with identifiers of grammar rules, and (pre-terminal) lexical nodes with class names for types of lexical entries.

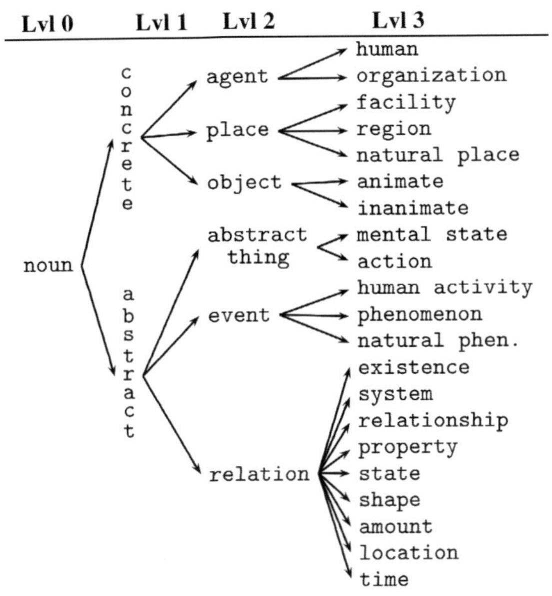

Figure 5: Top 3 levels of the GoiTaikei Ontology

didate analyses (for some Japanese string) according to JACY, the goal is to rank parse trees by their probability: training a stochastic parse selection model on the available treebank, we estimate statistics of various features of candidate analyses from the treebank. The definition and selection of features, thus, is a central parameter in the design of an effective parse selection model.

3.1 Syntactic Features

The first model that we trained uses syntactic features defined over HPSG derivation trees as summarized in Table 1. For the closely related purpose of parse selection over the English Redwoods treebank, Toutanova et al. (2005) train a discriminative log-linear model, using features defined over *derivation trees* with non-terminals representing the *construction types* and *lexical types* of the HPSG grammar. The basic feature set of our parse selection model for Japanese is defined in the same way (corresponding to the PCFG-S model of Toutanova et al. (2005)): each feature capturing a sub-tree from the deriva-

#	sample features
1	⟨0 rel-cl-sbj-gap hd-complement noun-le⟩
1	⟨1 frag-np rel-cl-sbj-gap hd-complement noun-le⟩
1	⟨2 △ frag-np rel-cl-sbj-gap hd-complement noun-le⟩
2	⟨0 rel-cl-sbj-gap hd-complement⟩
2	⟨0 rel-cl-sbj-gap noun-le⟩
2	⟨1 frag-np rel-cl-sbj-gap hd-complement⟩
2	⟨1 frag-np rel-cl-sbj-gap noun-le⟩
3	⟨1 conj-le ya⟩
3	⟨2 noun-le conj-le ya⟩
3	⟨3 ◁ noun-le conj-le ya⟩
4	⟨1 conj-le⟩
4	⟨2 noun-le conj-le⟩
4	⟨3 ◁ noun-le conj-le⟩

Table 1: Example structural features extracted from the derivation tree in Figure 3. The first column numbers the feature template corresponding to each example; in the examples, the first integer value is a parameter to feature templates, i.e. the depth of grandparenting (types #1 and#2) or *n*-gram size (types #3 and #4). The special symbols △ and ◁ denote the root of the tree and left periphery of the yield, respectively.

tion limited to depth one. Table 1 shows example features extracted from our running example (Figure 3 above) in our MaxEnt models, where the feature template #1 corresponds to local derivation subtrees. We will refer to the parse selection model using only local structural features as SYN-1.

3.1.1 Dominance Features

To reduce the effects of data sparseness, feature type #2 in Table 1 provides a back-off to derivation sub-trees, where the sequence of daughters is reduced to just the head daughter. Conversely, to facilitate sampling of larger contexts than just subtrees of depth one, feature template #1 allows optional grandparenting, including the upwards chain of dominating nodes in some features. In our experiments, we found that grandparenting of up to three dominating nodes gave the best balance of enlarged context *vs.* data sparseness. Enriching our basic model SYN-1 with these features we will henceforth call SYN-GP.

3.1.2 N-Gram Features

In addition to these dominance-oriented features taken from the derivation trees of each parse tree, our models also include more surface-oriented features, viz. *n*-grams of lexical types with or without lexicalization. Feature type #3 in Table 1 defines *n*-grams of variable size, where (in a loose analogy to part-of-speech tagging) sequences of lexical types capture syntactic category assignments. Feature templates #3 and #4 only differ with regard to lexicalization, as the former includes the surface token associated with the rightmost element of each *n*-gram (loosely corresponding to the emission probabilities in an HMM tagger). We used a maximum *n*-gram size of two in the experiments reported here, again due to its empirically determined best overall performance.

3.2 Semantic Features

In order to define semantic parse selection features, we use a reduction of the full semantic representation (MRS) into 'variable-free' *elementary dependencies*. The conversion centrally rests on a notion of one *distinguished* variable in each semantic relation. For most types of relations, the distinguished variable corresponds to the main index (ARG0 in the examples above), e.g. an event variable for verbal relations and a referential index for nominals. Assuming further that, by and large, there is a unique relation for each semantic variable for which it serves as the main index (thus assuming, for example, that adjectives and adverbs have event variables of their own, which can be motivated in predicative usages at least), an MRS can be broken down into a set of basic dependency tuples of the form shown in Figure 4 (Oepen and Lønning, 2006).

All predicates are indexed to the position of the word or words that introduced them in the input sentence (`<start:end>`). This allows us to link them to the sense annotations in the corpus.

3.2.1 Basic Semantic Dependencies

The basic semantic model, SEM-Dep, consists of features based on a predicate and its arguments taken from the elementary dependencies. For example, consider the dependencies for *densha ya jidousha-wo unten suru hito* "a person who drives a train or car" given in Figure 4. The predicate *unten* "drive" has two arguments: ARG1 *hito* "person" and ARG2 *jidousha* "car".

From these, we produce several features (See Table 2). One has all arguments and their labels (#20). We also produce various back offs: #21 introduces

#	sample features
20	⟨0 _unten_s ARG1 _hito_n_1 ARG2 _ya_p_conj⟩
20	⟨0 _ya_p_conj LIDX _densha_n_1 RIDX _jidousha_n_1⟩
21	⟨1 _unten_s ARG1 _hito_n_1⟩
21	⟨1 _unten_s ARG2 _jidousha_n_1⟩
21	⟨1 _ya_p_conj LIDX _densha_n_1⟩
21	⟨1 _ya_p_conj RIDX _jidousha_n_1⟩
22	⟨2 _unten_s _hito_n_1 _jidousha_n_1⟩
23	⟨3 _unten_s _hito_n_1⟩
23	⟨3 _unten_s _jidousha_n_1⟩
...	

Table 2: Example semantic features (SEM-Dep) extracted from the dependency tree in Figure 4.

only one argument at a time, #22 provides unlabeled relations, #23 provides one unlabeled relation at a time and so on.

Each combination of a predicate and its related argument(s) becomes a feature. These resemble the basic semantic features used by Toutanova et al. (2005). We further simplify these by collapsing some non-informative predicates, e.g. the `unknown` predicate used in fragments.

3.2.2 Word Sense and Semantic Class Dependencies

We created two sets of features based only on the word senses. For SEM-WS we used the sense annotation to replace each underspecified MRS predicate by a predicate indicating the word sense. This used the gold standard sense tags. For SEM-Class, we used the sense annotation to replace each predicate by its Goi-Taikei semantic class.

In addition, to capture more useful relationships, conjunctions were followed down into the left and right daughters, and added as separate features. The semantic classes for 電車$_1$*densha* "train" and 自動車$_1$*jidousha* "car" are both ⟨`988:land vehicle`⟩, while 運転$_1$ *unten* "drive" is ⟨`2003:motion`⟩ and 人$_4$ *hito* "person"is ⟨`4:human`⟩. The sample features of SEM-Class are shown in Table 3.

These features provide more specific information, in the case of the word sense, and semantic smoothing in the case of the semantic classes, as words are binned into only 2,700 classes.

3.2.3 Superordinate Semantic Classes

We further smooth these features by replacing the semantic classes with their hypernyms at a given level (SEM-L). We investigated levels 2 to 5. Predicates are binned into only 9 classes at level 2, 30 classes at level 3, 136 classes at level 4, and 392 classes at level 5.

#	sample features
40	⟨0 _unten_s ARG1 C4 ARG2 C988⟩
40	⟨1 C2003 ARG1 C4 ARG2 C988⟩
40	⟨1 C2003 ARG1 C4 ARG2 C988⟩
40	⟨0 _ya_p_conj LIDX C988 RIDX C988⟩
41	⟨2 _unten_s ARG1 C4⟩
41	⟨2 _unten_s ARG2 C988⟩
...	

Table 3: Example semantic class features (SEM-Class).

For example, at level 3, the hypernym class for ⟨`988:land vehicle`⟩ is ⟨`706:inanimate`⟩, ⟨`2003:motion`⟩ is ⟨`1236:human activity`⟩ and ⟨`4:human`⟩ is unchanged. So we used ⟨`706:inanimate`⟩ and ⟨`1236:human activity`⟩ to make features in the same way as Table 3.

An advantage of these underspecified semantic classes is that they are more robust to errors in word sense disambiguation — fine grained sense distinctions can be ignored.

3.2.4 Valency Dictionary Compatability

The last kind of semantic information we use is valency information, taken from the Japanese side of the Goi-Taikei Japanese-English valency dictionary as extended by Fujita and Bond (2004).This valency dictionary has detailed information about the argument properties of verbs and adjectives, including subcategorization and selectional restrictions. A simplified entry of the Japanese side for 運転する *unten-suru* "drive" is shown in Figure 6.

Each entry has a predicate and several case-slots. Each case-slot has information such as grammatical function, case-marker, case-role (N1, N2, ...) and semantic restrictions. The semantic restrictions are defined by the Goi-Taikei's semantic classes.

On the Japanese side of Goi-Taikei's valency dictionary, there are 10,146 types of verbs giving 18,512 entries and 1,723 types of adjectives giving 2,618 entries.

The valency based features were constructed by first finding the most appropriate pattern, and then recording how well it matched.

To find the most appropriate pattern, we extracted candidate dictionary entries whose lemma is the

```
PID:300513
┌ N1 <4:people> "が" ga
├ N2 <986:vehicles> "を" o
└ 運転する unten-suru
```

Figure 6: 運転する*unten-suru* "N1 drive N2". PID is the verb's Pattern ID

#	sample features
31	⟨0 High⟩
31	⟨1 300513 High⟩
31	⟨2 2⟩
31	⟨3 R:High⟩
31	⟨4 300513 R:High⟩
32	⟨1 _unten_s High⟩
32	⟨4 _unten_s R:High⟩
33	⟨5 N1 C High⟩
33	⟨7 C⟩
...	

Table 4: Example semantic features (SP)

same as the predicate in the sentence: for example we look up all entries for 運転する *unten-suru* "drive". Then, for each candidate pattern, we mapped its arguments to the target predicate's arguments via case-markers. If the target predicate has no suitable argument, we mapped to comitative phrase. Finally, for each candidate patterns, we calculate a matching score[1] and select the pattern which has the best score.

Once we have the most appropriate pattern, we then construct features that record how good the match is (Table 4). These include: the total score, with or without the verb's Pattern ID (High/Med/Low/Zero: #31 0,1), the number of filled arguments (#31 2), the fraction of filled arguments vs all arguments (High/Med/Low/Zero: #31 3,4), the score for each argument of the pattern (#32 5) and the types of matches (#32 5,7).

These scores allow us to use information about word usage in an exisiting dictionary.

4 Evaluation and Results

We trained and tested on a subset of the dictionary definition and example sentences in the Hinoki corpus. This consists of those sentences with ambiguous parses which have been annotated so that the number of parses has been reduced (Table 5). That is, we excluded unambiguous sentences (with a single parse), and those where the annotators judged that no parse gave the correct semantics. This does not necessarily mean that there is a single correct parse, we allow the annotator to claim that two or more parses are equally appropriate.

Corpus		# Sents	Length (Ave)	Parses/Sent (Ave)
Definitions	Train	30,345	9.3	190.1
	Test	2,790	10.1	177.0
Examples	Train	27,081	10.9	74.1
	Test	2,587	10.4	47.3

Table 5: Data of Sets for Evaluation

Dictionary definition sentences are a different genre to other commonly used test sets (e.g news-paper text in the Penn Treebank or travel dialogues in Redwoods). However, they are valid examples of naturally occurring texts and a native speaker can read and understand them without special training. The main differences with newspaper text is that the definition sentences are shorter, contain more fragments (especially NPs as single utterances) and fewer quoting and proper names. The main differences with travel dialogues is the lack of questions.

4.1 A Maximum Entropy Ranker

Log-linear models provide a very flexible framework that has been widely used for a range of tasks in NLP, including parse selection and reranking for machine translation. We use a *maximum entropy / minimum divergence* (MEMD) modeler to train the parse selection model. Specifically, we use the open-source **Toolkit for Advanced Discriminative Modeling** (TADM:[2] Malouf, 2002) for training, using its *limited-memory variable metric* as the optimization method and determining best-performing convergence thresholds and prior sizes experimentally. A comparison of this learner with the use of support vector machines over similar data found that the SVMs gave comparable results but were far slower (Baldridge and Osborne, 2007). Because we are investigating the effects of various different features, we chose the faster learner.

[1] The scoring method follows Bond and Shirai (1997), and depends on the goodness of the matches of the arguments.

[2] `http://tadm.sourceforge.net`

Method	Definitions		Examples	
	Accuracy (%)	Features (×1000)	Accuracy (%)	Features (×1000)
SYN-1	52.8	7	67.6	8
SYN-GP	62.7	266	76.0	196
SYN-ALL	**63.8**	316	**76.2**	245
SYN baseline	16.4	random	22.3	random
SEM-Dep	57.3	1,189	58.7	675
+SEM-WS	56.2	1,904	59.0	1,486
+SEM-Class	57.5	2,018	59.7	1,669
+SEM-L2	60.3	808	62.9	823
+SEM-L3	59.8	876	62.8	879
+SEM-L4	59.9	1,000	62.3	973
+SEM-L5	60.4	1,240	61.3	1,202
+SP	59.1	1,218	68.2	819
+SEM-ALL	**62.7**	3,384	**69.1**	2,693
SYN-SEM	**69.5**	2,476	**79.2**	2,126
SEM baseline	20.3	random	22.8	random

Table 6: Parse Selection Results

4.2 Results

The results for most of the models discussed in the previous section are shown in Table 6. The accuracy is exact match for the entire sentence: a model gets a point only if its top ranked analysis is the same as an analysis selected as correct in Hinoki. This is a stricter metric than component based measures (e.g., labelled precision) which award partial credit for incorrect parses. For the syntactic models, the baseline (random choice) is 16.4% for the definitions and 22.3% for the examples. Definition sentences are harder to parse than the example sentences. This is mainly because they have fewer relative clauses and coordinate NPs, both large sources of ambiguity. For the semantic and combined models, multiple sentences can have different parses but the same semantics. In this case all sentences with the correct semantics are scored as good. This raises the baselines to 20.3 and 22.8% respectively.

Even the simplest models (SYN-1 and SEM-Dep) give a large improvement over the baseline. Adding grandparenting to the syntactic model has a large improvement (SYN-GP), but adding lexical n-grams gave only a slight improvement over this (SYN-ALL).

The effect of smoothing by superordinate semantic classes (SEM-Class), shows a modest improvement. The syntactic model already contains a backoff to lexical-types, we hypothesize that the semantic classes behave in the same way. Surprisingly, as we add more data, the very top level of the semantic class hierarchy performs almost as well as the

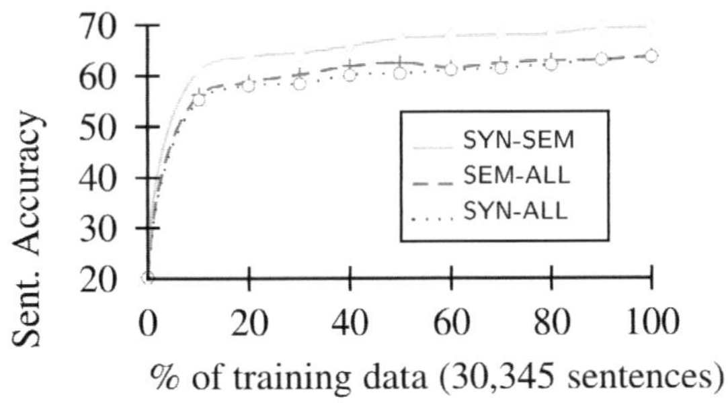

Figure 7: Learning Curves (Definitions)

more detailed levels. The features using the valency dictionary (SP) also provide a considerable improvement over the basic dependencies.

Combining all the semantic features (SEM-ALL) provides a clear improvement, suggesting that the information is heterogeneous. Finally, combing the syntactic and semantic features gives the best results by far (SYN-SEM: SYN-ALL + SEM-Dep + SEM-Class + SEM-L2 + SP). The definitions sentences are harder syntactically, and thus get more of a boost from the semantics. The semantics still improve performance for the example sentences.

The semantic class based sense features used here are based on manual annotation, and thus show an upper bound on the effects of these features. This is not an absolute upper bound on the use of sense information — it may be possible to improve further through feature engineering. The learning curves (Fig 7) have not yet flattened out. We can still improve by increasing the size of the training data.

5 Discussion

Bikel (2000) combined sense information and parse information using a subset of SemCor (with WordNet senses and Penn-II treebanks) to produce a combined model. This model did not use semantic dependency relations, but only syntactic dependencies augmented with heads, which suggests that the deeper structural semantics provided by the HPSG parser is important. Xiong et al. (2005) achieved only a very minor improvement over a plain syntactic model, using features based on both the correlation between predicates and their arguments, and between predicates and the hypernyms of their arguments (using HowNet). However, they do not investigate generalizing to different levels than a word's immediate hypernym.

Pioneering work by Toutanova et al. (2005) and Baldridge and Osborne (2007) on parse selection for an English HPSG treebank used simpler semantic features without sense information, and got a far less dramatic improvement when they combined syntactic and semantic information.

The use of hand-crafted lexical resources such as the Goi-Taikei ontology is sometimes criticized on the grounds that such resources are hard to produce and scarce. While it is true that valency lexicons and sense hierarchies are hard to produce, they are of such value that they have already been created for all of the languages we know of which have large treebanks. In fact, there are more languages with WordNets than large treebanks.

In future work we intend to confirm that we can get improved results with raw sense disambiguation results not just the gold standard annotations and test the results on other sections of the Hinoki corpus.

6 Conclusions

We have shown that sense-based semantic features combined with ontological information are effective for parse selection. Training and testing on the definition subset of the Hinoki corpus, a combined model gave a 5.6% improvement in parse selection accuracy over a model using only syntactic features (63.8% → 69.4%). Similar results (76.2% → 79.2%) were found with example sentences.

References

Jason Baldridge and Miles Osborne. 2007. Active learning and logarithmic opinion pools for HPSG parse selection. *Natural Language Engineering*, 13(1):1–32.

Daniel M. Bikel. 2000. A statistical model for parsing and word-sense disambiguation. In *Proceedings of the Joint SIGDAT Conference on Empirical Methods in Natural Language Processing and Very Large Corpora*, pages 155–163. Hong Kong.

Francis Bond, Sanae Fujita, and Takaaki Tanaka. 2007. The Hinoki syntactic and semantic treebank of Japanese. *Language Resources and Evaluation*. (Special issue on Asian language technology).

Francis Bond and Satoshi Shirai. 1997. Practical and efficient organization of a large valency dictionary. In *Workshop on Multilingual Information Processing — Natural Language Processing Pacific Rim Symposium '97: NLPRS-97*. Phuket.

Ann Copestake, Dan Flickinger, Carl Pollard, and Ivan A. Sag. 2005. Minimal Recursion Semantics. An introduction. *Research on Language and Computation*, 3(4):281–332.

Christine Fellbaum, editor. 1998. *WordNet: An Electronic Lexical Database*. MIT Press.

Sanae Fujita and Francis Bond. 2004. A method of creating new bilingual valency entries using alternations. In Gilles Sérasset, editor, *COLING 2004 Multilingual Linguistic Resources*, pages 41–48. Geneva.

Eduard Hovy, Mitchell Marcus, Martha Palmer, Lance Ramshaw, and Ralph Weischedel. 2006. Ontonotes: The 90% solution. In *Proceedings of the Human Language Technology Conference of the NAACL, Companion Volume: Short Papers*, pages 57–60. Association for Computational Linguistics, New York City, USA. URL `http://www.aclweb.org/anthology/N/N06/N06-2015`.

Satoru Ikehara, Masahiro Miyazaki, Satoshi Shirai, Akio Yokoo, Hiromi Nakaiwa, Kentaro Ogura, Yoshifumi Ooyama, and Yoshihiko Hayashi. 1997. *Goi-Taikei — A Japanese Lexicon*. Iwanami Shoten, Tokyo. 5 volumes/CDROM.

Kaname Kasahara, Hiroshi Sato, Francis Bond, Takaaki Tanaka, Sanae Fujita, Tomoko Kanasugi, and Shigeaki Amano. 2004. Construction of a Japanese semantic lexicon: Lexeed. In *IPSG SIG: 2004-NLC-159*, pages 75–82. Tokyo. (in Japanese).

Dan Klein and Christopher D. Manning. 2003. Accurate unlexicalized parsing. In Erhard Hinrichs and Dan Roth, editors, *Proceedings of the 41st Annual Meeting of the Association for Computational Linguistics*, pages 423–430. URL `http://www.aclweb.org/anthology/P03-1054.pdf`.

Robert Malouf. 2002. A comparison of algorithms for maximum entropy parameter estimation. In *CONLL-2002*, pages 49–55. Taipei, Taiwan.

Robert Malouf and Gertjan van Noord. 2004. Wide coverage parsing with stochastic attribute value grammars. In *IJCNLP-04 Workshop: Beyond shallow analyses - Formalisms and statistical modeling for deep analyses*. JST CREST. URL `http://www-tsujii.is.s.u-tokyo.ac.jp/bsa/papers/malouf.pdf`.

Stephan Oepen, Dan Flickinger, Kristina Toutanova, and Christoper D. Manning. 2004. LinGO redwoods: A rich and dynamic treebank for HPSG. *Research on Language and Computation*, 2(4):575–596.

Stephan Oepen and Jan Tore Lønning. 2006. Discriminant-based MRS banking. In *Proceedings of the 5th International Conference on Language Resources and Evaluation (LREC 2006)*. Genoa, Italy.

Carl Pollard and Ivan A. Sag. 1994. *Head Driven Phrase Structure Grammar*. University of Chicago Press, Chicago.

Melanie Siegel and Emily M. Bender. 2002. Efficient deep processing of Japanese. In *Proceedings of the 3rd Workshop on Asian Language Resources and International Standardization at the 19th International Conference on Computational Linguistics*, pages 1–8. Taipei.

Kristina Toutanova, Christopher D. Manning, Dan Flickinger, and Stephan Oepen. 2005. Stochastic HPSG parse disambiguation using the redwoods corpus. *Research on Language and Computation*, 3(1):83–105.

Deyi Xiong, Qun Liu Shuanglong Li and, Shouxun Lin, and Yueliang Qian. 2005. Parsing the Penn Chinese treebank with semantic knowledge. In Robert Dale, Jian Su Kam-Fai Wong and, and Oi Yee Kwong, editors, *Natural Language Processing — IJCNLP 005: Second International Joint Conference Proceedings*, pages 70–81. Springer-Verlag.

Deep Grammars in a Tree Labeling Approach to Syntax-based Statistical Machine Translation

Mark Hopkins
Department of Linguistics
University of Potsdam, Germany
hopkins@ling.uni-potsdam.de

Jonas Kuhn
Department of Linguistics
University of Potsdam, Germany
kuhn@ling.uni-potsdam.de

Abstract

In this paper, we propose a new syntax-based machine translation (MT) approach based on reducing the MT task to a tree-labeling task, which is further decomposed into a sequence of simple decisions for which discriminative classifiers can be trained. The approach is very flexible and we believe that it is particularly well-suited for exploiting the linguistic knowledge encoded in deep grammars whenever possible, while at the same time taking advantage of data-based techniques that have proven a powerful basis for MT, as recent advances in statistical MT show.

A full system using the Lexical-Functional Grammar (LFG) parsing system XLE and the grammars from the Parallel Grammar development project (ParGram; (Butt et al., 2002)) has been implemented, and we present preliminary results on English-to-German translation with a tree-labeling system trained on a small subsection of the Europarl corpus.

1 Motivation

Machine translation (MT) is probably the oldest application of what we call deep linguistic processing techniques today. But from its inception, there have been alternative considerations of approaching the task with data-based statistical techniques (cf. Warren Weaver's well-known memo from 1949). Only with fairly recent advances in computer technology have researchers been able to build effective statistical MT prototypes, but in the last few years, the statistical approach has received enormous research interest and made significant progress.

The most successful statistical MT paradigm has been, for a while now, the so-call phrase-based MT approach (Och and Ney, 2003). In this paradigm, sentences are translated from a source language to a target language through the repeated substitution of contiguous word sequences ("phrases") from the source language for word sequences in the target language. Training of the phrase translation model builds on top of a standard statistical word alignment over the training corpus of parallel text (Brown et al., 1993) for identifying corresponding word blocks, assuming no further linguistic analysis of the source or target language. In decoding, i.e. the application of the acquired translation model to unseen source sentences, these systems then typically rely on n-gram language models and simple statistical reordering models to shuffle the phrases into an order that is coherent in the target language.

An obvious advantage of statistical MT approaches is that they can adopt (often very idiomatic) translations of mid- to high-frequency constructions without requiring any language-pair specific engineering work. At the same time it is clear that a linguistics-free approach is limited in what it can ultimately achieve: only linguistically informed systems can detect certain generalizations from lower-frequency constructions in the data and successfully apply them in a similar but different linguistic context. Hence, the idea of "hybrid" MT, exploiting both linguistic and statistical information is fairly old. Here we will not consider classical, rule-based systems with some added data-based resource acquisition (although they may be among the best candidates for high-quality special-purpose translation – but adaption to new language pairs and sub-languages is very costly for these systems). The other form of hybridization – a statistical MT model that is based on a deeper analysis of the syntactic

Proceedings of the 5th Workshop on Important Unresolved Matters, pages 33–40,
Ann Arbor, June 2005. ©2005 Association for Computational Linguistics

structure of a sentence – has also long been identified as a desirable objective in principle (consider (Wu, 1997; Yamada and Knight, 2001)). However, attempts to retrofit syntactic information into the phrase-based paradigm have not met with enormous success (Koehn et al., 2003; Och et al., 2003)[1], and purely phrase-based MT systems continue to outperform these syntax/phrase-based hybrids.

In this work, we try to make a fresh start with syntax-based statistical MT, discarding the phrase-based paradigm and designing a MT system from the ground up, using syntax as our central guiding star – besides the word alignment over a parallel corpus. Our approach is compatible with and can benefit substantially from rich linguistic representations obtained from deep grammars like the ParGram LFGs. Nevertheless, contrary to classical interlingual or deep transfer-based systems, the generative stochastic model that drives our system is grounded only in the cross-language word alignment and a surface-based phrase structure tree for the source language and will thus degrade gracefully on input with parsing issues – which we suspect is an important feature for making the overall system competitive with the highly general phrase-based MT approach.

Preliminary evaluation of our nascent system indicates that this new approach might well have the potential to finally realize some of the promises of syntax in statistical MT.

2 General Task

We want to build a system that can learn to translate sentences from a source language to a destination language. The general set-up is simple.

Firstly, we have a training corpus of paired sentences f and e, where target sentence e is a gold standard translation of source sentence f. These sentence pairs are annotated with auxiliary information, which can include word alignments and syntactic information. We refer to these annotated sentence pairs as *complete translation objects*.

Secondly, we have an evaluation corpus of source sentences. These sentences are annotated with a subset of the auxiliary information used to annotate the training corpus. We refer to these partially annotated source sentences as *partial translation objects*.

[1](Chiang, 2005) also reports that with his hierarchical generalization of the phrase-based approach, the addition of parser information doesn't lead to any improvements.

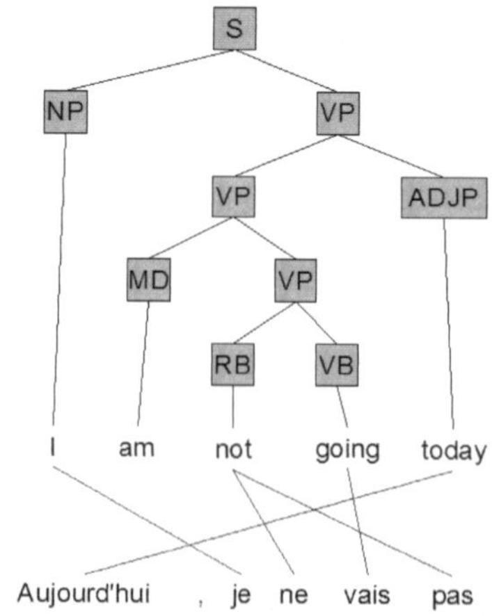

Figure 1: Example translation object.

The task at hand: use the training corpus to learn a procedure, through which we can successfully induce a complete translation object from a partial translation object. This is what we will define as *translation*.

3 Specific Task Addressed by this Paper

Before going on to actually describe a translation procedure (and how to induce it), we need to specify our prior assumptions about how the translation objects will be annotated. For this paper, we want to exploit the syntax information that we can gain from an LFG-parser, hence we will assume the following annotations:

(1) In the training and evaluation corpora, the source sentences will be parsed with the XLE-parser. The attribute-value information from LFG's f-structure is restructured so it is indexed by (c-structure) tree nodes; thus a tree node can bear multiple labels for various pieces of morphological, syntactic and semantic information.

(2) In the training corpus, the source and target sentence of every translation object will be aligned using GIZA++ (http://www.fjoch.com/).

In other words, our complete translation objects will be aligned tree-string pairs (for instance, Figure 1), while our partial translation objects will be trees (the tree portion of Figure 1). No other annotations will be assumed for this paper.

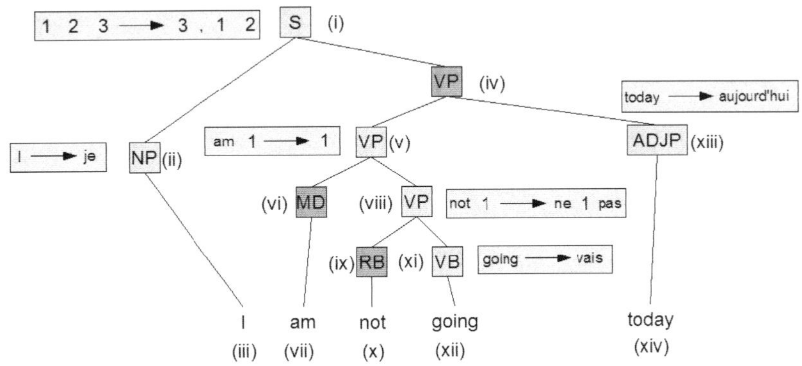

Figure 2: GHKM tree equivalent of example translation object. The light gray nodes are rule nodes of the GHKM tree.

4 Syntax MT as Tree Labeling

It is not immediately clear how one would learn a process to map a parsed source sentence into an aligned tree-string pair. To facilitate matters, we will map complete translation objects to an alternate representation. In (Galley et al., 2003), the authors give a semantics to aligned tree-string pairs by associating each with an annotated parse tree (hereafter called a *GHKM tree*) representing a specific theory about how the source sentence was translated into the destination sentence.

In Figure 1, we show an example translation object and in Figure 2, we show its associated GHKM tree. The GHKM tree is simply the parse tree f of the translation object, annotated with rules (hereafter referred to as *GHKM rules*). We will not describe in depth the mapping process from translation object to GHKM tree. Suffice it to say that the alignment induces a set of intuitive translation rules. Essentially, a rule like: "not 1 $\rightarrow$ ne 1 pas" (see Figure 2) means: if we see the word "not" in English, followed by a phrase already translated into French, then translate the entire thing as the word "ne" + the translated phrase + the word "pas." A parse tree node gets labeled with one of these rules if, roughly speaking, its span is still contiguous when projected (via the alignment) into the target language.

The advantage of using the GHKM interpretation of a complete translation object is that our translation task becomes simpler. Now, to induce a complete translation object from a partial translation object (parse tree), all we need to do is label the nodes of the tree with appropriate rules. We have reduced the vaguely defined task of translation to the concrete task of tree labeling.

5 The Generative Process

At the most basic level, we could design a naive generative process that takes a parse tree and then makes a series of decisions, one for each node, about what rule (if any) that node should be assigned. However it is a bit unreasonable to expect to learn such a decision without breaking it down somewhat, as there are an enormous number of rules that could potentially be used to label any given parse tree node. So let's break this task down into simpler decisions. Ideally, we would like to devise a generative process consisting of decisions between a small number of possibilities (ideally binary decisions).

We will begin by deciding, for each node, whether or not it will be annotated with a rule. This is clearly a binary decision. Once a generative process has made this decision for each node, we get a convenient byproduct. As seen in Figure 3, the LHS of each rule is already determined. Hence after this sequence of binary decisions, half of our task is already completed.

The question remains: how do we determine the RHS of these rules? Again, we could create a generative process that makes these decisions directly, but choosing the RHS of a rule is still a rather wide-open decision, so we will break it down further. For each rule, we will begin by choosing the *template* of its RHS, which is a RHS in which all sequences of variables are replaced with an empty slot into which variables can later be placed. For instance, the tem-

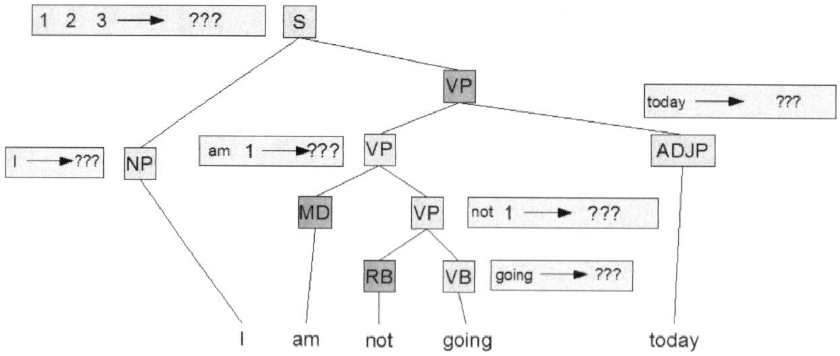

Figure 3: Partial GHKM tree, after rule nodes have been identified (light gray). Notice that once we identify the rule node, the rule left-hand sides are already determined.

plate of ⟨"ne", x_1, "pas"⟩ is ⟨"ne", X, "pas"⟩ and the template of ⟨x_3, ",", x_1, x_2⟩ is ⟨X, ",", X⟩, where X represents the empty slots.

Once the template is chosen, it simply needs to be filled with the variables from the LHS. To do so, we process the LHS variables, one by one. By default, they are placed to the right of the previously placed variable (the first variable is placed in the first slot). We repeatedly offer the option to push the variable to the right until the option is declined or it is no longer possible to push it further right. If the variable was not pushed right at all, we repeatedly offer the option to push the variable to the left until the option is declined or it is no longer possible to push it further left. Figure 4 shows this generative story in action for the rule RHS ⟨x_3, ",", x_1, x_2⟩.

These are all of the decisions we need to make in order to label a parse tree with GHKM rules. A trace of this generative process for the GHKM tree of Figure 2 is shown in Figure 5. Notice that, aside from the template decisions, all of the decisions are binary (i.e. feasible to learn discriminatively). Even the template decisions are not terribly large-domain, if we maintain a separate feature-conditional distribution for each LHS template. For instance, if the LHS template is ⟨"not", X⟩, then RHS template ⟨"ne", X, "pas"⟩ and a few other select candidates should bear most of the probability mass.

5.1 Training

Having established this generative story, training is straightforward. As a first step, we can convert each complete translation object of our training corpus to the trace of its generative story (as in Figure 5).

Decision to make	Decision	RHS so far
RHS template?	X , X	X , X
default placement of var 1		1 , X
push var 1 right?	yes	X , 1
default placement of var 2		X , 1 2
push var 2 left?	no	X , 1 2
default placement of var 3		X , 1 2 3
push var 3 left?	yes	X , 1 3 2
push var 3 left?	yes	X , 3 1 2
push var 3 left?	yes	3 , 1 2

Figure 4: Trace of the generative story for the right-hand side of a GHKM rule.

These decisions can be annotated with whatever feature information we might deem helpful. Then we simply divide up these feature vectors by decision type (for instance, rule node decisions, template decisions, etc.) and train a separate discriminative classifier for each decision type from the feature vectors. This method is quite flexible, in that it allows us to use any generic off-the-shelf classification software to train our system. We prefer learners that produce distributions (rather than hard classifiers) as output, but this is not required.

5.2 Exploiting deep linguistic information

The use of discriminative classifiers makes our approach very flexible in terms of the information that can be exploited in the labeling (or translation) process. Any information that can be encoded as features relative to GHKM tree nodes can be used. For the experiments reported in this paper, we parsed the source language side of a parallel corpus (a small subsection of the English-German Europarl corpus; (Koehn, 2002)) with the XLE system, using the ParGram LFG grammar and applying probabilistic disambiguation (Riezler et al., 2002) to obtain a single analysis (i.e., a c-structure [phrase structure tree] and an f-structure [an associated attribute-value matrix with morphosyntactic feature information and a shallow semantic interpretation]) for each sentence. A fall-back mechanism integrated in the parser/grammar ensures that even for sentences that do not receive a full parse, substrings are deeply parsed and can often be treated successfully.

We convert the c-structure/f-structure representation that is based on XLE's sophisticated word-internal analysis into a plain phrase structure tree representation based on the original tokens in the source language string. The morphosyntactic feature information from f-structure is copied as additional labeling information to the relevant GHKM tree nodes, and the f-structural dependency relation among linguistic units is translated into a relation among corresponding GHKM tree nodes. The relational information is then used to systematically extend the learning feature set for the tree-node based classifiers.

In future experiments, we also plan to exploit linguistic knowledge about the target language by factorizing the generation of target language words into separate generation of lemmas and the various morphosyntactic features. In decoding, a morphological generator will be used to generate a string of surface words.

5.3 Decoding

Because we have purposely refused to make any Markov assumptions in our model, decoding cannot be accomplished in polynomial time. Our hypothesis is that it is better to find a suboptimal solution of a high-quality model than the optimal solution of a poorer model. We decode through a simple search through the space of assignments to our generative process.

This is, potentially, a very large and intractible search space. However, if most assignment decisions can be made with relative confidence (i.e. the classifiers we have trained make fairly certain decisions), then the great majority of search nodes have values which are inferior to those of the best solutions. The standard search technique of *depth-first branch-and-bound search* takes advantage of search spaces with this particular characteristic by first finding greedy good-quality solutions and using their values to optimally prune a significant portion of the search space. Depth-first branch-and-bound search has the following advantage: it finds a good (suboptimal) solution in linear time and continually improves on this solution until it finds the optimal. Thus it can be run either as an optimal decoder or as a heuristic decoder, since we can interrupt its execution at any time to get the best solution found so far. Additionally, it takes only linear space to run.

6 Preliminary results

In this section, we present some preliminary results for an English-to-German translation system based on the ideas outlined in this paper.

Our data was a subset of the Europarl corpus consisting of sentences of lengths ranging from 8 to 17 words. Our training corpus contained 50000 sentences and our test corpus contained 300 sentences. We also had a small number of reserved sentences for development. The English sentences were parsed with XLE, using the English ParGram LFG grammar, and the sentences were word-aligned with GIZA++. We used the WEKA machine learning package (Witten and Frank, 2005) to train the distributions (specifically, we used model trees).

For comparison, we also trained and evaluated the phrase-based MT system Pharaoh (Koehn, 2005) on this limited corpus, using Pharaoh's default parameters. In a different set of MT-as-Tree-Labeling experiments, we used a standard treebank parser trained on the PennTreebank Wall Street Journal section. Even with this parser, which produces less detailed information than XLE, the results are competitive when assessed with quantitative measures: Pharaoh achieved a BLEU score of 11.17 on the test set, whereas our system achieved a BLEU score of 11.52. What is notable here is not the scores themselves (low due to the size of the training corpus). However our system managed to perform comparably with Pharaoh in a very early stage of its development, with rudimentary features and without the benefit of an n-gram language model.

For the XLE-based system we cannot include quantitative results for the same experimental setup at the present time. As a preliminary qualitative

Decision to make	Decision	Active features
rule node (i)?	YES	NT="S"; HEAD = "am"
rule node (ii)?	YES	NT="NP"; HEAD = "I"
rule node (iv)?	NO	NT="VP"; HEAD = "am"
rule node (v)?	YES	NT="VP"; HEAD = "am"
rule node (vi)?	NO	NT="MD"; HEAD = "am"
rule node (viii)?	YES	NT="VP"; HEAD = "going"
rule node (ix)?	NO	NT="RB"; HEAD = "not"
rule node (xi)?	YES	NT="VB"; HEAD = "going"
rule node (xiii)?	YES	NT="ADJP"; HEAD = "today"
RHS template? (i)	X , X	NT="S"
push var 1 right? (i)	YES	VARNT="NP"; PUSHPAST= ","
push var 2 left? (i)	NO	VARNT="VP"; PUSHPAST= "NP"
push var 3 left? (i)	YES	VARNT="ADJP"; PUSHPAST= "VP"
push var 3 left? (i)	YES	VARNT="ADJP"; PUSHPAST= "NP"
push var 3 left? (i)	YES	VARNT="ADJP"; PUSHPAST= ","
RHS template? (ii)	je	NT="NP"; WD="I"
RHS template? (v)	X	NT="VP"
RHS template? (viii)	ne X pas	NT="VP"; WD="not"
RHS template? (xi)	vais	NT="VB"; WD="going"
RHS template? (xiii)	aujourd'hui	NT="ADJP"; WD="today"

Figure 5: Trace of a top-down generative story for the GHKM tree in Figure 2.

evaluation, let's take a closer look at the sentences produced by our system, to gain some insight as to its current strengths and weaknesses.

Starting with the English sentence (1) (note that all data is lowercase), our system produces (2).

(1) i agree with the spirit of those amendments .

(2) ich stimme die geist dieser änderungsanträge zu .
I vote the.FEM spirit.MASC these change-proposals to .

The GHKM tree is depicted in Figure 6. The key feature of this translation is how the English phrase "agree with" is translated as the German "stimme ... zu" construction. Such a feat is difficult to produce consistently with a purely phrase-based system, as phrases of arbitrary length can be placed between the words "stimme" and "zu", as we can see happening in this particular example. By contrast, Pharaoh opts for the following (somewhat less desirable) translation:

(3) ich stimme mit dem geist dieser änderungsanträge .
I vote with the.MASC spirit.MASC these change-proposals .

A weakness in our system is also evident here. The German noun "Geist" is masculine, thus our system uses the wrong article (a problem that Pharaoh, with its embedded n-gram language model, does not encounter).

In general, it seems that our system is superior to Pharaoh at figuring out the proper way to arrange the words of the output sentence, and inferior to Pharaoh at finding what the actual translation of those words should be.

Consider the English sentence (4). Here we have an example of a modal verb with an embedded infinitival VP. In German, infinite verbs should go at the end of the sentence, and this is achieved by our system (translating "shall" as "werden", and "submit" as "vorlegen"), as is seen in (5).

(4)) we shall submit a proposal along these lines before the end of this year .

(5) wir werden eine vorschlag in dieser haushaltslinien vor die ende dieser jahres vorlegen .
we will a.FEM proposal.MASC in these budget-lines before the.FEM end.NEUT this.FEM year.NEUT submit .

Pharaoh does not manage this (translating "submit" as "unterbreiten" and placing it mid-sentence).

(6) werden wir unterbreiten eine vorschlag in dieser haushaltslinien vor ende dieser jahr .
will we submit a proposal in these budget-lines before end this.FEM year.NEUT .

It is worth noting that while our system gets the word order of the output system right, it makes sev-

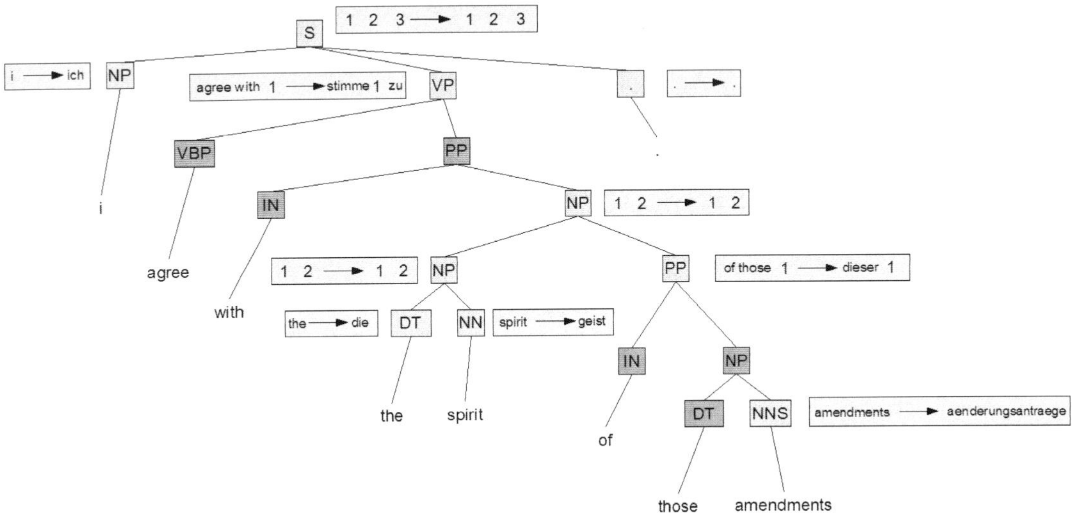

Figure 6: GHKM tree output for a test sentence.

eral agreement mistakes and (like Pharaoh) doesn't get the translation of "along these lines" right.

In Figure 7, we show sample translations by the three systems under discussion for the first five sentences in our evaluation set. For the LFG-based approach, we can at this point present only results for a version trained on 10% of the sentence pairs. This explains why more source words are left untranslated. But note that despite the small training set, the word ordering results are clearly superior for this system: the syntax-driven rules place the untranslated English words in the correct position in terms of German syntax.

The translations with Pharaoh contain relatively few agreement mistakes (note that it exploits a language model of German trained on a much larger corpus). The phrase-based approach does however skip words and make positioning mistakes some of which are so serious (like in the last sentence) that they make the result hard to understand.

7 Discussion

In describing this pilot project, we have attempted to give a "big picture" view of the essential ideas behind our system. To avoid obscuring the presentation, we have avoided many of the implementation details, in particular our choice of features. There are exactly four types of decisions that we need to train: (1) whether a parse tree node should be a rule node, (2) the RHS template of a rule, (3) whether a rule variable should be pushed left, and (4) whether a rule variable should be pushed right. For each of these decisions, there are a number of possible features that suggest themselves. For instance, recall that in German, embedded infinitival verbs get placed at the end of the sentence or clause. So when the system is considering whether to push a rule's noun phrase to the left, past an existing verb, it would be useful for it to consider (as a feature) whether that verb is the first or second verb of its clause and what the morphological form of the verb is.

Even in these early stages of development, the MT-as-Tree-Labeling system shows promise in using syntactic information flexibly and effectively for MT. Our preliminary comparison indicates that using deep syntactic analysis leads to improved translation behavior. We hope to develop the system into a competitive alternative to phrase-based approaches.

References

P.F. Brown, S. A. Della Pietra, V. J. Della Pietra, and R. L. Mercer. 1993. The mathematics of statistical machine translation: Parameter estimation. *Computational Linguistics*, 19(2):263–311.

Miriam Butt, Helge Dyvik, Tracy Holloway King, Hiroshi Masuichi, and Christian Rohrer. 2002. The parallel gram-

source	we believe that this is a fundamental element .
professional translation	wir denken , dass dies ein grundlegender aspekt ist .
PHARAOH (50k)	wir halten dies für eine grundlegende element .
TL-WSJ (50k)	wir glauben , dass diesen ist ein grundlegendes element .
TL-LFG (5k)	wir meinen , dass dies eine grundlegende element ist .
source	it is true that lisbon is a programme for ten years .
professional translation	nun ist lissabon ein programm für zehn jahre .
PHARAOH (50k)	es ist richtig , dass lissabon ist eine programm für zehn jahren .
TL-WSJ (50k)	es ist richtig , dass lissabon ist eine programm für zehn jahren .
TL-LFG (5k)	es ist *true* , dass *lisbon* eine programm für zehn jahren ist .
source	i completely agree with each of these points .
professional translation	ich bin mit jeder einzelnen dieser aussagen voll und ganz einverstanden .
PHARAOH (50k)	ich ..... völlig einverstanden mit jedem dieser punkte .
TL-WSJ (50k)	ich bin völlig mit jedes diese fragen einer meinung .
TL-LFG (5k)	ich *agree completely* mit jeder dieser punkte .
source	however , i would like to add one point .
professional translation	aber ich möchte gern einen punkt hinzufügen .
PHARAOH (50k)	allerdings möchte ich noch eines sagen .
TL-WSJ (50k)	ich möchte jedoch ~~an~~ noch einen punkt hinzufügen .
TL-LFG (5k)	allerdings möchte ich einen punkt *add* .
source	this is undoubtedly a point which warrants attention .
professional translation	ohne jeden zweifel ist dies ein punkt , der aufmerksamkeit verdient .
PHARAOH (50k)	das ist sicherlich eine punkt .... rechtfertigt das aufmerksamkeit .
TL-WSJ (50k)	das ist ohne zweifel eine punkt , die *warrants* beachtung .
TL-LFG (5k)	das ist *undoubtedly* .... sache , die *attention warrants* .

Figure 7: Sample translations by (1) the PHARAOH system, (2) our system with a treebank parser (TL-WSJ), (3) our system with the XLE parser (TL-LFG). (1) and (2) were trained on 50,000 sentence pairs, (3) just on (3) sentence pairs. Error coding: wrong morphological form, incorrectly positioned word, *untranslated source word*, missed word: ...., ~~extra word~~.

mar project. In *Proceedings of COLING-2002 Workshop on Grammar Engineering and Evaluation*, pages 1–7.

David Chiang. 2005. A hierarchical phrase-based model for statistical machine translation. In *Proceedings of ACL*, pages 263–270.

Michel Galley, Mark Hopkins, Kevin Knight, and Daniel Marcu. 2003. What's in a translation rule? In *Proc. NAACL*.

Philipp Koehn, Franz Josef Och, and Daniel Marcu. 2003. Statistical phrase-based translation. In *Proceedings of the Human Language Technology Conference 2003 (HLT-NAACL 2003)*, Edmonton, Canada.

Philipp Koehn. 2002. Europarl: A multilingual corpus for evaluation of machine translation. Ms., University of Southern California.

Philipp Koehn. 2005. Pharaoh: a beam search decoder for phrase-based statistical machine translation models. In *Proceedings of the Sixth Conference of the Association for Machine Translation in the Americas*, pages 115–124.

Franz Josef Och and Hermann Ney. 2003. A systematic comparison of various statistical alignment models. *Computational Linguistics*, 29(1):19–51.

F. J. Och, D. Gildea, S. Khudanpur, A. Sarkar, K. Yamada, A. Fraser, S. Kumar, L. Shen, D. Smith, K. Eng, Viren Jain, Z.Jin, and D. Radev. 2003. Syntax for statistical machine translation. Technical report, Center for Language and Speech Processing, Johns Hopkins University, Baltimore. Summer Workshop Final Report.

Stefan Riezler, Dick Crouch, Ron Kaplan, Tracy King, John Maxwell, and Mark Johnson. 2002. Parsing the Wall Street Journal using a Lexical-Functional Grammar and discriminative estimation techniques. In *Proceedings of the 40th Annual Meeting of the Association for Computational Linguistics (ACL'02), Pennsylvania, Philadelphia*.

Ian H. Witten and Eibe Frank. 2005. *Data Mining: Practical machine learning tools and techniques*. Morgan Kaufmann.

Dekai Wu. 1997. Stochastic inversion transduction grammars and bilingual parsing of parallel corpora. *Computational Linguistics*, 23(3):377–403.

Kenji Yamada and Kevin Knight. 2001. A syntax-based statistical translation model. In *Proceedings of the 39th Annual Meeting of the Association for Computational Linguistics*, pages 523–530.

Question Answering based on Semantic Roles

Michael Kaisser **Bonnie Webber**
University of Edinburgh
2 Buccleuch Place
Edinburgh EH8 9LW
Scotland
m.kaisser@sms.ed.ac.uk, bonnie@inf.ed.ac.uk

Abstract

This paper discusses how lexical resources based on semantic roles (i.e. FrameNet, PropBank, VerbNet) can be used for Question Answering, especially Web Question Answering. Two algorithms have been implemented to this end, with quite different characteristics. We discuss both approaches when applied to each of the resources and a combination of these and give an evaluation. We argue that employing semantic roles can indeed be highly beneficial for a QA system.

1 Introduction

A large part of the work done in NLP deals with exploring how different tools and resources can be used to improve performance on a task. The quality and usefulness of the resource certainly is a major factor for the success of the research, but equally so is the creativity with which these tools or resources are used. There usually is more than one way to employ these, and the approach chosen largely determines the outcome of the work.

This paper illustrates the above claims with respect to three lexical resources – FrameNet (Baker et al., 1998), PropBank (Palmer et al., 2005) and VerbNet (Schuler, 2005) – that convey information about lexical predicates and their arguments. We describe two new and complementary techniques for using these resources and show the improvements to be gained when they are used individually and then together. We also point out problems that must be overcome to achieve these results.

Compared with WordNet (Miller et al., 1993)–which has been used widely in QA–FrameNet, PropBank and VerbNet are still relatively new, and therefore their usefulness for QA has still to be proven. They offer the following features which can be used to gain a better understanding of questions, sentences containing answer candidates, and the relations between them:

- They all provide verb-argument structures for a large number of lexical entries.
- FrameNet and PropBank contain semantically annotated sentences that exemplify the underlying frame.
- FrameNet contains not only verbs but also lexical entries for other part-of-speeches.
- FrameNet provides inter-frame relations that can be used for more complex paraphrasing to link the question and answer sentences.

In this paper we describe two methods that use these resources to annotate both questions and sentences containing answer candidates with semantic roles. If these annotations can successfully be matched, an answer candidate can be extracted. We are able, for example, to give a complete frame-semantic analysis of the following sentences and to recognize that they all contain an answer to the question "When was Alaska purchased?":

The United States purchased Alaska in 1867.
Alaska was bought from Russia in 1867.
In 1867, Russia sold Alaska to the United States.
The acquisition of Alaska by the United States in 1867 is known as "Seward's Folly.

Proceedings of the 5th Workshop on Important Unresolved Matters, pages 41–48,
Ann Arbor, June 2005.

The first algorithm we present uses the three lexical resources to generate potential answer-containing templates. While the templates contain holes – in particular, for the answer – the parts that are known can be used to create exact quoted search queries. Sentences can then be extracted from the output of the search engine and annotated with respect to the resource being used. From this, an answer candidate (if present) can be extracted. The second algorithm analyzes the dependency structure of the annotated example sentences in FrameNet and PropBank. It then poses rather abstract queries to the web, but can in its candidate sentence analysis stage deal with a wider range of syntactic possibilities. As we will see, the two algorithms are nicely complementary.

2 Method 1: Question Answering by Natural Language Generation

The first method implemented uses the data available in the resources to generate potential answer sentences to the question. While at least one component of such a sentence (the answer) is yet unknown, the remainder of the sentence can be used to query a web search engine. The results can then be analyzed, and if they match the originally-proposed answer sentence structure, an answer candidate can be extracted.

The first step is to annotate the question with its semantic roles. For this task we use a classical semantic role labeler combined with a rule-based approach. Keep in mind that our task is to annotate questions, not declarative sentences. This is important for several reasons:

1. The role labeler we use is trained on FrameNet and PropBank data, i.e. mostly on declarative sentences, whose syntax often differs considerably from the sytax of questions. Aa a result, the training and test set differ substantially in nature.
2. Questions tend to be shorter and simpler syntactically than declarative sentences–especially those occurring in news corpora.
3. Questions contain one semantic role that has to be annotated but which is not or is only implicitly (through the question word) mentioned – the answer.

Because of these reasons and especially because many questions tend to be gramatically simple, we found that a few simple rules can help the question annotation process dramatically. We rely on MiniPar (Lin, 1998) to find the question's head verb, e.g. "purchase" for "Who purchased YouTube?" (In the following we will often refer to this question to illustrate our approach.) We then look up all entries in one of the resources, and for FrameNet and PropBank we simplify the annotated sentences until we achieve a set of abstract frame structures, similar to those in VerbNet. By doing this we intentionally remove certain levels of information that were present in the original data, i.e. tense, voice, mood and negation. (In a later step we will reintroduce some of it.) Here is what we find in FrameNet for "purchase":

```
Buyer[Subj,NP] VERB Goods[Obj,NP]
Buyer[Subj,NP] VERB Goods[Obj,NP]
                    Seller[Dep,PP-from]
Buyer[Subj,NP] VERB Goods[Obj,NP]
                    Money[Dep,PP-for]
Buyer[Subj,NP] VERB Goods[Obj,NP]
                    Recipient[Dep,PP-for]
 ...
```

A syntactic analysis of the question (also obtained from MiniPar) shows that "Who" is the (deep) subject and "YouTube", the (deep) object. The first of the above frames fits this analysis best, because it lists only the two roles with the desired grammatical functions. By mapping the question analysis to this frame, we can assign the roles *Goods* to "YouTube" and *Buyer* to "Who". From this we can conclude that the question asks for the *Buyer* role.

An additional point suitable to illustrate why a few simple rules can achieve in many cases more that a statistical classifier, are *When*- and *Where*-questions. Here, the hint that leads to the correct detection of the answer role lies in the question word, which is of course not present in the answer sentence. Furthermore, the answer role in an answer sentence will usually be realized as a PP with a totally different dependency path than the one of question's question word. In contrast, a rule that states that whenever a temporal or location question is detected the answer role becomes, in FrameNet terms, *Place* or *Time*, respectively, is very helpful here.

Once the role assignment is complete, we use all abstract frames which contain the roles found in the question to generate potential answer templates.

This is also the point where we reintroduce tense and voice information:[1] If the question was asked in the a past tense, we will now create from each abstract frame, all surface realizations in all past tenses, both in active and passive voice. If we had used the annotated data directly without the detour over the abstract frames, we would have difficulty sorting out negated sentences, those in undesired moods and those in unsuitable tenses. In contrast our approach guarantees that all possible tenses in both voices are generated, and no meaning-altering information like mood and negation is present. For the example given above we would create *inter alia* the following answer templates:

```
ANSWER[NP] purchased YouTube
YouTube was purchased by ANSWER[NP]
ANSWER[NP] had purchased YouTube
...
```

The part (or parts) of the templates that are known are quoted and sent to a search engine. For the second example, this would be `"YouTube was purchased by"`. From the snippets returned by the search engine, we extract candidate sentences and match them against the abstract frame structure from which the queries were originally created. In this way, we annotate the candidate sentences and are now able to identify the filler of the answer role. For example, the above query returns "On October 9, 2006, YouTube was purchased by Google for an incredible US$1.65 billion", from which we can extract "Google", because it is the NP filling the buyer role.

So far, we have mostly discussed questions whose answer role is an argument of the head verb. However, for questions like "When was YouTube purchased?" this assumption does not hold. Here, the question asks for an adjunct. This is an important difference for at least three reasons:

1. FrameNet and VerbNet do not or only sparsely annotate peripheral adjuncts. (PropBank however does.)
2. In English, the position of adjuncts varies much more than those of arguments.
3. In English, different kinds of adjuncts can occupy the same position in a sentence, although naturally not at the same time.

[1]While we strip off mood and negation during the creation of the abstract frames, we have not yet reintroduced them.

The following examples illustrate point 2:

YouTube was purchased by Google on October 9.
On October 9, YouTube was purchased by Google.
YouTube was purchased on October 9 by Google.

All variations are possible, although they may differ in frequency. PPs conveying other peripheral adjuncts (e.g. "for $1.65 billion") could replace all the above temporals PPs, or they could be added at other positions.

The special behavior of these types of questions has not only to be accounted for when annotating the question with semantic roles, but also and when creating and processing potential answer sentences. We use an abstract frame structure like the following to create the queries:

```
Buyer[Subj,NP,unknown]
      VERB Goods[Obj,NP,"YouTube"]
```

While this lacks a role for the answer, we can still use it to create, for example, the query `"has purchased YouTube"`. When sentences returned from the search engine are then matched against the abstract structure, we can extract all PPs directly before the Buyer role, between the Buyer role and the verb and directly behind the Goods role. Then we can check all these PPs on their semantic types and keep only those that match the answer type of the question (if any).

3 Making use of FrameNet Frames and Inter-Frame Relations

The method presented so far can be used with all three resources. But FrameNet goes a step further than just listing verb-argument structures: It organizes all of its lexical entries in frames[2], with relations between frames that can be used for a wider paraphrasing and inference. This section will explain how we make use of these relations.

The *purchase.v* entry is organized in a frame called *Commerce_buy* which also contains the entries for *buy.v* and *purchase_((act)).n*. Both these entries are annotated with the same frame elements as *purchase.v*. This makes it possible to formulate alternative answer templates, for example: `YouTube was bought by ANSWER[NP]` and

[2]Note the different meaning of *frame* in FrameNet and PropBank/VerbNet respectively.

`ANSWER[NP-Genitive] purchase of YouTube.` The latter example illustrates that we can also generate target paraphrases with heads which are not verbs. Handling these is usually easier than sentences based on verbs, because no tense/voice information has to be introduced.

Furthermore, frames themselves can stand in different relations. The frame *Commerce_goods-transfer*, for example, relates both to the already mentioned *Commerce_buy* frame and to *Commerce_sell* in an *is_perspectivized_in* relation. The latter contains the lexical entries *retail.v*, *retailer.n*, *sale.n*, *sell.v*, *vend.v* and *vendor.n*. Again, the frame elements used are the same as for *purchase.v*. Thus we can now create answer templates like `YouTube was sold to ANSWER[NP]`. Other templates created from this frame seem odd, e.g. `YouTube has been retailed to ANSWER[NP].` because the verb "to retail" usually takes mass-products as its object argument and not a company. But FrameNet does not make such fine-grained distinctions. Interestingly, we did not come across a single example in our experiments where such a phenomenon caused an overall wrong answer. Sentences like the one above will most likely not be found on the web (just because they are in a narrow semantic sense not well-formed). Yet even if we would get a hit, it probably would be a legitimate to count the odd sentence "YouTube had been retailed to Google" as evidence for the fact that Google bought YouTube.

4 Method 2: Combining Semantic Roles and Dependency Paths

The second method we have implemented compares the dependency structure of example sentences found in PropBank and FrameNet with the dependency structure of candidate sentences. (VerbNet does not list example sentences for lexical entries, so could not be used here.)

In a pre-processing step, all example sentences in PropBank and FrameNet are analyzed and the dependency paths from the head to each of the frame elements are stored. For example, in the sentence "The Soviet Union has purchased roughly eight million tons of grain this month" (found in PropBank), "purchased" is recognized as the head, "The Soviet Union" as *ARG0*, "roughly eight million tons of grain" as *ARG1*, and "this month" as an adjunct of type *TMP*. The stored paths to each are as follows:

headPath = $\downarrow i$
role = *ARG0*, paths = $\{\downarrow s, \downarrow subj\}$
role = *ARG1*, paths = $\{\downarrow obj\}$
role = *TMP*, paths = $\{\downarrow mod\}$

This says that the head is at the root, ARG0 is at both surface subject (*s*) and deep subject (*subj*) position[3], ARG1 is the deep object (*obj*), and TMP is a direct adjunct (*mod*) of the head.

Questions are annotated as described in Section 2. Sentences that potentially contain answer candidates are then retrieved by posing a rather abstract query consisting of key words from the question. Once we have obtained a set of candidate-containing sentences, we ask the following questions of their dependency structures compared with those of the example sentences from PropBank[4]:

- 1a Does the candidate-containing sentence share the same head verb as the example sentence?
- 1b Do the candidate sentence and the example sentence share the same path to the head?
- 2a In the candidate sentence, do we find one or more of the example's paths to the answer role?
- 2b In the candidate sentence, do we find all of the example's paths to the answer role?
- 3a Can some of the paths for the other roles be found in the candidate sentence?
- 3b Can all of the paths for the other roles be found in the candidate sentence?
- 4a Do the surface strings of the other roles partially match those of the question?
- 4b Do the surface strings of the other roles completely match those of the question?

Tests 1a and 2a of the above are required criteria: If the candidate sentence does not share the same head verb or if we can find no path to the answer role, we exclude it from further processing.

[3] MiniPar allows more than one path between nodes due, for example, to traces. The given example is MiniPar's way of indicating that this is a sentence in active voice.

[4] Note that our proceeding is not too different from what a classical role labeler would do: Both approaches are primarily based on comparing dependency paths. However, a standard role labeler would not take tests 3a, 3b, 4a and 4b into account.

Each sentence that passes steps 1a and 2a is assigned a weight of 1. For each of the remaining tests that succeeds, we multiply that weight by 2. Hence a candidate sentence that passes all the tests is assigned a weight 64 times higher than a candidate that only passes tests 1a and 2a. We take this as reasonable, as the evidence for having found a correct answer is indeed very weak if only tests 1a and 2a succeeded and very high if all tests succeed. Whenever condition 2a holds, we can extract an answer candidate from the sentence: It is the phrase that the answer role-path points to. All extracted answers are stored together with their weights, if we retrieve the same answer more than once, we simple add the new weight to the old ones. After all candidate sentences have been compared with all pre-extracted structures, the ones that do not show the correct semantic type are removed. This is especially important for answers that are realized as adjuncts, see Section 2. We choose the answer candidate with the highest score as the final answer.

We now illustrate this method with respect to our question "Who purchased YouTube?" The roles assignment process produces this result: "YouTube" is *ARG1* and the answer is *ARG0*. From the web we retrieve *inter alia* the following sentence: "Their aim is to compete with YouTube, which Google recently purchased for more than $1 billion." The dependency analysis of the relevant phrases is:

headPath = $\downarrow i \downarrow i \downarrow pred \downarrow i \downarrow mod \downarrow pcom\text{-}n \downarrow rel \downarrow i$
phrase = "Google", paths = $\{\downarrow s, \downarrow subj\}$
phrase = "which", paths = $\{\downarrow obj\}$
phrase = "YouTube", paths = $\{\uparrow i \uparrow rel\}$
phrase = "for more than $1 billion", paths = $\{\downarrow mod\}$

If we annotate this sentence by using the analysis from the above example sentence ("The Soviet Union has purchased ...") we get the following (partially correct) role assignment: "Google" is *ARG0*, "which" is *ARG1*, "for more than $1 billion" is *TMP*.

The following table shows the results of the 8 tests described above:

1a	OK	2a	OK	3a	OK	4a	–
1b	–	2b	OK	3b	OK	4b	–

Test 1a and 2a succeeded, so this sentence is assigned an initial weight of 1. However, only three other tests succeed as well, so its final weight is 8. This rather low weight for a positive candidate sentence is due to the fact that we compared it against a dependency structure which it only partially matched. However, it might very well be the case that another of the annotated sentences shows a perfect fit. In such a case this comparison would result in a weight of 64. If these were the only two sentences that produce a weight of 1 or greater, the final weight for this answer candidate would be $8 + 64 = 72$.

5 Evaluation

We choose to evaluate our experiments with the TREC 2002 QA test set because test sets from 2004 and beyond contain question series that pose problems that are separate from the research described in this paper. While we participated in TREC 2004, 2005 and 2006, with an anaphora-resolution component that performed quite well, we feel that if one wants to evaluate a particular method, adding an additional module, unrelated to the actual problem, can distort the results. Additionally, because we are searching for answers on the web rather than in the AQUAINT corpus, we do not distinguish between supported and unsupported judgments.

Of the 500 questions in the TREC 2002 test set, 236 have *be* as their head verb. As the work described here essentially concerns **verb** semantics, such questions fall outside its scope. Evaluation has thus been carried out on only the remaining 264 questions.

For the first method (cf. Section 2), we evaluated system accuracy separately for each of the three resources, and then together, obtaining the following values:

FrameNet	PropBank	VerbNet	combined
0.181	0.227	0.223	0.261

For the combined run we looked up the verb in all three resources simultaneously and all entries from every resource were used. As can be seen, PropBank and VerbNet perform equally well, while FrameNet's performance is significantly lower. These differences are due to coverage issues: FrameNet is still in development, and further versions with a higher coverage will be released. However, a closer look shows that coverage is a problem for all of the resources. The following table shows the percentage of the head verbs that were looked up during the above experiments based on the 2002 question set, that could not be found (*not found*). It also lists the percentage of lexical entries that contain no annotated sentences ($s = 0$), five or fewer ($s <= 5$), ten or fewer ($s <= 10$), or more than 50 ($s > 50$). Furthermore, the table lists the average number of lexical entries found per head verb (*avg senses*) and the average number of annotated sentences found per lexical entry (*avg sent*). [5]

	FrameNet	PropBank
not found	11%	8%
$s = 0$	41%	7%
$s <= 5$	48%	35%
$s <= 10$	57%	45%
$s > 50$	8%	23%
avg senses	2.8	4.4
avg sent.	16.4	115.0

The problem with lexical entires only containing a small number of annotated sentences is that these sentences often do not exemplify common argument structures, but rather seldom ones. As a solution to this coverage problem, we experimented with a cautious technique for expanding coverage. Any head verb, we assumed displays the following three patterns:

intransitive: [ARG0] VERB
transitive: [ARG0] VERB [ARG1]
ditransitive: [ARG0] VERB [ARG1] [ARG2]

During processing, we then determined whether the question used the head verb in a standard intransitive, transitive or ditransitive way. If it did, and that pattern for the head verb was not contained in the resources, we temporarily added this abstract frame to the list of abstract frames the system used. This method rarely adds erroneous data, because the question shows that such a verb argument structure exists for the verb in question. By applying this technique, the combined performance increased from 0.261 to 0.284.

In Section 2 we reported on experiments that make use of FrameNet's inter-frame relations. The next table lists the results we get when (a) using only the question head verb for the reformulations, (b) using the other entries in the same frame as well, (c) using all entries in all frames to which the starting frame is related via the *Inheritance*, *Perspective_on* and *Using* relations (by using only those frames which show the same frame elements).

(a)	only question head verb	0.181
(b)	all entries in frame	0.204
(c)	all entries in related frames (with same frame elements)	0.215

Our second method described in Section 4, can only be used with FrameNet and PropBank, because VerbNet does not give annotated example sentences. Here are the results:

FrameNet	PropBank
0.030	0.159

Analysis shows that PropBank dramatically outperforms FrameNet for three reasons:

1. PropBank's lexicon contains more entries.
2. PropBank provides many more example sentences for each entry.
3. FrameNet does not annotate peripheral adjuncts, and so does not apply to When- or Where-questions.

The methods we have described above are complementary. When they are combined so that when method 1 returns an answer it is always chosen as the final one, and only if method 1 did not return an answer were the results from method 2 used, we obtain a combined accuracy of 0.306 when only using PropBank. When using method 1 with all three resources and our cautious coverage-extension strategy, with all additional reformulations that FrameNet can produce and method 2, using PropBank and FrameNet, we achieve an accuracy of 0.367.

We also evaluated how much increase the described approaches based on semantic roles bring to our existing QA system. This system is completly web-based and employs two answer finding strategies. The first is based on syntactic reformulation rules, which are similar to what we described in section 2. However, in contrast to the work described in this paper, these rules are manually created. The second strategy uses key words from the question as queries, and looks for frequently occuring n-grams in the snippets returned by the search engine. The system received the fourth best result for factoids in TREC 2004 (Kaisser and Becker, 2004) (where both

[5] As VerbNet contains no annotated sentences, it is not listed. Note also, that these figures are not based on the resources in total, but on the head verbs we looked up for our evaluation.

just mentioned approaches are described in more detail) and TREC 2006 (Kaisser et al., 2006), so it in itself is a state-of-the-art, high performing QA system. We observe an increase in performance by 21% over the mentioned baseline system. (Without the components based on semantic roles 130 out of 264 questions are answered correct, with these components 157.)

6 Related Work

So far, there has been little work at the intersection of QA and semantic roles. Fliedner (2004) describes the functionality of a planned system based on the German version of FrameNet, SALSA, but no so far no paper describing the completed system has been published.

Novischi and Moldovan (2006) use a technique that builds on a combination of lexical chains and verb argument structures extracted from VerbNet to re-rank answer candidates. The authors' aim is to recognize changing syntactic roles in cases where an answer sentence shows a head verb different from the question (similar to work described here in Section 2). However, since VerbNet is based on *thematic* rather than *semantic* roles, there are problems in using it for this purpose, illustrated by the following VerbNet pattern for *buy* and *sell*:

```
[Agent] buy [Theme] from [Source]
[Agent] sell [Recipient] [Theme]
```

Starting with the sentence "Peter bought a guitar from Johnny", and mapping the above roles for *buy* to those for *sell*, the resulting paraphrase in terms of *sell* would be "Peter sold UNKNOWN a guitar". That is, there is nothing blocking the Agent role of *buy* being mapped to the Agent role of *sell*, nor anything linking the Source role of *buy* to any role in *sell*. There is also a coverage problem: The authors report that their approach only applies to 15 of 230 TREC 2004 questions. They report a performance gain of 2.4% (MMR for the top 50 answers), but it does not become clear whether that is for these 15 questions or for the complete question set.

The way in which we use the web in our first method is somewhat similar to (Dumais et al., 2002). However, our system allows control of verb argument structures, tense and voice and thus we can create a much larger set of reformulations.

Regarding our second method, two papers describe related ideas: Firstly, in (Bouma et al., 2005) the authors describe a Dutch QA system which makes extensive use of dependency relations. In a pre-processing step they parsed and stored the full text collection for the Dutch CLEF QA-task. When their system is asked a question, they match the dependency structure of the question against the dependency structures of potential answer candidates. Additionally, a set of 13 equivalence rules allows transformations of the kind "the coach of Norway, Egil Olsen" ⇔ "Egil Olsen, the coach of Norway".

Secondly, Shen and Klakow (2006) use dependency relation paths to rank answer candidates. In their work, a candidate sentence supports an answer if relations between certain phrases in the candidate sentence are similar to the corresponding ones in the question.

Our work complements that described in both these papers, based as it is on a large collection of semantically annotated example sentences: We only require a candidate sentence to match one of the annotated example sentences. This allows us to deal with a much wider range of syntactic possibilities, as the resources we use do not only document verb argument structures, but also the many ways they can be syntactically realized.

7 Discussion

Both methods presented in this paper employ semantic roles but with different aims in mind: The first method focuses on creating obvious answer-containing sentences. Because in these sentences, the head and the semantic roles are usually adjacent, it is possible to create exact search queries that will lead to answer candidates of a high quality. Our second method can deal with a wider range of syntactic variations but here the link to the answer sentences' surface structure is not obvious, thus no exact queries can be posed.

The overall accuracy we achieved suggests that employing semantic roles for question answering is indeed useful. Our results compare nicely to recent TREC evaluation results. This is an especially strong point, because virtually all high performing TREC systems combine miscellaneous strategies, which are already know to perform well. Because the research question driving this work was to determine how semantic roles can benefit QA, we deliberately designed our system to *only* build on semantic roles. We did not chose to extend an already existing system, using other methods with a few features based on semantic roles.

Our results are convincing qualitatively as well as quantitatively: Detecting paraphrases and drawing inferences is a key challenge in question answering, which our methods achieve in various ways:

- They both recognize different verb-argument structures of the same verb.
- Method 1 controls for tense and voice: Our system will not take a future perfect sentence for an answer to a present perfect question.
- For method 1, no answer candidates altered by mood or negation are accepted.
- Method 1 can create and recognize answer sentences, whose head is synonymous or related in meaning to the answers head. In such transformations, we are also aware of potential changes in the argument structure.
- The annotated sentences in the resources enables method 2 to deal with a wide range of syntactic phenomena.

8 Conclusion

This paper explores whether lexical resources like FrameNet, PropBank and VerbNet are beneficial for QA and describes two different methods in which they can be used. One method uses the data in these resources to generate potential answer-containing sentences that are searched for on the web by using exact, quoted search queries. The second method uses only a keyword-based search, but it can annotate a larger set of candidate sentences. Both methods perform well solemnly and they nicely complement each other. Our methods based on semantic roles alone achieves an accuracy of 0.39. Furthermore adding the described features to our already existing system boosted accuracy by 21%.

Acknowledgments

This work was supported by Microsoft Research through the European PhD Scholarship Programme.

References

Colin F. Baker, Charles J. Fillmore, and John B. Lowe. 1998. The Berkeley FrameNet Project. In *Proceedings of COLING-ACL.*

Gosse Bouma, Jori Mur, Gertjan van Noord, Lonneke van der Plas, and Jörg Tiedemann. 2005. Question Answering for Dutch using Dependency Relations. In *Proceedings of the CLEF 2005 Workshop.*

Susan Dumais, Michele Bankom, Eric Brill, Jimmy Lin, and Andrew Ng. 2002. Web Question Answering: Is More Always Better? *Proceedings of UAI 2003.*

Gerhard Fliedner. 2004. Towards Using FrameNet for Question Answering. In *Proceedings of the LREC 2004 Workshop on Building Lexical Resources from Semantically Annotated Corpora.*

Michael Kaisser and Tilman Becker. 2004. Question Answering by Searching Large Corpora with Linguistic Methods. In *The Proceedings of the 2004 Edition of the Text REtrieval Conference, TREC 2004.*

Michael Kaisser, Silke Scheible, and Bonnie Webber. 2006. Experiments at the University of Edinburgh for the TREC 2006 QA track. In *The Proceedings of the 2006 Edition of the Text REtrieval Conference, TREC 2006.*

Dekang Lin. 1998. Dependency-based Evaluation of MINIPAR. In *Workshop on the Evaluation of Parsing Systems.*

George A. Miller, Richard Beckwith, Christiane Fellbaum, Derek Gross, and Katherine Miller. 1993. Introduction to WordNet: An On-Line Lexical Database.

Adrian Novischi and Dan Moldovan. 2006. Question Answering with Lexical Chains Propagating Verb Arguments. In *Proceedings of the 21st International Conference on Computational Linguistics and 44th Annual Meeting of the ACL.*

Martha Palmer, Daniel Gildea, and Paul Kingsbury. 2005. The Proposition Bank: An Annotated Corpus of Semantic Roles. *Computational Linguistics*, 31(1):71–106.

Karin Kipper Schuler. 2005. *VerbNet: A Broad-Coverage, Comprehensive Verb Lexicon.* Ph.D. thesis, University of Pennsylvania.

Dan Shen and Dietrich Klakow. 2006. Exploring Correlation of Dependency Relation Paths for Answer Extraction. In *Proceedings of the 21st International Conference on Computational Linguistics and 44th Annual Meeting of the ACL.*

Deep Linguistic Processing for Spoken Dialogue Systems

James Allen
Department of Computer Science
University of Rochester
james@cs.rochester.edu

Myroslava Dzikovska
ICCS-HCRC
University of Edinburgh
mdzikovs@inf.ed.ac.uk

Mehdi Manshadi
Department of Computer Science
University of Rochester
mehdih@cs.rochester.edu

Mary Swift
Department of Computer Science
University of Rochester
swift@cs.rochester.edu

Abstract

We describe a framework for deep linguistic processing for natural language understanding in task-oriented spoken dialogue systems. The goal is to create domain-general processing techniques that can be shared across all domains and dialogue tasks, combined with domain-specific optimization based on an ontology mapping from the generic LF to the application ontology. This framework has been tested in six domains that involve tasks such as interactive planning, coordination operations, tutoring, and learning.

1 Introduction

Deep linguistic processing is essential for spoken dialogue systems designed to collaborate with users to perform collaborative tasks. We describe the TRIPS natural language understanding system, which is designed for this purpose. As we develop the system, we are constantly balancing two competing needs: (1) deep semantic accuracy: the need to produce the semantically and pragmatically deep interpretations for a specific application; and (2) portability: the need to reuse our grammar, lexicon and discourse interpretation processes across domains.

We work to accomplish portability by using a multi-level representation. The central components are all based on domain general representations, including a linguistically based detailed semantic representation (the Logical Form, or LF), illocutionary acts, and a collaborative problem-solving model. Each application then involves using a domain-specific ontology and reasoning components.

The generic LF is linked to the domain-specific representations by a set of ontology mapping rules that must be defined for each domain. Once the ontology mapping is defined, we then can automatically specialize the generic grammar to use the stronger semantic restrictions that arise from the specific domain. In this paper we mainly focus on the generic components for deep processing. The work on ontology mapping and rapid grammar adaptation is described elsewhere (Dzikovska et al. 2003; forthcoming).

2 Parsing for deep linguistic processing

The parser uses a broad coverage, domain-independent lexicon and grammar to produce the LF. The LF is a flat, unscoped representation that includes surface speech act analysis, dependency information, word senses (semantic types) with semantic roles derived from the domain-independent language ontology, tense, aspect, modality, and implicit pronouns. The LF supports fragment and ellipsis interpretation, discussed in Section 5.2

2.1 Semantic Lexicon

The content of our semantic representation comes from a domain-independent ontology linked to a domain-independent lexicon. Our syntax relies on a frame-based design in the LF ontology, a common representation in semantic lexicons (Baker et al., 1998, Kipper et al., 2000). The LF type hierarchy is influenced by argument structure, but provides a more detailed level of semantic analysis than found in most broad coverage parsers as it distinguishes senses even if the senses take the same argument structure, and may collapse lexical entries with different argument structures to the same sense. As a very simple example, the generic lexicon includes the senses for the verb *take* shown

Proceedings of the 5th Workshop on Important Unresolved Matters, pages 49–56,
Ann Arbor, June 2005.

in Figure 1. Our generic senses have been inspired by FrameNet (Baker et al., 1998).

In addition, types are augmented with semantic features derived from EuroWordNet (Vossen et al., 1997) and extended. These are used to provide selectional restrictions, similar to VerbNet (Kipper et al., 2000). The constraints are intentionally weak, excluding utterances unsuitable in most contexts (*the idea slept*) but not attempting to eliminate borderline combinations.

The generic selectional restrictions are effective in improving overall parsing accuracy, while remaining valid across multiple domains. An evaluation with an earlier version of the grammar showed that if generic selectional restrictions were removed, full sentence semantic accuracy decreased from 77.8% to 62.6% in an emergency rescue domain, and from 67.9 to 52.5% in a medical domain (using the same versions of grammar and lexicon) (Dzikovska, 2004).

The current version of our generic lexicon contains approximately 6400 entries (excluding morphological variants), and the current language ontology has 950 concepts. The lexicon can be supplemented by searching large-scale lexical resources such as WordNet (Fellbaum, 1998) and Comlex (Grisham et al., 1994). If an unknown word is encountered, an underspecified entry is generated on the fly. The entry incorporates as much information from the resource as possible, such as part of speech and syntactic frame. It is assigned an underspecified semantic classification based on correspondences between our language ontology and WordNet synsets.

2.2 Grammar

The grammar is context-free, augmented with feature structures and feature unification, motivated from X-bar theory, drawing on principles from GPSG (e.g., head and foot features) and HPSG. A detailed description of an early non-lexicalized version of the formalism is in (Allen, 1995). Like HPSG, our grammar is strongly lexicalized, with the lexical features defining arguments and complement structures for head words. Unlike HPSG,

CONSUME	*Take an aspirin*
MOVE	*Take it to the store*
ACQUIRE	*Take a picture*
SELECT	*I'll take that one*
COMPATIBLE WITH	*The projector takes 100 volts*
TAKE-TIME	*It took three hours*

Figure 1: Some generic senses of take in lexicon

however, the features are not typed and rather than multiple inheritance, the parser supports a set of orthogonal single inheritance hierarchies to capture different syntactic and semantic properties. Structural variants such as passives, dative shifts, gerunds, and so on are captured in the context-free rule base. The grammar has broad coverage of spoken English, supporting a wide range of conversational constructs. It also directly encodes conventional conversational acts, including standard surface speech acts such as inform, request and question, as well as acknowledgments, acceptances, rejections, apologies, greetings, corrections, and other speech acts common in conversation.

To support having both a broad domain-general grammar and the ability to produce deep domain-specific semantic representations, the semantic knowledge is captured in three distinct layers (Figure 2), which are compiled together before parsing to create efficient domain-specific interpretation. The first level is primarily encoded in the grammar, and defines an interpretation of the utterance in terms of generic grammatical relations. The second is encoded in the lexicon and defines an interpretation in terms of a generic language-based ontology and generic roles. The third is encoded by a set of ontology-mapping rules that are defined for each domain, and defines an interpretation in terms of the target application ontology. While these levels are defined separately, the parser can produce all three levels simultaneously, and exploit domain-specific semantic restrictions to simultaneously improve semantic accuracy and parsing efficiency. In this paper we focus on the middle level, the generic LF.

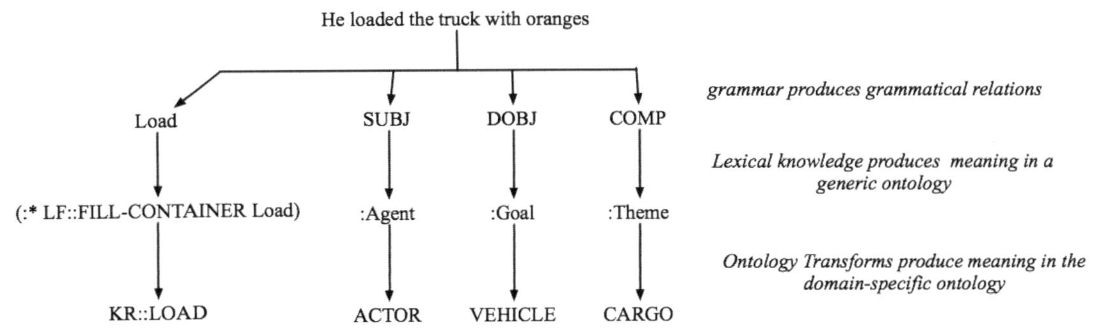

Figure 2: The Levels of Representation computed by the Parser

The rules in the grammar are weighted, and weights are combined, similar to how probabilities are computed in a PCFG. The weights, however, are not strictly probabilities (e.g., it is possible to have weights greater than 1); rather, they encode structural preferences. The parser operates in a best-first manner and as long as weights never exceed 1.0, is guaranteed to find the highest weighted parse first. If weights are allowed to exceed 1.0, then the parser becomes more "depth-first" and it is possible to "garden-path" and find globally sub-optimal solutions first, although eventually all interpretations can still be found.

The grammar used in all our applications uses these hand-tuned rule weights, which have proven to work relatively well across domains. We do not use a statistical parser based on a trained corpus because in most dialogue-system projects, sufficient amounts of training data are not available and would be too time consuming to collect. In the one domain in which we have a reasonable amount of training data (about 9300 utterances), we experimented with a PCFG using trained probabilities with the Collins algorithm, but were not able to improve on the hand-tuned preferences in overall performance (Elsner et al., 2005).

Figure 3 summarizes some of the most important preferences encoded in our rule weights. Because we are dealing with speech, which is often ungrammatical and fragmented, the grammar includes "robust" rules (e.g., allowing dropped determiners) that would not be found in a grammar of written English.

3 The Logical Form Language

The logical form language captures a domain-independent semantic representation of the utterance. As shown later in this paper, it can be seen as a variant of MRS (Copestake et al., 2006) but is expressed in a frame-like notation rather than predicate calculus. In addition, it has a relatively simple method of computing possible quantifier scoping, drawing from the approaches by (Hobbs & Shieber, 1987) and (Alshawi, 1990).

A logical form is set of terms that can be viewed as a rooted graph with each term being a node identified by a unique ID (the variable). There are three types of terms. The first corresponds to generalized quantifiers, and is on the form (<quant> <id> <type> <modifiers>*). As a simple example, the NP *Every dog* would be captured by the term (Every d1 DOG). The second type of term is the propositional term, which is represented in a neo-Davidsonian representation (e.g., Parsons, 1990) using reified events and properties. It has the form (F <id> <type> <arguments>*). The propositional terms produced from *Every dog hates a cat* would be (F h1 HATE :Experiencer d1 :Theme c1). The third type of term is the speech act, which has the same form as propositional terms except for the initial indicator SA identifying it as a performed speech act. The speech act for Every dog hates a cat would be (SA sa1 INFORM :content h1). Putting this all together, we get the following (condensed) LF representation from the parser for *Every large dog hates a cat* (shown in graphical

Prefer

- Interpretations without gaps to those with gaps
- Subcategorized interpretations over adjuncts
- Right attachment of PPs and adverbials
- Fully specified constituents over those with dropped or "implicit" arguments
- Adjectival modification over noun-noun modification
- Standard rules over "robust" rules

Figure 3: Some Key Preferences used in Parsing

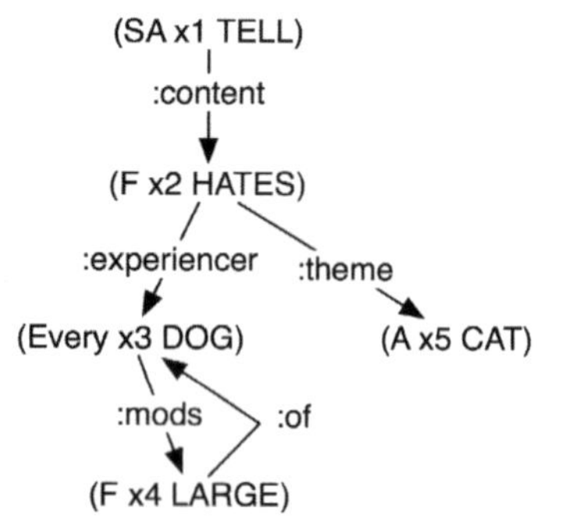

Figure 4: The LF in graphical form

form in Figure 4).

(SA x1 TELL :content x2)
(F x2 HATE :experience x3 :theme x5)
(Every x3 DOG :mods (x4))
(F x4 LARGE :of x3)
(A x5 CAT)

4 Comparison of LF and MRS

Minimal Recursion Semantics (MRS) (Copestake et al. 2006) is a semantic formalism which has been widely adopted in the last several years. This has motivated some research on how this formalism compares to some traditional semantic formalisms. For example, Fuchss et al. (2004) formally show that the translation from MRS to Dominance Constraints is feasible. We have also found that MRS is very similar to LF in its descriptive power. In fact, we can convert every LF to an equivalent MRS structure with a simple algorithm.

First, consider the sentence *Every dog hates a cat*. Figure 5 shows the LF and MRS representations for this sentence.

(SA :content v1)	*h1 : Every(x, h2, h3)*
(F v1 Hate :Experiencer x :Theme y)	*h4: Dog(x)*
(Every x Dog)	*h5: A(y, h6, h7)*
(A y Cat)	*h8: Cat(y)*
	h9: hate(x, y)
	{h0 =q h9, h2 =q h4, h6 =q h8}

Figure 5: The LF (left) and MRS (right) representations for the sentence "Every dog hates a cat."

The first step toward converting LF to MRS is to express LF terms as n-ary relationships. For example we express the LF term *(F v1 Hate :Experiencer x :Theme y)* as *Hate(x, y)*. For quantifier terms, we break the LF term into two relations: one for the quantifier itself and one for the restriction. For example *(Every x Dog)* is converted to *Every(x) and Dog(x)*.

There is a small change in the conversion procedure when the sentence contains some modifiers. Consider the modifier *large* in the sentence *Every large dog hates a cat.* In the LF, we bring the modifier in the term which defines the semantic head, using a *:MODS* slot. In the MRS, however, modifiers are separate EPs labeled with same handle as the head's. To cover this, for each LF term T which has a (*:MODS* v_k) slot, and the LF term T1 which defines the variable v_k, we assign the same handle to both T and T1. For example for the terms *(F x Dog :MODS v2)* and *(F v2 Large :OF x)*, we assign the same handle to both *Dog(x)* and *Large(x)*. Similar approach applies when the modifier itself is a scopal term, such as in the sentence *Every cat in a room sleeps*. Figure 7 shows LF and MRS representations for this sentence. Figure 8, summarizes all these steps as an algorithm which takes a LF representation as the input and generates its equivalent MRS.

There is a small change in the conversion procedure when the sentence contains some modifiers. Consider the modifier *large* in the sentence *Every large dog hates a cat.* In the LF, we bring the modifier in the term which defines the semantic head, using a *:MODS* slot. In the MRS, however, modifiers are separate EPs labeled with same handle as the head's. To cover this, for each LF term T which has a (*:MODS* v_k) slot, and the LF term T1 which defines the variable v_k, we assign the same handle to both T and T1. For example for the terms *(F x Dog :MODS v2)* and *(F v2 Large :OF x)*, we assign the same handle to both *Dog(x)* and *Large(x)*. Similar approach applies when the modifier itself is a scopal term, such as in the sentence *Every cat in a room sleeps*. Figure 7 shows LF and MRS representations for this sentence. Figure 8, summarizes all these steps as an algorithm which takes a LF representation as the input and generates its equivalent MRS.

The next step is to bring handles into the repre-

Step 1:	*Step 2:*	
Hate(x,y)	*h1: Hate(x, y)*	*h0 =*
Every(x), Dog(x)	*h2: Every(x, h6, h7)*	*h6 =*
	h3: Dog(x)	
A(y), Cat(y)	*h4: A(y, h8, h9)*	*h8 =*
	h5: Cat(y)	

Figure 6: The steps of converting the LF for "Every cat hates a cat" to its MRS representation

sentation. First, we assign a different handle to each term. Then, for each quantifier term such as *Every(x)*, we add two handles as the arguments of the relation: one for the restriction and one for the body as in *h2: Every(x, h6, h7)*. Finally, we add the handle constraints to the MRS. We have two types of handle constraint. The first type comes from the restriction of each quantifier. We add a qeq relationship between the restriction handle argument of the quantifier term and the handle of the actual restriction term. The second type of constraint is the qeq relationship which defines the top handle of the MRS. The speech act term in every LF refers to a formula term as content (*:content* slot), which is actually the heart of the LF. We build a qeq relationship between h0 (the top handle) and the handle of this formula term. Figure 6 shows the effect of applying these steps to the above example.

(SA :content v1)	*h1 : Every(x, h2, h3)*
(F v1 Sleep :Theme x)	*h4: Cat(x)*
(Every x Cat :MODS v2)	*h4: In(x,y)*
(F v2 In :OF x :VAL y)	*h5: A(y, h6, h7)*
(A y Room)	*h8: Room(y)*
	h9: Sleep(x)
	{h0 =q h9, h2 =q h4, h6 =q h8}

Figure 7: The LF and MRS representations for the sentence "Every cat in a room sleeps."

Another interesting issue about these two formalisms is that the effect of applying the simple scoping algorithms referred in section 3 to generate all possible interpretations of a LF is the same as applying MRS axioms and handle constraints to generate all scope-resolved MRSs. For instance, the example in (Copestake et al. 2006), *Every nephew of some famous politician saw a pony* has the same 5 interpretations using either approach.

As the last point here, we need to mention that the algorithm in Figure 8 does not consider fixed-scopal terms such as scopal adverbials or negation. However, we believe that the framework itself is able to support these types of scopal term and with a small modification, the scoping algorithm will work well in assigning different possible interpretations. We leave the full discussion about these details as well as the detailed proof of the other claims we made here to another paper.

5 Generic Discourse Interpretation

With a generic semantic representation, we can then define generic discourse processing capabilities that can be used in any application. All of these methods have a corresponding capability at the domain-specific level for an application, but we will not discuss this further here. We also do not discuss the support for language generation which uses the same discourse context.

There are three core discourse interpretation capabilities that the system provides: reference resolution, ellipsis processing, and speech act interpretation. All our different dialog systems use the same discourse processing, whether the task involves collaborative problem solving, learning from instruction or automated tutoring.

5.1 Reference Resolution

Our domain-independent representation supports reference resolution in two ways. First, the quantifiers and dependency structure extracted from the sentence allow for implementing reference resolution algorithms based on extracted syntactic features. The system uses different strategies for re-

Input: LF, list of all logical form terms,
Output: MRS structure

1. Initialize MRS to <h0, EP={}, C={}>
2. Find the SPEECHACT term T in the form (SA … :content V_i) and the formula term T1 which defines variable V_i. Define a new handle h_j and assign it to T1; then add $h_0 =_q h_j$ to C
3. While LF is not empty, remove a term T from LF
   - 3.1. If T is a formula term in the form
     (F V_i Rel_1(…) Rel_2(…) …Rel_n(…) :MODS(u_1) :MODS(u_2) … MODS(u_m))
     - 3.1.1. If T has not already been assigned a handle h_j, define a new handle h_j and assign it to T
     - 3.1.2. Add h_j:Rel_1(…), h_j:Rel_2(…), … to EP
     - 3.1.3. For each variable u_l, find the formula term T_l which defines u_l and assign h_j to T_l
   - 3.2. If T is a quantifier term T in the form (Q V_i Rel_1(…) … Rel_n(…) :MODS(u_1) … MODS(u_m))
     - 3.2.1. Define new handles h_j, h_l, h_1 and h_m
     - 3.2.2. Add h_j: Q(v_i, h_l, h_1) , h_m:Rel_1(…), h_m:Rel_2(…), …. to EP and $h_l =_q h_m$ to C
     - 3.2.3. For each variable u_l, find the formula term T_l which defines u_l and assign h_m to T_l

Figure 8: The LF-MRS conversion algorithm

solving each type of referring expression along the lines described in (Byron, 2002).

Second, domain-independent semantic information helps greatly in resolving pronouns and definite descriptions. The general capability provided for resolving referring expressions is to search through the discourse history for the most recent entity that matches the semantic requirements, where recency within an utterance may be reordered to reflect focusing heuristics (Tetreault, 2001). For definite descriptions, the semantic information required is explicit in the lexicon. For pronouns, the parser can often compute semantic features from verb argument restrictions. For instance, the pronoun *it* carries little semantic information by itself, but in the utterance *Eat it* we know we are looking for an edible object. This simple technique performs well in practice.

Because of the knowledge in the lexicon for role nouns such as *author*, we can also handle simple bridging reference. Consider the discourse fragment *That book came from the library. The author* .... The semantic representation of *the author* includes its implicit argument, e.g., (The x1 AUTHOR :of b1). Furthermore, the term b1 has the semantic feature INFO-CONTENT, which includes objects that "contain" information such as books, articles, songs, etc.., which allows the pronoun to correctly resolve via bridging to the book in the previous utterance.

5.2 Ellipsis

The parser produces a representation of fragmentary utterances similar to (Schlangen and Lascarides, 2003). The main difference is that instead of using a single underspecified *unknown_rel* predicate to resolve in discourse context, we use a speech act term as the underspecified relation, differentiating between a number of common relations such as acknowledgments, politeness expressions, noun phrases and underspecified predicates (PP, ADJP and VP fragments). The representations of the underspecified predicates also include an IMPRO in place of the unspecified argument.

We currently handle only a few key cases of ellipsis. The first is question/answer pairs. By retaining the logical form of the question in the discourse history, it is relatively easy to reconstruct the full content of short answers (e.g., in *Who ate the pizza? John?* the answer maps to the representation that John ate the pizza). In addition, we handle common follow-up questions (e.g., *Did John buy a book? How about a magazine?)* by performing a semantic closeness matching of the fragment into the previous utterance and substituting the most similar terms. The resulting term can then be used to update the context. This process is similar to the resolution process in (Schlangen and Lascarides, 2003), though the syntactic parallelism constraint is not checked. It could also be easily extended to cover other fragment types, as the grammar provides all the necessary information.

5.3 Speech Act Interpretation

The presence of domain-independent semantic classes allows us to encode a large set of these common conversational pattern independently of the application task and domain. These include rules to handle short answers to questions, acknowledgements and common politeness expressions, as well as common inferences such as interpreting *I need to do X* as *please do X*.

Given our focus on problem solving domains, we are generally interested in identifying more than just the illocutionary force of an utterance. For instance, in a domain for planning how to evacuate people off an island, the utterance *Can we remove the people by helicopter?* is not only ambiguous between being a true Y-N question or a suggestion of a course of action, but at the problem solving level it might intended to (1) introduce a new goal, (2) elaborate or extend the solution to the current problem, or (3) suggest a modification to an existing solution (e.g., moving them by truck). One can only choose between these readings using domain specific reasoning about the current task. The point here is that the interpretation rules are still generic across all domains and expressed using the generic LF, yet the interpretations produced are evaluated using domain-specific reasoning. This interleaving of generic interpretation and domain-specific reasoning is enabled by our ontology mappings.

Similarly, in tutoring domains students often phrase their answers as check questions. In an answer to the question *Which components are in a closed path*, the student may say *Is the bulb in 3 in a closed path?* The domain-independent representation is used to identify the surface form of this utterance as a yes-no question. The dialogue manager then formulates two hypotheses: that this is a hedged answer, or a real question. If a domain-specific tutoring component confirms the former hypothesis, the dialogue manager will proceed with verifying answer correctness and carrying on remediation as necessary. Otherwise (such as for *Is the bulb in 5 connected to a battery* in the same context), the utterance is a question that can be answered by querying the domain reasoner.

5.4 A Note on Generic Capabilities

A key point is that these generic discourse interpretation capabilities are enabled because of the detailed generic semantic interpretation produced by the parser. If the parser produced a more shallow representation, then the discourse interpretation techniques would be significantly degraded. On the other hand, if we developed a new representation for each domain, then we would have to rebuild all the discourse processing for the domain.

6 Evaluation

Our evaluation is aimed at assessing two main features of the grammar and lexicon: portability and accuracy. We use two main evaluation criteria: full sentence accuracy, that takes into account both syntactic and semantic accuracy of the system, and sense tagging accuracy, to demonstrate that the word senses included in the system can be distinguished with a combination of syntactic and domain-independent semantic information.

As a measure of the breadth of grammatical coverage of our system, we have evaluated our coverage on the CSLI LKB (Linguistic Knowledge Building) test suite (Copestake, 1999). The test suite contains approximately 1350 sentences, of which about 400 are ungrammatical. We use a full-sentence accuracy measure to evaluate our coverage, since this is the most meaningful measure in terms of what we require as parser output in our applications. For a sentence representation to be counted as correct by this measure, both the syntactic structure and the semantic representation must be correct, which includes the correct assignment of word senses, dependency relations among terms, and speech act type. Our current coverage for the diverse grammatical phenomena in the corpus is 64% full-sentence accuracy.

We also report the number of spanning parses found, because in our system there are cases in which the syntactic parse is correct, but an incorrect word sense may have been assigned, since we disambiguate senses using not only syntactic structure but also semantic features as selectional restrictions on arguments. For example, in *The manager interviewed Browne after working*, the parser assigns *working* the sense LF::FUNCTION, used with non-agentive subjects, instead of the correct sense for agentive subjects, LF::WORKING. For the grammatical utterances in the test suite, our parser found spanning parses for 80%.

While the ungrammatical sentences in the set are an important tool for constraining grammar output, our grammar is designed to find a reasonable interpretation for natural speech, which often is less than perfect. For example, we have low preference grammar rules that allow dropped subjects, missing determiners, and wrong subject verb agreement. In addition, utterances are often fragmentary, so even those without spanning parses may be considered correct. Our grammar allows all major constituents (NP, VP, ADJP, ADVP) as valid utterances. As a result, our system produces spanning parses for 46% of the "ungrammatical" utterances. We have not yet done a detailed error analysis.

As a measure of system portability to new domains, we have evaluated our system coverage on the ATIS (Airline Travel Information System) speech corpus, which we have never used before. For this evaluation, the proper names (cities, airports, airline companies) in the ATIS corpus were added to our lexicon, but no other development work was performed. We parsed 116 randomly selected test sentences and hand-checked the results using our full-sentence accuracy measure. Our baseline coverage of these utterances is 53% full-sentence semantic accuracy. Of the 55 utterances that were not completely correct, we found spanning parses for 36% (20). Reasons that spanning parses were marked as wrong include incorrect word senses (e.g., for *stop* in *I would like it to have a stop in Phoenix*) or PP-attachment. Reasons that no spanning parse was found include missing senses for existing words (e.g., *serve* as in *Does that flight serve dinner*).

7 Discussion

We presented a deep parser and semantic interpreter for use in dialogue systems. An important question to ask is how it compares to other existing formalisms. At present there is no easy way to make such comparison. One possible criterion is grammatical coverage. Looking at the grammar coverage/accuracy on the TSNLP suite that was used to evaluate the LINGO ERG grammar, our grammar demonstrates 80% coverage (number of spanning parses). The reported figure for LINGO ERG coverage of CSLI is 77% (Oepen, 1999), but this number has undoubtedly improved in the 9-year development period. For example, the current reported coverage figures on spoken dialogue corpora are close to 90% (Oepen et al., 2002).

However, the grammar coverage alone is not a satisfactory measure for a deep NLP system for use in practical applications, because the logical forms and therefore the capabilities of deep NLP systems differ significantly. A major distinguishing feature of our system is that the logical form it outputs uses semantically motivated word senses. LINGO ERG, in contrast, contains only syntactically motivated word senses. For example, the words *end* and *finish* are not related in any obvious way. This reflects a difference in underlying philosophy. LINGO ERG aims for linguistic precision, and as can be seen from our experiments, requiring the parser to select correct domain-independent word senses lowers accuracy.

Our system, however, is built with the goal of easy portability within the context of dialogue systems. The availability of word senses simplifies the design of domain-independent interpretation components, such as reference resolution and speech act interpretation components that use domain-independent syntactic and semantic information to encode conventional interpretation rules.

If the LINGO ERG grammar were to be put in a dialogue system that requires domain interpretation and reasoning, an additional lexical interpretation module would have to be developed to perform word sense disambiguation as well as interpretation, something that has not yet been done.

Acknowledgments

We thank 3 reviewers for helpful comments. This work was supported by NSF IIS-0328811, DARPA NBCHD30010 via subcontract to SRI #03-000223 and ONR N00014051004-3 and –8.

References

H. Alshawi. 1990. Resolving Quasi Logical Forms. *Computational Linguistics* 16(3):133-144.

W. Baker, C. Fillmore and J. B. Lowe. 1998. The Berkeley FrameNet Project. *COLING-ACL'98*, Montréal.

D. Byron. 2002. Resolving Pronominal Reference to Abstract Entities. *ACL-02*, Philadelphia.

A. Copestake. 1999. *The (New) LKB System*. CSLI.

A. Copestake, D. Flickinger, C. Pollard and I. Sag. 2006. Minimal Recursion Semantics: An Introduction. *Research on Language and Computation*, 3(4):281-332.

M. Dzikovska. 2004. *A Practical Semantic Representation for Natural Language Parsing*. Ph.D. Thesis, University of Rochester.

M. Dzikovska, J. Allen and M. Swift. Forthcoming. Linking Semantic and Knowledge Representations in a Multi-domain Dialogue System. *Journal of Logic and Computation*.

M. Dzikovska, J. Allen and M. Swift. 2003. Integrating Linguistic and Domain Knowledge for Spoken Dialogue Systems in Multiple Domains. *Workshop on Knowledge and Reasoning in Practical Dialogue Systems, IJCAI-2003*, Acapulco.

M. Elsner, M. Swift, J. Allen and D. Gildea. 2005. Online Statistics for a Unification-based Dialogue Parser. *IWPT05*, Vancouver.

C. Fellbaum. 1998. *WordNet: An Electronic Lexical Database*. MIT Press.

R. Fuchss, A. Koller, J. Niehren, S. Thater. 2004. Minimal Recursion Semantics as Dominance Constraints. *ACL-04*, Barcelona.

R. Grisham, C. Macleod and A. Meyers. 1994. Comlex Syntax: Building a Computational Lexicon. *COLING 94*, Kyoto.

J. Hobbs and S. Shieber. 1987. An Algorithm for Generating Quantifier Scopings. *Computational Linguistics* 13(1-2):47-63.

K. Kipper, H. T. Dang and M. Palmer. 2000. Class-based Construction of a Verb Lexicon. *AAAI-2000*.

S. Oepen, D. Flickinger, K. Toutanova and C. Manning. 2002. Lingo Redwoods: A Rich and Dynamic Treebank for HPSG. *First Workshop on Treebanks and Linguistic Theories* (TLT2002).

S. Oepen (1999). [incr tsdb()] User Manual. www.delph-in.net/itsdb/publications/manual.ps.gz.

T. Parsons. 1990. *Events in the Semantics of English. A Study in Subatomic Semantics*. MIT Press.

D. Schlangen and A. Lascarides 2003. The Interpretation of Non-Sentential Utterances in Dialogue. *SIGDIAL-03*, Sapporo.

J. Tetreault. 2001. A Corpus-Based Evaluation of Centering and Pronoun Resolution. *Computational Linguistics*. 27(4):507-520.

Vossen, P. (1997) EuroWordNet: A Multilingual Database for Information Retrieval. In *Proc. of the Delos workshop on Cross-language Information Retrieval*.

Self- or Pre-Tuning?
Deep linguistic processing of language variants

António Branco
Universidade de Lisboa
Antonio.Branco@di.fc.ul.pt

Francisco Costa
Universidade de Lisboa
fcosta@di.fc.ul.pt

Abstract

This paper proposes a design strategy for deep language processing grammars to appropriately handle language variants. It allows a grammar to be restricted as to what language variant it is tuned to, but also to detect the variant a given input pertains to. This is evaluated and compared to results obtained with an alternative strategy by which the relevant variant is detected with current language identification methods in a pre-processing step.

1 Introduction

This paper addresses the issue of handling different variants of a given language by a deep language processing grammar for that language.

In the benefit of generalization and grammar writing economy, it is desirable that a grammar can handle language variants – that share most grammatical structures and lexicon – in order to avoid endless multiplication of individual grammars, motivated by inessential differences.

From the viewpoint of analysis, however, increased variant coverage typically opens the way to increased spurious overgeneration. Consequently, the ability for the grammar to be tuned to the relevant dialect of the input is important to control overgeneration arising from its flexibility.

Control on what is generated is also desirable. In general one wants to be able to parse as much variants as possible, but at the same time be selective in generation, by consistently generating only in a given selected variant.

Closely related to the setting issue (addressed in the next Section 2) is the tuning issue: if a system can be restricted to a particular variety, what is the best way to detect the variety of the input? We discuss two approaches to this issue.

One of them consists in using pre-processing components that can detect the language variety at stake. This pre-tuning approach explores the hypothesis that methods developed for language identification can be used also to detect language variants (Section 5).

The other approach is to have the computational grammar prepared for self-tuning to the language variant of the input in the course of processing that input (Section 4).

We evaluate the two approaches and compare them (last Section 6).

2 Variant-sensitive Grammar

In this Section, we discuss the design options for a deep linguistic processing grammar allowing for its appropriate tuning to different language variants. For the sake of concreteness of the discussion, we assume the HPSG framework (Pollard and Sag, 1994) and a grammar that handles two close variants of the same language, European and Brazilian Portuguese. These assumptions are merely instrumental, and the results obtained can be easily extended to other languages and variants, and to other grammatical frameworks for deep linguistic processing.

A stretch of text from a language L can display grammatical features common to all variants of L, or contain a construction that pertains to some or only one of its variants. Hence, undesirable overgeneration due to the grammar readiness to cope with all language variants can

Proceedings of the 5th Workshop on Important Unresolved Matters, pages 57–64,
Ann Arbor, June 2005.

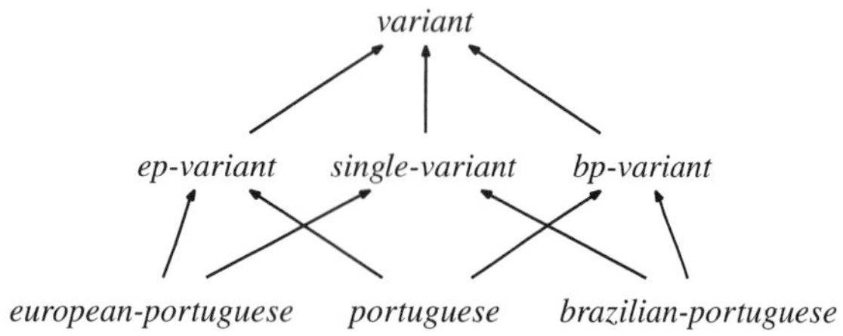

Figure 1: Type hierarchy under *variant*.

be put in check by restricting the grammar to produce variant-"consistent" analyses. More precisely, if the input string contains an element that can only be found in variety v_1 and that input string yields ambiguity in a different stretch but only in varieties v_k other than v_1, this ambiguity will not give rise to multiple analyses if the grammar can be designed so that it can be constrained to accept strings with marked elements of at most one variety, v_1.

The approach we propose seeks to implement this mode of operation in analysis, with the important effect of permitting also to control the variant under which generation should be performed. It relies on the use of a feature VARIANT to model variation. This feature is appropriate for all signs and declared to be of type *variant*. Given the working language variants assumed here, its values are presented in Figure 1.

This attribute is constrained to take the appropriate value in lexical items and constructions specific to one of the two varieties. For example, a hypothetical lexical entry for the lexical item *autocarro* (*bus*, exclusive to European Portuguese) would include the constraint that the attribute VARIANT has the value *ep-variant* and the corresponding Brazilian Portuguese entry for ˆ*onibus*would constrain the same feature to bear the value *bp-variant*. The only two types that are used to mark signs are *ep-variant* and *bp-variant*. The remaining types presented in Figure 1 are used to constrain grammar behavior, as explained below.

Lexical items are not the only elements that can have marked values in the VARIANT feature. Lexical and syntax rules can have them, too. Such constraints model constructions that markedly pertain to one of the dialects.

Feature VARIANT is structure-shared among all signs comprised in a full parse tree. This is achieved by having all lexical or syntactic rules unifying their VARIANT feature with the VARIANT feature of their daughters.

If two signs (e.g. from lexical items and syntax rules) in the same parse tree have different values for feature VARIANT (one has *ep-variant* and the other *bp-variant*), they will unify to *portuguese*, as can be seen from Figure 1. This type means that lexical items or constructions specific to two different varieties are used together. Furthermore, since this feature is shared among all signs, it will be visible everywhere, for instance in the root node.

It is possible to constrain feature VARIANT in the root condition of the grammar so that the grammar works in a variant-"consistent" fashion: this feature just has to be constrained to be of type *single-variant* (in root nodes) and the grammar will accept either European Portuguese or Brazilian Portuguese. Furthermore, in the non natural condition where the input string bears marked properties of both variants, that string will receive no analysis: feature VARIANT will have the value *portuguese* in this case, and there is no unifier for *portuguese* and *single-variant*.

If this feature is constrained to be of type *european-portuguese* in the root node, the grammar will not accept any sentence with features of Brazilian Portuguese, since they will be marked to have a VARIANT of type *bp-variant*, which is incompatible with *european-portuguese*. It is also possible to have the grammar reject European Portuguese (using type *brazilian-portuguese*) or to ignore variation completely by not constraining this feature in the start symbol.

With this grammar design it is thus possible to control beforehand the mode of operation for the grammar, either for it to handle only one variant or several. But it is also possible to use the grammar to detect to which variety input happens to belong. This self-tuning of the grammar to the relevant variant is done by parsing that input and placing no constraint on feature VARIANT of root nodes, and then reading the value of attribute VARIANT from the resulting feature structure: values *ep-variant* and *bp-variant* result from parsing text with properties specific to European Portuguese or Brazilian Portuguese respectively; value *variant* indicates that no marked elements were detected and the text can be from both variants. Also here where the language variant of the input is detected by the grammar, the desired variant-"consistent" behavior of the grammar is enforced.

If the input can be known to be specifically European or Brazilian Portuguese before it is parsed, the constraints on feature VARIANT can be set accordingly to improve efficiency: When parsing text known to be European Portuguese, there is no need to explore analyses that are markedly Brazilian Portuguese, for instance.

It is thus important to discuss what methods for language variant detection can be put in place that support a possible pre-processing step aimed at pre-tuning the grammar for the relevant variant of the input. It is also important to gain insight on the quality of the performance of this method and on how the performance of this pre-tuning setup compares with the self-tuning approach. This is addressed in the next Sections.

3 Experimental setup

Before reporting on the results obtained with the experiments on the performance of the two approaches (self- and pre-tuning), it is important to introduce the experimental conditions under which such exercises were conducted.

3.1 Data

To experiment with any of these two approaches to variant-tuning, two corpora of newspaper text were used, CETEMPublico (204M tokens) and CETENFolha (32M tokens). The first contains text from the European newspaper *O Público*, and the latter from the South American *Folha de São Paulo*. These corpora are only minimally annotated (paragraph and sentence boundaries, *inter alia*), but are very large.

Some preprocessing was carried out: XML-like tags, like the `<s>` and `</s>` tags marking sentence boundaries, were removed and each individual sentence was put in a single line.

Some heuristics were also employed to remove loose lines (parts of lists, etc.) so that only lines ending in `.`, `!` and `?`, and containing more than 5 tokens (whitespace delimited) were considered. Other character sequences that were judged irrelevant and potential misguiders for the purpose at hand were normalized: URLs were replaced by the sequence `URL`, e-mail addresses by `MAIL`, hours and dates by `HORA` and `DATA`, etc. Names at the beginning of lines indicating speaker (in an interview, for instance) were removed, since they are frequent and the grammar that will be used is not intended to parse name plus sentence strings.

The remaining lines were ordered by length in terms of words and the smallest 200K lines from each of the two corpora were selected. Small lines were preferred as they are more likely to receive an analysis by the grammar.

Given the methods we will be employing for pre-tuning reportedly perform well even with small training sets (Section 5), only a modest portion of text from these corpora was needed.

In the benefit of comparability of the two approaches for grammar tuning, it is important that all the lines in the working data are parsable by the grammar. Otherwise, even if in the pre-tuning approach the pre-processor gets the classification right for non parsable sentences, this will be of no use since the grammar will not produce any result out of that. 90K lines of text were thus randomly selected from each corpus and checked as to whether they could be parsed by the grammar. 25K of parsable lines of the American corpus and 21K of parsable lines of the European corpus were obtained (46K lines out of 180K, representing 26% rate of parsability for the grammar used – more details on this grammar in the next Section).

It is worth noting that the use of two corpora, one from an European newspaper and the other from an American newspaper, without further annotation, does not allow their appropriate use in the present set of experiments. The reason is that if a sentence is found in the European corpus, one can have almost absolute certainty that it is possible in European Portuguese, but one does not know if it is Brazilian Portuguese, too. The same is true of any sentences in the American corpus — it can also be a sentence of European Portuguese in case it only contains words and structures common to both variants.

In order to prepare the data, a native speaker of European Portuguese was asked to manually decide from sentences found in the American corpus whether they are markedly Brazilian Portuguese. Conversely, a Brazilian informant detected markedly European Portuguese sentences from the European corpus.

From these parsed lines we drew around 1800 random lines of text from each corpus, and had them annotated. The lines coming from the American corpus were annotated for whether they are markedly Brazilian Portuguese, and vice-versa for the other corpus. Thus a three-way classification is obtained: any sentence was classified as being markedly Brazilian Portuguese, European Portuguese or common to both variants.

The large majority of the sentences were judged to be possible in both European and Brazilian Portuguese. 16% of the sentences in the European corpus were considered not belonging to Brazilian Portuguese, and 21% of the sentences in the American corpus were judged as not being European Portuguese.[1] Overall, 81% of the text was common to both varieties.

10KB of text from each one of the three classes were obtained. 140 lines, approximately 5KB, were reserved for training and another 140 for test. In total, the 30 K corpus included 116, 170, 493 and 41 sentence tokens for, respectively, 8, 7, 6 and 5 word length sentence types.

3.2 Variation

These training corpora were submitted to manual inspection in order to identify and quantify the sources of variant specificity. This is important to help interpret the experimental results and to gain insight on the current coverage of the grammar used in the experiment.

This analysis was performed over the 140 lines selected as markedly Brazilian Portuguese, and assumed that the sources of variant specificity should have broadly the same distribution in the other 140K lines markedly European Portuguese.

1. Mere orthographic differences (24%) e.g. *ação* vs. *acção* (*action*)

2. Phonetic variants reflected in orthography (9.3%) e.g. *irônico* vs. *irónico* (*ironic*)

3. Lexical differences (26.9% of differences)
   (a) Different form, same meaning (22.5%) e.g. *time* vs. *equipa* (*team*)
   (b) Same form, different meaning (4.4%) e.g. *policial* (*policeman/criminal novel*

4. Syntactic differences (39.7%)
   (a) Possessives w/out articles (12.2%)
   (b) In subcategorization frames (9.8%)
   (c) Clitic placement (6.4%)
   (d) Singular bare NPs (5.4%)
   (e) In subcat and word sense (1.9%)
   (f) Universal *todo* + article (0.9%)
   (g) Contractions of Prep+article (0.9%)
   (h) Questions w/out SV inversion (0.9%)
   (i) Postverbal negation (0.5%)
   (j) other (0.5%)

About 1/3 of the differences found would disappear if a unified orthography was adopted. Differences that are reflected in spelling can be modeled via multiple lexical entries, with constraints on feature VARIANT reflecting the variety in which the item with that spelling is used.

Interestingly, 40% of the differences are syntactic in nature. These cases are expected to be more difficult to detect with stochastic approaches than with a grammar.

4 Self-tuning

4.1 Grammar and baseline

The experiments on the self-tuning approach were carried out with a computational grammar for Portuguese developed with the LKB platform (Copestake, 2002) that uses MRS for semantic representation (Copestake et al., 2001) (Branco and Costa, 2005). At the time of the experiments reported here, this grammar was of modest size. In terms of linguistic phenomena, it covered basic declarative sentential structures and basic phrase structure of all categories, with a fully detailed account of the structure of NPs. It contained 42 syntax rules, 37 lexical rules (mostly inflectional) and a total of 2988 types, with 417 types for lexical entries. There were 2630 hand-built lexical entries, mostly nouns, with 1000 entries. It was coupled with a POS tagger for Portuguese, with 97% accuracy (Branco and Silva, 2004).

[1] A hypothetical explanation for this asymmetry (16% vs. 21%) is that one of the most pervasive differences between European and Brazilian Portuguese, clitic placement, is attenuated in writing: Brazilian text often displays word order between clitic and verb similar to European Portuguese, and different from oral Brazilian Portuguese. Therefore, European text displaying European clitic order tends not be seen as markedly European. In fact, we looked at the European sentences with clitic placement characteristic of European Portuguese that were judged possible in Brazilian Portuguese. If they were included in the markedly European sentences, 23% of the European text would be unacceptable Brazilian Portuguese, a number closer to the 21% sentences judged to be exclusively Brazilian Portuguese in the American corpus.

In terms of the sources of variant specificity identified above, this grammar was specifically designed to handle the co-occurrence of prenominal possessives and determiners and most of the syntactic constructions related to clitic-verb order. As revealed by the study of the training corpus, these constructions are responsible for almost 20% of marked sentences.

The lexicon contained lexical items markedly European Portuguese and markedly Brazilian Portuguese. These were taken from the Portuguese Wiktionary, where this information is available. Leaving aside the very infrequent items, around 740 marked lexical items were coded. Items that are variant specific found in the training corpora (80 more) were also entered in the lexicon.

These items, markedly belonging to one variant, were declined into their inflected forms and the resulting set Lex_{bsl} was used in the following baseline for dialect tuning: for a sentence s and N_{ep}, resp. N_{bp}, the number of tokens of items in Lex_{bsl} markedly European, resp. Brazilian Portuguese, occurring in s, s is tagged as European Portuguese if $N_{ep} > N_{bp}$, or vice-versa, or else, "common" Portuguese if $N_{ep} = N_{bp} = 0$.

Known class	*Predicted class* EP	BP	Common	Recall
EP	45	0	95	0.32
BP	3	45	92	0.32
Common	4	4	132	0.94
Precision	0.87	0.98	0.41	

Table 1: Baseline: Confusion matrix.

For this baseline, the figure of 0.53 of overall accuracy was obtained, detailed in Table 1.[2]

4.2 Results with self-tuning

The results obtained for the self-tuning mode of operation are presented in Table 2.[3] When the grammar produced multiple analyses for a given sentence, that sentence was classified as markedly European, resp. Brazilian, Portuguese if all the parses produced VARIANT with type *ep-variant*, resp. *bp-variant*. In all other cases, the sentence would be classified as common to both variants.

Known class	*Predicted class* EP	BP	Common	Recall
EP	53	1	86	0.38
BP	6	61	73	0.44
Common	14	1	125	0.89
Precision	0.73	0.97	0.44	

Table 2: Self-tuning: Confusion matrix.

Every sentence in the test data was classified, and the figure of 0.57 was obtained for overall accuracy. The analysis of errors shows that the sentence belonging to Brazilian Portuguese or to "common" Portuguese wrongly classified as European Portuguese contain clitics following the European Portuguese syntax, and some misspellings conforming to the European Portuguese orthography.

5 Pre-tuning

5.1 Language Detection Methods

Methods have been developed to detect the language a given text is written in. They have also been used to discriminate varieties of the same language, although less often. (Lins and Gonçalves, 2004) look up words in dictionaries to discriminate among languages, and (Oakes, 2003) runs stochastic tests on token frequencies, like the chi-square test, in order to differentiate between European and American English.

Many methods are based on frequency of byte n-grams in text because they can simultaneously detect language and character encoding (Li and Momoi, 2001), and can reliably classify short portions of text. They have been applied in web browsers (to identify character encodings) and information retrieval systems.

We are going to focus on methods based on character n-grams. Because all information used for classification is taken from characters, and they can be found in text in much larger quantities than words or phrases, problems of scarcity of data are attenuated. Besides, training data can also be easily found in large amounts because corpora do not need to be annotated (it is

[2]Naturally, extending the operation of this baseline method beyond the terms of comparability with grammars that handle each sentence at a time, namely by increasingly extending the number of sentences in the stretch of text being classified, will virtually lead it to reach optimal accuracy.

[3]These figures concern the test corpus, with the three conditions represented by 1/3 of the sentences, which are all parsable. Hence, actual recall over a naturally occurring text is expected to be lower. Using the estimate that only 26% of input receives a parse, that figure for recall would lie somewhere around 0.15 (= 0.57 x 0.26).

only necessary to know the language they belong to). More importantly, methods based on character n-grams can reliably classify small portions of text. The literature on automatic language identification mentions training corpora as small as 2K producing classifiers that perform with almost perfect accuracy for test strings as little as 500 Bytes (Dunning, 1994) and considering several languages. With more training data (20K-50K of text), similar quality can be achieved for smaller test strings (Prager, 1999).

Many n-gram based methods have been explored besides the one we opted for.[4] Many can achieve perfect or nearly perfect classification with small training corpora on small texts. In previous work (Branco and Costa, 2007), we did a comparative study on two classifiers that use approaches very well understood in language processing and information retrieval, namely Vector Space and Bayesian models. We retain here the latter as this one scored comparatively better for the current purposes.

In order to know which language $L_i \in L$ generated string s, Bayesian methods can be used to calculate the probabilities $P(s|L_i)$ of string s appearing in language L_i for all $L_i \in L$, the considered language set, and decide for the language with the highest score (Dunning, 1994). That is, in order to compute $P(L_i|s)$, we only compute $P(s|L_i)$. The Bayes rule allows us to cast the problem in terms of $\frac{P(s|L_i)P(L_i)}{P(s)}$, but as is standard practice, the denominator is dropped since we are only interested here in getting the highest probability, not its exact value. The prior $P(L_i)$ is also ignored, corresponding to the simplifying assumption that all languages are equally probable for the operation of the classifier. The way $P(s|L_i)$ is calculated is also the standard way to do it, namely assuming independence and just multiplying the probabilities of character c_i given the preceding *n-1* characters (using n-grams), for all characters in the input (estimated from n-gram counts in the training set).

For our experiments, we implemented the algorithm described in (Dunning, 1994). Other common strategies were also used, like prepending $n-1$ special characters to the input string to harmonize calculations, summing logs of probabilities instead of multiplying them to avoid underflow errors, and using Laplace smoothing to reserve probability mass to events not seen in training.

[4]See (Sibun and Reynar, 1996) and (Hughes et al., 2006) for surveys.

5.2 Calibrating the implementation

5.2.1 Detection of languages

First of all, we want to check that the language identification methods we are using, and have implemented, are in fact reliable to identify different languages. Hence, we run the classifier on three languages showing strikingly different characters and character sequences. This is a deliberately easy test to get insight into the appropriate setting of the two parameters at stake here, size of of the n-gram in the training phase, and size of the input in the running phase.

For this test, we used the Universal Declaration of Human Rights texts.The languages used were Finnish, Portuguese and Welsh.[5]

Several tests were conducted, splitting the test data in chunks 1, 5, 10 and 20 lines long. The classifier obtained perfect accuracy on all test conditions (all chunk sizes), for all values of n between 1 and 7 (inclusively). For $n = 8$ and $n = 9$ there were errors only when classifying 1 line long items.

The average line length for the test corpora was 138 characters for Finnish, 141 for Portuguese and 121 for Welsh (133 overall). In the corpora we will be using in the following experiments, average line length is much lower (around 40 characters per line). To become closer to our experimental conditions, we also evaluated this classifiers with the same test corpora, but truncated each line beyond the first 50 characters, yielding test corpora with an average line length around 38 characters (since some were smaller than that). The results are similar. The Bayesian classifier performed with less than perfect accuracy also with $n = 7$ when classifying 1 line at a time.

Our classifier was thus performing well at discriminating languages with short values of n, and can classify short bits of text, even with incomplete words.

[5]The Preamble and Articles 1–19 were used for training (8.1K of Finnish, 6.9K of Portuguese, and 6.1K of Welsh), and Articles 20–30 for testing (4.6K of Finnish, 4.7K of Portuguese, and 4.0K of Welsh).

5.2.2 Detection of originating corpus

In order to study its suitability to discriminate also the two Portuguese variants, we experimented our implementation of the Bayesian classifiers on 200K lines of text from each of the two corpora. We randomly chose 20K lines for testing and the remaining 180K for training. A classification is considered correct if the classifier can guess the newspaper the text was taken from.

The average line length of the test sentences is 43 characters. Several input lengths were tried out by dividing the test data into various sets with varying size. Table 3 summarizes the results obtained.

	Length of Test Item			
	1 line	5 lines	10 lines	20 lines
$n = 2$	0.84	0.99	**1**	**1**
$n = 3$	**0.96**	0.99	1	1
$n = 4$	**0.96**	**1**	1	1
$n = 5$	0.94	**1**	1	1
$n = 6$	0.92	0.99	1	1
$n = 7$	0.89	0.98	0.99	1

Table 3: Originating corpora: Accuracy

The accuracy of the classifier is surprisingly high given that the sentences that cannot be attributed to a single variety are estimated to be around 81%.

5.2.3 Scaling down the training data

A final check was made with the classifier to gain further insight on the comparability of the results obtained under the two tuning approaches. It was trained on the data prepared for the actual experiment, made of the 10K with lines that have the shortest length and are parsable, but using only the markedly European and Brazilian Portuguese data (leaving aside the sentences judged to be common to both). This way the two setups can be compared, since in the test of the Subsection just above much more data was available for training.

Results are in Table 4. As expected, with a much smaller amount of training data there is an overall drop in the accuracy, with a noticed bias at classifying items as European Portuguese. The performance of the classifier degrades with larger values of n. Nevertheless, the classifier is still very good with bigrams, with an

	Length of Test Item			
	1 line	5 lines	10 lines	20 lines
$n = 2$	**0.86**	**0.98**	**0.96**	**1**
$n = 3$	0.82	0.73	0.64	0.5
$n = 4$	0.68	0.55	0.5	0.5

Table 4: Two-way classification: Accuracy

almost optimal performance, only slightly worse than the one observed in the previous Subsection, when it was trained with more data.

From these preliminary tests, we learned that we could expect a quasi optimal performance of the classifier we implemented to act as a preprocessor in the pre-tuning approach, when $n = 2$ and it is run under conditions very close to the ones it will encounter in the actual experiment aimed at comparing the two tuning approaches.

5.3 Results with pre-tuning

In the final experiment, the classifier should discriminate between three classes, deciding whether the input is either specifically European or Brazilian Portuguese, or else whether it belongs to both variants. It was trained over the 15K tokens/420 lines of training data, and tested over the held out test data of identical size.

	Length of Test Item			
	1 line	5 lines	10 lines	20 lines
$n = 2$	**0.59**	**0.67**	**0.76**	**0.76**
$n = 3$	0.55	0.52	0.45	0.33
$n = 4$	0.48	0.39	0.33	0.33

Table 5: Three-way classification: Accuracy

The results are in Table 5. As expected, the classifier based in bigrams has the best performance for every size of the input, which improves from 0.59 to 0.76 as the size of the input gets from 1 line to 20 lines.

6 Discussion and conclusions

From the results above for pre-tuning, it is the value 0.59, obtained for 1 line of input, that can be put on a par with the value of 0.57 obtained for self-tuning — both of them to be appreciated against the baseline of 0.53.

Interestingly, the performance of both approaches are quite similar, and quite encouraging given the limitations under which the present pilot exercise was executed. But this is also the reason why they should be considered with the appropriate *grano salis.*

Note that there is much room for improvement in both approaches. From the several sources of variant specificity, the grammar used was prepared to cope only with grammatical constructs that are responsible for at most 20% of them. Also the lexicon, that included a little more than 800 variant-distinctive items, can be largely improved.

As to the classifier used for pre-tuning, it implements methods that may achieve optimal accuracy with training data sets of modest size but that need to be nevertheless larger than the very scarce 15K tokens used this time. Using backoff and interpolation will help to improve as well.

Some features potentially distinguish, however, the pre-tuning based on Bayesian classifier from the self-tuning by the grammar.

Language detection methods are easy to scale up with respect to the number of variants used. In contrast, the size of the type hierarchy under *variant* is exponential on the number of language variants if all combinations of variants are taken into account, as it seems reasonable to do.

N-grams based methods are efficient and can be very accurate. On the other hand, like any stochastic method, they are sensitive to training data and tend to be much more affected than the grammar in self-tuning by a change of text domain. Also in dialogue settings with turns from different language variants, hence with small lengths of texts available to classify and successive alternation between language variants, n-grams are likely to show less advantage than self-tuning by fully fledged grammars.

These are issues over which more acute insight will be gained in future work, which will seek to improve the contributions put forward in the present paper.

Summing up, a major contribution of the present paper is a design strategy for type-feature grammars that allows them to be appropriately set to the specific language variant of a given input. Concomitantly, this design allows the grammars either to be pre-tuned or to self-tune to that dialect – which, to the best of our knowledge, consists in a new kind of approach to handling language variation in deep processing.

In addition, we undertook a pilot experiment which can be taken as setting the basis for a methodology to comparatively assess the performance of these different tuning approaches and their future improvements.

References

António Branco and Francisco Costa. 2005. LX-GRAM – deep linguistic processing of Portuguese with HSPG. Technical report, Dept. of Informatics, University of Lisbon.

António Branco and Francisco Costa. 2007. Handling language variation in deep processing. In *Proc. CLIN2007.*

António Branco and João Silva. 2004. Evaluating solutions for the rapid development of state-of-the-art POS taggers for Portuguese. In *Proc. LREC2004.*

Ann Copestake, Dan Flickinger, Carl Pollard, and Ivan Sag. 2001. Minimal Recursion Semantics: An introduction. *Language and Computation*, 3.

Ann Copestake. 2002. *Implementing typed feature structure grammars.* CSLI.

Ted Dunning. 1994. Statistical identification of language. Technical Report MCCS-94-273, Computing Research Lab, New Mexico State Univ.

Baden Hughes, Timothy Baldwin, Steven Bird, Jeremy Nicholson, and Andrew MacKinlay. 2006. Reconsidering language identification for written language resources. In *Proc. LREC2006.*

Shanjian Li and Katsuhiko Momoi. 2001. A composite approach to language/encoding detection. In *Proc. 19th International Unicode Conference.*

Rafael Lins and Paulo Gonçalves. 2004. Automatic language identification of written texts. In *Proc. 2004 ACM Symposium on Applied Computing.*

Michael P. Oakes. 2003. Text categorization: Automatic discrimination between US and UK English using the chi-square test and high ratio pairs. *Research in Language*, 1.

Carl Pollard and Ivan Sag. 1994. *Head-driven phrase structure grammar.* CSLI.

John M. Prager. 1999. Linguini: Language identification for multilingual documents. *Journal of Management Information Systems*, 16(3).

Penelope Sibun and Jeffrey C. Reynar. 1996. Language identification: Examining the issues. In *5th Symposium on Document Analysis and IR.*

Pruning the Search Space of a Hand-Crafted Parsing System with a Probabilistic Parser

Aoife Cahill
Dublin City University
acahill@computing.dcu.ie

Tracy Holloway King
PARC
thking@parc.com

John T. Maxwell III
PARC
maxwell@parc.com

Abstract

The demand for deep linguistic analysis for huge volumes of data means that it is increasingly important that the time taken to parse such data is minimized. In the XLE parsing model which is a hand-crafted, unification-based parsing system, most of the time is spent on unification, searching for valid f-structures (dependency attribute-value matrices) within the space of the many valid c-structures (phrase structure trees). We carried out an experiment to determine whether pruning the search space at an earlier stage of the parsing process results in an improvement in the overall time taken to parse, while maintaining the quality of the f-structures produced. We retrained a state-of-the-art probabilistic parser and used it to pre-bracket input to the XLE, constraining the valid c-structure space for each sentence. We evaluated against the PARC 700 Dependency Bank and show that it is possible to decrease the time taken to parse by ∼18% while maintaining accuracy.

1 Introduction

When deep linguistic analysis of massive data is required (e.g. processing Wikipedia), it is crucial that the parsing time be minimized. The XLE English parsing system is a large-scale, hand-crafted, deep, unification-based system that processes raw text and produces both constituent-structures (phrase structure trees) and feature-structures (dependency attribute-value matrices). A typical breakdown of parsing time of XLE components is Morphology (1.6%), Chart (5.8%) and Unifier (92.6%).

The unification process is the bottleneck in the XLE parsing system. The grammar generates many valid c-structure trees for a particular sentence: the Unifier then processes all of these trees (as packed structures), and a log-linear disambiguation module can choose the most probable f-structure from the resulting valid f-structures. For example, the sentence "Growth is slower." has 84 valid c-structure trees according to the current English grammar;[1] however once the Unifier has processed all of these trees (in a packed form), only one c-structure and f-structure pair is valid (see Figure 1). In this instance, the log-linear disambiguation does not need to choose the most probable result.

The research question we pose is whether the search space can be pruned earlier before unification takes place. Bangalore and Joshi (1999), Clark and Curran (2004) and Matsuzaki et al. (2007) show that by using a super tagger before (CCG and HPSG) parsing, the space required for discriminitive training is drastically reduced. Supertagging is not widely used within the LFG framework, although there has been some work on using hypertags (Kinyon, 2000). Ninomiya et al. (2006) propose a method for faster HPSG parsing while maintaining accuracy by only using the probabilities of lexical entry selections (i.e. the supertags) in their discriminitive model. In the work presented here, we con-

[1] For example, *is* can be a copula, a progressive auxiliary or a passive auxiliary, while *slower* can either be an adjective or an adverb.

Proceedings of the 5th Workshop on Important Unresolved Matters, pages 65–72,
Ann Arbor, June 2005.

centrate on reducing the number of c-structure trees that the Unifier has to process, ideally to one tree. The hope was that this would speed up the parsing process, but how would it affect the quality of the f-structures? This is similar to the approach taken by Cahill et al. (2005) who do not use a hand-crafted complete unification system (rather an automatically acquired probabilistic approximation). They parse raw text into LFG f-structures by first parsing with a probabilistic CFG parser to choose the most probable c-structure. This is then passed to an automatic f-structure annotation algorithm which deterministically generates one f-structure for that tree.

The most compact way of doing this would be to integrate a statistical component to the parser that could rank the c-structure trees and only pass the most likely forward to the unification process. However, this would require a large rewrite of the system. So, we first wanted to investigate a "cheaper" alternative to determine the viability of the pruning strategy; this is the experiment reported in this paper. This is implemented by stipulating constituent boundaries in the input string, so that any c-structure that is incompatible with these constraints is invalid and will not be processed by the Unifier. This was done to some extent in Riezler et al. (2002) to automatically generate training data for the log-linear disambiguation component of XLE. Previous work obtained the constituent constraints (i.e. brackets) from the gold-standard trees in the Penn-II Treebank. However, to parse novel text, gold-standard trees are unavailable.

We used a state-of-the-art probabilistic parser to provide the bracketing constraints to XLE. These parsers are accurate (achieving accuracy of over 90% on Section 23 WSJ text), fast, and robust. The idea is that pre-parsing of the input text by a fast and accurate parser can prune the c-structure search space, reducing the amount of work done by the Unifier, speed up parsing and maintain the high quality of the f-structures produced.

The structure of this paper is as follows: Section 2 introduces the XLE parsing system. Section 3 describes a baseline experiment and based on the results suggests retraining the Bikel parser to improve results (Section 4). Section 5 describes experiments on the development set, from which we evaluate the most successful system against the PARC 700 test set (Section 6). Finally, Section 7 concludes.

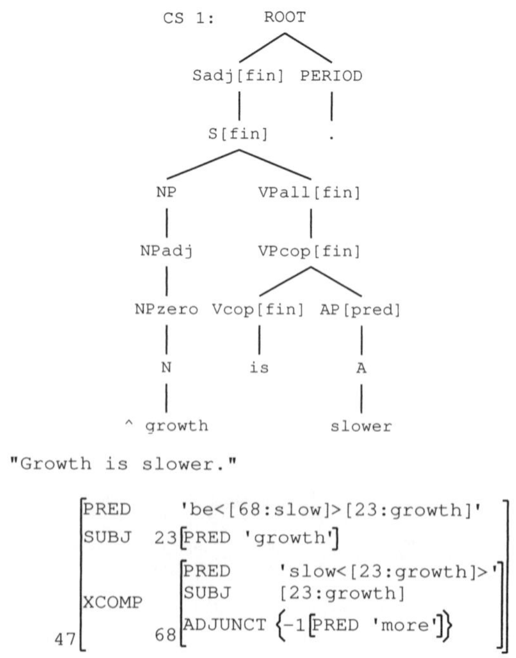

Figure 1: C- and F-Structure for "Growth is slower."

2 Background

In this section we introduce Lexical Functional Grammar, the grammar formalism underlying the XLE, and briefly describe the XLE parsing system.

2.1 Lexical Functional Grammar

Lexical Functional Grammar (LFG) (Kaplan and Bresnan, 1982) is a constraint-based theory of grammar. It (minimally) posits two levels of representation, c(onstituent)-structure and f(unctional)-structure. C-structure is represented by context-free phrase-structure trees, and captures surface grammatical configurations such as word order. The nodes in the trees are annotated with functional equations (attribute-value structure constraints) which are resolved to produce an f-structure. F-structures are recursive attribute-value matrices, representing abstract syntactic functions. F-structures approximate basic predicate-argument-adjunct structures or dependency relations. Figure 1 shows the c- and f-structure for the sentence "Growth is slower.".

```
Parser Output: (S1 (S (NP (NN Growth)) (VP (AUX is) (ADJP (JJR slower))) (. .)))
      Labeled: \[S1 \[S Growth \[VP is \[ADJP slower\] \].\] \]
    Unlabeled: \[ \[ Growth \[ is \[ slower\] \].\] \]
```

Figure 2: Example of retained brackets from parser output to constrain the XLE parser

2.2 The XLE Parsing System

The XLE parsing system is a deep-grammar-based parsing system. The experiments reported in this paper use the English LFG grammar constructed as part of the ParGram project (Butt et al., 2002). This system incorporates sophisticated ambiguity-management technology so that all possible syntactic analyses of a sentence are computed in an efficient, packed representation (Maxwell and Kaplan, 1993). In accordance with LFG theory, the output includes not only standard context-free phrase-structure trees (c-structures) but also attribute-value matrices (f-structures) that explicitly encode predicate-argument relations and other meaningful properties. The f-structures can be deterministically mapped to dependency triples without any loss of information, using the built-in ordered rewrite system (Crouch et al., 2002). XLE selects the most probable analysis from the potentially large candidate set by means of a stochastic disambiguation component based on a log-linear probability model (Riezler et al., 2002) that works on the packed representations. The underlying parsing system also has built-in robustness mechanisms that allow it to parse strings that are outside the scope of the grammar as a list of fewest well-formed "fragments". Furthermore, performance parameters that bound parsing and disambiguation can be tuned for efficient but accurate operation. These parameters include at which point to timeout and return an error, the amount of stack memory to allocate, the number of new edges to add to the chart and at which point to start skimming (a process that guarantees XLE will finish processing a sentence in polynomial time by only carrying out a bounded amount of work on each remaining constituent after a time threshold has passed). For the experiments reported here, we did not fine-tune these parameters due to time constraints; so default values were arbitrarily set and the same values used for all parsing experiments.

3 Baseline experiments

We carried out a baseline experiment with two state-of-the-art parsers to establish what effect pre-bracketing the input to the XLE system has on the quality and number of the solutions produced. We used the Bikel () multi-threaded, head-driven chart-parsing engine developed at the University of Pennsylvania. The second parser is that described in Charniak and Johnson (2005). This parser uses a discriminative reranker that selects the most probable parse from the 50-best parses returned by a generative parser based on Charniak (2000).

We evaluated against the PARC 700 Dependency Bank (King et al., 2003) which provides gold-standard analyses for 700 sentences chosen at random from Section 23 of the Penn-II Treebank. The Dependency Bank was bootstrapped by parsing the 700 sentences with the XLE English grammar, and then manually correcting the output. The data is divided into two sets, a 140-sentence development set and a test set of 560 sentences (Kaplan et al., 2004).

We took the raw strings from the 140-sentence development set and parsed them with each of the state-of-the-art probabilistic parsers. As an upper bound for the baseline experiment, we use the brackets in the original Penn-II treebank trees for the 140 development set.

We then used the brackets from each parser output (or original treebank trees) to constrain the XLE parser. If the input to the XLE parser is bracketed, the parser will only generate c-structures that respect these brackets (i.e., only c-structures with brackets that are compatible with the input brackets are considered during the unification stage). Figure 2 gives an example of retained brackets from the parser output. We do not retain brackets around PRN (parenthetical phrase) or NP nodes as their structure often differed too much from XLE analyses of the same phrases. We passed pre-bracketed strings to the XLE and evaluated the output f-structures in terms of dependency triples against the 140-sentence subset of

	Non-Fragment		Fragment	
	Penn-XLE (lab.)	Penn-XLE (unlab.)	Penn-XLE (lab.)	Penn-XLE (unlab.)
Total XLE parses (/140)	0	89	140	140
F-Score of subset	0	84.11	53.92	74.87
Overall F-Score	0	58.91	53.92	74.87

Table 1: Upper-bound results for original Penn-II trees

	Non-Fragment			Fragment		
	XLE	Bikel-XLE (lab.)	Bikel-XLE (unlab.)	XLE	Bikel-XLE (lab.)	Bikel-XLE (unlab.)
Total XLE Parses (/140)	119	0	84	135	140	140
F-Score of Subset	81.57	0	84.23	78.72	54.37	73.71
Overall F-Score	72.01	0	55.06	76.13	54.37	*73.71
	XLE	CJ-XLE (lab.)	CJ-XLE (unlab.)	XLE	CJ-XLE (lab.)	CJ-XLE (unlab.)
Total XLE Parses (/140)	119	0	86	135	139	139
F-Score of Subset	81.57	0	86.57	78.72	53.96	75.64
Overall F-Score	72.01	0	58.04	76.13	53.48	*74.98

Table 2: Bikel (2002) and Charniak and Johnson (2005) out-of-the-box baseline results

the PARC 700 Dependency Bank.

The results of the baseline experiments are given in Tables 1 and 2. Table 1 gives the upper bound results if we use the gold standard Penn treebank to bracket the input to XLE. Table 2 compares the XLE (fragment and non-fragment) grammar to the system where the input is pre-parsed by each parser. XLE fragment grammars provide a back-off when parsing fails: the grammar is relaxed and the parser builds a fragment parse of the well-formed chunks. We compare the parsers in terms of total number of parses (out of 140) and the f-score of the subset of sentences successfully parsed. We also combine these scores to give an overall f-score, where the system scores 0 for each sentence it could not parse. When testing for statistical significance between systems, we compare the overall f-score values. Figures marked with an asterisk are not statistically significantly different at the 95% level.[2]

The results show that using unlabeled brackets achieves reasonable f-scores with the non-fragment grammar. Using the labeled bracketing from the output of both parsers causes XLE to always fail when parsing. This is because the labels in the output of parsers trained on the Penn-II treebank differ considerably from the labels on c-structure trees produced by XLE. Interestingly, the f-scores for both the CJ-XLE and Bikel-XLE systems are very similar to the upper bounds. The gold standard upper bound is not as high as expected because the Penn trees used to produce the gold bracketed input are not always compatible with the XLE-style trees. As a simple example, the tree in Figure 1 differs from the parse tree for the same sentence in the Penn Treebank (Figure 3). The most obvious difference is the labels on the nodes. However, even in this small example, there are structural differences, e.g. the position of the period. In general, the larger the tree, the greater the difference in both labeling and structure between the Penn trees and the XLE-style trees. Therefore, the next step was to retrain a parser to produce trees with structures the same as XLE-style trees and with XLE English grammar labels on the nodes. For this experiment we use the Bikel () parser, as it is more suited to being retrained on a new treebank annotation scheme.

4 Retraining the Bikel parser

We retrained the Bikel parser so that it produces trees like those outputted by the XLE parsing system (e.g. Figure 1). To do this, we first created a training corpus, and then modified the parser to deal with this new data.

Since there is no manually-created treebank of

[2]We use the approximate randomization test (Noreen, 1989) to test for significance.

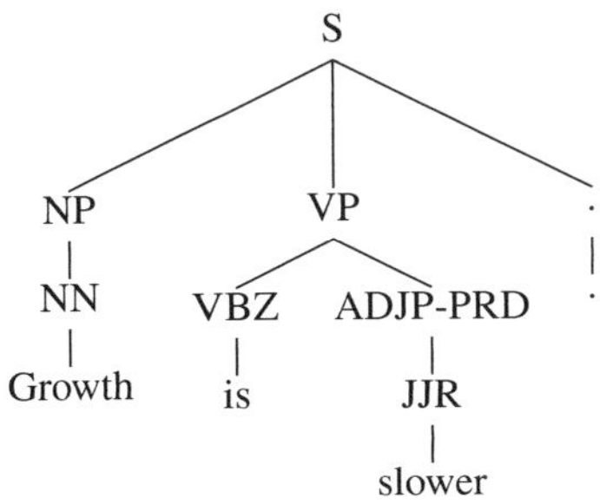

Figure 3: Penn Treebank tree for "Growth is slower."

XLE-style trees, we created one automatically from sections 02-21 of the Penn-II Treebank. We took the raw strings from those sections and marked up NP and SBAR constituents using the brackets from the gold standard Penn treebank. The NP constituents are labeled, and the SBAR unlabeled (i.e. the SBAR constituents are forced to exist in the XLE parse, but the label on them is not constrained to be SBAR). We also tagged verbs, adjectives and nouns, based on the gold standard POS tags.

We parsed the 39,832 marked-up sentences in the standard training corpus and used the XLE disambiguation module to choose the most probable c- and f-structure pair for each sentence. Ideally we would have had an expert choose these. We automatically extracted the c-structure trees produced by the XLE and performed some automatic post-processing.[3] This resulted in an automatically created training corpus of 27,873 XLE-style trees. The 11,959 missing trees were mainly due to the XLE parses not being compatible with the bracketed input, but sometimes due to time and memory constraints.

Using the automatically-created training corpus of XLE-style trees, we retrained the Bikel parser on this data. This required adding a new language module ("XLE-English") to the Bikel parser, and regenerating head-finding rules for the XLE-style trees.

5 Experiments

Once we had a retrained version of the Bikel parser that parses novel text into XLE-style trees, we carried out a number of experiments on our development set in order to establish the optimum settings

	All Sentences	
	XLE	Bikel-XLE
	Non-fragment grammar Labeled brackets	
Total Parsing Time	964	336
Total XLE Parses (/140)	119	77
F-Score of Subset	81.57	86.11
Overall F-Score	72.01	52.84
	Non-fragment grammar Unlabeled brackets	
Total Parsing Time	964	380
Total XLE Parses (/140)	119	89
F-Score of Subset	81.57	85.62
Overall F-Score	72.01	59.34
	Fragment grammar Labeled brackets	
Total Parsing Time	1143	390
Total XLE Parses (/140)	135	140
F-Score of Subset	78.72	71.86
Overall F-Score	76.13	71.86
	Fragment grammar Unlabeled brackets	
Total Parsing Time	1143	423
Total XLE Parses (/140)	135	140
F-Score of Subset	78.72	74.51
Overall F-Score	76.13	*74.51

Table 3: Bikel-XLE Initial Experiments

for the evaluation against the PARC 700 test set.

5.1 Pre-bracketing

We automatically pre-processed the raw strings from the 140-sentence development set. This made systematic changes to the tokens so that the retrained Bikel parser can parse them. The changes included removing quotes, converting *a* and *an* to *_a*, converting *n't* to *_not*, etc. We parsed the pre-processed strings with the new Bikel parser.

We carried out four initial experiments, experimenting with both labeled and unlabeled brackets and XLE fragment and non-fragment grammars. Table 3 gives the results for these experiments. We compare the parsers in terms of time, total number of parses (out of 140), the f-score of the subset of sentences successfully parsed and the overall f-score if the system achieves a score of 0 for all sentences it does not parse. The time taken for the Bikel-XLE system includes the time taken for the Bikel parser to parse the sentences, as well as the time taken for XLE to process the bracketed input.

Table 3 shows that using the non-fragment grammar, the Bikel-XLE system performs better on the

[3] The postprocessing included removing morphological information and the brackets from the original markup.

subset of sentences parsed than XLE system alone, though the results are not statistically significantly better overall, since the coverage is much lower. The number of bracketed sentences that can be parsed by XLE increases if the brackets are unlabeled. The table also shows that the XLE system performs much better than Bikel-XLE when using the fragment grammars. Although the Bikel-XLE system is quite a bit faster, there is a drop in f-score; however this is not statistically significant when the brackets are unlabeled.

5.2 Pre-tagging

We performed some error analysis on the output of the Bikel-XLE system and noticed that a considerable number of errors were due to mis-tagging. So, we pre-tagged the input to the Bikel parser using the MXPOST tagger (Ratnaparkhi, 1996). The results for the non-fragment grammars are presented in Table 4. Pre-tagging with MXPOST, however, does not result in a statistically significantly higher result than parsing untagged input, although more sentences can be parsed by both systems. Pre-tagging also adds an extra time overhead cost.

		No pretags	MXPOST tags
	XLE	Bikel-XLE	Bikel-XLE
	Unlabeled		
Total Parsing Time	964	380	493
# XLE Parses (/140)	119	89	92
F-Score of Subset	81.57	85.62	84.98
Overall F-Score	72.01	59.34	*61.11
	Labeled		
Total Parsing Time	964	336	407
# XLE Parses (/140)	119	77	80
F-Score of Subset	81.57	86.11	85.87
Overall F-Score	72.01	52.84	*54.91

Table 4: MXPOST pre-tagged, Non-fragment grammar

5.3 Pruning

The Bikel parser can be customized to allow different levels of pruning. The above experiments were carried out using the default level. We carried out experiments with three levels of pruning.[4] The results are given in Table 5 for the experiment with labeled brackets and the non-fragment XLE grammar. More pruning generally results in fewer and lower-quality parses. The biggest gain is with pruning level 1, where the number and quality of bracketed sentences that can be parsed with XLE remains the same as with the default level. This is because Bikel with pruning level 1 does not relax the constraints when parsing fails and does not waste time parsing sentences that cannot be parsed in bracketed form by XLE.

	Default	L1	L2	L3
Total Parsing Time	336	137	137	106
# XLE Parses (/140)	77	77	76	75
F-Score of Subset	86.11	86.11	86.04	85.87
Overall F-Score	52.84	*52.84	*52.43	*52.36

Table 5: Pruning with Non-fragment grammar, Labeled brackets, Levels default-3

5.4 Hybrid systems

Although pre-parsing with Bikel results in faster XLE parsing time and high-quality f-structures (when examining only the quality of the sentences that can be parsed by the Bikel-XLE system), the coverage of this system remains poor, therefore the overall f-score remains poor. One solution is to build a hybrid two-pass system. During the first pass all sentences are pre-parsed by Bikel and the bracketed output is parsed by the XLE non-fragment grammar. In the second pass, the sentences that were not parsed during the first pass are parsed with the XLE fragment grammar. We carried out a number of experiments with hybrid systems and the results are given in Table 6.

The results show that again labeled brackets result in a statistically significant increase in f-score, although the time taken is almost the same as the XLE fragment grammar alone. Coverage increases by 1 sentence. Using unlabeled brackets results in 3 additional sentences receiving parses, and parsing time is improved by $\sim$12%; however the increase in f-score is not statistically significant.

Table 7 gives the results for hybrid systems with pruning using labeled brackets. The more pruning that the Bikel parser does, the faster the system, but the quality of the f-structures begins to deteri-

[4]The default level of pruning starts at 3.5, has a maximum of 4 and relaxes constraints when parsing fails. Level 1 pruning is the same as the default except the constraints are never relaxed. Level 2 pruning has a start value of 3.5 and a maximum value of 3.5. Level 3 pruning has a start and maximum value of 3.

	XLE (frag)	Bikel-XLE hybrid (labeled)	Bikel-XLE hybrid (unlabeled)
Total Parsing Time	1143	1121	1001
Total XLE Parses (/140)	135	136	138
F-Score of Subset	78.72	79.85	79.51
Overall F-Score	76.13	77.61	*78.28

Table 6: Hybrid systems compared to the XLE fragment grammar alone

	XLE (frag)	Bikel-XLE hybrid (level 1)	Bikel-XLE hybrid (level 2)	Bikel-XLE hybrid (level 3)
Total Parsing Time	1143	918	920	885
Total XLE Parses (/140)	135	136	136	136
F-Score of Subset	78.72	79.85	79.79	79.76
Overall F-Score	76.13	77.61	77.55	77.53

Table 7: Hybrid systems with pruning compared to the XLE fragment grammar alone

orate. The best system is the Bikel-XLE hybrid system with labeled brackets and pruning level 1. This system achieves a statistically significant increase in f-score over the XLE fragment grammar alone, decreases the time taken to parse by almost 20% and increases coverage by 1 sentence. Therefore, we chose this system to perform our final evaluation against the PARC 700 Dependency Bank.

6 Evaluation against the PARC 700

We evaluated the system that performs best on the development set against the 560-sentence test set of the PARC 700 Dependency Bank. The results are given in Table 8. The hybrid system achieves an 18% decrease in parsing time, a slight improvement in coverage of 0.9%, and a 1.12% improvement in overall f-structure quality.

	XLE (frag)	Bikel-XLE hybrid (labeled, prune 1)
Total Parsing Time	4967	4077
Total XLE Parses (/560)	537	542
F-Score of Subset	80.13	80.63
Overall F-Score	77.04	78.16

Table 8: PARC 700 evaluation of the Hybrid system compared to the XLE fragment grammar alone

7 Conclusions

We successfully used a state-of-the-art probabilistic parser in combination with a hand-crafted system to improve parsing time while maintaining the quality of the output produced. Our hybrid system consists of two phases. During phase one, pre-processed, tokenized text is parsed with a retrained Bikel parser. We use the labeled brackets in the output to constrain the c-structures generated by the XLE parsing system. In the second phase, we use the XLE fragment grammar to parse any remaining sentences that have not received a parse in the first phase.

Given the slight increase in overall f-score performance, the speed up in parsing time (∼18%) can justify more complicated processing architecture for some applications.[5] The main disadvantage of the current system is that the input to the Bikel parser needs to be tokenized, whereas XLE processes raw text. One solution to this is to use a state-of-the-art probabilistic parser that accepts untokenized input (such as Charniak and Johnson, 2005) and retrain it as described in Section 4.

Kaplan et al. (2004) compared time and accuracy of a version of the Collins parser tuned to maximize speed and accuracy to an earlier version of the XLE parser. Although the XLE parser was more accurate, the parsing time was a factor of 1.49 slower (time converting Collins trees to dependencies was not counted in the parse time; time to produce f-structures from c-structures was counted in the XLE parse time). The hybrid system here narrows the speed gap while maintaining greater accuracy.

The original hope behind using the brackets to constrain the XLE c-structure generation was that

[5]For example, in massive data applications, if the parsing task takes 30 days, reducing this by 18% saves more than 5 days.

the brackets would force the XLE to choose only one tree. However, the brackets were sometimes ambiguous, and sometimes more than one valid tree was found. In the final evaluation against the PARC 700 test set, the average number of optimal solutions was 4.05; so the log-linear disambiguation module still had to chose the most probable f-structure. However, this is considerably less to choose from than the average of 341 optimal solutions produced by the XLE fragment grammar for the same sentences when unbracketed.

Based on the results of this experiment we have integrated a statistical component into the XLE parser itself. With this architecture the packed c-structure trees are pruned before unification without needing to preprocess the input text. The XLE c-structure pruning results in a $\sim$30% reduction in parse time on the Wikipedia with little loss in precision. We hope to report on this in the near future.

Acknowledgments

The research in this paper was partly funded by Science Foundation Ireland grant 04/BR/CS0370.

References

Srinivas Bangalore and Aravind K. Joshi. 1999. Supertagging: An approach to alsmost parsing. *Computational Linguistics*, 25(2):237–265.

Dan Bikel. Design of a Multi-lingual, Parallel-processing Statistical Parsing Engine. In *Proceedings of HLT, YEAR = 2002, pages = 24–27, address = San Diego, CA,.*

Miriam Butt, Helge Dyvik, Tracy Holloway King, Hiroshi Masuichi, and Christian Rohrer. 2002. The Parallel Grammar Project. In *Proceedings of Workshop on Grammar Engineering and Evaluation*, pages 1–7, Taiwan.

Aoife Cahill, Martin Forst, Michael Burke, Mairead McCarthy, Ruth O'Donovan, Christian Rohrer, Josef van Genabith, and Andy Way. 2005. Treebank-based acquisition of multilingual unification grammar resources. *Journal of Research on Language and Computation*, pages 247–279.

Eugene Charniak and Mark Johnson. 2005. Coarse-to-Fine n-Best Parsing and MaxEnt Discriminative Reranking. In *Proceedings of ACL*, pages 173–180, Ann Arbor, Michigan.

Eugene Charniak. 2000. A maximum entropy inspired parser. In *Proceedings of NAACL*, pages 132–139, Seattle, WA.

Stephen Clark and James R. Curran. 2004. The Importance of Supertagging for Wide-Coverage CCG Parsing . In *Proceedings of COLING*, pages 282–288, Geneva, Switzerland, Aug 23–Aug 27. COLING.

Richard Crouch, Ron Kaplan, Tracy Holloway King, and Stefan Riezler. 2002. A comparison of evaluation metrics for a broad coverage parser. In *Proceedings of the LREC Workshop: Beyond PARSEVAL*, pages 67–74, Las Palmas, Canary Islands, Spain.

Ron Kaplan and Joan Bresnan. 1982. Lexical Functional Grammar, a Formal System for Grammatical Representation. In Joan Bresnan, editor, *The Mental Representation of Grammatical Relations*, pages 173–281. MIT Press, Cambridge, MA.

Ron Kaplan, Stefan Riezler, Tracy Holloway King, John T. Maxwell, Alexander Vasserman, and Richard Crouch. 2004. Speed and Accuracy in Shallow and Deep Stochastic Parsing. In *Proceedings of HLT-NAACL*, pages 97–104, Boston, MA.

Tracy Holloway King, Richard Crouch, Stefan Riezler, Mary Dalrymple, and Ron Kaplan. 2003. The PARC 700 dependency bank. In *Proceedings of LINC*, pages 1–8, Budapest, Hungary.

Alexandra Kinyon. 2000. Hypertags. In *Proceedings of COLING*, pages 446–452, Saarbrücken.

Takuya Matsuzaki, Yusuke Miyao, and Jun'ichi Tsujii. 2007. Efficient HPSG Parsing with Supertagging and CFG-filtering. In *Proceedings of IJCAI*, pages 1671–1676, India.

John T. Maxwell and Ronald M. Kaplan. 1993. The interface between phrasal and functional constraints. *Computational Linguistics*, **19**(4):571–590.

Takashi Ninomiya, Takuya Matsuzaki, Yoshimasa Tsuruoka, Yusuke Miyao, and Jun'ichi Tsujii. 2006. Extremely Lexicalized Models for Accurate and Fast HPSG Parsing. In *Proceedings of EMNLP*, pages 155–163, Australia.

Eric W. Noreen. 1989. *Computer Intensive Methods for Testing Hypotheses: An Introduction*. Wiley, New York.

Adwait Ratnaparkhi. 1996. A Maximum Entropy Part-Of-Speech Tagger. In *Proceedings of EMNLP*, pages 133–142, Philadelphia, PA.

Stefan Riezler, Tracy King, Ronald Kaplan, Richard Crouch, John T. Maxwell, and Mark Johnson. 2002. Parsing the Wall Street Journal using a Lexical-Functional Grammar and Discriminative Estimation Techniques. In *Proceedings of ACL*, pages 271–278, Philadelphia, PA.

Semantic composition with (Robust) Minimal Recursion Semantics

Ann Copestake
Computer Laboratory, University of Cambridge
JJ Thomson Avenue, Cambridge, UK
aac@cl.cam.ac.uk

Abstract

We discuss semantic composition in Minimal Recursion Semantics (MRS) and Robust Minimal Recursion Semantics (RMRS). We demonstrate that a previously defined formal algebra applies to grammar engineering across a much greater range of frameworks than was originally envisaged. We show how this algebra can be adapted to composition in grammar frameworks where a lexicon is not assumed, and how this underlies a practical implementation of semantic construction for the RASP system.

1 Introduction

Minimal Recursion Semantics (MRS: Copestake et al. (2005)) is a flat semantic representation which factors semantics into elementary predications (EPs) and allows for underspecification of scope. It has been widely used, especially for HPSG. Robust Minimal Recursion Semantics (RMRS: Copestake (2003)) is a variant of MRS which takes this factorisation further to allow underspecification of relational information as well. While MRS has generally been used with hand-built HPSG grammars, RMRS is also suitable for use with shallower approaches to analysis, including part-of-speech tagging, noun phrase chunking and stochastic parsers which operate without detailed lexicons. MRSs can be converted into RMRSs: RMRS output from shallower systems is less fully specified than the output from deeper systems, but in principle fully compatible. In our work, the semantics produced by a deep grammar is taken as normative when developing semantic representations from shallower processing. For English, the target semantic representations are those produced by the English Resource Grammar (ERG, Flickinger (2000)). The MRS/RMRS approach has been adopted as a common framework for the DELPH-IN initiative (Deep Linguistic Processing with HPSG: `http://www.delph-in.net`). An algebra for MRS was defined by Copestake et al. (2001) (henceforth CLF) and forms the starting point for the work reported here.

The aim of CLF was to formalise the notion of semantic composition within grammars expressed in a typed feature structure (TFS) logic. Here, we extend that work to non-lexicalist approaches and also describe how the formal principles of composition used in MRS can be adapted to produce a formalism for RMRS composition. Thus we demonstrate that the algebra applies to grammar engineering across a much wider range of frameworks than was originally envisaged. Besides its theoretical interest, this result has practical benefits when combining multiple processing systems in that it allows compatible semantic representations at a phrasal level as well as at a sentence level.

The next section (§2) describes the most important features of MRS, RMRS and the earlier work on the algebra. We then outline how the algebra can be used for implementing deep non-TFS approaches (§3) and explain how it works with RMRS (§4). This is followed by discussion of the extension to grammars without a detailed lexicon (§5). To briefly illustrate the practical applications, section (§6) outlines how RMRS semantics is constructed from RASP (Robust accurate domain-independent statistical parsing: Briscoe and Carroll (2002)).

2 MRS, RMRS and the algebra

Details of MRS, RMRS and the algebra are given in the cited papers, but we will briefly introduce them here for convenience. Fig. 1 illustrates an MRS from a deep grammar (based on the ERG output, but simplified for expository purposes), an equivalent RMRS and a very underspecified RMRS, derived from a POS tagger.

MRS achieves a flat representation via the use of labels on EPs, thus factoring out scopal relationships. Scope constraints (HCONS) are shown as qeq relationships ($=_q$ equality modulo quantifiers: the

Proceedings of the 5th Workshop on Important Unresolved Matters, pages 73–80,
Ann Arbor, June 2005.

MRS representation:
$l0$: _the_q$(x0, h01, h02)$, $l1$: _fat_j$(x1)$, $l2$: _cat_n$(x2)$, $l3$: _sit_v_1$(e3, x3)$, $l4$: _on_p$(e4, e41, x4)$,
$l5$: _a_q$(x5, h51, h52)$, $l6$: _mat_n_1$(x6)$,
$h01 =_q l1, h51 =_q l6$
$x0 = x1 = x2 = x3, e3 = e41, x4 = x5 = x6, l1 = l2, l3 = l4$
RMRS equivalent to the MRS above:
$l0$: $a0$: _the_q$(x0)$, $l0$: $a0$: RSTR$(h01)$, $l0$: $a0$: BODY$(h02)$, $l1$: $a1$: _fat_j$(x1)$, $l2$: $a2$: _cat_n$(x2)$,
$l3$: $a3$: _sit_v_1$(e3)$, $l3$: $a3$: ARG1$(x31)$, $l4$: $a4$: _on_p$(e4, e41, x4)$, $l4$: $a4$: ARG1$(e41)$, $l4$: $a4$: ARG2$(x4)$,
$l5$: $a5$: _a_q$(x5)$, $l5$: $a5$: RSTR$(h51)$, $l5$: $a5$: BODY$(h52)$, $l6$: $a6$: _mat_n_1$(x6)$,
$h01 =_q l1, h51 =_q l6$
$x0 = x1 = x2 = x3, e3 = e41, x4 = x5 = x6, l1 = l2, l3 = l4$
Highly underspecified RMRS output:
$l0$: $a0$: _the_q$(x0)$, $l1$: $a1$: _fat_j$(x1)$, $l2$: $a2$: _cat_n$(x2)$, $l3$: $a3$: _sit_v$(e3)$, $l4$: $a4$: _on_p$(e4)$,
$l5$: $a5$: _a_q$(x5)$, $l6$: $a6$: _mat_n$(x6)$

Figure 1: MRS and RMRS for *the fat cat sat on a mat*

details are not important to understand this paper). In MRS, implicit conjunction is indicated by equality between labels. For instance, the labels on $l1$: fat(x) and $l2$: cat1(x) are equated. In this figure, we show MRS using explicit equalities (eqs: $=$) rather than coindexation of variables since this corresponds to the formalism used in the algebra.

RMRS uses the same approach to scope but adopts a variant of a neo-Davidsonian representation, where arguments (ARGs) are represented as distinct elements. In the very underspecified RMRS at the bottom of Fig.1, no relational information is known so there are no ARGs. Separating out ARGs from the EPs and allowing them to be omitted permits a straightforward notion of a specificity hierarchy in terms of information content. ARGs may also be underspecified: e.g., ARGn indicates that there is some argument relationship, but it is unknown whether it is an ARG1, ARG2 or ARG3. In the version of RMRS described in this paper, the ARGs are related to the main EPs via an 'anchor' element. An EP and its associated ARGs share a unique anchor. This version of RMRS uses exactly the same mechanism for conjunction as does MRS: the anchor elements are required so that ARGs can still be associated with a single EP even if the label of the EP has been equated with another EP. This is a change from Copestake (2003): the reasons for this proposal are discussed in §4, below. The conjunction information is not available from a POS tagger alone and so is not present in the second RMRS in Fig.1.

The naming convention adopted for the relations (e.g., _sit_v) allows them to be constructed without access to a lexicon. '_v' etc are indications of the coarse-grained sense distinctions which can be inferred from part-of-speech information. Deep grammars can produce finer-grained sense distinctions, indicated by '_1' etc, and there is an implicit hierarchy such that _sit_v_1 is taken as being more specific than _sit_v. However, in what follows, we will use simple relation names for readability. MRS and RMRS both assume an inventory of features on variables which are used to represent tense etc, but these will not be discussed in this paper.

2.1 The MRS algebra

In the algebra introduced by CLF, semantic structures (SEMENTS) for phrases consist of five parts:

1. Hooks: can be thought of as pointers into the relations list. In a full grammar, hooks consist of three parts: a label (l), an index (i) and an external argument (omitted here for simplicity).
2. Slots: structures corresponding to syntactic/semantic unsaturation — they specify how the semantics is combined. A slot in one sign is instantiated by being equated with the hook of another sign. (CLF use the term 'hole' instead of 'slot'.) For the TFS grammars considered in CLF, the slot corresponds to the part of the TFS accessed via a valence feature. The inventory of slot labels given by CLF is SUBJ, SPR, SPEC, COMP1, COMP2, COMP3 and MOD.

3. rels: The bag of EPs.
4. hcons: qeq constraints ($=_q$).
5. eqs: the variable equivalences which are the results of equating slots and hooks.

SEMENTs are: $[l, i]\{slots\}[eps][hcons]\{eqs\}$.

Some rules contribute their own semantics (construction semantics: e.g., compound nouns). However, the MRS approach requires that this can always be treated as equivalent to having an additional daughter in the rule. Thus construction semantics need not be considered separately in the formal algebra, although it does result in some syntactically binary rules being semantically ternary (and so on).

The principles of composition are:

1. A (syntactically specified) slot in one structure (the daughter which corresponds to the **semantic head**) is filled by the hook of the other structure (by adding equalities).
2. The hook of the phrase is the semantic head's hook.
3. The eps of the phrase is equal to appending the eps of the daughters.
4. The eqs of the phrase is equal to appending the eqs of the daughters plus any eqs contributed by the filling of the slot.
5. The slots of the phrase are the unfilled slots of the daughters (although see below).
6. The hcons of the phrase is equal to appending the hcons of the daughters.

Formally, the algebra is defined in terms of a series of binary operations, such as op_{spec}, which each correspond to the instantiation of a particular labelled slot.

Fig. 2 illustrates this. The hook of *cat* instantiates the SPEC slot of *a*, which is the semantic head (though not the syntactic head in the ERG). This leads to the equalities between the variables in the result. Since the SPEC slot has been filled, it is not carried up to the phrase. Thus, abstractly at least, the semantics of the HPSG specifier-head rule corresponds to op_{spec}.[1]

[1]As usual in MRS, in order to allow scope underspecification, the label l4 of the quantifier's hook is not coindexed with any EP.

The MRS algebra was designed to abstract away from the details of the syntax and of the syntax-semantics interface, so that it can be applied to grammars with differing feature geometry. The assumption in CLF is simply that the syntax selects the appropriate *op* and its arguments for each application. i.e., semantic operations are associated with HPSG constructions so that there is a mapping from the daughters of the construction to the arguments of the operation. The algebra does not attempt to completely replicate all aspects of semantic construction: e.g., the way that the features (representing tense and so on) are instantiated on variables is not modelled. However, it does constrain semantic construction compared with the possibilities for TFS semantic compositional in general. For instance, as discussed by CLF, it enforces a strong monotonicity constraint. The algebra also contributes to limiting the possibilities for specification of scope. These properties can be exploited by algorithms that operate on MRS: e.g., generation, scope resolution.

2.2 The MRS algebra and the syntax-semantics interface

CLF did not discuss the syntax-semantics interface in detail, but we do so here for two reasons. Firstly, it is a preliminary for discussing the use of the algebra in frameworks other than HPSG in the following sections. Secondly, as CLF discuss, the constraints that the algebra imposes cannot be fully implemented in a TFS. Thus, for grammar engineering in TFS frameworks, an additional automatic checker is needed to determine whether a grammar meets the algebra's constraints. This requires specification of the syntax-semantics interface so that the checker can extract the slots from the TFSs and determine the slot operation(s) corresponding to a rule.

Unfortunately, CLF are imprecise about the algebra in several respects. One problem is that they gloss over the issue of slot propagation in real grammars. CLF state that for an operation op_x, the slot corresponding to op_x on the semantic head is instantiated and all other slots appear on the result. For instance, the definition of op_{spec} states that for all labels $l \neq spec$: $slot_l(op_{\text{spec}}(a_1, a_2)) = slot_l(a_1) \cup slot_l(a_2)$. However, this is inadequate for real grammars, if a simple correspondence between the slot names and the valence paths in the feature structure

	hook	slots	rels	eqs	hcons
cat :	$[l1, x1]$	$\{\}$	$[l1 : \text{cat}(x1)]$	$\{\}$	$[]$
a :	$[l4, x2]$	$\{[l3, x2]_{spec}\}$	$[l2 : \text{a}(x2, h2, h3)]$	$\{\}$	$[h2 =_q l3]$
a cat :	$[l4, x2]$	$\{\}$	$[l2 : \text{a}(x2, h2, h3), l1 : \text{cat}(x1)]$	$\{l3 = l1, x2 = x1\}$	$[h2 =_q l3]$

Figure 2: Example of the MRS algebra

is assumed. For instance, the passive rule involves coindexing a COMP in the original lexical sign with the SUBJ of the passive (informally, the complement 'becomes' the subject).

There are two ways round this problem. The first is to keep the algebra unchanged, but to assume that, for instance, the subject-head grammar rule corresponds to op_{subj} in the algebra for non-passivized cases and to op_{comp1} for passives of simple transitives and so on. Though possible formally, this is not in accord with the spirit of the approach since selection of the appropriate algebra operation in the syntax-semantics interface would require non-local information. Practically, it also precludes the implementation of an algebra checker, since keeping track of the slot uses would be both complex and grammar-specific. The alternative is to extend the algebra to allow for slot renaming. For instance, $op_{\text{comp1-subj}}$ can be defined so that the COMP1 slot on the daughter is a SUBJ slot on the mother.

1. For all labels $l \neq compl$, $l \neq subj$:
   $slot_l(op_{\text{comp1-subj}}(a)) = slot_l(a)$
2. $slot_{\text{subj}}(op_{\text{comp1-subj}}(a)) = slot_{\text{comp1}}(a)$

This means extending the inventory of operations, but the choice of operation is then locally determinable from the rule (e.g., the passive rule would specify $op_{\text{comp1-subj}}$ to be its operation).

Another issue arises in grammars which allow for optional complements. For instance, one approach to a verb like *eat* is to give it a single lexical entry which corresponds to both transitive and intransitive uses. The complement is marked as optional and the corresponding variable in the semantics is assumed to be discourse bound if there is no syntactic complement in the phrase. Optional complements can be discharged by a construction. This approach is (arguably) appropriate for *eat* because the intransitive use involves an implicit patient (e.g., *I already ate* means *I already ate something*), in contrast to a verb like *kick*. CLF do not discuss optionality but it can be formalised in the algebra in terms of a construction-specified sement which has a hook containing the discourse referent and is otherwise empty. For instance, an optional complement construction corresponds to $op_{\text{comp1}}(a_1, a_2)$ where a_1 is the head (and the only daughter appearing in the TFS for the construction) and a_2 is stipulated by the rule to be $[l, d]\{\}[][]\{\}$, where d is the discourse-bound referent.

3 The algebra in non-lexicalist grammars

CLF motivate the MRS algebra in terms of formalisation of the semantics of constraint-based grammars, such as HPSG, but, as we outline here, it is equally applicable to non-lexicalist frameworks. With a suitable definition of the syntax-semantics interface, the algebra can be used with non-TFS-based grammars. Fig. 3 sketches an example of MRS semantics for a CFG. A syntax-semantic interface component of the rule (shown in the second line of the figure) specifies the ops and their daughters: the IOBJ slot of the verb is instantiated with the first NP's hook and the OBJ slot of the result is instantiated with the hook of the second NP. The idea is extremely similar to the use of the algebra with TFS but note that with the addition of this syntax-semantic interface, the algebra can be used directly to implement semantic composition for a CFG.

This still relies on the assumption that all slots are known for every lexical item: semantically the grammar is lexicalist even though it is not syntactically. In fact this is analogous to semantic composition in GPSG (Gazdar et al., 1985) in that conventional lambda calculus also assumes that the semantic properties are known at the lexical level.

4 RMRS composition with deep grammars

The use of the CLF algebra in RMRS composition with deep lexicalist grammars is reasonably straight-

VP -> Vditrans NP1 NP2

$op_{\mathrm{obj}}(op_{\mathrm{iobj}}(\mathrm{Vditrans}, \mathrm{NP1}), \mathrm{NP2})$

MRSs for application of the rule to *give a cat a rat.*

	hook	slots	rels	eqs
give :	$[l1, e1]$	$\{[l1, x12]_{subj},$ $[l1, x13]_{obj}, [l1, x14]_{iobj}\}$	$[l1 : \mathrm{give}(e1, x12, x13, x14)]$	$\{\}$
a cat :	$[l4, x2]$	$\{\}$	$[l2 : \mathrm{a}(x2, h2, h3), l1 : \mathrm{cat}(x1)]$	$\{l3 = l1, x2 = x1\}$
a rat :	$[l7, x5]$	$\{\}$	$[l5 : \mathrm{a}(x5, h5, h6), l4 : \mathrm{rat}(x4)]$	$\{l6 = l4, x5 = x4\}$
iobj :	$[l1, e1]$	$\{[l1, x12]_{subj}, [l1, x13]_{obj}\}$	$[l1 : \mathrm{give}(e1, x12, x13, x14),$ $l2 : \mathrm{a}(x2, h2, h3), l1 : \mathrm{cat}(x1)]$	$\{l3 = l1, x2 = x1,$ $l1 = l4, x14 = x2\}$
obj :	$[l1, e1]$	$\{[l1, x12]_{subj}\}$	$[l1 : \mathrm{give}(e1, x12, x13, x14),$ $l2 : \mathrm{a}(x2, h2, h3), l1 : \mathrm{cat}(x1),$ $l5 : \mathrm{a}(x5, h5, h6), l4 : \mathrm{rat}(x4)]$	$\{l3 = l1, x2 = x1,$ $l1 = l4, x14 = x2,$ $l1 = l7, x13 = x5\}$

Figure 3: MRS algebra with a CFG (hcons omitted for clarity)

forward.[2] The differences between MRS and RMRS are that RMRS uses anchors and factors out the ARGs. Thus for RMRS, we need to redefine the notion of a semantic entity from the MRS algebra to add anchors. An RMRS EP thus contains:

1. a handle, which is the label of the EP
2. an anchor (a)
3. a relation
4. up to one argument of the relation

Hooks also include anchors: $\{[l, a, i]\}$ is a hook. Instead of the rels list only containing EPs, such as l1:chase(e,x,y), it contains a mixture of EPs and ARGs, with associated anchors, such as l1:a1:chase(e), l1:a1:ARG1(x), l1:a1:ARG2(y). But formally ARGs are EPs according to the definition above, so this requires no amendment of the algebra. Fig. 4 shows the RMRS version of Fig. 2.

As mentioned above, earlier forms of RMRS used an explicit representation for conjunction: the in-group, or in-g. Reasons to avoid explicit binary conjunction were discussed with respect to MRS by Copestake et al. (2005) and readers are referred to that paper for an explanation: essentially the problem is that the syntactic assumptions influence the semantic representation. e.g., the order of combination of intersective modifiers affects the semantic representation, though it has no effect on denotation. The binary in-g suffers from this problem.

One alternative would be to use an n-ary conjunction symbol. However such representations cannot be constructed compositionally if modification is binary branching as there is no way of incrementally adding the conjuncts. Another option we considered was the use of, possibly redundant, conjunction relations associated with each element which could be combined to produce a flat conjunction. This leads to a spurious in-g in the case where there is no modifier. This looks ugly, but more importantly, does not allow for incremental specialisation, although the demonstration of this would take us too far from the main point of this paper.

We therefore assume a modified version of RMRS which drops in-g symbols but uses anchors instead. This means that RMRS and MRS TFS grammars can be essentially identical apart from lexical types. Furthermore, it turns out that, for composition without a lexicon, an anchor is needed in the hook regardless of the treatment of conjunction (see below).

5 RMRS composition without a lexicon

We now discuss the algebra for grammars which do not have access to subcategorization information and thus are neither syntactically nor semantically lexicalist. We concentrate in particular on composition for the grammar used in the RASP system. RASP consists of a tokenizer, POS tagger, lemmatizer, tag sequence grammar and statistical disambiguator. Of the robust analysers we have looked at, RASP pro-

[2] Current DELPH-IN grammars generally construct MRSs which may be converted into RMRSs. However, RMRS has potential advantages, for instance in allowing more extensive lexical underspecification than is possible with MRS: e.g., (Haugereid, 2004).

	hook	slots	rels	eqs	hcons
cat :	$[l1, a1, x1]$	$\{\}$	$[l1 : a1 : \text{cat}(x1)]$	$\{\}$	$[]$
a :	$[l4, a2, x2]$	$\{[l3, a2, x2]_{spec}\}$	$[l2 : a2 : \text{a}(x2),$ $l2 : a2 : \text{rstr}(h2), l2 : a2 : \text{body}(h2)]$	$\{\}$	$[h2 =_q l3]$
a cat :	$[l4, a4, x2]$	$\{\}$	$[l1 : a1 : \text{cat}(x1), l2 : a2 : \text{a}(x2),$ $l2 : a2 : \text{rstr}(h2), l2 : a2 : \text{body}(h2)$	$\{l3 = l1,$ $x2 = x1]$	$[h2 =_q l3]$

Figure 4: Example of the RMRS algebra.

vides the biggest challenge for the RMRS approach because it provides quite detailed syntactic analyses which are somewhat dissimilar to the ERG: it is an intermediate rather than a shallow processor. The RMRS approach can only be fully successful to the extent that it abstracts away from the differences in syntactic analyses assumed by different systems, so intermediate processors are more difficult to deal with than shallow ones.

Instead of normal lexical entries, RASP uses the POS tags for the words in the input. For the example in Fig. 1, the output of the POS tagging phase is:

the_AT fat_JJ cat_NN1 sit+ed_VVD on_II a_AT1 mat_NN1

The semantics associated with the individual words in the sentence can be derived from a 'lexicon' of POS tags, which defines the EPs. Schematically:

AT	lexrel_q(x)	NN1	lexrel_n(x)
AT1	lexrel_q(x)	VVD	lexrel_v(e_{past})
JJ	lexrel_j(x)	II	lexrel_p(e)

Here, 'lexrel' is a special symbol, which is to be replaced by the individual lemma (with a leading underscore) — e.g., lexrel_v(e_{past}) yields l1:a1:_sit_v(e). Producing the semantics from the tagger output and this lexicon is a simple matter of substitution. All EPs are labelled with unique labels and all variables are different unless repeated in the same lexical entry.

If the analysis were to stop at POS tagging, the semantic composition rules would apply trivially. There are no slots, the hooks are irrelevant and there are no equalities. The composition principle of accumulation of elementary predications holds, so the semantics of the result involves an accumulation of the rels (see the example at the bottom of Fig. 1).

When using the full RASP parser, although we cannot expect to obtain all the details available from deep grammars, we can derive some relational structure. For instance, given a sentence such as *the cat chased the rat*, it should be possible to derive the ARG1 and ARG2 for *chase* by associating the ARG1 with the application of the `S/np_vp` RASP rule (i.e., `S->NP VP`) and the ARG2 with the application of the `V1/v_np` rule. But since there can be no slot information in the lexical structures (at least not for open-class words), it is necessary to modify the lexicalist approach to semantics taken so far.

We assume that both the ARGs and the slots are specified at a phrasal level rather than lexically. As mentioned in §2.1, the MRS algebra allows for rules to contribute semantics as though they were normal phrases. The central idea in the application of the algebra to RASP is to make use of construction semantics in all rules. Fig. 5 illustrates this with the `V1/v_np` rule (the NP has been simplified for clarity) assuming the same sort of syntax-semantics interface specification as shown earlier for the CFG. This is semantically ternary because of the rule semantics. The rule has an ARG2 slot plus a slot R which is instantiated by the verb's hook. In effect, the rule adds a slot to the verb.

It is necessary for the anchor of the argument-taking structure to be visible at all points where arguments may be attached. For instance, in the example above, the anchor of the verb *chase* has to be accessible when the ARG1 relation is introduced. Although generally the anchor will correspond to the anchor of the semantic head daughter, this is not the case if there is a scopal modifier (consider *a cat did not chase a rat*: the ARG1 must be attached to *chase* rather than to *not*). This is illustrated by *not sleep* in Fig. 6. Because *not* is associated with a unique tag in RASP, it can be assigned a slot and an ARG1 directly. The anchor of the result is equated with the label of *sleep* and thus the subject ARG1 can be appropriately attached. So the hook would have to include an anchor even if explicit conjunction were used instead of equating labels.

$$\text{VP -> V NP}$$
$$op_{\text{arg2}}(op_{\text{r}}(\text{rule}, \text{V}), \text{NP})$$

chase :	$[l1, a1, e1]$	$\{\}$	$[l1 : a1 : \text{chase}(e1)]$	$\{\}$
rule :	$[l2, a2, e2]$	$\{[l2, a2, e2]_r, [l4, a4, x2]_{arg2}\}$	$[l2 : a2 : \text{ARG2}(x2)]$	$\{\}$
(rule V)/r :	$[l2, a2, e2]$	$\{[l4, x2]_{arg2}\}$	$[l2 : a1 : \text{ARG2}(x2), l1 : a1 : \text{chase}(e1)]$	$\{l1 = l2, e2 = e1\}$
it :	$[l3, a3, x3]$	$\{\}$	$[l3 : a3 : \text{pron}(x3)]$	$\{\}$
chase it :	$[l2, a2, e2]$	$\{\}$	$[l2 : a2 : \text{ARG2}(x2), l1 : a1 : \text{chase}(e1), l3 : a3 : \text{pron}(x3)]$	$\{l1 = l2, e2 = e1, l4 = l3, x2 = x3\}$

Figure 5: RASP-RMRS algebra (hcons omitted)

not :	$[l1, a2, e2]$	$\{[l2, a3, e2]_{mod}\}$	$[l1 : a1 : \text{not}(e2), l1 : a1 : \text{ARG1}(h4)]$	$\{\}$	$[h4 =_q l2]$
sleep :	$[l2, a2, e2]$	$\{\}$	$[l2 : a2 : \text{sleep}(e2)]$	$\{\}$	$[]$
not sleep :	$[l1, a2, e2]$	$\{\}$	$[l1 : a1 : \text{not}(e2), l1 : a1 : \text{ARG1}(h4), l2 : a2 : \text{sleep}(e2)]$	$\{\}$	$[h4 =_q l3]$

Figure 6: RASP-RMRS illustrating the use of the anchor

6 Experiments with RASP-RMRS

In this section, we outline the practical implementation of the algebra for RASP-RMRS. The RASP tag sequence grammar is formally equivalent to a CFG: it uses phrase structure rules augmented with features. As discussed, the algebra requires that ops are specified for each rule application, and the easiest way of achieving this is to associate semantic composition rules with each rule name. Composition operates on the tree output from RASP, e.g.,:

```
(|T/txt-sc1/----|
 (|S/np_vp|
  (|NP/det_n1| |Every:1_AT1|
   (|N1/n| |cat:2_NN1|))
  (|V1/v| |bark+ed:3_VVD|)))
```

Composition operates bottom-up: the semantic structures derived from the tags are combined according to the semantics associated with the rule. The implementation corresponds very directly to the algebra, although the transitive closure of the equalities is computed on the final structure, since nothing requires that it be available earlier.

The notation used to specify semantics associated with the rules incorporates some simplifications to avoid having to explicitly specify the slot and ops. The specification of equalities between variables and components of the individual daughters' hooks is a convenient shorthand for the full algebra.

```
rule V1/v_np
daughters V NP
semhead V
hook [l,a,e] rels {l:a:ARG2(x)}
eqs {x=NP.index,l=V.label,
     a=V.anchor}
```

If no semantic rule is specified corresponding to a rule used in a tree, the rels are simply appended. Semantic composition is thus robust to omissions in the semantic component of the grammar. In fact, semantic rules can be constructed semi-automatically, rather than fully manually, although we do not have space to discuss this in detail here.

There are cases of incompatibility between RASP-RMRS and ERG-RMRS. For example, the ERG treats *it* as expletive in *it rains*: the lexical entry for *rain* specifies an expletive subject (i.e., a semantically empty *it*). RASP makes no such distinction, since it lacks the lexical information and thus the sentence has extraneous relations for the pronoun and an incorrect ARG1 for *rain*. This is an inevitable consequence of the lack of lexical information in RASP. However, from the perspective of the evaluation of the revised algebra, the issue is whether there are any cases where compositional construction of RASP-RMRSs which match ERG-RMRSs is impossible due to the restrictions imposed by the algebra. No such cases have been found.

7 Related work

Bos et al. (2004) and Bos (2005) derive semantic interpretations from a wide-coverage categorial grammar. There are several differences between this and RASP-RMRS, but the most important arise from the differences between CCG and RASP. The CCG parser relies on having detailed subcategorization information (automatically derived from the CCG Bank which was semi-automatically constructed from the Penn Treebank), and thus semantic construction can assume that the arity of the predicate is lexically available. However, because CCG is purely lexicalist, phenomena that we expect to have construction semantics (e.g., compound nouns, larger numbers) have to be dealt with in a post-parsing phase rather than compositionally.

Spreyer and Frank (2005) demonstrate RMRS construction from TIGER dependencies, but do not attempt to match a deep parser output.

8 Conclusion

We have demonstrated that the MRS algebra, originally intended as a formalisation of some aspects of semantic composition in constraint-based grammars, can be extended to RMRS and other types of grammar framework and can be used as the basis of a full implementation of composition. The algebra can thus be used much more widely than originally envisaged and could be exploited by a wide range of parsers. Useful properties concerning monotonicity and scope (see Fuchss et al. (2004)) are thus guaranteed for a range of grammars. Phrasal-level compatibility of RMRS (to the extent that this is syntactically possible) is also an important result. The main practical outcome of this work so far has been a semantic component for the RASP system which produces representations compatible with that of the ERG without compromising RASP speed or robustness. RASP-RMRSs have already been used in systems for question answering, information extraction, email response, creative authoring and ontology extraction (e.g., Uszkoreit et al. (2004), Watson et al. (2003), Herbelot and Copestake (2006)).

Acknowledgements

This work was funded by EPSRC (EP/C010035/1). I am very grateful to the anonymous reviewers for their insightful comments, which sadly I have had to ignore due to the constraints of time and space. I hope to address them in a later paper.

References

Johan Bos, Stephen Clark, Mark Steedman, James R. Curran and Julia Hockenmaier 2004. Wide-Coverage Semantic Representations from a CCG Parser. COLING '04, Geneva.

Johan Bos. 2005. Towards Wide-Coverage Semantic Interpretation. Sixth International Workshop on Computational Semantics IWCS-6. 42–53.

Ted Briscoe and John Carroll. 2002. Robust accurate statistical annotation of general text. LREC-2002, Las Palmas, Gran Canaria.

Ann Copestake, Alex Lascarides, and Dan Flickinger. 2001. An Algebra for Semantic Construction in Constraint-based Grammars. ACL-01, Toulouse.

Ann Copestake. 2003. Report on the design of RMRS. DeepThought project deliverable.

Ann Copestake, Dan Flickinger, Ivan Sag, and Carl Pollard. 2005. Minimal Recursion Semantics: An introduction. *Research in Language and Computation* 3(2–3), 281–332.

Dan Flickinger 2000. On building a more efficient grammar by exploiting types. *Natural Language Engineering*,**6:1**,15–28.

Ruth Fuchss, Alexander Koller, Joachim Niehren, and Stefan Thater 2004. Minimal Recursion Semantics as Dominance Constraints: Translation, Evaluation, and Analysis. Proceedings of the 42nd ACL, Barcelona.

Gerald Gazdar, Ewan Klein, Geoffrey Pullum and Ivan Sag 1985. Generalized Phrase Structure Grammar. Basil Blackwell, Oxford

Petter Haugereid 2004. Linking in Constructions. HPSG2004, Leuven.

Aurelie Herbelot and Ann Copestake 2006. Acquiring Ontological Relationships from Wikipedia Using RMRS. ISWC 2006 Workshop on Web Content Mining with Human Language Technologies, Athens, Georgia.

Kathrin Spreyer and Anette Frank. 2005 Projecting RMRS from TIGER Dependencies. HPSG 2005, Lisbon. 354–363.

Hans Uszkoreit, Ulrich Callmeier, Andreas Eisele, Ulrich Schfer, Melanie Siegel, Jakob Uszkoreit. 2004. Hybrid Robust Deep and Shallow Semantic Processing for Creativity Support in Document Production. KONVENS 2004, Vienna, Austria, 209–216.

Rebecca Watson, Judita Preiss and EJ Briscoe. 2003. The Contribution of Domain-independent Robust Pronominal Anaphora Resolution to Open-Domain Question-Answering. Int. Symposium on Reference Resolution and its Application to Question-Answering and Summarisation, Venice.

A Task-based Comparison of Information Extraction Pattern Models

Mark A. Greenwood and **Mark Stevenson**
Department of Computer Science
University of Sheffield
Sheffield, S1 4DP, UK
{m.greenwood, marks}@dcs.shef.ac.uk

Abstract

Several recent approaches to Information Extraction (IE) have used dependency trees as the basis for an extraction pattern representation. These approaches have used a variety of pattern models (schemes which define the parts of the dependency tree which can be used to form extraction patterns). Previous comparisons of these pattern models are limited by the fact that they have used indirect tasks to evaluate each model. This limitation is addressed here in an experiment which compares four pattern models using an unsupervised learning algorithm and a standard IE scenario. It is found that there is a wide variation between the models' performance and suggests that one model is the most useful for IE.

1 Introduction

A common approach to Information Extraction (IE) is to (manually or automatically) create a set of patterns which match against text to identify information of interest. Muslea (1999) reviewed the approaches which were used at the time and found that the most common techniques relied on lexico-syntactic patterns being applied to text which has undergone relatively shallow linguistic processing. For example, the extraction rules used by Soderland (1999) and Riloff (1996) match text in which syntactic chunks have been identified. More recently researchers have begun to employ deeper syntactic analysis, such as dependency parsing (Yangarber et al., 2000; Stevenson and Greenwood, 2005; Sudo et al., 2001; Sudo et al., 2003; Yangarber, 2003). In these approaches extraction patterns are essentially parts of the dependency tree. To perform extraction they are compared against the dependency analysis of a sentence to determine whether it contains the pattern.

Each of these approaches relies on a *pattern model* to define which parts of the dependency tree can be used to form the extraction patterns. A variety of pattern models have been proposed. For example the patterns used by Yangarber et al. (2000) are the subject-verb-object tuples from the dependency tree (the remainder of the dependency parse is discarded) while Sudo et al. (2003) allow any subtree within the dependency parse to act as an extraction pattern. Stevenson and Greenwood (2006) showed that the choice of pattern model has important implications for IE algorithms including significant differences between the various models in terms of their ability to identify information of interest in text.

However, there has been little comparison between the various pattern models. Those which have been carried out have been limited by the fact that they used indirect tasks to evaluate the various models and did not compare them in an IE scenario. We address this limitation here by presenting a direct comparison of four previously described pattern models using an unsupervised learning method applied to a commonly used IE scenario.

The remainder of the paper is organised as follows. The next section presents four pattern models which have been previously introduced in the litera-

Proceedings of the 5th Workshop on Important Unresolved Matters, pages 81–88,
Ann Arbor, June 2005. ©2005 Association for Computational Linguistics

ture. Section 3 describes two previous studies which compared these models and their limitations. Section 4 describes an experiment which compares the four models on an IE task, the results of which are described in Section 5. Finally, Section 6 discusses the conclusions which may be drawn from this work.

2 IE Pattern Models

In dependency analysis (Mel'čuk, 1987) the syntax of a sentence is represented by a set of directed binary links between a word (the head) and one of its modifiers. These links may be labelled to indicate the relation between the head and modifier (e.g. subject, object). An example dependency analysis for the sentence *"Acme hired Smith as their new CEO, replacing Bloggs."* is shown Figure 1.

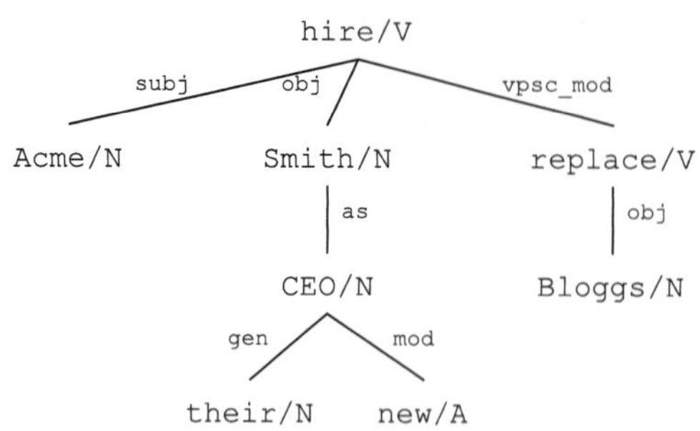

Figure 1: An example dependency tree.

The remainder of this section outlines four models for representing extraction patterns which can be derived from dependency trees.

Predicate-Argument Model (SVO): A simple approach, used by Yangarber et al. (2000), Yangarber (2003) and Stevenson and Greenwood (2005), is to use subject-verb-object tuples from the dependency parse as extraction patterns. These consist of a verb and its subject and/or direct object. Figure 2 shows the two SVO patterns[1] which are produced for the dependency tree shown in Figure 1.

This model can identify information which is expressed using simple predicate-argument constructions such as the relation between *Acme* and *Smith* in the dependency tree shown in Figure 1. However, the SVO model cannot represent information described using other linguistic constructions such as nominalisations or prepositional phrases. For example the SVO model would not be able to recognise that Smith's new job title is CEO since these patterns ignore the part of the dependency tree containing that information.

Chains: A pattern is defined as a path between a verb node and any other node in the dependency tree passing through zero or more intermediate nodes (Sudo et al., 2001). Figure 2 shows examples of the chains which can be extracted from the tree in Figure 1.

Chains provide a mechanism for encoding information beyond the direct arguments of predicates and includes areas of the dependency tree ignored by the SVO model. For example, they can represent information expressed as a nominalisation or within a prepositional phrase, e.g. "*The resignation of Smith from the board of Acme ...*" However, a potential shortcoming of this model is that it cannot represent the link between arguments of a verb. Patterns in the chain model format are unable to represent even the simplest of sentences containing a transitive verb, e.g. *"Smith left Acme"*.

Linked Chains: The linked chains model (Greenwood et al., 2005) represents extraction patterns as a pair of chains which share the same verb but no direct descendants. Example linked chains are shown in Figure 2. This pattern representation encodes most of the information in the sentence with the advantage of being able to link together event participants which neither of the SVO or chain model can, for example the relation between *"Smith"* and *"Bloggs"* in Figure 1.

Subtrees: The final model to be considered is the subtree model (Sudo et al., 2003). In this model any subtree of a dependency tree can be used as an extraction pattern, where a subtree is any set of nodes in the tree which are connected to one another. Single nodes are not considered to be subtrees. The subtree model is a richer representation than those discussed so far and can represent any part of a dependency tree. Each of the previous models form a proper subset of the subtrees. By choosing an appropriate subtree it is possible to link together any pair of nodes in a tree and consequently this model can

[1] The formalism used for representing dependency patterns is similar to the one introduced by Sudo et al. (2003). Each node in the tree is represented in the format `a[b/c]` (e.g. `subj[N/Acme]`) where `c` is the lexical item (`Acme`), `b` its grammatical tag (`N`) and `a` the dependency relation between this node and its parent (`subj`). The relationship between nodes is represented as `X(A+B+C)` which indicates that nodes `A`, `B` and `C` are direct descendents of node `X`.

SVO

```
[V/hire](subj[N/Acme]+obj[N/Smith])
[V/replace](obj[N/Bloggs])
```

Chains

```
[V/hire](subj[N/Acme])
[V/hire](obj[N/Smith])
[V/hire](obj[N/Smith](as[N/CEO]))
[V/hire](obj[N/Smith](as[N/CEO](gen[N/their])))
```

Linked Chains

```
[V/hire](subj[N/Acme]+obj[N/Smith])
[V/hire](subj[N/Acme]+obj[N/Smith](as[N/CEO]))
[V/hire](obj[N/Smith]+vpsc_mod[V/replace](obj[N/Bloggs]))
```

Subtrees

```
[V/hire](subj[N/Acme]+obj[N/Smith]+vpsc_mod[V/replace])
[V/hire](subj[N/Acme]+vpsc_mod[V/replace](obj[N/Bloggs]))
[N/Smith](as[N/CEO](gen[N/their]+mod[A/new]))
```

Figure 2: Example patterns for four models

represent the relation between any set of items in the sentence.

3 Previous Comparisons

There have been few direct comparisons of the various pattern models. Sudo et al. (2003) compared three models (SVO, chains and subtrees) on two IE scenarios using a entity extraction task. Models were evaluated in terms of their ability to identify entities taking part in events and distinguish them from those which did not. They found the SVO model performed poorly in comparison with the other two models and that the performance of the subtree model was generally the same as, or better than, the chain model. However, they did not attempt to determine whether the models could identify the relations between these entities, simply whether they could identify the entities participating in relevant events.

Stevenson and Greenwood (2006) compared the four pattern models described in Section 2 in terms of their complexity and ability to represent relations found in text. The complexity of each model was analysed in terms of the number of patterns which would be generated from a given dependency parse. This is important since several of the algorithms which have been proposed to make use of dependency-based IE patterns use iterative learning (e.g. (Yangarber et al., 2000; Yangarber, 2003; Stevenson and Greenwood, 2005)) and are unlikely to cope with very large sets of candidate patterns. The number of patterns generated therefore has an effect on how practical computations using that model may be. It was found that the number of patterns generated for the SVO model is a linear function of the size of the dependency tree. The number of chains and linked chains is a polynomial function while the number of subtrees is exponential.

Stevenson and Greenwood (2006) also analysed the representational power of each model by measuring how many of the relations found in a standard IE corpus they are expressive enough to represent. (The documents used were taken from newswire texts and biomedical journal articles.) They found that the SVO and chain model could only represent a small proportion of the relations in the corpora. The subtree model could represent more of the relations than any other model but that there was no statistical difference between those relations and the ones covered by the linked chain model. They concluded that the linked chain model was optional since it is expressive enough to represent the information of interest without introducing a potentially unwieldy number of patterns.

There is some agreement between these two studies, for example that the SVO model performs poorly in comparison with other models. However, Stevenson and Greenwood (2006) also found that the coverage of the chain model was significantly worse than the subtree model, although Sudo et al.

(2003) found that in some cases their performance could not be distinguished. In addition to these disagreements, these studies are also limited by the fact that they are indirect; they do not evaluate the various pattern models on an IE task.

4 Experiments

We compared each of the patterns models described in Section 2 using an unsupervised IE experiment similar to one described by Sudo et al. (2003).

Let D be a corpus of documents and R a set of documents which are relevant to a particular extraction task. In this context "relevant" means that the document contains the information we are interested in identifying. D and R are such that $D = R \cup \bar{R}$ and $R \cap \bar{R} = \emptyset$. As assumption behind this approach is that useful patterns will be far more likely to occur in R than D overall.

4.1 Ranking Patterns

Patterns for each model are ranked using a technique inspired by the tf-idf scoring commonly used in Information Retrieval (Manning and Schütze, 1999). The score for each pattern, p, is given by:

$$score(p) = tf_p \times \left(\frac{N}{df_p}\right)^{\beta} \quad (1)$$

where tf_p is the number of times pattern p appears in relevant documents, N is the total number of documents in the corpus and df_p the number of documents in the collection containing the pattern p.

Equation 1 combines two factors: the *term frequency* (in relevant documents) and *inverse document frequency* (across the corpus). Patterns which occur frequently in relevant documents without being too prevalent in the corpus are preferred. Sudo et al. (2003) found that it was important to find the appropriate balance between these two factors. They introduced the β parameter as a way of controlling the relative contribution of the *inverse document frequency*. β is tuned for each extraction task and pattern model combination.

Although simple, this approach has the advantage that it can be applied to each of the four pattern models to provide a direct comparison.

4.2 Extraction Scenario

The ranking process was applied to the IE scenario used for the sixth Message Understanding conference (MUC-6). The aim of this task was to identify management succession events from a corpus of newswire texts. Relevant information describes an executive entering or leaving a position within a company, for example *"Last month Smith resigned as CEO of Rooter Ltd."*. This sentence described as event involving three items: a person (*Smith*), position (*CEO*) and company (*Rooter Ltd*). We made use of a version of the MUC-6 corpus described by Soderland (1999) which consists of 598 documents.

For these experiments relevant documents were identified using annotations in the corpus. However, this is not necessary since Sudo et al. (2003) showed that adequate knowledge about document relevance could be obtained automatically using an IR system.

4.3 Pattern Generation

The texts used for these experiments were parsed using the Stanford dependency parser (Klein and Manning, 2002). The dependency trees were processed to replace the names of entities belonging to specific semantic classes with a general token. Three of these classes were used for the management succession domain (`PERSON`, `ORGANISATION` and `POST`). For example, in the dependency analysis of *"Smith will became CEO next year"*, *"Smith"* is replaced by `PERSON` and *"CEO"* by `POST`. This process allows more general patterns to be extracted from the dependency trees. For example, `[V/become](subj[N/PERSON]+obj[N/POST])`. In the MUC-6 corpus items belonging to the relevant semantic classes are already identified.

Patterns for each of the four models were extracted from the processed dependency trees. For the SVO, chain and linked chain models this was achieved using depth-first search. However, the enumeration of all subtrees is less straightforward and has been shown to be a $\#P$-complete problem (Goldberg and Jerrum, 2000). We made use of the *rightmost extension* algorithm (Abe et al., 2002; Zaki, 2002) which is an efficient way of enumerating all subtrees. This approach constructs subtrees iteratively by combining together subtrees which have already been observed. The algorithm starts with a set of trees, each of which consists of a single node. At each stage the known trees are extended by the addition of a single node. In order to avoid duplication the extension is restricted to allowing nodes only to be added to the nodes on the rightmost path of the tree. Applying the process recursively creates a search space in which all subtrees are enumerated with minimal duplication.

The rightmost extension algorithm is most suited to finding subtrees which occur multiple times and, even using this efficient approach, we were unable to generate subtrees which occurred fewer than four times in the MUC-6 texts in a reasonable time. Similar restrictions have been encountered within other approaches which have relied on the generation of a comprehensive set of subtrees from a parse forest. For example, Kudo et al. (2005) used subtrees for parse ranking but could only generate subtrees which appear at least ten times in a 40,000 sentence corpus. They comment that the size of their data set meant that it would have been difficult to complete the experiments with less restrictive parameters. In addition, Sudo et al. (2003) only generated subtrees which appeared in at least three documents. Kudo et al. (2005) and Sudo et al. (2003) both used the rightmost extension algorithm to generate subtrees.

To provide a direct comparison of the pattern models we also produced versions of the sets of patterns extracted for the SVO, chain and linked chain models in which patterns which occurred fewer than four times were removed. Table 1 shows the number of patterns generated for each of the four models when the patterns are both filtered and unfiltered. (Although the set of unfiltered subtree patterns were not generated it is possible to determine the number of patterns which would be generated using a process described by Stevenson and Greenwood (2006).)

Model	Filtered	Unfiltered
SVO	9,189	23,128
Chains	16,563	142,019
Linked chains	23,452	493,463
Subtrees	369,453	1.69×10^{12}

Table 1: Number of patterns generated by each model

It can be seen that the various pattern models generate vastly different numbers of patterns and that the number of subtrees is significantly greater than the other three models. Previous analysis (see Section 3) suggested that the number of subtrees which would be generated from a corpus could be difficult to process computationally and this is supported by our findings here.

4.4 Parameter Tuning

The value of β in equation 1 was set using a separate corpus from which the patterns were generated, a methodology suggested by Sudo et al. (2003). To generate this additional text we used the Reuters Corpus (Rose et al., 2002) which consists of a year's worth of newswire output. Each document in the Reuters corpus has been manually annotated with topic codes indicating its general subject area(s). One of these topic codes (`C411`) refers to management succession events and was used to identify documents which are relevant to the MUC6 IE scenario. A corpus consisting of 348 documents annotated with code `C411` and 250 documents without that code, representing irrelevant documents, were taken from the Reuters corpus to create a corpus with the same distribution of relevant and irrelevant documents as found in the MUC-6 corpus. Unlike the MUC-6 corpus, items belonging to the required semantic classes are not annotated in the Reuters Corpus. They were identified automatically using a named entity identifier.

The patterns generated from the MUC-6 texts were ranked using formula 1 with a variety of values of β. These sets of ranked patterns were then used to carry out a document filtering task on the Reuters corpus - the aim of which is to differentiate documents based on whether or not they contain a relation of interest. The various values for β were compared by computing the area under the curve. It was found that the optimal value for β was 2 for all pattern models and this setting was used for the experiments.

4.5 Evaluation

Evaluation was carried out by comparing the ranked lists of patterns against the dependency trees for the MUC-6 texts. When a pattern is found to match against a tree the items which match any semantic classes in the pattern are extracted. These items are considered to be related and compared against the gold standard data in the corpus to determine whether they are in fact related.

The precision of a set of patterns is computed as the proportion of the relations which were identified that are listed in the gold standard data. The recall is the proportion of relations in the gold standard data which are identified by the set of patterns.

The ranked set of patterns are evaluated incrementally with the precision and recall of the first (highest ranked) pattern computed. The next pattern is then added to the relations extracted by both are evaluated. This process continues until all patterns are exhausted.

5 Results

Figure 3 shows the results when the four filtered pattern models, ranked using equation 1, are compared.

A first observation is that the chain model performs poorly in comparison to the other three models. The highest precision achieved by this model is 19.9% and recall never increases beyond 9%. In comparison the SVO model includes patterns with extremely high precision but the maximum recall achieved by this model is low. Analysis showed that the first three SVO patterns had very high precision. These were `[V/succeed](subj[N/PERSON]+obj[N/PERSON])`, `[V/be](subj[N/PERSON]+obj[N/POST])` and `[V/become](subj[N/PERSON]+obj[N/POST])`, which have precision of 90.1%, 80.8% and 78.9% respectively. If these high precision patterns are removed the maximum precision of the SVO model is around 32%, which is comparable with the linked chain and subtree models. This suggests that, while the SVO model includes very useful extraction patterns, the format is restrictive and is unable to represent much of the information in this corpus.

The remaining two pattern models, linked chains and subtrees, have very similar performance and each achieves higher recall than the SVO model, albeit with lower precision. The maximum recall obtained by the linked chain model is slightly lower than the subtree model but it does maintain higher precision at higher recall levels.

The maximum recall achieved by all four models is very low in this evaluation and part of the reason for this is the fact that the patterns have been filtered to allow direct comparison with the subtree model. Figure 4 shows the results when the unfiltered SVO, chain and linked chain patterns are used. (Performance of the filtered subtrees are also included in this graph for comparison.)

This result shows that the addition of extra patterns for each model improves recall without effecting the maximum precision achieved. The chain model also performs badly in this experiment. Precision of the SVO model is still high (again this is due to the same three highly accurate patterns) however the maximum recall achieved by this model is not particularly increased by the addition of the unfiltered patterns. The linked chain model benefits most from the unfiltered patterns. The extra patterns lead to a maximum recall which is more than double any of the other models without overly degrading precision. The fact that the linked chain model is able to achieve such a high recall shows that it is able to represent the relations found in the MUC-6 text, unlike the SVO and chain models. It is likely that the subtrees model would also produce a set of patterns with high recall but the number of potential patterns which are allowable within this model makes this impractical.

6 Discussion and Conclusions

Some of the results reported for each model in these experiments are low. Precision levels are generally below 40% (with the exception of the SVO model which achieves high precision using a small number of patterns). One reason for this that the the patterns were ranked using a simple unsupervised learning algorithm which allowed direct comparison of four different pattern models. This approach only made use of information about the distribution of patterns in the corpus and it is likely that results could be improved for a particular pattern model by employing more sophisticated approaches which make use of additional information, for example the structure of the patterns.

The results presented here provide insight into the usefulness of the various pattern models by evaluating them on an actual IE task. It is found that SVO patterns are capable of high precision but that the

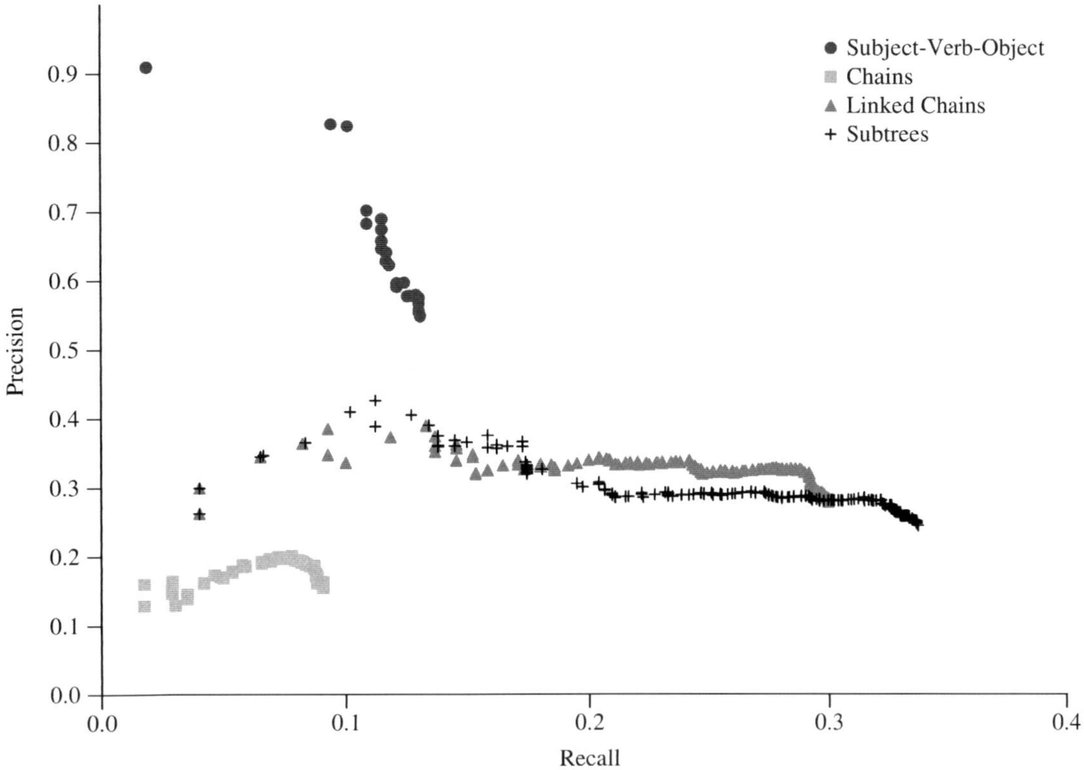

Figure 3: Comparisons of filtered pattern models.

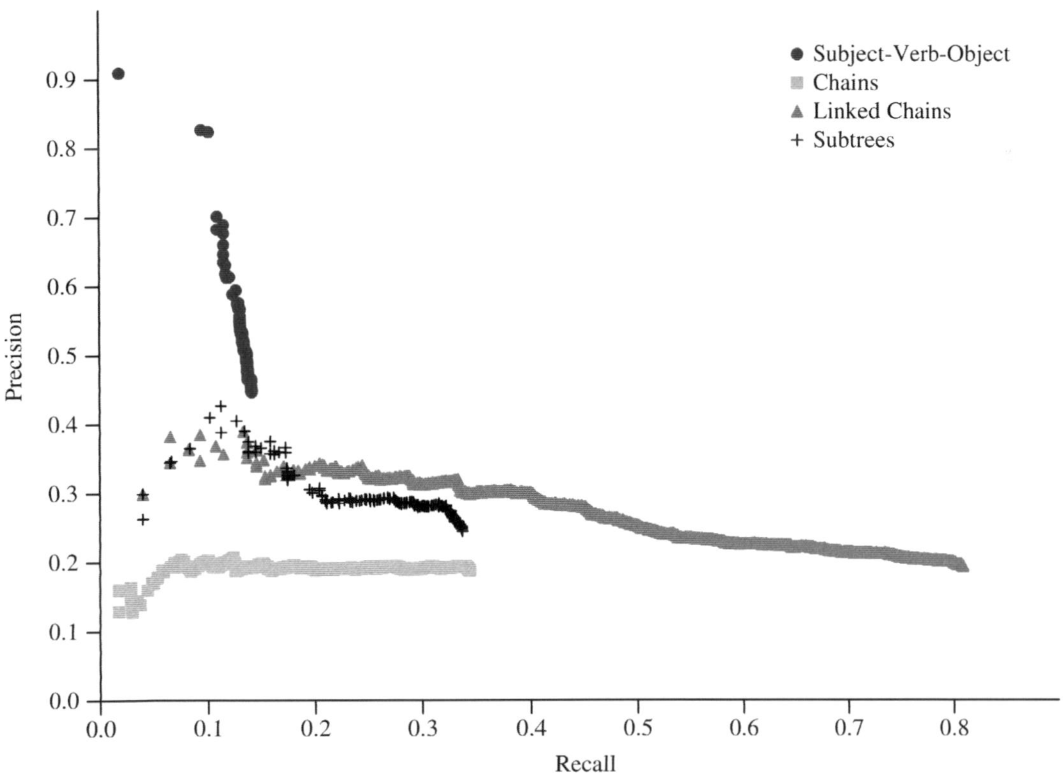

Figure 4: Comparison of unfiltered models.

restricted set of possible patterns leads to low recall. The chain model was found to perform badly with low recall and precision regardless of whether the patterns were filtered. Performance of the linked chain and subtree models were similar when the patterns were filtered but unfiltered linked chains were capable of achieving far higher recall than the filtered subtrees.

These experiments suggest that the linked chain model is a useful one for IE since it is simple enough for an unfiltered set of patterns to be extracted and able to represent a wider range of information than the SVO and chain models.

References

Kenji Abe, Shinji Kawasoe, Tatsuya Asai, Hiroki Arimura, and Setsuo Arikawa. 2002. Optimised Substructure Discovery for Semi-Structured Data. In *Proceedings of the 6th European Conference on Principles and Practice of Knowledge in Databases (PKDD-2002)*, pages 1–14.

Leslie Ann Goldberg and Mark Jerrum. 2000. Counting Unlabelled Subtrees of a Tree is $\#P$-Complete. *London Mathmatical Society Journal of Computation and Mathematics*, 3:117–124.

Mark A. Greenwood, Mark Stevenson, Yikun Guo, Henk Harkema, and Angus Roberts. 2005. Automatically Acquiring a Linguistically Motivated Genic Interaction Extraction System. In *Proceedings of the 4th Learning Language in Logic Workshop (LLL05)*, Bonn, Germany.

Dan Klein and Christopher D. Manning. 2002. Fast Exact Inference with a Factored Model for Natural Language Parsing. In *Advances in Neural Information Processing Systems 15 (NIPS 2002)*, Vancouver, Canada.

Taku Kudo, Jun Suzuki, and Hideki Isozaki. 2005. Boosting-based Parse Reranking with Subtree Features. In *Proceedings of the 43rd Annual Meeting of the Association for Computational Linguistics*, pages 189–196, Ann Arbour, MI.

Chritopher Manning and Hinrich Schütze. 1999. *Foundations of Statistical Natural Language Processing*. MIT Press, Cambridge, MA.

Igor Mel'čuk. 1987. *Dependency Syntax: Theory and Practice*. SUNY Press, New York.

Ion Muslea. 1999. Extraction Patterns for Information Extraction: A Survey. In *Proceedings of the AAAI-99 workshop on Machine Learning for Information Extraction*, Orlando, FL.

Ellen Riloff. 1996. Automatically Generating Extraction Patterns from Untagged Text. In *Thirteenth National Conference on Artificial Intelligence (AAAI-96)*, pages 1044–1049, Portland, OR.

Tony Rose, Mark Stevenson, and Miles Whitehead. 2002. The Reuters Corpus Volume 1 - from Yesterday's News to Tomorrow's Language Resources. In *Proceedings of the Third International Conference on Language Resources and Evaluation (LREC-02)*, pages 827–832, La Palmas de Gran Canaria.

Stephen Soderland. 1999. Learning Information Extraction Rules for Semi-structured and Free Text. *Machine Learning*, 31(1-3):233–272.

Mark Stevenson and Mark A. Greenwood. 2005. A Semantic Approach to IE Pattern Induction. In *Proceedings of the 43rd Annual Meeting of the Association for Computational Linguistics*, pages 379–386, Ann Arbor, MI.

Mark Stevenson and Mark A. Greenwood. 2006. Comparing Information Extraction Pattern Models. In *Proceedings of the Information Extraction Beyond The Document Workshop (COLING/ACL 2006)*, pages 12–19, Sydney, Australia.

Kiyoshi Sudo, Satoshi Sekine, and Ralph Grishman. 2001. Automatic Pattern Acquisition for Japanese Information Extraction. In *Proceedings of the Human Language Technology Conference (HLT2001)*, San Diego, CA.

Kiyoshi Sudo, Satoshi Sekine, and Ralph Grishman. 2003. An Improved Extraction Pattern Representation Model for Automatic IE Pattern Acquisition. In *Proceedings of the 41st Annual Meeting of the Association for Computational Linguistics (ACL-03)*, pages 224–231, Sapporo, Japan.

Roman Yangarber, Ralph Grishman, Pasi Tapanainen, and Silja Huttunen. 2000. Unsupervised Discovery of Scenario-level Patterns for Information Extraction. In *Proceedings of the Applied Natural Language Processing Conference (ANLP 2000)*, pages 282–289, Seattle, WA.

Roman Yangarber. 2003. Counter-training in the Discovery of Semantic Patterns. In *Proceedings of the 41st Annual Meeting of the Association for Computational Linguistics (ACL-03)*, pages 343–350, Sapporo, Japan.

Mohammed Zaki. 2002. Effectively Mining Frequent Trees in a Forest. In *8th ACM SIGKDD International Conference on Knowledge Discovery and Data Mining*, pages 71–80, Edmonton, Canada.

Creating a Systemic Functional Grammar Corpus from the Penn Treebank

Matthew Honnibal and **James R. Curran**
School of Information Technologies
University of Sydney
NSW 2006, Australia
{mhonn, james}@it.usyd.edu.au

Abstract

The lack of a large annotated systemic functional grammar (SFG) corpus has posed a significant challenge for the development of the theory. Automating SFG annotation is challenging because the theory uses a minimal constituency model, allocating as much of the work as possible to a set of hierarchically organised features.

In this paper we show that despite the unorthodox organisation of SFG, adapting existing resources remains the most practical way to create an annotated corpus. We present and analyse SFGBank, an automated conversion of the Penn Treebank into systemic functional grammar. The corpus is comparable to those available for other linguistic theories, offering many opportunities for new research.

1 Introduction

Systemic functional grammar (Halliday and Matthiessen, 2004) aims to describe the set of meaningful choices a speaker makes when putting a thought into words. Each of these choices is seen as a resource for shaping the meaning in a particular way, and the selection will have a distinct grammatical outcome as well as a semantic implication. The choices are presented hierarchically, so that early selections restrict other choices. For instance, if a speaker chooses imperative mood for a clause, they cannot choose a tense. Each selection is linked to a syntactic expression rule. When imperative mood is selected, the subject of the clause is suppressed; when interrogative mood is selected, the order of the subject and first auxiliary are reversed.

Systemic grammars are very different from grammars influenced by the formalist tradition. Systemic analysis locates a constituent within a typology, and yields a set of features that describe its salient properties. These features have proven useful for research in applied linguistics, on topics such as stylistics, discourse analysis and translation. As a generative theory, systemic grammars are less effective. There have been a few attempts, such as those discussed by O'Donnell and Bateman (2005), but as yet a wide coverage systemic grammar that can be used for tractable parsing has not been developed.

The lack of a corpus and parser has limited research on systemic grammars, as corpus studies have been restricted to small samples of manually coded examples, or imprecise queries of unannotated data. The corpus we present, obtained by converting the Penn Treebank, addresses this issue. It also suggests a way to automatically code novel text, by converting the output of a parser for a different formalism. This would also allow the use of SFG features for NLP applications to be explored, and support current research using SFG for applied linguistics.

The conversion process relies on a set of manually coded rules. The first step of the process is to collect SFG clauses and their constituents from parses in the Penn Treebank. Each clause constituent is then assigned up to three function labels, for the three simultaneous semantic and pragmatic structures Halliday (1970) describes. Finally, the system features are calculated, using rules referring to the function labels assigned in the previous step. This paper extends the work described in Honnibal (2004).

Proceedings of the 5th Workshop on Important Unresolved Matters, pages 89–96,
Ann Arbor, June 2005.

2 Related Work

Converting the Penn Treebank is the standard approach to creating a corpus annotated according to a specific linguistic theory. This has been the method used to create LTAG (Frank, 2001), LFG (Frank et al., 2003) and CCG (Hockenmaier and Steedman, 2005) corpora, among others. We employ a similar methodology, converting the corpus using manually specified rules.

Since the SFG annotation is semantically oriented, the work also bears some resemblance to Propbank (Palmer et al., 2005). However, Propbank is concerned with manually adding information to the Penn Treebank, rather than automatically reinterpreting the same information through the lens of a different linguistic theory.

We chose not to base our conversion on the Propbank annotation, as it does not currently cover the Brown or Switchboard sections of the Treebank. The wider variety of genres provided by these sections makes the corpus much more useful for SFG, since the theory devotes significant attention to pragmatic phenomena and stylistic variation.

3 Systemic Functional Grammar

Generating a constituent using a systemic functional grammar involves traversing a decision-tree-like structure referred to as a *system network*. The nodes of this tree are referred to as *systems*, and the options from the systems are referred to as *features*. At each system, the feature selected may add constraints on the type, number or order of the internal structure of the constituent. When the entire network has been traversed, the constraints are unified, and the required constituents generated.

In order to annotate a sentence according to a systemic functional grammar, we must specify the set of features encountered as the system network is traversed, and apply function labels to each constituent. The function labeling is required because the constraints are always specified according to the child constituents' function, rather than their form.

Constituents may have more than one function label, as SFG describes three *metafunctions*, following Halliday's (1969) argument that a clause is structured simultaneously as a communicative act, a piece of information, and a representation of reality.

Interpersonal function labels are assigned to clause constituents in determining the clause's communicative status. The most important interpersonal functions are *Subject* and *Finite*, since the relative position of the constituents bearing these labels largely determines whether the clause will be a question, statement or command.

The *textual* structure of the clause includes the functions *Theme* and *Rheme*, following Halliday's (1970) theory of information structure.

Finally, the *experiential* function of a constituent is its semantic role, described in terms of a small set of labels that are only minimally sensitive to the semantics of the predicate.

4 Annotation Implemented

We base our annotation on the clause network in the Nigel grammar (Mann and Matthiessen, 1983), as it is freely available and discussed at length in Matthiessen (1995). It is difficult to include annotation from the group and phrase networks, because of the flat bracketing of constituents in the Penn Treebank. The converted corpus has full coverage over all sections of the Penn Treebank 3 corpus.

We implement features from 41 systems from the clause network, out of a possible 62. The most prominent missing features relate to process type. The process type system classifies clauses as one of four broad semantic types: material, mental, verbal or relational, with subsequent systems making finer grained distinctions. This is mostly determined by the argument structure of the verb, but also depends on its lexical semantics. Process type assignment therefore suffers from word sense ambiguity, so we are unable to select from this system or others which depend on its result. Figure 1 gives an example of a clause with interpersonal, textual and experiential function labels applied to its constituents.

5 Creating the Corpus

SFG specifies the structure of a clause from 'above', by setting constraints that are imposed by the set of features selected from the system network. These constraints describe the structure in terms of interpersonal, textual and experiential function labels. These functions then determine the boundaries of the clause, by specifying its constituents.

Constituent	Interpersonal	Textual	Ideational
and	–	Txt. Theme	–
last year	Adjunct	Top. Theme	Circumstance
prices	Subject	Rheme	Participant
were	Finite	Rheme	–
quickly	Adjunct	Rheme	Circumstance
plummeting	Predicator	Rheme	Process

Table 1: SFG function labels assigned to clause constituents.

```
preprocess(parse)
clauses = []
for word in parse.words():
  if isPredicate(word):
    constituents = getConstituents(word)
      clauses.append(constituents)
```

Figure 2: Conversion algorithm.

The Penn Treebank provides rich syntactic trees, specifying the structure of the sentence. We therefore proceed from 'below', using the Penn Treebank to find clauses and their constituents, then applying function labels to them, and using the function labels as the basis for rules to traverse the system network.

5.1 Finding Constituents

In this stage, we search the Treebank parse for SFG clauses, and collect their constituents. Clauses are identified by searching for predicates that head them, and constituents are collecting by traversing upwards from the predicate, collecting the nodes' siblings until we hit an S node.

There are a few common constructions which present problems for one or both of these procedures. These exceptions are handled by pre-processing the Treebank tree, changing its structure to be compatible with the predicate and constituent extraction algorithms. Figure 2 describes the conversion process more formally.

5.1.1 Finding predicates

A predicate is the main verb in the clause. In the Treebank annotation, the predicate will be the word attached to the lowest node in a VP chain, because auxiliaries attach higher up. Figure 3 describes the function to decide whether a word is a predicate. Essentially, we want words that are the last word attached to a VP, that do not have a VP sibling.

Figure 1 marks the predicates and constituents in a Treebank parse. The predicates are underlined, and the constituents numbered to match the predicate.

```
if verb.parent.label == 'VP':
  for sibling in verb.parent.children:
    if sibling.isWord():
      if sibling.offset > verb.offset:
        return False
    if sibling.label == 'VP':
      return False
return True
```

Figure 3: Determining whether a word is a predicate.

```
node = predicate
constituents = [predicate]
while node.label not in clauseLabels:
  for sibling in node.parent.children:
    if sibling != node:
      constituents.append(sibling)
for sibling in node.parent.children:
  if sibling != node
  and sibling.label in conjOrWHLabels:
    constituents.append(sibling)
```

Figure 4: Finding constituents.

5.1.2 Getting Constituents

Once we have a predicate, we can traverse the tree around it to collect the constituents in the clause it heads. We do this by collecting its siblings and moving up the tree, collecting the 'uncle' nodes, until we hit the top of the clause. Figure 4 describes the process more formally. The final loop collects conjunctions and WH constituents that attach alongside the clause node, such as the 'which' in Figure 1.

5.1.3 Pre-processing Ellipsis and Gapping

Ellipsis and gapping involve two or more predicates sharing some constituents. When the sharing can be denoted using the tree structure, by placing the shared items above the point where the VPs fork, we refer to the construction as ellipsis. Figure 5 shows a sentence with a subject and an auxiliary shared between two predicates. 3.4% of predicates share at least one constituent with another clause via ellipsis. We pre-process ellipsis constructions by inserting an S node above each VP after the first, and adding traces for the shared constituents.

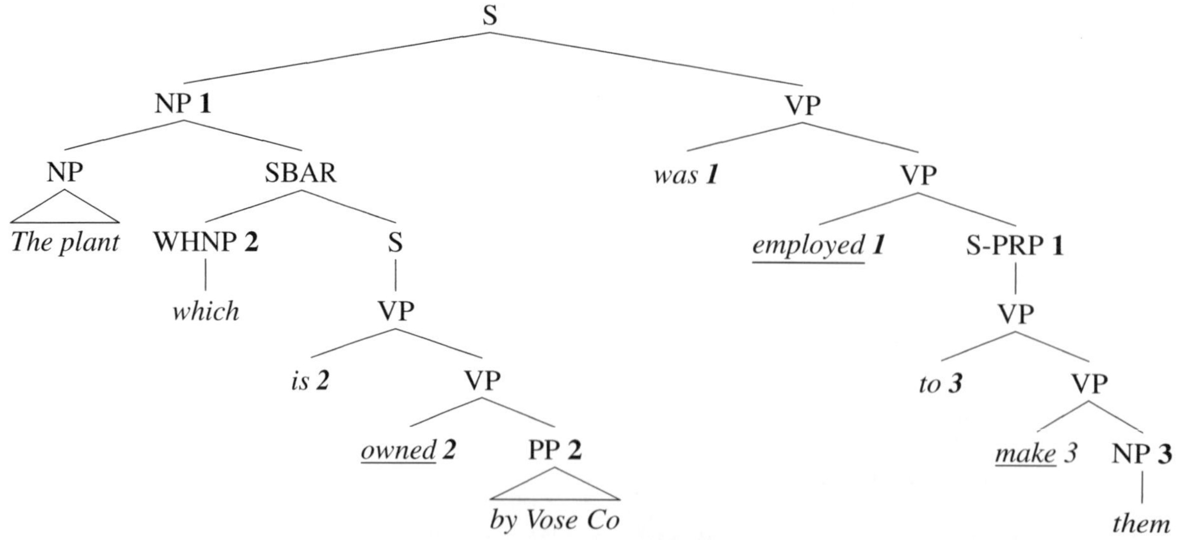

Figure 1: A parse tree with predicates underlined and constituents numbered.

In gapping constructions, the shared constituent is the predicate itself, and what differs between the two clauses are the arguments. The Treebank uses special trace rules to describe which arguments must be copied across to the gapped clause. We create traces to the shared constituents and add them to each gapped clause, so that the trace of the verb will be picked up as a predicate later on. Gapping is a very rare phenomenon – only 0.02% clauses have gapped predicates.

5.1.4 Pre-processing Semi-auxiliaries

In Figure 6 the verb 'continue' will match our rules for predicate extraction, described in Section 5.1. SFG analyses this and other 'semi-auxiliaries' (Quirk et al., 1991) as a serial verb construction, rather than a matrix clause and a complement clause. Since we want to treat the finite verb as though it were an auxiliary, we pre-process these cases by simply deleting the S node, and attaching its children directly to the semi-auxiliary's VP.

Defining the semi-auxiliary constructions is not so simple, however. Quirk et al. note that some of these verbs are more like auxiliaries than others, and organise them into a rough gradient according to their formal properties. The problem is that there is not clear agreement in the SFG literature about where the line should be drawn. Matthiessen (1995) describes all non-finite sentential complements as serial-verb constructions. Martin et al. (1997) argue that verbs such as 'want' impose selectional restrictions on the subject, and therefore should be treated as full verbs with a clause complement. Other compromises are possible as well.

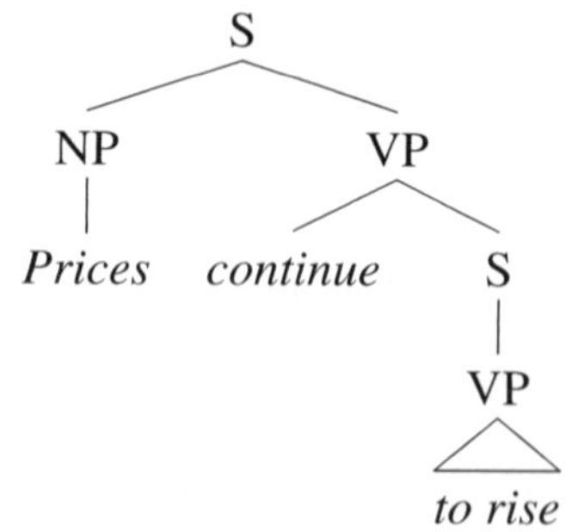

Figure 6: Treebank representation of a sentence with a semi-auxiliary.

Using Matthiessen's definition, we collect 5.3% fewer predicates than if we treated all semi-auxiliaries as main verbs. If the complement clause has a different subject from the parent clause, when the two are merged the new verb will seem to have extra arguments. 58% of these mergings introduce an extra argument in this way. For example,

Investors want the market to boom

will be analysed as though *boom* has two arguments, *investors* and *market*. We prevent this from occurring by adding an extra condition for merging clauses, stating that the subject of the embedded clause should be a trace co-indexed with the subject of the parent clause.

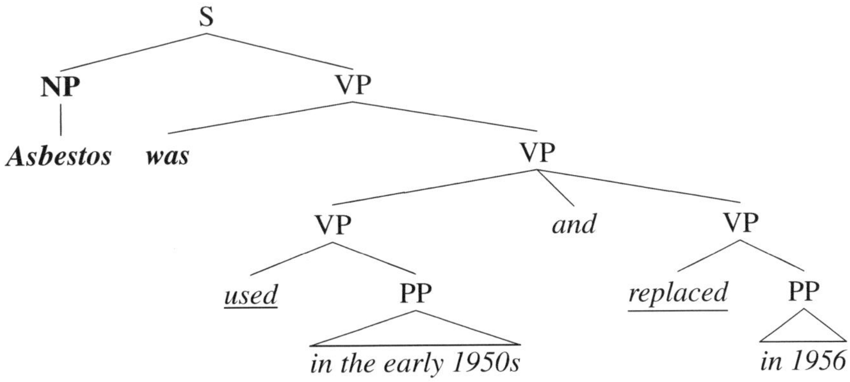

Figure 5: Treebank representation of ellipsis. Predicates are underlined, shared items are in bold.

5.2 Constituent functions

As discussed above, we attach up to three function labels to each clause constituent, one for each *metafunction*. The rules to do this rely on the order of constituents and the function dash-tags in the Penn Treebank. Some experiential function rules also refer to interpersonal labels, and some textual function rules refer to experiential labels.

5.2.1 Interpersonal Function Labels

The possible interpersonal function labels we assign are *Subject*, *Complement*, *Adjunct*, *Finite*, and *Predicator*. The Finite and Predicator are the first tensed verb, and the predicate respectively. If there are no auxiliary verbs, Halliday and Matthiessen (2004) describes the predicate as functioning both as Finite and Predicator. Since this is the only case in which a constituent would receive multiple labels from a single metafunction, we instead assign the single label *Finite/Predicator*.

For NPs, Subjects, Complements and Adjuncts are distinguished using the Penn Treebank's dash-tag function labels. SFG always assigns prepositional phrases the label Adjunct. All NP constituents that are not marked with an adverbial function tag in the Treebank are labeled *Complement*. Conjunctions are not assigned interpersonal functions.

5.2.2 Experiential Function Labels

The experiential function labels we assign are *Participant*, *Process* and *Circumstance*. This is a simplification of the function labels described by Halliday and Matthiessen (2004), as Participants are usually subdivided into what other linguistic theories refer to as semantic roles. SFG has its own semantic role description, which relies on *process type* features. For instance, Participants in a *verbal* process like 'say' have the role options *Sayer*, *Target*, *Receiver* and *Verbiage*.

Distinguishing process types requires a word sense disambiguated corpus and a word sense sensitive process type lexicon. While there is a significant intersection between the Penn Treebank and the Semcor word sense disambiguated corpus, there is currently no suitable process type lexicon. Consequently, Participants have not been subtyped. The Process is simply the verb phrase, while the Subject and Complements are Participants.

5.2.3 Textual Function labels

The textual metafunction describes the information structure of the clause. Halliday's textual function labels are *Textual Theme*, *Interpersonal Theme*, *Topical Theme* and *Rheme*. Theme and Rheme are often referred to as Topic and Comment in other theories of information structure (Vallduvi, 1993). Theories also disagree about exactly where to draw the boundary between the two.

In Halliday's theory, the Rheme begins after the first full constituent with an experiential function label, and extends to the end of the clause. The first constituent with an experiential function is labeled Topical Theme. Constituents before it are labeled either Interpersonal Theme or Textual Theme. Auxiliaries and vocatives are labeled Interpersonal Theme, while conjunctions are labeled Textual Theme.

System	Null %	Feature 1	Feature 2
clause class	0%	major (86%)	minor (13%)
agency	13%	effective (52%)	middle (34%)
conjunction	13%	non-conjuncted (64%)	conjuncted (21%)
finiteness	13%	finite (67%)	non-finite (19%)
polarity	13%	positive (81%)	negative (4%)
rank	13%	ranking (66%)	shifted (19%)
secondary/beta clause	13%	false (58%)	true (28%)
status	13%	bound (45%)	free (41%)
deicticity	32%	temporal (60%)	modal (7%)
person	32%	non-interactant (54%)	interactant (13%)
theme selection	32%	unmarked (58%)	marked (9%)
voice	47%	active (45%)	passive (6%)
embed type	80%	nominal qualifier (15%)	other qualifier (3%)
theme role	90%	as adjunct (7%)	as process (1%)
passive agency	93%	non-agentive (5%)	agentive (1%)

Table 2: Selected systems and how often their features are selected.

5.3 System Selections

As discussed above, the system features are organised into hierarchies, with every feature assuming a null value unless its system's entry condition is met. We therefore approach the system network much like a decision tree, using rules to control how the network is traversed.

The rules used to traverse the network cannot be explained here in full, as there are 41 such decision functions currently implemented. Table 2 lists a few of the systems we implement, along with how often their features are selected. Because the system network is organised hierarchically, a selection will not always be made from a given system, since the 'entry condition' may not be met. For instance, the feature agency=effective is an entry condition for the voice system, so if a clause is middle, no voice will be selected. The Null % column describes how often the entry condition of the clause is not met. Systems further down the heirarchy will obviously be relevant less often, as will systems which describe a finer grained distinction for an already rare feature.

The following sections describe the system network in terms of four general regions. The systems within each region largely sub-categorise each other, or relate to the same grammatical phenomenon.

5.4 Mood systems

Assuming the clause is independent, the major mood options are declarative, interrogative and imperative. Deciding between these is quite simple: in interrogative clauses, the Subject occurs after the first auxiliary. Imperative clauses have no Subject.

There are a few more granular systems for interrogative clauses, recording whether the question is polar or WH. If the clause is WH interrogative, there are two further features recording whether the requested constituent functions as Subject, Adjunct or Complement. The values of these features are quite simple to calculate, by finding the WH element among the constituents and retrieving its interpersonal function.

If the clause is not imperative, there are systems recording the person (first, second or third) of the subject, and whether the first auxiliary is modal, present tense, past tense, or future tense. SFG describes three tenses in English, regarding 'will' and 'shall' auxiliaries as future tense markers, rather than modals.

If the clause is imperative, there is a further system recording whether the clause is the 'jussive' imperative with 'let's', an 'oblative' imperative with 'let me', or a second person imperative. If the imperative is second person, a further feature records whether the 'you' is explicit or implied.

There are also features recording the 'polarity' of the clause: whether it is positive or negative, and, if negative, whether the negative marker is full-formed or cliticised as -n't.

5.5 Voice systems

In the Nigel grammar, the first voice distinction drawn is not between active and passive, but between transitive and intransitive clauses. Intransitive clauses cannot be passivised, as there is no Complement to shift to Subject. It therefore makes sense to carve these off first. If the clause is transitive, another system records whether it is active or passive. The rules to draw this distinction simply look at the verb phrase, checking whether the last auxiliary is a form of the verb 'be' and the lexical verb has a past participle part-of-speech tag. Finally, a further system records whether passive clauses have an agent introduced by 'by'.

5.6 Theme systems

Theme systems record what occurs at the start of the clause. Typically in English, the first major constituent will be the logical subject, and hence also the Topical Theme. A system records whether this is or is not the case. If the clause is finite and the logical subject is not the Topical Theme, the clause is said to have a 'marked' theme. Verb phrase Topical Themes are considered unmarked if the clause is imperative. A further system records whether the Topical Theme is the logical object (as in passivisation), or whether it is a fronted Adjunct. Passive clauses may have a fronted Adjunct, so does not necessarily have a logical object as Topical Theme. There are two further systems recording whether the clause has a Textual Theme and/or an Interpersonal Theme.

5.7 Taxis systems

Taxis systems record dependency relationships between clauses. There are two types of information: whether the attachment is made through coordination or subordination, and the semantic type of the attachment. Broadly, semantic type is between 'expansion' and 'projection', projection being reported (or quoted) speech or thought. A further system records the subtype of expansion clauses, which is quite a subtle distinction. Unfortunately Halliday chose thoroughly unhelpful terminology for this distinction: his subtypes of expansion are elaboration, enhancement and extension. Enhancing clauses are essentially adverbial, and are almost always subordinate. Extending clauses, by contrast, are approximately the 'and' relationship, and are almost always coordinate. Elaborating clauses qualify or further define the information in the clause they are attached to. Elaborating clauses can be either subordinate or coordinate. Subordinate elaborating clauses are non-defining relative clauses, while coordinate elaborating clauses are usually introduced by a conjunctive adjunct, like 'particularly'.

6 Accuracy

In order to evaluate the accuracy of the conversion process, we manually evaluated the constituency structure of a randomly selected sample of 200 clauses. The conversion heuristics were developed on section 00 of the Wall Street Journal and section 2 of Switchboard, while the evaluation sentences were sampled from the rest of the Penn Treebank.

We limited evaluation to the constituency conversion process, in order to examine more clauses. The function labels are calculated from the constituency conversion, while the system features are calculated from the function labels and other system features. Since the system network is like a decision tree, whether a feature is null-valued depends on prior feature decisions. These dependencies in the annotation mean that evaluating all of it involves some redundancy. We therefore evaluated the constituency structure, since it did not depend on any of the other annotation, and the conversion heuristics involved in calculating it were more complicated than those for the function labels and system features.

In the 200 clause sample, we found three clauses with faulty constituency structures. One of these was the result of a part-of-speech tag error in the Treebank. The other two errors were conjunctions that were incorrectly replicated in ellipsis clauses.

7 Conclusion

The Penn Treebank was designed as a largely theory neutral corpus. In deciding on an annotation scheme, it emphasised the need to have its annotators work quickly and consistent, rather than fidelity to any particular linguistic theory (Marcus et al., 1994).

The fact that it has been successfully converted to so many other annotation schemes suggests that its annotation is indeed consistent and fine grained. It is therefore unsurprising that it is possible to convert it to SFG as well. Despite historically different concerns, SFG still fundamentally agrees with other theories about which constructions are syntactically distinct — it simply has an unorthodox strategy for representing that variation, delegating more work to feature structures and less work to the syntactic representation.

Now that a sizable SFG corpus has been created, it can be put to use for linguistic and NLP research. Linguistically, we suggest that it would be interesting to use the corpus to explore some of the assertions in the literature that have until now been untestable. For instance, Halliday and Matthiessen (2004) suggests that the motivation for passivisation is largely structural — what comes first in a clause is an important choice in English. This implies that the combination of passive voice and a fronted adjunct should be unlikely. There should be many such simple queries that can shed interesting light on abstract claims in the literature.

Large annotated corpora are currently very important for parsing research, making this work a vital first step towards exploring whether SFG annotation can be automated. The fact that Treebank parses can be converted into SFG annotation suggests it can be, although most parsers do not replicate the dash-tags attached to Treebank labels, which are necessary to distinguish SFG categories in our conversion system.

Even without automating annotation, the corpus offers some potential for investigating how useful SFG features are for NLP tasks. The Penn Treebank includes texts from a variety of genres, including newspaper text, literature and spoken dialogue. The Switchboard section of the corpus also comes with various demographic properties about the speakers, and is over a million words. We therefore suggest that gold standard SFG features could be used in some simple document classification experiments, such as predicting the gender or education level of speakers in the Switchboard corpus.

8 Acknowledgments

We would like to thanks the anonymous reviewers for their helpful comments. James Curran was funded under ARC Discovery grants DP0453131 and DP0665973.

References

Anette Frank. 2001. Treebank conversion: Converting the NEGRA treebank to an LTAG grammar. In *Proceedings of the EUROLAN Workshop on Multi-layer Corpus-based Analysis*. Iasi, Romania.

Anette Frank, Louisa Sadler, Josef van Genabith, and Andy Way. 2003. *From Treebank Resources To LFG F-Structures - Automatic F-Structure Annotation of Treebank Trees and CFGs extracted from Treebanks*. Kluwer, Dordrecht.

Michael A. K. Halliday. 1969. Options and functions in the English clause. *Brno Studies in English*, 8:82–88. Reprinted in Halliday and Martin (eds.)(1981) Readings in Systemic Linguistics, Batsford, London.

Michael A. K. Halliday. 1970. Language structure and language function. In John Lyons, editor, *New Horizons in Linguistics*. Penguin, Harmondsworth.

Michael A. K. Halliday and Christian M. I. M. Matthiessen. 2004. *An Introduction to Functional Grammar*. Edward Arnold, London, third edition.

Julia Hockenmaier and Mark Steedman. 2005. Ccgbank manual. Technical Report MS-CIS-05-09, University of Pennsylvania.

Matthew Honnibal. 2004. Converting the Penn Treebank to Systemic Sunctional Grammar. In *Proceedings of the Australasian Language Technology Workshop (ALTW04)*.

William C. Mann and Christian M. I. M. Matthiessen. 1983. An overview of the Nigel text generation grammar. Technical Report RR-83-113, USC/Information Sciences Institute.

Mitchell P. Marcus, Beatrice Santorini, and Mary Ann Marcinkiewicz. 1994. Building a large annotated corpus of English: The Penn Treebank. *Computational Linguistics*, 19(2):313–330.

James R. Martin, Christian M. I. M. Matthiessen, and Clare Painter. 1997. *Working with Functional Grammar*. Arnold, London.

Christian Matthiessen. 1995. *Lexicogrammatical Cartography*. International Language Sciences Publishers, Tokyo, Taipei and Dallas.

Michael O'Donnell and John A. Bateman. 2005. SFL in computational contexts: a contemporary history. In J. Webster, R. Hasan, and C. M. I. M. Matthiessen, editors, *Continuing Discourse on Language: A functional perspective*, pages 343–382. Equinox, London.

Martha Palmer, Daniel Gildea, and Paul Kingsbury. 2005. The proposition bank: An annotated corpus of semantic roles. *Computational Linguistics*, 31(1):71–106.

Randolph Quirk, Sidney Greenbaum, Geoffrey Leech, and Jan Svartvik. 1991. *A Grammar of Contemporary English*. Longman, London.

Enric Vallduvi. 1993. Information packing: A survey. Technical Report HCRC/RP-44, Universiy of Edinburgh.

Verb Valency Semantic Representation for Deep Linguistic Processing

Aleš Horák[1], Karel Pala[1], Marie Duží[2], Pavel Materna[1]

1: Faculty of Informatics, Masaryk University
Botanicka 68a
602 00 Brno
Czech Republic
{hales,pala}@fi.muni.cz

2: VSB-Technical University of Ostrava
17.listopadu 15
708 33 Ostrava-Poruba
Czech Republic
marie.duzi@vsb.cz

Abstract

In the paper, we describe methods for exploitation of a new lexical database of valency frames (VerbaLex) in relation to Transparent Intensional Logic (TIL). We present a detailed description of the Complex Valency Frames (CVF) as they appear in VerbaLex including basic ontology of the VerbaLex semantic roles.

TIL is a typed logical system developed for natural language semantic representation using TIL logical forms known as constructions. TIL is well suited to handle the difficult language phenomena such as temporal relations, intensionality and propositional attitudes. Here we make use of the long-term development of the Normal Translation Algorithm aimed at automatic translation of natural language sentences into TIL constructions.

We examine the relations between CVFs and TIL constructions of predicate-argument structures and discuss the procedure of automatic acquisition of the verbal object constructions. The exploitation of CVFs in the syntactic parsing is also briefly mentioned.

1 Introduction

In the paper we propose a method to integrate the logical analysis of sentences with the linguistic approach to semantics, exploiting the complex valency frames (CVFs) in the VerbaLex verb valency lexicon, see (Hlaváčková, Horák, Kadlec 2006). To this end we first present a brief survey of the logic we are going to use, namely Transparent Intensional Logic (TIL), which was originated by P. Tichý (Tichý 1988). Theoretical aspects of TIL were further developed in particular by P. Materna (Materna 1998) and also by co-authors of this paper (see, Materna, Duží 2005, Horák 2002). A question may be asked why we do not exploit first order predicate logic (PL1) where some of the presented problems have already been explored and PL1 has been used to represent logical forms. It is a well established fact that PL1 is not able to handle systematically the phenomena like propositional verbs (which, of course, appear in our valency frames), grammatical tenses and modalities (modal verbs and modal particles in natural language). On the other hand, since TIL works with types these problems either do not arise or they can be solved in an intuitive way (see Tichý 1988).

In the second linguistic section we present CVFs by means of which the semantics of verbs in natural language such as Czech or English can be described.

In Section 3 we show how CVFs describe the surface valencies of verbs (i.e. their respective morphological cases in Czech) as well as the semantics of their predicate-argument structure. Concerning the latter we make use of the deep semantic roles expressed by two-level labels based partly on the Top Ontology (EuroWordNet) and partly on the selected literals from Princeton WordNet.

Since so far these two ways of description, namely the logical and linguistic one, have been treated separately, the task we set is to propose a method

Proceedings of the 5th Workshop on Important Unresolved Matters, pages 97–104,
Ann Arbor, June 2005.

of their interrelation and coordination. Needless to say that both ways of description of verb semantics are useful.

Hence we are going to show how to combine a logical description using mostly terms like types, individuals, classes, relations, propositions, or, in general, constructions of these entities, with the linguistic framework capturing the idiosyncratic semantic features of the verbs such as SUBS(liquid:1) or AG(person:1|animal:1).

In Section 4 we adduce an example of the analysis of selected English and Czech verbs for which the above mentioned integration has been proposed.

2 Basics of Transparent Intensional Logic

In this Section we provide an introductory explanation of the main notions of Transparent Intensional Logic (TIL). For exact definitions and details see, e.g., Tichý (1988), Tichý (2004), Materna (1998), Materna (2004) and Materna, Duží (2005). TIL approach to knowledge representation can be characterised as the 'top-down approach'. TIL 'generalises to the hardest case' and obtains the 'less hard cases' by lifting various restrictions that apply only higher up. This way of proceeding is opposite to how semantic theories tend to be built up. The standard approach (e.g. predicate logic) consists in beginning with atomic sentences, then proceeding to molecular sentences formed by means of truth-functional connectives or by quantifiers, and from there to sentences containing modal operators and, finally, attitudinal operators.

Thus, to use a simple case for illustration, once a vocabulary and rules of formation have been laid down, semantics gets off the ground by analysing an atomic sentence as follows:

(1) "Charles is happy": Fa

And further upwards:

(2) "Charles is happy, and Thelma is grumpy": $Fa \wedge Gb$

(3) "Somebody is happy": $\exists x\,(Fx)$

(4) "Possibly, Charles is happy": $\Diamond\,(Fa)$

(5) "Thelma believes that Charles is happy": $Bb\,(Fa)$.

In non-hyperintensional (i.e., non-procedural) theories of formal semantics, attitudinal operators are swallowed by the modal ones. But when they are not, we have three levels of granularity: the coarse level of truth-values, the fine-grained level of truth-conditions (propositions, truth-values-in-intension), and the very fine-grained level of hyper-propositions, i.e., *constructions* of propositions. TIL operates with these three levels of granularity. We start out by analysing sentences from the uppermost end, furnishing them with a hyperintensional[1] semantics, and working our way downwards, furnishing even the lowest-end sentences (and other empirical expressions) with a hyperintensional semantics. That is, the sense of a sentence such as "Charles is happy" is a hyper-proposition, namely the *construction of the denoted proposition* (i.e., the *instruction* how to evaluate the truth-conditions of the sentence in any state of affairs).

When assigning a construction to an expression as its meaning, we specify a *procedural know-how*, which must not be confused with the respective *performancy know-how*. Distinguishing performatory know-how from procedural know-how, the latter could be characterised "that a knower x knows how A is done in the sense that x can spell out instructions for doing A." For instance, to *know* what Goldbach Conjecture *means* is to understand the instruction to find whether 'all positive even integers ≥ 4 can be expressed as the sum of two primes'. It does not include either actually finding out (whether it is true or not by following a procedure or by luck) or possessing the skill to do so.[2]

Furthermore, the sentence "Charles is happy" is an 'intensional context', in the sense that its logical analysis must involve reference to empirical parameters, in this case both possible worlds and instants of time. Charles is only *contingently* happy; i.e., he is only happy at some worlds and only sometimes. The other reason is because the *analysans* must be capable of figuring as an argument for functions whose domain are propositions rather than truth-values. Construing 'Fa' as a name of a truth-value works only in the case of (1), (2) and (3). It won't work in (5), since truth-values are not the sort of thing that can be

1 The term 'hyperintensional' has been introduced by Max Cresswell in Cresswell (1975). See also Cresswell (1985).

2 For details on TIL handling knowledge see Duží, Jespersen, Müller (2005).

believed. Nor will it work in (4), since truth-values are not the sort of thing that can be possible.

Constructions are procedures, or instructions, specifying how to arrive at less-structured entities. Being procedures, constructions are structured from the algorithmic point of view, unlike set-theoretical objects. The TIL 'language of constructions' is a modified hyper-intensional version of the typed λ-calculus, where Montague-like λ-terms denote, not the functions constructed, but the constructions themselves. Constructions *qua* procedures operate on input objects (of any type, even on constructions of any order) and yield as output (or, in well defined cases fail to yield) objects of any type; in this way constructions construct *partial* functions, and functions, rather than relations, are basic objects of our ontology.

By claiming that constructions are algorithmically structured, we mean the following: a construction *C* — being an instruction — consists of particular steps, i.e., sub-instructions (or, *constituents*) that have to be executed in order to execute *C*. The concrete/abstract objects an instruction operates on are not its constituents, they are just mentioned. Hence objects have to be supplied by another (albeit trivial) construction. The constructions themselves may also be only mentioned: therefore one should not conflate *using* constructions as constituents of composed constructions and *mentioning* constructions that enter as input into composed constructions, so we have to strictly distinguish between *using* and *mentioning* constructions. Just briefly: Mentioning is, in principle, achieved by using atomic constructions. A construction is atomic if it is a procedure that does not contain any other construction as a used subconstruction (a constituent). There are two atomic constructions that supply objects (of any type) on which complex constructions operate: *variables* and *trivializations.*

Variables are constructions that construct an object dependently on *valuation*: they *v-construct,* where *v* is the parameter of valuations. When X is an object (including constructions) of any type, the *Trivialization* of X, denoted $^0\boldsymbol{X}$, constructs X without the mediation of any other construction. ^{0}X is the atomic concept of X: it is the primitive, non-perspectival mode of presentation of X.

There are three *compound* constructions, which consist of other constructions: *Composition*, *Closure* and Double Execution. Composition $[X\ Y_1 \ldots Y_m]$ is the procedure of applying a function *f* *v*-constructed by *X* to an argument A *v*-constructed by $Y_1,\ldots,Y_m$, i.e., the instruction to apply *f* to A to obtain the value (if any) of *f* at A. Closure $[\lambda x_1 \ldots x_m\ Y]$ is the procedure of constructing a function by abstracting over variables, i.e., the instruction to do so. Finally, higher-order construction *X* can be used twice over as a constituent of a composed construction. This is achieved by the fifth construction called *Double Execution* $^2\boldsymbol{X}$.

TIL constructions, as well as the entities they construct, all receive a type. On the ground level of the type-hierarchy, there are entities unstructured from the algorithmic point of view belonging to a *type of order 1*. Given a so-called *epistemic (or 'objectual') **base** of **atomic types*** (ο-truth values, ι-individuals, τ-time moments / real numbers, ω-possible worlds), mereological complexity is increased by the induction rule for forming partial functions: where $\alpha, \beta_1,\ldots,\beta_n$ are types of order 1, the set of partial mappings from $\beta_1 \times\ldots\times \beta_n$ to α, denoted $(\alpha\beta_1\ldots\beta_n)$, is a type of order 1 as well. Constructions that construct entities of order 1 are *constructions of order 1*. They belong to a *type of order 2*, denoted by $*_1$. Inductively we define *type of order n,* $*_n$.

TIL is specific in a precise solution for intensions as non-empirical objects of the real world. Intensions are qualified as functions of a type ((ατ)ω), i.e., functions from possible worlds to *chronologies* of the type α (in symbols: $\alpha_{\tau\omega}$), where a chronology is a function of type (ατ). Some important kinds of intensions are:

Propositions, type $o_{\tau\omega}$ (shortened as π). They are denoted by empirical (declarative) sentences.

Properties of members of a type α, or simply *α-properties,* type $(o\alpha)_{\tau\omega}$.[3] General terms (some substantives, intransitive verbs) denote properties, mostly of individuals.

Relations-in-intension, type $(o\beta_1\ldots\beta_m)_{\tau\omega}$. For example transitive empirical verbs, also attitudinal verbs denote these relations. Omitting $_{\tau\omega}$ we get the type $(o\beta_1\ldots\beta_m)$ of *relations-in-extension* (to be met mainly in mathematics).

---

[3] Collections, sets, classes of 'α-objects' are members of type (οα); TIL handles classes (subsets of a type) as characteristic functions. Similarly relations (-in-extension) are of type(s) $(o\beta_1\ldots\beta_m)$.

α-roles or offices, type $\alpha_{\tau\omega}$, where $\alpha \neq (o\beta)$. Frequently $\iota_{\tau\omega}$ (an individual office). Often denoted by concatenation of a superlative and a noun ("*the highest mountain*"). Individual roles correspond to what Church calls an "*individual concept*".

3 The Complex Valency Frames

Valency frames have been built in several projects (VALLEX for Czech PDT (Žabokrtský 2005) or VerbNet (Kipper et al 2006)). Motivation for the VerbaLex project came from comparing Czech WordNet verb frames with VALLEX. The main goal of VerbaLex is an automatic processing of verb phrases exploiting explicit links to Princeton WordNet. The complex valency frames we are working with can be characterized as data structures (tree graphs) describing predicate-argument structure of a verb which contains the verb itself and the arguments determined by the verb meaning (their number usually varies from 1-5). The argument structure also displays the semantic preferences on the arguments. On the syntactic (surface) level the arguments are most frequently expressed as noun or pronominal groups in one of the seven cases (in Czech) and also as prepositional cases or adverbials.
An example of a complex valency frame for the verb *zabít (kill)* looks like:
usmrtit:1/zabít:1/dostat:11 (kill:1)
-frame: AG<person:1|animal:1>$_{who\_nom}^{obl}$
VERB^{obl}
PAT<person:1|animal:1>$_{whom\_acc}^{obl}$
INS<instrument:1>$_{with\_what\_ins}^{opt}$
-example: vrah zabil svou oběť nožem (A murderer has killed the victim with a knife).
-synonym:
-use: prim
More examples of CVFs for some selected verbs can be found below in Section 4.
The semantics of the arguments is typically labeled as belonging to a given semantic role (or deep case), which represents a general role plus subcategorization features (or selectional restrictions). Thus valency frames in Verbalex include information about:

1. the syntactic (surface) information about the syntactic valencies of a verb, i.e. what **morphological cases** (direct and prepositional ones in highly inflected languages such as Czech) are associated with (required by) a particular verb, and also **adverbials**,
2. **semantic roles** (deep cases) that represent the integration of the general labels with subcategorization features (or selectional restrictions) required by the meaning of the verb.

The inventory of the semantic roles is partly inspired by the Top Ontology and Base Concepts as they have been defined within EuroWordNet project. Thus we work with the general or 'large' roles like AG, ART(IFACT), SUBS(TANCE), PART, CAUSE, OBJ(ECT) (natural object), INFO(RMATION), FOOD, GARMENT, VEHICLE and others. They are combined with the literals from Princeton WordNet 2.0 where literals represent subcategorization features allowing us to climb down the hypero/hyponymical trees to the individual lexical units. For example, we have AG(person:1|animal:1) or SUBS(liquid:1) that can be used within the individual CVFs.
The verb entries are linked to the Czech and Princeton WordNet 2.0, i.e. they are organized around the respective lemma in synsets with numbered senses.
The Czech lexical resource being now developed is then a list of Czech CVFs – this work is going on within the Verbalex project at FI MU (Hlaváčková, Horák, 2005). Verbalex now contains approx. 11000 verb literals organized in synsets. The current goal is to enlarge the lexicon to 15 000 verbs.
The inventory of the semantic roles we work with clearly represents a sort of ontology which tries to cover word stock of Czech verbs and can be used as a base for a semantic classification and subclassification of the verbs. The ontologies represent theoretical constructs designed from the „top" and as such they are not directly based on the empirical evidence, i.e. corpus data. Thus there is a need to confront the ontologies and the inventories of the semantic roles that can be derived from them with the corpus data and see how well they can correspond to them. For this purpose we are experimenting with the corpus data obtained from the Word Sketch Engine (Kilgarriff, Rychlý, Smrž, Tugwell 2006).

4 Logical Analysis Using CVFs

In this section we describe the translation of VerbaLex CVFs into a verb phrase, which is a core of a sentence logical analysis.

TIL comes with a dissociation of significant verbs into two groups according to the classification of their meaning:

1. *by attributive verbs* we ascribe qualities or properties to objects. Attributive verbs are typically expressed by the respective form of the verb 'to be' combined with an expression denoting a property; examples: 'to be red' or 'to be mellow' or with a general substantive like 'to be a traitor', 'to be a tree'.
2. *episodic verbs*, on the other hand, specify actions performed by a subject.

An episodic verb does not describe its subject's state in any moment of time, it rather describes an episode of doing something at the certain time moment (and necessarily some time before that moment plus the expectation that it will last also in the next few moments, at least). *TIL* provides a complex handling of episodic verbs including the verb tense, aspect (perfective/imperfective) or active/passive state. All these features are concentrated around the so called *verbal object*, the construction of which (i.e., the meaning of a particular verb phrase) is the application of (the construction of) the verb to (the constructions of) the verb's arguments.

Since the analysis of attributive verbs is usually quite simple, we will concentrate in the following text on the examples of selected episodic verbs from VerbaLex and their logical analysis using the complex valency frames.

The TIL type of episodic verbal objects is $(o(o\pi)(o\pi))_{\omega}$, where π is the type of propositions ($o_{\tau\omega}$). See (Horák 2002, pp. 64-73) and (Tichý 1980) for detailed explanation. Our analysis is driven by a linguistic (syntactic) context that signals the *semantic fact that there is always a function involved here,* so that we have to ascribe types to its arguments and value.

4.1 Examples of Logical Analysis

We have chosen cca 10 verbs with their verb frames from VerbaLex and we will use them as examples of the algorithm for determining the verb type in the TIL logical analysis procedure.

dát (give)

dát:2 / dávat:2 / darovat:1 / věnovat:1 (give:8, gift:2, present:7)

-frame: DON<organization:1>$_{what\_nom}^{obl}$ VERB^{obl} OBJ<object:1>$_{what\_acc}^{obl}$ BEN<person:1>$_{to\_whom\_dat}^{obl}$

-example: firma věnovala zaměstnancům nová auta (a company gave new cars to the employees)

-use: prim

The verb arguments in this frame are: *who, to whom, what* (all obligatory) with (at least) two options: a) *to whom* is an individual, b) *to whom* is a class of individuals. The respective verb types are ad a): $((o(o\pi)(o\pi))_{\omega}\iota\iota\iota)$,

ad b): $((o(o\pi)(o\pi))_{\omega}\iota(o\iota)\iota)$.

For example *to whom* = to the employees of a given institution. To be an employee of the institution XY is a property, say Z / $(o\iota)_{\tau\omega}$. So "The company gave to the employees of XY...", not taking into account grammatical tenses and omitting trivializations we get $\lambda w \lambda t$ [Give$_{wt}$ XY Z$_{wt}$ etc.] (XY has the type ι here, being a collective rather than a class.)

With this example, we can show that CVFs are used not only for determining the verbal object type, but also for stating additional *prerequisities* (necessary conditions) for the sentence constituents. The full analysis using the verb frame above thus contains, except the verb phrase part, the conditions saying that "*X gives Y to Z* $\wedge$ *organization(X)* $\wedge$ *object(Y)* $\wedge$ *person(Z)*". The predicates *organization*, *object* and *person* here represent the properties denoted by the corresponding terms in the wordnet hypero-hyponymical hierarchy.

dát:15 / dávat:15 / nabídnout:3 / nabízet:3 (give:37)

-frame: AG<person:1>$_{who\_nom}^{obl}$ VERB^{obl} ABS<abstraction:1>$_{what\_acc}^{obl}$ REC<person:1>$_{to\_whom\_dat}^{obl}$

-example: dal jí své slovo (he gave her his word)

-example: nabídl jí své srdce (he offered her his heart)

-use: fig

Here we have an idiom ("to give word"), which corresponds to an (episodic) relation between two individuals. Thus the type of the verb is $((o(o\pi)(o\pi))_{\omega}\iota\iota)$, the second ι corresponds to *to whom*.

bránit (prevent)
bránit:1 / zabránit:2 / zabraňovat:2 / zamezit:2 / zamezovat:2 (prevent:2, keep:4)
-frame: AG<person:1>$_{who\_nom}^{obl}$ VERB^{obl} PAT<person:1>$_{to\_whom\_dat}^{obl}$ ACT<act:1>$_{inf}^{obl}$
-example: zabránila mu uhodit syna (she prevented him from hitting the son)
-use: prim

bránit:1 / zabránit:2 / zabraňovat:2 / zamezit:2 / zamezovat:2 (prevent:2, keep:4)
-frame: AG<institution:1>$_{what\_nom}^{obl}$ VERB^{obl} PAT<person:1>$_{to\_whom\_dat}^{obl}$ ACT<act:2>$_{in\_what\_loc}^{opt}$
-example: policie mu zabránila v cestě do zahraničí (police prevented him from going abroad)
-use: prim

Here, arguments of the verb correspond to the phrases *who, to whom, in (from)*. The third argument has the type of an activity given, of course, by an episodic verb *hit the son, travel abroad* (the substantive form *travelling abroad* can be construed as that activity). The type of the verb is $((o(o\pi)(o\pi))_{\omega}\iota\iota((o(o\pi)(o\pi))_{\omega}))$.

říct (say)
říct:1 / říkat:1 / říci:1 / říkat:1 / pravit:1 (say:6)
-frame: AG<person:1>$_{who\_nom}^{obl}$ VERB^{obl} COM<speech act:1>$_{what\_acc,that,dsp}^{obl}$ ADR<person:1>$_{to\_whom\_dat}^{opt}$
-example: říct kolegovi dobrý den (say hello to a colleague)
-example: řekl, že to platí (he said that it holds)
-example: pravil: "Dobrý den" (he said: "Good day")
-use: prim

The case questions for the corresponding arguments of the verb *říct* are *a) who, what*$_1$, *b) who, what*$_2$, *c) who, to whom, what*$_1$, and *d) who, to whom, what*$_2$. Examples of instantiated sentences can be a) *Charles says „Hello"*, b) *Charles says that he is ill,* c) *Charles says to his colleague "Hello"*, or d) *Charles says to his colleague that he is ill.*

The quotation context (*ad* a), c)) is normally impossible to type. Unless we want to go into some deep analyses we can ascribe to any quoted expression the type of individual. The relation to and unquoted subordinate clause is analysed as a general construction of type $*_n$. The resulting types of verbs are then
a) $((o(o\pi)(o\pi))_{\omega}\iota\iota)$,
b) $((o(o\pi)(o\pi))_{\omega}\iota *_n)$,
c) $((o(o\pi)(o\pi))_{\omega}\iota\iota\iota)$,
d) $((o(o\pi)(o\pi))_{\omega}\iota\iota *_n)$.

brečet$_1$ (cry) because of something, for something
brečet:1 / plakat:1 (cry:2, weep:1)
-frame: AG<person:1>$_{who\_nom}^{obl}$ VERB^{obl} CAUSE<cause:4>$_{due+to+what\_dat,over+what\_ins,for+what\_acc}^{obl}$
-example: brečela kvůli zničeným šatům (she cried for spoiled clothes)
-example: plakal nad svou chudobou (he cried over his poverty)
-example: plakal pro své hříchy (he cried for his sins)
-use: prim

brečet$_2$ (cry) for somebody
brečet:1 / plakat:1 (cry:2, weep:1)
-frame: AG<person:1>$_{who\_nom}^{obl}$ VERB^{obl} ENT<person:1>$_{for+whom\_acc}^{obl}$
-example: plakala pro milého (she cried for her boy)
-use: prim

If I cry *because of, for* etc., then the role of causing is played by this *because of.* Crying is an episodic verb, whereas *because of* etc. is a relation between propositions, often between events. We have therefore *because of* / $(o\pi\pi)_{\tau\omega}$, where the first $\pi(=o_{\tau\omega})$ belongs to the proposition denoted, e.g., by *clothes have been spoiled* or that *the respective individual is poor, sinful* etc., and the second π to the proposition *that the respective individual cries.* In case of *to cry for somebody* the respective type is again a "relation" $((o(o\pi)(o\pi))_{\omega}\iota\iota)$, although this *for* hides some cause, which is, however, not mentioned.
With this verb, we will describe the analysis of verb entailment handling in TIL. If we analyse a general case of the above mentioned meanings of cry (cry$_1$-because of something, cry$_2$-for

somebody) simply *to cry,* (*He cries all the time*). This verb's type is a verbal object without arguments, $(o(o\pi)(o\pi))_{\omega}$. In addition to this the following rule holds: *If X cries because of... or X cries for..., then X cries.* In this way the semantic dependence between the three cases of crying is given; otherwise we would not be able to detect this connection, e.g. between **brečet$_1$** and **brečet$_2$**.

absolvovat (undergo)
absolvovat:2 / prožít:1 / prožívat:1 (experience:1, undergo:2, see:21, go through:1)
-frame: AG<person:1>$_{who\_nom}^{obl}$ VERB^{obl} EVEN<experience:3>$_{what\_acc}^{obl}$ LOC<location:1>$_{in\_what\_loc}^{opt}$
-example: absolvoval vyšetření na psychiatrické klinice (he went through investigation in a psychiatric clinic)
-use: prim

In general it is an episodic relation to an event (type π)[4], so the type is $((o(o\pi)(o\pi))_{\omega}\iota\pi)$. In some cases we may also use a relation to an episode (specific class of events, type $(o\pi)$), then the type is $((o(o\pi)(o\pi))_{\omega}\iota(o\pi))$, and *investigation in a clinic* has to be defined as a sequence of events.

akceptovat (accept)
akceptovat:3 / přijmout:6 / přijímat:6 (accept:4)
-frame: AG<person:1|social group:1>$_{who\_nom}^{obl}$ VERB^{obl} STATE<state:4>|EVEN<event:1>|INFO<info:1>$_{what\_acc}^{obl}$
-example: akceptujeme jeho povahu (we accept his character)
-example: lidé přijali nový zákon s nadšením (people accepted new law with enthusiasm)
-use: prim

We can accept nearly anything. Here we meet the problem of type-theoretical polymorphism, which is handled here as a type *scheme* $((o(o\pi)(o\pi))_{\omega}\iota\alpha)$, for an arbitrary type α. A quintessence of such a polymorphism: *think on (about)* — one can think of an object of any kind.

učit (teach)
naučit:1 / učit:2 / vyučovat:1 (teach:1, learn:5, instruct:1)
-frame: AG<person:1>$_{who\_nom}^{obl}$ VERB^{obl} PAT<person:1>$_{whom\_acc}^{opt}$ KNOW<subject:3>$_{what\_acc,to\_what\_dat}^{obl}$
-example: naučil dítě abecedu (he educated a children in the alphabet)
-example: učí studenty matematiku (he teaches mathematics for students)
-example: vyučuje dějepisu (he/she teaches history)
-use: prim

If understood as in "*What does (s)he live off? (S)he teaches.*" it is the case of *cry$_3$* (see above). *To teach* understood as in "*He teaches history, maths*", etc., the analysis depends on which type is given to the school subjects, disciplines. One possibility is to analyse them as properties of a set of propositions, $(o(o\pi))_{\tau\omega}$. Then *to teach* receives the type $((o(o\pi)(o\pi))_{\omega}\iota(o(o\pi))_{\tau\omega})$. If "*teaches alphabet*" is the case then we have to decide what we mean by *alphabet*. Here the point is to *teach (learn)* to associate symbols and sounds (phonemes?), so the respective type of alphabet is $(\alpha\beta)$, where α is the type of symbols, β the type of sounds. In the analysis of "*to educate somebody in something*" the verb takes an individual as its additional argument: $((o(o\pi)(o\pi))_{\omega}\iota\iota\alpha)$, where α is the type of the discipline.

In all the examples, we have displayed the relations between the two-level semantic roles used in the VerbaLex verb frames and the resulting logical analysis types of the verbal object as the main part of the clause's logical construction. The algorithmisation of this procedure uses a list of all roles used in the lexicon (there are about 200 roles used) with the corresponding (ambiguous) logical types of the constituents. In this way we can form a basic skeleton of the automatic translation of text to logical constructions.

5 Conclusions

The paper presented a first outline of comparison and integration of the two approaches, namely logical and linguistic, to the semantics of verbs in a natural language (English and Czech). We are aware that this work is still in a great progress and the results so presented rather fragmentary. Still, we are convinced that the research project we aim at is a relevant contribution to the semantics of natural language.

---

4 see (Horák 2002, p. 65) and (Tichý 1980).

We have shown that pursuing such a research is reasonable and comes up with a new viewpoint to the meaning of verbs. In this way we extend our knowledge in the important way. Actually, we are dealing with two deep levels of the meaning description and a question may be asked which one is deeper and better. Our answer is, do not contrast the two levels, and make use of both of them. In this way we believe to integrate them into one compact whole and perhaps obtain a unique data structure. The results of the presented research can be immediately applied in the area of knowledge representation and in the long-term Normal Translation System project that is being prepared.
We have not tackled the other deep descriptions, such as the method that exploits the tectogramatical level as it is presently applied in PDT (Hajič 2004). This, obviously, is a topic of another paper.

Acknowledgments

This work has been supported by the Academy of Sciences of the Czech Republic, project No. T100300414, by the Ministry of Education of CR within the Center of basic research LC536, by the program 'Information Society' of Czech Academy of Sciences, project No. 1ET101940420 "Logic and Artificial Intelligence for multi-agent systems", and by the Czech Science Foundation under the project 201/05/2781.

References

Cresswell, M.J. (1975): 'Hyperintensional Logic'. *Studia Logica* 34, pp.25-38.

Cresswell, M.J. (1985): *Structured meanings.* MIT Press, Cambridge, Mass.

Duží, M., Jespersen, B., Müller, J. (2005): Epistemic Closure and Inferable Knowledge. *The Logica Yearbook 2004*, ed. L. Běhounek, M. Bílková, Filosofia Prague, pp. 125-140.

Fellbaum, C., editor. 1998. *WordNet: An Electronic Lexical Database.* The MIT Press, Cambridge, Massachusetts, London, England.

Hajič, Jan (2004): *Complex Corpus Annotation: The Prague Dependency Treebank*, Jazykovedny Ustav L.Stura, Bratislava, Slovakia, 2004.

Hlaváčková, Dana - Horák, Aleš - Kadlec, Vladimír (2006). Exploitation of the VerbaLex Verb Valency Lexicon in the Syntactic Analysis of Czech. Lecture Notes in Artificial Intelligence, Proceedings of Text, Speech and Dialogue 2006, Berlin, Heidelberg : Springer, 2006.

Horák, Aleš (2002). *The Normal Translation Algorithm in Transparent Intensional Logic for Czech*, Ph.D. Dissertation, Masaryk University, Brno, 2002.

Kilgarriff, Adam - Rychlý, Pavel - Smrž, Pavel - Tugwell, David (2006). *The Sketch Engine.* In Proceedings of the Eleventh EURALEX International Congress. Lorient, France : Universite de Bretagne-Sud, pp. 105-116, 2004.

Karin Kipper, Anna Korhonen, Neville Ryant, and Martha Palmer (2006): Extensive Classifications of English verbs. *Proceedings of the 12th EURALEX International Congress.* Turin, Italy. September, 2006.

Materna, P. (1998): *Concepts and Objects.* Acta Philosophica Fennica, Vol. 63, Helsinki.

Materna, P. (2004): *Conceptual Systems.* Logos Verlag, Berlin.

Materna, P., Duží, M. (2005): Parmenides Principle. *Philosophia,* vol. 32 (1-4), pp. 155-180.

Tichý, P. (1988): *The Foundations of Frege's Logic*, Berlin, New York: DeGruyter.

Tichý, P. (1980): The Semantics of Episodic Verbs, *Theoretical Linguistics 7*, pp. 263-296, 1980.

Tichý, P. (2004): *Collected Papers in Logic and Philosophy*, V. Svoboda, B. Jespersen, C. Cheyne (eds.), Prague: Filosofia, Czech Academy of Sciences, and Dunedin: University of Otago Press

Žabokrtský, Z. (2005): *Valency Lexicon of Czech Verbs.* Ph.D. Thesis, Faculty of Mathematics and Physics, Charles University in Prague, 2005.

The Spanish Resource Grammar: pre-processing strategy and lexical acquisition

Montserrat Marimon, Núria Bel, Sergio Espeja, Natalia Seghezzi
IULA - Universitat Pompeu Fabra
Pl. de la Mercè, 10-12
08002-Barcelona
{montserrat.marimon,nuria.bel,sergio.espeja,natalia.seghezzi}@upf.edu

Abstract

This paper describes work on the development of an open-source HPSG grammar for Spanish implemented within the LKB system. Following a brief description of the main features of the grammar, we present our approach for pre-processing and ongoing research on automatic lexical acquisition.[1]

1 Introduction

In this paper we describe the development of the Spanish Resource Grammar (SRG), an open-source[2] medium-coverage grammar for Spanish. The grammar is grounded in the theoretical framework of HPSG (*Head-driven Phrase Structure Grammar*; Pollard and Sag, 1994) and uses *Minimal Recursion Semantics* (MRS) for the semantic representation (Copestake et al, 2006). The SRG is implemented within the *Linguistic Knowledge Building* (LKB) system (Copestake, 2002), based on the basic components of the grammar Matrix, an open–source starter-kit for the development of HPSG grammars developed as part of the LinGO consortium's multilingual grammar engineering (Bender et al., 2002).

The SRG is part of the DELPH-IN open-source repository of linguistic resources and tools for writing (the LKB system), testing (The [incr tsbd()]; Oepen and Carroll, 2000) and efficiently processing HPSG grammars (the PET system; Callmeier, 2000). Further linguistic resources that are available in the DELPH-IN repository include broad-coverage grammars for English, German and Japanese as well as smaller grammars for French, Korean, Modern Greek, Norwegian and Portuguese .[3]

The SRG has a full coverage of closed word classes and it contains about 50,000 lexical entries for open classes (roughtly: 6,600 verbs, 28,000 nouns, 11,200 adjectives and 4,000 adverbs). These lexical entries are organized into a type hierachy of about 400 leaf types (defined by a type hierarchy of around 5,500 types). The grammar also has 40 lexical rules to perform valence changing operations on lexical items and 84 structure rules to combine words and phrases into larger constituents and to compositionally build up the semantic representation.

We have been developing the SRG since January 2005. The range of linguistic phenomena that the grammar handles includes almost all types of subcategorization structures, valence alternations, subordinate clauses, raising and control, determination, null-subjects and impersonal constructions, compound tenses, modification, passive constructions, comparatives and superlatives, cliticization, relative and interrogative clauses and sentential adjuncts, among others.

Together with the linguistic resources (grammar and lexicon) we provide a set of controlled hand-constructed test suites. The construction of the test suites plays a major role in the development of the SRG, since test suites provide a fine-grained diag-

[1] This research was supported by the Spanish *Ministerio de Educación y Ciencia*: Project AAILE (HUM2004-05111-C02-01), *Ramon y Cajal*, *Juan de la Cierva* programmes and PTA-CTE/1370/2003 with *Fondo Social Europeo*.

[2] The Spanish Resource Grammar may be downloaded from: http://www.upf.edu/pdi/iula/montserrat.marimon/.

[3] See http://www.delph-in.net/.

Proceedings of the 5th Workshop on Important Unresolved Matters, pages 105–111,
Ann Arbor, June 2005. ©2005 Association for Computational Linguistics

nosis of grammar performance and they allow us to compare the SRG with other DELPH-IN grammars. In building the test suites we aimed at (a) testing specific phenomena in isolation or in controlled interaction, (b) providing test cases which show systematic and exhaustive variations over each phenomenon, including infrequent phenomena and variations, (c) avoiding irrelevant variation (i.e. different instances of the same lexical type), (d) avoiding ambiguity, and (e) including negative or ungrammatical data. We have about 500 test cases which are distributed by linguistic phenomena (we have 17 files). Each test case includes a short linguistic annotation describing the phenomenon and the number of expected results when more than one analysis cannot be avoided (e.g. testing optionality).

Test suites are not the only source of data we have used for testing the SRG. Hand-constructed sentences were complemented by real corpus cases from: (a) the Spanish questions from the Question Answering track at CLEF (CLEF-2003, CLEF-2004, CLEF-2005 and CLEF-2006), and (b) the *general* sub-corpus of the *Corpus Tècnic de l'IULA* (IULA's Technical Corpus; Cabré and Bach, 2004); this sub-corpus includes newspaper articles and it has been set up for contrastive studies. CLEF cases include short queries showing little interaction of phenomena and an average of 9.2 words; newspaper articles show a high level of syntactic complexity and interaction of phenomena, sentences are a bit longer, ranging up to 35 words. We are currently shifting to much more varied corpus data of the *Corpus Tècnic de l'IULA,* which includes specialized corpus of written text in the areas of computer science, environment, law, medicine and economics, collected from several sources, such as legal texts, textbooks, research reports, user manuals, ... In these texts sentence length may range up to 70 words.

The rest of the paper describes the pre-processing strategy we have adopted and on our on-going research on lexical acquisition.

2 Pre-processing in the SRG

Following previous experiments within the *Advanced Linguistic Engineering Platform* (ALEP) platform (Marimon, 2002), we have integrated a shallow processing tool, the FreeLing tool, as a pre-processing module of the grammar.

The FreeLing tool is an open-source[4] language analysis tool suite (Atserias et al., 2006) perfoming the following functionalities (though disambiguation, named entity classification and the last three functionalities have not been integrated):

- Text tokenization (including MWU and contraction splitting).
- Sentence splitting.
- Morpho-syntactic analysis and disambiguation.
- Named entity detection and classification.
- Date/number/currency/ratios/physical magnitude (speed, weight, temperature, density, etc.) recognition.
- Chart-based shallow parsing.
- WordNet-based sense annotation.
- Dependency parsing.

FreeLing also includes a guesser to deal with words which are not found in the lexicon by computing the probability of each possible PoS tag given the longest observed termination string for that word. Smoothing using probabilities of shorter termination strings is also performed. Details can be found in Brants (2000) and Samuelson (1993).

Our system integrates the FreeLing tool by means of the LKB *Simple PreProcessor Protocol* (SPPP; http://wiki.delph-in.net/moin/LkbSppp), which assumes that a preprocessor runs as an external process to the LKB system, and uses the LKB inflectional rule component to convert the PoS tags delivered by the FreeLing tool into partial descriptions of feature structures.

2.1 The integration of PoS tags

The integration of the morpho-syntactic analysis in the LKB system using the SPPP protocol means defining inflectional rules that propagate the morpho-syntactic information associated to full-forms, in the form of PoS tags, to the morpho-syntactic features of the lexical items. (1) shows the rule propagating the tag AQMS (adjective qualitative masculine singular) delivered by FreeLing. Note

[4] The FreeLing tool may be downloaded from http://www.garraf.epsevg.upc.es/freeling/.

that we use the tag as the rule identifier (i.e. the name of the inflectional rule in the LKB).

```
(1) aqms :=
    %suffix ()
    [SYNSEM.LOCAL[CAT adj,
                  AGR.PNG[PN 3sg,
                          GEN masc]]]
```

In Spanish, when the verb is in non-finite form, such as infinitive or gerund, or it is in the imperative, clitics[5] take the form of enclitics. That is, they are attached to the verb forming a unique word, e.g. *hacerlo* (*hacer+lo*; to do it), *gustarle* (*gustar+le*; to like to him). FreeLing does not split verbs and pronouns, but uses complex tags that append the tags of each word. Thus, the form *hacerlo* gets the tag *VMN+PP3MSA* (verb main infinitive + personal pronoun 3rd masculine singular accusative). In order to deal with these complex tags, the SRG includes a series of rules that build up the same type of linguistic structure as that one built up with the structure rules attaching affixes to the left of verbal heads. Since the application of these rules is based on the tag delivered by FreeLing, they are included in the set of inflectional rules and they are applied after the set of rules dealing with complement cliticization.

Apart from avoiding the implementation of inflectional rules for such a highly inflected language, the integration of the morpho-syntactic analysis tags will allow us to implement default lexical entries (i.e. lexical entry templates that are activated when the system cannot find a particular lexical entry to apply) on the basis of the category encoded to the lexical tag delivered by FreeLing, for virtually unlimited lexical coverage.[6]

2.2 The integration of multiword expressions

All multiword expressions in FreeLing are stored in a file. The format of the file is one multiword per line, having three fields each: form, lemma and PoS.[7] (2) shows two examples of multiword fixed expressions; i.e. the ones that are fully lexicalized and never show morpho-syntactic variation, *a través de* (through) and *a buenas horas* (finally).

```
(2) a_través_de a_través_de SPS00
    a_buenas_horas a_buenas_horas RG
```

The multiword form field may admit lemmas in angle brackets, meaning that any form with that lemma will be a valid component for the multiword. Tags are specified directly or as a reference to the tag of some of the multiword components. (3) builds a multiword with both singular and plural forms (*apartado(s) de correos* (P.O Box)). The tag of the multiform is that of its first form ($1) which starts with NC and takes the values for number depending on whether the form is singular or plural.

```
(3) <apartado>_de_correos apar-
tado_de _correos \$1:NC
```

Both fixed expressions and semi-fixed expressions are integrated by means of the inflectional rules that we have described in the previous subsection and they are treated in the grammar as word complex with a single part of speech.

2.3 The integration of messy details and named entities

FreeLing identifies, classifies and, when appropriate, normalizes special text constructions that may be considered peripheral to the lexicon, such as dates, numbers, currencies, ratios, physical magnitudes, etc. FreeLing also identifies and classifies named entities (i.e. proper names); however, we do not activate the classification functionality, since high performance of that functionality is only achieved with PoS disambiguated contexts.

To integrate these messy details and named entities into the grammar, we require special inflectional rules and lexical entry templates for each text construction tag delivered by FreeLing. Some of these tags are: W for dates, Z for numbers, Zm for currencies, ... In order to define one single entry for each text construct, we identify the tag and the STEM feature. (4) shows the lexical entry for dates.[8]

[5] Actually, Spanish weak pronouns are considered *pronominal affixes* rather than *pronominal clitics*.

[6] The use of underspecified default lexical entries in a highly lexicalized grammar, however, may increase ambiguity and overgeneration (Marimon and Bel, 2004).

[7] FreeLing only handles continuous multiword expressions.

[8] Each lexical entry in the SRG consists of a unique identifier, a lexical type, an orthography and a semantic relation.

```
(4)
date := date_le &
[STEM <"w">,
SYNSEM.LKEY.KEYREL.PRED time_n_rel]
```

The integration of these messy details allows us to release the analysis process from certain tasks that may be reliably dealt with by shallow external components.

3 Automatic Lexical Acquisition

We have investigated Machine Learning (ML) methods applied to the acquisition of the information contained in the lexicon of the SRG.

ML applied to lexical acquisition is a very active area of work linked to deep linguistic analysis due to the central role that lexical information has in lexicalized grammars and the costs of handcrafting them. Korhonen (2002), Carroll and Fang (2004), Baldwin (2005), Blunsom and Baldwin (2006), and Zhang and Kordoni (2006) are just a few examples of reported research work on deep lexical acquisition.

The most successful systems of lexical acquisition are based on the linguistic idea that the contexts where words occur are associated to particular lexical types. Although the methods are different, most of the systems work upon the syntactic information on words as collected from a corpus, and they develop different techniques to decide whether this information is relevant for type assignment or it is noise, especially when there are just a few examples. In the LKB grammatical framework, lexical types are defined as a combination of grammatical features. For our research, we have looked at these morpho-syntactically motivated features that can help in discriminating the different types that we will ultimately use to classify words. Thus, words are assigned a number of grammatical features, the ones that define the lexical types.

Table 1 and Table 2 show the syntactic features that we use to characterize 6 types of adjectives and 7 types of nouns in Spanish, respectively.[9] As can be observed, adjectives are cross-classified according to their syntactic position within the NP, i.e. (*preN*(ominal)) vs *postN*(ominal), the possibility of co-occurring in predicative constructions (*pred*) and being modified by degree adverbs (*G*), and their subcategorization frame (*pcomp*); whereas lexical types for nouns are basically defined on the basis of the *mass/countable* distinction and valence information. Thus, an adjective like *bonito* (nice), belonging to the type *a_qual_intr*, may be found both in pre-nominal and post-nominal position or in predicative constructions, it may also be modified by degree adverbs, this type of adjectives, however, does not take complements. Nouns belonging to the type *n_intr_count*, like *muchacha* (girl), are countable intransitive nouns.

TYPE/SF	preN	postN	pred	G	pcomp
a_adv_int	yes	no	no	no	no
a_adv_event	yes	yes	no	no	no
a_rel_nonpred	no	yes	no	no	no
a_rel_pred	no	yes	yes	no	no
a_qual_intr	yes	yes	yes	yes	no
a_qual_trans	yes	yes	yes	yes	yes

Table 1. Some adjectival types of the SRG

TYPE/SF	mass	count	intr	trans	pcomp
n_intr_mass	yes	no	yes	no	no
n_intr_count	no	yes	yes	no	no
n_intr_cnt-mss	yes	yes	yes	no	no
n_trans_mass	yes	no	no	yes	no
n_trans_count	no	yes	no	yes	no
n_ppde_pcomp_count	no	yes	no	yes	yes
n_ppde_pcomp_mss	yes	no	no	yes	yes

Table 2. Some nominal types of the SRG

We have investigated two methods to automatically acquire such linguistic information for Spanish nouns and adjectives: a Bayesian model and a decision tree. The aim of working with these two methods was to compare their performance taking into account that while the decision tree gets the information from previously annotated data, the Bayesian method learns it from the linguistic typology as defined by the grammar. These methods are described in the following subsections.

3.1 A Bayesian model for lexical acquisition

We have used a Bayesian model of inductive learning for assigning grammatical features to words occurring in a corpus. Given a hypothesis space (the linguistic features of words according to its lexical type) and one or more occurrences of the

[9] The SRG has 35 types for nouns and 44 types for adjectives.

word to classify, the learner evaluates all hypotheses for word features and values by computing their posterior probabilities, proportional to the product of prior probabilities and likelihood.

In order to obtain the likelihood, grammatical features are related to the expected contexts where their instances might appear. The linguistic typology provides likelihood information that is the learner's expectation about which contexts are likely to be observed given a particular hypothesis of a word type. This likelihood is used as a substitute of the computations made by observing directly the data, which is what a supervised machine learning method does. As said, our aim was to compare these two strategies.

The decision on a particular word is determined by averaging the predictions of all hypothesis weighted by their posterior probabilities. More technically, for each syntactic feature $\{sf_1, sf_2, ..., sf_n\}$ of the set SF (Syntactic Features) represented in the lexical typology, we define the goal of our system to be the assignment of a value, {*no*, *yes*}, that maximizes the result of a function $f: \sigma \rightarrow SF$, where σ is the collection of its occurrences ($\sigma = \{v_1, v_2, ..., v_z\}$), each being a *n*-dimensional vector. The decision on value assignment is achieved by considering every occurrence as a cumulative evidence in favour or against of having each syntactic feature. Thus, our function $Z'(SF, \sigma)$, shown in (5), will assess how much relevant information is got from all the vectors. A further function, shown in (8), will decide on the maximal value in order to assign $sf_{i,x}$.

$$(5)\quad Z'(sf_{i,x}, \sigma) = \sum_{j}^{z} P(sf_{i,x} \mid v_j)$$

To assess $P(sf_{i,x}|v_j)$, we use (6), which is the application of Bayes Rule for solving the estimation of the probability of a vector conditioned to a particular feature and value.

$$(6)\quad P(sf_{i,x} \mid v_j) = \frac{P(v_j \mid sf_{i,x}) P(sf_{i,x})}{\sum_k P(v_j \mid sf_{i,k}) P(sf_{i,k})}$$

For solving (6), the prior $P(sf_{i,x})$ is computed on the basis of a lexical typology too, assuming that what is more frequent in the typology will correspondingly be more frequent in the data. For computing the likelihood $P(v_j|sf_{i,x})$, as each vector is made of *m* components, that is, the linguistic cues $v_z = \{lc_1, lc_2, ..., lc_m\}$, we proceed as in (7) on the basis of $P(lc_l|sf_{i,x})$; i.e. the likelihood of finding the word in a particular context given a particular syntactic feature.

$$(7)\quad P(v_j \mid sf_{i,x}) = \prod_{l=1}^{m} P(lc_l \mid sf_{i,x})$$

Finally Z, as in (8), is the function that assigns the syntactic features to σ.[10]

$$(8)\quad Z = \begin{cases} Z'(sf_{i,x=yes} \mid \sigma) > Z'(sf_{i,x=no} \mid \sigma) \rightarrow yes \\ Z'(sf_{i,x=no} \mid \sigma) > Z'(sf_{i,x=yes} \mid \sigma) \rightarrow no \end{cases}$$

For computing the likelihood, we count on the conditional probabilities of the correlations between features as defined in the typology. We use these correlations to infer the expectation of observing the linguistic cues associated to particular syntactic features, and to make it to be conditional to a particular feature and value. However, linguistic cues and syntactic features are in two different dimensions; syntactic features are properties of lexical items, while linguistic cues show the characteristics of actual occurrences. As we assume that each syntactic feature must have at least one corresponding linguistic cue, we must tune the probability to acknowledge the factors that affect linguistic cues. For such a tuning, we have considered the following two issues: (i) to include in the assessments the known uncertainty of the linguistic cues that can be present in the occurrence or not; and (ii) to create a dummy variable to deal with the fact that, while syntactic features in the typology are independent from one another, evidences in text are not so.

We have also observed that the information that can be gathered by looking at all word occurrences as a complex unit have a conclusive value. Take for instance the case of prepositions. The observation of a given prepositions in different occurrences of the same word is a conclusive evidence for considering it a bound preposition. In order to take this into account, we have devised a function that acts as a dynamic weighting module. The function $app\_lc(sf_i, \sigma)$ returns the number of contexts where the cue is found. In the case that in a

[10] In the theoretical case of having the same probability for *yes* and for *no*, *Z* is undefined.

particular signature there is no context with such a *lc*, it returns '1'. Thus, *app_lc* is used to reinforce this conclusive evidence in (5), which is now (9).

(9)

$$Z'(sf_{i,x=yes},\sigma) = \left(\sum_{j}^{z} P(sf_{i,x=yes} \mid v_j)\right) * app\_lc(sf_i,\sigma)$$

$$Z'(sf_{i,x=no},\sigma) = \sum_{j}^{z} P(sf_{i,x=no} \mid v_j)$$

3.2 A Decision tree

Linguistic motivated features have also been evaluated using a C4.5 Decision Tree (DT) classifier (Quinlan, 1993) in the Weka implementation (Witten and Frank, 2005). These features correspond to the expected contexts for the different nominal and adjectival lexical types.

We have trained the DT with all the vectors of the word occurrences that we had in the different gold-standards, using their encoding for the supervised experiment in a 10-fold cross-validation testing (Bel et al. 2007).

3.3 Evaluation and Results

For the evaluation, we have applied both methods to the lexical acquisition of nouns and adjectives.

We have worked with a PoS tagged corpus of 1,091,314 words. Datasets of 496 adjectives and 289 nouns were selected among the ones that had occurrences in the corpus. Some manual selection had to be done in order to have all possible types represented but still it roughly corresponds to the distribution of features in the existing lexicon.

We evaluated by comparing with Gold-standard files; i.e. the manually encoded lexicon of the SRG. The usual accuracy measures as *type precision* (percentage of feature values correctly assigned to all values assigned) and *type recall* (percentage of correct feature values found in the dictionary) have been used. F1 is the usual score combining precision and recall.

Table 3 shows the results in terms of F1 score for the different methods and PoS for feature assignment. From these data, we concluded that the probabilistic information inferred from the lexical typology defined in our grammar is a good source of knowledge for lexical acquisition.

PoS	noun	adj
Z	0.88	0.87
DT	0.89	0.9

Table 3. F1 for different methods and PoS.

Table 4 shows more details of the results comparing between DT and Z for Spanish adjectives.

	SF = no		SF = yes	
	Z	DT	Z	DT
prep_a	0.98	0.97	0.72	0.44
prep_en	0.98	0.99	0.27	0
prep_con	0.99	0.99	0.60	0
prep_para	0.98	0.99	0.51	0.53
prep_de	0.88	0.97	0.34	0.42
postN	0	0	0.99	0.99
preN	0.75	0.83	0.44	0.80
Pred	0.50	0.41	0.59	0.82
G	0.85	0.80	0.75	0.72
Sent	0.97	0.97	0.55	0.44

Table 4. F1 for Spanish adjectival features.

Finally, Table 5 shows the results for 50 Spanish nouns with only one occurrence in the corpus. These results show that grammatical features can be used for lexical acquisition of low frequency lexical items, providing a good hypothesis for ensuring grammar robustness and adding no overgeneration to parsing results.

	DT			*Z*		
	prec.	*rec.*	*F*	*prec.*	*rec.*	*F*
MASS	0.50	0.16	0.25	0.66	0.25	0.36
COUNT	0.97	1.00	0.98	1.00	0.96	0.98
TRANS	0.75	0.46	0.57	0.68	0.73	0.71
INTRANS	0.85	0.95	0.89	0.89	0.76	0.82
PCOMP	0	0	0	0.14	0.20	0.16

Table 5. Results of 50 unseen nouns with a single occurrence.

4 Future Work

We have presented work on the development of an HPSG grammar for Spanish; in particular, we have described our approach for pre-processing and ongoing research on automatic lexical acquisition. Besides extending the coverage of the SRG and continuing research on lexical acquisition, the specific aims of our future work on the SRG are:

- Treebank development.

- To extend the shallow/deep architecture and integrate the structures generated by partial parsing, to provide robust techniques for infrequent structural constructions. The coverage of these linguistic structures by means of structure rules would increase both processing time and ambiguity.
- To use ML methods for disambiguation; i.e. for ranking possible parsings according to relevant linguistic features, thus enabling the setting of a threshold to select the n-best analyses.
- The development of error mining techniques (van Noord, 2004) to identify erroneous and incomplete information in the linguistic resources which cause the grammar to fail.

References

J. Atserias, B. Casas, E. Comelles, M. González, L. Padró and M. Padró. 2006. FreeLing 1.3: Syntactic and semantic services in an open-source NLP library. 5*th International Conference on Language Resources and Evaluation*. Genoa, Italy.

T. Baldwin. 2005. Bootstrapping Deep Lexical Resources: Resources for Courses, *ACL-SIGLEX 2005. Workshop on Deep Lexical Acquisitio*n. Ann Arbor, Michigan.

N. Bel, S. Espeja, M. Marimon. 2007. Automatic Acquisition of Grammatical Types for Nouns. *Human Language Technologies: The Annual Conference of the North American Chapter of the Association for Computational Linguistics*. Rochester, NY, USA,

E.M. Bender, D. Flickinger and S. Oepen. 2002. The grammar Matrix. An open-source starter-kit for the rapid development of cress-linguistically consistent broad-coverage precision grammar. *Workshop on Grammar Engineering and Evaluation, 19th International Conference on Computational Linguistics*. Taipei, Taiwan.

P. Blunsom and T. Baldwin. 2006. Multilingual Deep Lexical Acquisition for HPSGs via Supertagging. *Conference on Empirical Methods in Natural Language Processing*. Sydney, Australia.

T. Brants. 2000. TnT: A statistical part-of-speech tagger. *6th Conference on Applied Natural Language Processing*. Seattle, USA.

T. Cabré and C. Bach, 2004. El corpus tècnic de l'IULA: corpus textual especializado plurilingüe. *Panacea, V*. 16, pages 173-176.

U. Callmeier. 2000. Pet – a platform for experimentation with efficient HPSG processing. *Journal of Natural Language Engineering 6(1): Special Issue on Efficient Processing with HPSG: Methods, System, Evaluation*, pages 99-108.

A. Copestake, D. Flickinger, C. Pollard and I.A. Sag. 2006. Minimal Recursion Semantics: An Introduction. *Research on Language and Computation* 3.4:281-332.

A. Copestake. 2002. I*mplementing Typed Features Structure Grammars*. CSLI Publications.

A. Korhonen. 2002. 'Subcategorization acquisition'. As Technical Report UCAM-CL-TR-530, University of Cambridge, UK.

M. Marimon. 2002. Integrating Shallow Linguistic Processing into a Unification-based Spanish Grammar. *9th International Conference on Computational Linguistics*. Taipei, Taiwan.

M. Marimon and N. Bel. 2004. Lexical Entry Templates for Robust Deep Parsing. *4th International Conference on Language Resources and Evaluation*. Lisbon, Portugal.

S. Oepen and J. Carroll. 2000. Performance Profiling for Parser Engineering. *Journal of Natural Language Engineering 6(1): Special Issue on Efficient Processing with HPSG: Methods, System, Evaluation*, pages 81-97.

C.J. Pollard and I.A. Sag. 1994. *Head-driven Phrase Structure Grammar*. The University of Chicago Press, Chicago.

R.J. Quinlan 1993. C4.5: Programs for Machine Learning. Series in Machine Learning. Morgan Kaufman, San Mateo, CA.

C. Samuelson. 1993. Morphological tagging based entirely on Bayesian inference. *9th Nordic Conference on Computational Linguistics*. Stockholm, Sweden.

I.H. Witten and E. Frank. 2005. *Data Mining: Practical machine learning tools and techniques*. Morgan Kaufmann, San Francisco.

G. van Noord. 2004. Error mining for wide-coverage grammar engineering. *42th Annual Meeting of the ACL*. Barcelona, Spain.

Y. Zhang and V. Kordoni. 2006. Automated deep lexical acquisition for robust open text processing. 5*th International Conference on Language Resources and Evaluation*. Genoa, Italy.

Extracting a verb lexicon for deep parsing from FrameNet

Mark McConville and **Myroslava O. Dzikovska**
School of Informatics
University of Edinburgh
2 Buccleuch Place, Edinburgh EH8 9LW, Scotland
{Mark.McConville,M.Dzikovska}@ed.ac.uk

Abstract

We examine the feasibility of harvesting a wide-coverage lexicon of English verbs from the FrameNet semantically annotated corpus, intended for use in a practical natural language understanding (NLU) system. We identify a range of constructions for which current annotation practice leads to problems in deriving appropriate lexical entries, for example imperatives, passives and control, and discuss potential solutions.

1 Introduction

Although the lexicon is the primary source of information in lexicalised formalisms such as HPSG or CCG, constructing one manually is a highly labour-intensive task. Syntactic lexicons *have* been derived from other resources — the LinGO ERG lexicon (Copestake and Flickinger, 2000) contains entries extracted from ComLex (Grishman et al., 1994), and Hockenmaier and Steedman (2002) acquire a CCG lexicon from the Penn Treebank. However, one thing these resources lack is information on how the syntactic subcategorisation frames correspond to meaning.

The output representation of many "deep" wide coverage parsers is therefore limited with respect to argument structure — sense distinctions are strictly determined by syntactic generalisations, and are not always consistent. For example, in the logical form produced by the LinGO ERG grammar, the verb *end* can have one of two senses depending on its subcategorisation frame: `end_v_1_rel` or `end_v_cause_rel`, corresponding to *the celebrations ended* and *the storm ended the celebrations* respectively. Yet a very similar verb, *stop*, has a single sense, `stop_v_1_rel`, for both *the celebrations stopped* and *the storm stopped the celebrations*. There is no direct connection between these different verbs in the ERG lexicon, even though they are intuitively related and are listed as belonging to the same or related word classes in semantic lexicons/ontologies such as VerbNet (Kipper et al., 2000) and FrameNet (Baker et al., 1998).

If the output of a deep parser is to be used with a knowledge representation and reasoning component, for example in a dialogue system, then we need a more consistent set of word senses, linked by specified semantic relations. In this paper, we investigate how straightforward it is to harvest a computational lexicon containing this kind of information from FrameNet, a semantically annotated corpus of English. In addition, we consider how the FrameNet annotation system could be made more transparent for lexical harvesting.

Section 2 introduces the FrameNet corpus, and section 3 discusses the lexical information required by frame-based NLU systems, with particular emphasis on linking syntactic and semantic structure. Section 4 presents the algorithm which converts the FrameNet corpus into a frame-based lexicon, and evaluates the kinds of entries harvested in this way. We then discuss a number of sets of entries which are inappropriate for inclusion in a frame-based lexicon: (a) 'subjectless' entries; (b) entries derived from passive verbs; (c) entries subcategorising for modifiers; and (d) entries involving 'control' verbs.

Proceedings of the 5th Workshop on Important Unresolved Matters, pages 112–119,
Ann Arbor, June 2005.

2 FrameNet

FrameNet[1] is a corpus of English sentences annotated with both syntactic and semantic information. Underlying the corpus is an ontology of 795 'frames' (or semantic *types*), each of which is associated with a set of 'frame elements' (or semantic *roles*). To take a simple example, the `Apply_heat` frame describes a situation involving frame elements such as a `COOK`, some `FOOD`, and a `HEATING_INSTRUMENT`. Each frame is, in addition, associated with a set of 'lexical units' which are understood as *evoking* it. For example, the `Apply_heat` frame is evoked by such verbs as *bake*, *blanch*, *boil*, *broil*, *brown*, *simmer*, *steam*, etc.

The FrameNet corpus proper consists of 139,439 sentences (mainly drawn from the British National Corpus), each of which has been hand-annotated with respect to a particular target word in the sentence. Take the following example: *Matilde fried the catfish in a heavy iron skillet*. The process of annotating this sentence runs as follows: (a) identify a target word for the annotation, for example the main verb *fried*; (b) identify the semantic frame which is evoked by the target word in this particular sentence – in this case the relevant frame is `Apply_heat`; (c) identify the sentential constituents which realise each frame element associated with the frame, i.e.:

[`COOK` *Matilde*] [`Apply_heat` ***fried***] [`FOOD` *the catfish*] [`HEATING_INSTR` *in a heavy iron skillet*]

Finally, some basic syntactic information about the target word and the constituents realising the various frame elements is also added: (a) the part-of-speech of the target word (e.g. `V`, `N`, `A`, `PREP`); (b) the syntactic *category* of each constituent realising a frame element (e.g. `NP`, `PP`, `VPto`, `Sfin`); and (c) the syntactic *role*, with respect to the target word, of each constituent realising a frame element (e.g. `Ext`, `Obj`, `Dep`). Thus, each sentence in the corpus can be seen to be annotated on at least three independent 'layers', as exemplified in Figure 1.

3 Frame-based NLU

The core of any frame-based NLU system is a parser which produces domain-independent semantic representations like the following, for the sentence *John billed the champagne to my account*:

$$\begin{bmatrix} \textit{commerce-pay} & \\ \text{AGENT} & \textit{John} \\ \text{THEME} & \textit{champagne} \\ \text{SOURCE} & \begin{bmatrix} \textit{account} & \\ \text{OWNER} & \textit{me} \end{bmatrix} \end{bmatrix}$$

Deep parsers/grammars such as the ERG, OpenCCG (White, 2006) and TRIPS (Dzikovska, 2004) produce more sophisticated representations with scoping and referential information, but still contain a frame-based representation as their core. The lexical entries necessary for constructing such representations specify information about orthography, part-of-speech, semantic type and subcategorisation properties, including a mapping between a syntactic subcategorisation frame and the semantic frame.

An example of a TRIPS lexical entry is presented in Figure 2, representing the entry for the verb *bill* as used in the sentence discussed above. Note that for each subcategorised argument the syntactic role, syntactic category, and semantic role are specified. Much the same kind of information is included in ERG and OpenCCG lexical entries.

When constructing a computational lexicon, there are a number of issues to take into account, several of which are pertinent to the following discussion. Firstly, computational lexicons typically list only the 'canonical' subcategorisation frames, corresponding to a declarative sentence whose main verb is in the active voice, as in Figure 1. Other variations, such as passive forms, imperatives and dative alternations are generated automatically, for example by lexical rules. Secondly, parsers that build semantic representations typically make a distinction between 'complements' and 'modifiers'. Complements are those dependents whose meaning is completely determined by the verb, for example the PP *on him* in the sentence *Mary relied on him*, and are thus listed in lexical entries. Modifiers, on the other hand, are generally not specified in verb entries — although they may be associated with the underlying verb frame, their meaning is determined independently, usually by the preposition, such as the time adverbial *next week* in *I will see him next week*.

Finally, for deep parsers, knowledge about which argument of a matrix verb 'controls' the implicit

[1]The version of FrameNet discussed in this paper is FrameNet II release 1.3 from 22 August 2006.

	Matilde	*fried*	*the catfish*	*in a heavy iron skillet*
target		`Apply_heat`		
frame element	`COOK`		`FOOD`	`HEATING_INSTR`
syntactic category	`NP`	`V`	`NP`	`PP`
syntactic role	`Ext`		`Obj`	`Dep`

Figure 1: A FrameNet annotated sentence

$$\begin{bmatrix} \text{ORTH} & \langle \textit{bill} \rangle \\ \text{SYNCAT} & \textit{v} \\ \text{SEMTYPE} & \begin{bmatrix} \textit{commerce-pay} & \\ \text{ASPECT} & \textit{bounded} \\ \text{TIME-SPAN} & \textit{atomic} \end{bmatrix} \\ \text{ARGS} & \left\langle \begin{bmatrix} \text{SYNROLE} & \textit{subj} \\ \text{SYNCAT} & \textit{np} \\ \text{SEMROLE} & \textit{agent} \end{bmatrix}, \begin{bmatrix} \text{SYNROLE} & \textit{obj} \\ \text{SYNCAT} & \textit{np} \\ \text{SEMROLE} & \textit{theme} \end{bmatrix}, \begin{bmatrix} \text{SYNROLE} & \textit{comp} \\ \text{SYNCAT} & \begin{bmatrix} \textit{pp} & \\ \text{PTYPE} & \textit{to} \end{bmatrix} \\ \text{SEMROLE} & \textit{source} \end{bmatrix} \right\rangle \end{bmatrix}$$

Figure 2: A TRIPS lexical entry

subject of an embedded complement verb phrase is necessary in order to to build the correct semantic form. In a unification parser such as TRIPS, control is usually represented by a relation of token-identity (i.e. feature structure reentrancy) between the subject or object of a control verb and the subject of a verbal complement.

4 Harvesting a computational lexicon from FrameNet

In order to harvest a computational lexicon from the FrameNet corpus, we took each of the 60,309 annotated sentences whose target word is a verb and derived a lexical entry directly from the annotated information. For example, from the sentence in Figure 1, the lexical entry in Figure 3 is derived.[2]

In order to remove duplicate entries, we made two assumptions: (a) the value of the ARGS feature is a *set* of arguments, rather than, say, a list or multiset; and (b) two arguments are identical just in case they specify the same syntactic role and semantic role. These assumptions prevent a range of inappropriate entries from being created, for example entries derived from sentences involving a 'split' argument, both parts of which are annotated independently in FrameNet, e.g. [`Ext` *Serious concern*] ***arose*** [`Ext` *about his motives*]. A second group of inappropriate entries which are thus avoided are those deriving from relative clause constructions, where the relative pronoun and its antecedent are also annotated separately:

[`Ext Perp` *The two boys*] [`Ext Perp` *who*] ***abducted*** [`Obj Victim` *James Bulger*] *are likely to have been his murderers*

Finally, assuming that the arguments constitute a set means that entries derived from sentences involving both canonical[3] and non-canonical word order are treated as equivalent. The kinds of construction implicated here include 'quotative inversion' (e.g. *"Or Electric Ladyland," added Bob*), and leftwards extraction of objects and dependents, for example:

Are there [`Obj` *any places*] [`Ext` *you*] *want to* ***praise*** [`Dep` *for their special facilities*]?

In this paper we are mainly interested in extracting the possible syntax-semantics mappings from FrameNet, rather than the precise details of their relative ordering. Since dependents in the harvested

[2]Our original plan was to use the automatically generated 'lexical entry' files included with the most recent FrameNet release as a basis for deep parsing. However, these entries contain so many inappropriate subcategorisation frames, of the types discussed in this paper, that we decided to start from scratch with the corpus annotations.

[3]The canonical word order in English involves a pre-verbal subject, with all other dependents following the verb.

```
[ORTH      ⟨fry⟩
 SYNCAT    V
 SEMTYPE   Apply_heat
 ARGS      ⟨ [SYNROLE Ext      [SYNROLE Obj      [SYNROLE Dep
              SYNCAT  NP   ,    SYNCAT  NP   ,    SYNCAT  PP
              SEMROLE Cook]     SEMROLE Food]     SEMROLE Heating_Instr] ⟩ ]
```

Figure 3: The lexical entry derived from Figure 1

lexicon are fully specified for semantic role, syntactic category *and* syntactic role, post-verbal constituent ordering can-be regulated extra-lexically by means of precedence rules. For example, for the TRIPS and LFG formalisms, there is a straightforward correspondence between their native syntactic role specifications and the FrameNet syntactic roles.

After duplicate entries were removed from the resulting lexicon, we were left with 26,022 distinct entries. The harvested lexicon incorporated 2,002 distinct orthographic forms, 358 distinct frames, and 2,661 distinct orthography-frame pairs, giving a functionality ratio (average number of lexical entries per orthography-type pair) of 9.8.

Next, we evaluated a random sample of the derived lexical entries by hand. The aim here was to identify general classes of the harvested verb entries which are not appropriate for inclusion in a frame-based verb lexicon, and which would need to be identified and fixed in some way. The main groups identified were: (a) entries with no `Ext` argument (section 4.1); (b) entries derived from verbs in the passive voice (section 4.2); (c) entries which subcategorise for modifiers (section 4.3); and (d) entries for control verbs (section 4.4).

4.1 Subjectless entries

The harvested lexicon contains 2,201 entries (i.e. 9% of the total) which were derived from sentences which do *not* contain an argument labelled with the `Ext` syntactic role, in contravention of the generally accepted constraint on English verbs that they always have a subject.

Three main groups of sentences are implicated here: (a) those featuring *imperative* uses of the target verb, e.g. *Always* ***moisturise*** *exposed skin with an effective emollient like E45*; (b) those featuring other *non-finite* forms of the target verb whose understood subject is not controlled by (or even coreferential with) some other constituent in the sentence, e.g. *Being* ***accused*** *of not having a sense of humour is a terrible insult*; and (c) those involving a non-referential subject *it*, for example *It is* ***raining*** *heavily* or *It is to be* ***regretted*** *that the owner should have cut down the trees*. In FrameNet annotations, non-referential subjects are not identified on the syntactic role annotation layer, and this makes it more difficult to harvest appropriate lexical entries for these verbs from the corpus.

These entries are easy to locate in the harvested lexicon, but more difficult to repair. Typically one would want to discard the entries generated from (a) and (b) as they will be derived automatically in the grammar, but keep the entries generated from (c) while adding a non-referential *it* as a subject.

Although the FrameNet policy is to annotate the (a) and (b) sentences as having a 'non-overt' realisation of the relevant frame element, this is confined to the frame element annotation layer itself, with the syntactic role and syntactic category layers containing *no* clues whatsoever about understood subjects. One rather roundabout way of differentiating between these cases would involve attempting to identify the syntactic category and semantic role of the missing `Ext` argument by looking at other entries with the same orthography and semantic type. However, this whole problem could be avoided if understood and expletive subjects were identified on the *syntactic* layers in FrameNet annotations.

4.2 'Passive' entries

Many entries in the harvested lexicon were derived from sentences where the target verb is used in the passive voice, for example:

[`Ext NP Victim` *The men*] *had allegedly been* ***abducted*** [`Dep PP Perp` *by Mrs Mandela's body-*

guards] [Dep PP Time *in 1988*]

As discussed above, computational lexicons do not usually list the kinds of lexical entry derived directly from such sentences. Thus, it is necessary to identify and correct or remove them.

In FrameNet annotated sentences, the voice of target verbs is not marked explicitly.[4] We applied the following simple diagnostic to identify 'passive' entries: (a) there is an Ext argument realising frame element e; and (b) there is some other entry with the same orthographic form and semantic frame, which has an Obj argument realising frame element e.

Initially we applied this diagnostic to the entries in the harvested lexicon together with a part-of-speech tag filter. The current FrameNet release includes standard POS-tag information for each word in each annotated sentence. We considered only those lexical entries derived from sentences whose target verb is tagged as a 'past-participle' form (i.e. VVN). This technique identified 4,160 entries in the harvested lexicon (i.e. 16% of the total) as being 'passive'. A random sample of 10% of these was examined and *no* false positives were found.

The diagnostic test was then repeated on the remaining lexical entries, this time *without* the POS-tag filter. This was deemed necessary in order to pick up false negatives caused by the POS-tagger having assigned the wrong tag to a passive target verb (generally the past tense form tag VVD). This test identified a further 1007 entries as 'passive' (4% of the total entries). As well as mis-tagged instances of normal passives, this test picked up a further three classes of entry derived from target verbs appearing in passive-related constructions. The first of these involves cases where the target verb is in the complement of a 'raising adjective' (e.g. *tough, difficult, easy, impossible*), for example:

[Ext NP Goal *Both planning and control*] *are difficult to* ***achieve*** [Dep PP Circs *in this form of production*]

The current FrameNet annotation guidelines (Ruppenhofer et al., 2006) state that the extracted object in these cases *should* be tagged as Obj. However, in practice, the majority of these instances appear to have been tagged as Ext.

[4]Whilst there are dedicated subcorpora containing *only* passive targets, it is not the case that *all* passive targets are in these.

The second group of passive-related entries involve verbs in the *need -ing* construction[5], e.g.:

[Ext NP Content *Many private problems*] *need* ***airing*** [Dep PP Medium *in the family*]

The third group involved sentences where the target verb is used in the 'middle' construction:

[Ext Experiencer *You*] ***frighten*** [Dep Manner *easily*]

Again, linguistically-motivated grammars generally treat these three constructions in the rule component rather than the lexicon. Thus, the lexical entries derived from these sentences need to be located and repaired, perhaps by comparison with other entries.

Of the 1007 lexical entries identified by the second, weaker form of the passive test, 224 (i.e. 22%) turn out to be false positives. The vast majority of these involve verbs implicated in the causative-inchoative alternation (e.g. *John's back arched* vs. *John arched his back*). The official FrameNet policy is to distinguish between frames encoding a change-of-state and those encoding the causation of such a change, for example Amalgamation versus Cause_to_amalgamate, Motion versus Cause_motion etc. In each case, the two frames are linked by the Causative_of frame relation. Most of the false positives are the result of a failure to consistently apply this principle in annotation practice, for example where no causative counterpart has been defined for a particular inchoative frame, or where an inchoative target has been assigned to a causative frame, or a causative target to an inchoative frame. For example, 94 of the false positives are accounted for simply by the lack of a causative counterpart for the Body_movement frame, meaning that both inchoative and causative uses of verbs like *arch, flutter* and *wiggle* have all been assigned to the same frame.

For reasons of data sparsity, it is expected that the approach to identifying passive uses of target verbs discussed here will result in false negatives, since it relies on there being at least one corresponding active use in the corpus. We checked a random sample of 400 of the remaining entries in the harvested lexicon and found nine false negatives, suggesting that

[5]Alternatively *merit -ing, bear -ing* etc.

the test successfully identifies 91% of those lexical entries derived from passive uses of target verbs.

4.3 Modifiers

General linguistic theory makes a distinction between two kinds of non-subject dependent of a verb, depending on the notional 'closeness' of the semantic relation — complements vs. modifiers. Take for example the following sentence:

[`Ext Performer` *She*]*'s* [`Dep Time` *currently*] ***starring*** [`Dep Performance` *in The Cemetery Club*] [`Dep Place` *at the Wyvern Theatre*]

Of the three constituents annotated here as `Dep`, only one is an complement (the `Performance`); the `Time` and `Place` dependents are modifiers. Frame-based NLU systems do not generally list modifiers in the argument structure of a verb's lexical entry. Thus, we need to find a means of identifying those dependents in the harvested lexicon which are actually modifiers.

The FrameNet ontology provides some information to help differentiate complements and modifiers. A frame element can be marked as `Core`, signifying that it "instantiates a conceptually necessary component of a frame, while making the frame unique and different from other frames". The annotation guidelines state that the distinction between `Core` and non-`Core` frame elements covers "the semantic spirit" of the distinction between complements and modifiers. Thus, for example, obligatory dependents are always `Core`, as are: (a) those which, when omitted, receive a definite interpretation (e.g. the `Goal` in *John arrived*); and (b) those whose semantics cannot be predicted from their form. In the `Performers_and_roles` frame used in the example above, the `Performer` and `Performance` frame elements are marked as `Core`, whilst `Time` and `Place` are not.

However, it is not clear that the notion of ontological 'coreness' used in FrameNet corresponds well with the intuitive distinction between syntactic complements and modifiers. This is exemplified by the existence of numerous constituents in the corpus which have been marked as direct objects, despite invoking non-*Core* frame elements, for example:

[`Agent` *I*] **ripped** [`Subregion` *the top*] [`Patient` *from my packet of cigarettes*]

The relevant frame here is `Damaging`, where the `Subregion` frame element is marked as non-`Core`, based on examples like *John ripped his trousers* [*below the knee*]. Thus in this case, the decision to retain all senses of the verb *rip* within the same frame has led to a situation where semantic and syntactic coreness have become dislocated. Thus, although the `Core` vs. non-`Core` property on frame elements *does* yield a certain amount of information about which arguments are complements and which are modifiers, greater care needs to be taken when assigning different subcategorisation alternants to the same frame. For example, it would have been more convenient to have assigned the verb *rip* in the above example to the `Removing` frame, where the direct object would then be assigned the `Core` frame element `Theme`.

In the example discussed above, FrameNet does provide syntactic role information (`Obj`) allowing us to infer that a non-`Core` role is a complement rather than a modifier. Where the syntactic role is simply marked as `Dep` however, it is not possible to make the decision without recourse to other lexical resources (e.g. ComLex). Since different parsers may utilise different criteria for distinguishing complements from modifiers, it might be better to postpone this task to the syntactic alignment module.

4.4 Control verbs

Unification-based parsers generally handle the distinction between subject (*John promised Mary to go*) and object (*John persuaded Mary to go*) control verbs in the lexicon, using coindexation of the subject/object of the control verb and the understood subject of the embedded verb. The parser can use this lexical information to assign the correct referent to the understood subject in a sentence like *John asked Mary to go*:

$$\begin{bmatrix} \textit{command} & \\ \text{AGENT} & \textit{John} \\ \text{THEME} & \textit{Mary}\boxed{1} \\ \text{EFFECT} & \begin{bmatrix} \textit{motion} \\ \text{THEME}\ \boxed{1} \end{bmatrix} \end{bmatrix}$$

Control verbs are annotated in FrameNet in the following manner:

Perhaps [`Ext NP Speaker` *we*] *can* **persuade** [`Obj NP Addressee` *Tammuz*] [`Dep VPto`

`Content` *to entertain him*]

The lexical entries for transitive control verbs that we can harvest directly from these annotations thus fail to identify whether it is the subject or the direct object which controls the understood subject of the embedded verb.

We attempted to automatically distinguish subject from object control in FrameNet by looking for the annotated sentences that contain independently annotated argument structures for both the control verb and embedded verb. For example, let's assume the following annotation also exists in the corpus:

Perhaps we can persuade [`Ext NP Agent` *Tammuz*] *to* ***entertain*** [`Obj NP Experiencer` *him*]

We can then use the fact that it is the *object* of the control verb which is coextensive with the `Ext` of the embedded verb to successfully identify *persuade* as an object-control verb.

The problem with this approach is data sparsity. The harvested lexicon contains 135 distinct verbs which subcategorise for both a direct object and a controlled VP complement. In a random sample of ten of these *none* of the annotated sentences had been annotated independently from the perspective of the governed verb. As the proportion of the FrameNet corpus which involves annotation of running text, rather than cherry-picked example sentences, increases, we would expect this to improve.[6]

5 Implementation and discussion

The revised version of the harvested lexicon contains 9,019 entries for 2,626 orthography-frame pairs, yielding a functionality ratio of 3.4.

This lexicon still requires a certain amount of cleaning up. For example, the verb *accompany* is assigned to a number of distinct lexical entries depending on the semantic role associated with the PP complement (i.e. `Goal`, `Path` or `Source`). Cases like this, where the role name is determined by the particular choice of preposition, could be handled outside the lexicon. Alternatively, it may be possible to use the 'core set' feature of the FrameNet ontology (which groups together roles that are judged to be equivalent in some sense) to locate this kind of redundancy. Other problems involve sentences where a possessive determiner has been annotated as the subject of a verb, e.g. *It was [his] intention to* ***aid*** *Larsen*, resulting in numerous spurious entries.

The harvested lexical entries are encoded according to a framework-independent XML schema, which we developed with the aim of deriving lexicons for use with a diverse range of parsers. At the moment, several additional steps are required to convert the entries we extracted into a format suitable for a particular parser.

Firstly, the syntactic categories used by FrameNet and the target lexicon have to be reconciled. While basic constituent types such as noun and adjective phrases do not change between the theories, small differences may still exist. For example, the TRIPS parser classifies all *wh*-clauses such as *what he did* in *I saw what he did* and *What he did was good* as noun phrases, the LinGO ERG grammar interprets them as either noun phrases or clauses depending on the context, and FrameNet annotation classifies all of them as clauses. The alignment, however, should be relative straightforward as there is, in general, good agreement on the basic syntactic categories.[7]

Secondly, the information relevant to constituent ordering may need to be derived, as discussed in Section 4. Finally, the more abstract features such as control have to be converted into feature structures appropriate for the unification parsers. Our schema incorporates the possibility for embedded category structure, as in the treatment of control verbs in CCG and HPSG where the verbal complement is an 'unsaturated' category. We plan to use our schema as a platform for deriving richer lexical representations from the 'flatter' entries harvested directly from FrameNet.

As part of our future work, we expect to create generic algorithms that help automate these steps. In particular, we plan to include a domain-independent set of constituent categories and syntactic role labels, and add algorithms that convert between a linear ordering and a set of functional labels, for example (Crabbé et al., 2006). We also plan to develop algorithms to import information from other seman-

[6]An alternative approach would be to consult an external lexical resource, e.g. the LinGO ERG lexicon, which has good coverage of control verbs.

[7]http://www.cl.cam.ac.uk/users/alk23/classes/Classes2.txt contains a list of mappings between three different deep parsers and ComLex subcategorisation frames

tic lexicons such as VerbNet into the same schema.

Currently, we have implemented an algorithm for converting the harvested entries into the TRIPS lexicon format, resulting in a 6133 entry verb lexicon involving 2654 distinct orthography-type pairs. This lexicon has been successfully used with the TRIPS parser, but additional work remains to be done before the conversion process is complete. For example, we need a more sophisticated approach to resolving the complement-modifier distinction, along with a means of integrating the FrameNet semantic types with the TRIPS ontology so the parser can use selectional restrictions to disambiguate.

The discussion in this paper has been mainly focused on extracting entries for a deep lexicons using frame-based NLU, but similar issues have been faced also by the developers of shallow semantic parsers from semantically annotated corpora. For example, Gildea and Jurafsky (2002) found that identifying passives was important in training a semantic role classifier from FrameNet, using a parser trained on the Penn Treebank along with a set of templates to distinguish passive constructions from active ones. Similarly, Chen and Rambow (2003) argue that the kind of deep linguistic features we harvest from FrameNet is beneficial for the successful assignment of PropBank roles to constituents, in this case using TAGs generated from PropBank to generate the relevant features. From this perspective, our harvested lexicon can be seen as providing a 'cleaned-up', filtered version of FrameNet for training semantic interpreters. It may also be utilised to provide information for a separate lexical interpretation and disambiguation module to be built on top of a syntactic parser.

6 Conclusion

We have developed both a procedure and a framework-independent representation schema for harvesting lexical information for deep NLP systems from the FrameNet semantically annotated corpus. In examining the feasibility of this approach to increasing lexical coverage, we have identified a number of constructions for which current FrameNet annotation practice leads to problems in deriving appropriate lexical entries, for example imperatives, passives and control.

7 Acknowledgements

The work reported here was supported by grants N000140510043 and N000140510048 from the Office of Naval Research.

References

C. F. Baker, C. Fillmore, and J. B. Lowe. 1998. The Berkeley FrameNet Project. In *Proceedings of COLING-ACL'98, Montreal*, pages 86–90.

J. Chen and O. Rambow. 2003. Use of deep linguistic features for the recognition and labeling of semantic arguments. In *Proceedings of EMNLP'03, Sapporo, Japan.*

A. Copestake and D. Flickinger. 2000. An open-source grammar development environment and broad-coverage English grammar using HPSG. In *Proceedings of LREC'00, Athens, Greece*, pages 591–600.

B. Crabbé, M. O. Dzikovska, W. de Beaumont, and M. Swift. 2006. Increasing the coverage of a domain independent dialogue lexicon with VerbNet. In *Proceedings of ScaNaLU'06*, New York City.

M. O. Dzikovska. 2004. *A Practical Semantic Representation for Natural Language Parsing*. Ph.D. thesis, University of Rochester, Rochester NY.

D. Gildea and D. Jurafsky. 2002. Automatic labeling of semantic roles. *Computational Linguistics*, 28(3):245–288.

R. Grishman, C. MacLeod, and A. Meyers. 1994. Comlex syntax: Building a computational lexicon. In *Proceedings of COLING'94, Kyoto, Japan*, pages 268–272.

J. Hockenmaier and M. Steedman. 2002. Acquiring Compact Lexicalized Grammars from a Cleaner Treebank. In *Proceedings of LREC'02, Las Palmas, Spain.*

K. Kipper, H. T. Dang, and M. Palmer. 2000. Class-based construction of a verb lexicon. In *Proceedings of AAAI'00, Austin TX.*

J. Ruppenhofer, M. Ellsworth, M. R. L. Petruck, C. R. Johnson, and J. Scheffczyk, 2006. *FrameNet II: Extended Theory and Practice*. The Berkeley FrameNet Project, August.

M. White. 2006. Efficient realization of coordinate structures in Combinatory Categorial Grammar. *Research on Language and Computation*, 4(1):39–75.

Fips, a "Deep" Linguistic Multilingual Parser

Eric Wehrli
LATL-Dept. of Linguistics
University of Geneva
Eric.Wehrli@lettres.unige.ch

Abstract

The development of robust "deep" linguistic parsers is known to be a difficult task. Few such systems can claim to satisfy the needs of large-scale NLP applications in terms of robustness, efficiency, granularity or precision. Adapting such systems to more than one language makes the task even more challenging.

This paper describes some of the properties of Fips, a multilingual parsing system that has been for a number of years (and still is) under development at LATL. Based on Chomsky's generative grammar for its grammatical aspects, and on object-oriented (OO) sofware engineering techniques for its implementation, Fips is designed to efficiently parse the four Swiss "national" languages (German, French, Italian and English) to which we also added Spanish and (more recently) Greek.

1 Introduction

This papers describes the Fips project, which aims at developing a robust, multilingual "deep" linguistic parsing system efficient enough for a wide-range of NLP applications. The system is currently available for six languages (English, French, German, Italian, Spanish and Greek), and has been extensively used for terminology extraction (Seretan & Wehrli, 2006), as well as for terminology assistance and translation (Wehrli, 2004, 2006).

This paper is organized as follows. The next section gives an overview of the Fips parser, describing some of its linguistic properties and its main processes. In section 3, we present the object-oriented design adopted for the project. Section 4 discusses some cases of cross-linguistic syntactic variation. Finally, section 5 provides some details about the results and presents an evaluation of the parser for the six languages.

2 The Fips parser

Fips is a robust "deep" linguistic parser which assigns to an input sentence an enriched S-structure type of representation, along with a predicate-argument representation. Fips can also be used as a tagger, outputing for each word of a given sentence a POS-tag and optionally the grammatical function (associated to the first word of a constituent), the base form (citation form) of the word, and whether a word is part of an expression or a collocation.

As an illustation, figure 1 shows the enriched structure representation and figure 2 the POS-tags returned by Fips for sentence (1). Notation is explained below.

(1) The record she broke was very old.

$[_{\mathrm{TP}}\ [_{\mathrm{DP}}$ the $[_{\mathrm{NP}}$ record$_i$ $[_{\mathrm{CP}}\ [_{\mathrm{DP}}$ e $]_i$ $[_{\mathrm{TP}}\ [_{\mathrm{DP}}$ she] broke $[_{\mathrm{DP}}$ e $]_i$]]]] was $[_{\mathrm{FP}}\ [_{\mathrm{AP}}\ [_{\mathrm{Adv}}$ very] old]]]

Figure 1: Enriched S-Structure representation for sentence (1)

The linguistic assumptions used in this project correspond roughly to a free-adaptation of Chomsky's generative linguistics, borrowing concepts from the *Minimalist* model (Chomsky, 1995, 2004), from the *Simpler Syntax* model (Culicover & Jackendoff, 2005), as well as from *Lexical Functional Grammar* (Bresnan, 1982, 2001).

Proceedings of the 5th Workshop on Important Unresolved Matters, pages 120–127,
Ann Arbor, June 2005. ©2005 Association for Computational Linguistics

word	tag	expression
the	DET-SIN	
record	NOM-SIN	break-record
she	PRO-PER-SIN-FEM	
broke	VER-PAS-3-SIN	break-record
was	VER-PAS-3-SIN	
very	ADV	
old	ADJ	

Figure 2: POS-tag output for sentence (1)

Roughly, the grammar is lexicalist, exploiting a rich lexicon which specifies, among others,

- the selectional properties of functional elements such as prepositions, auxiliaries, determiners, etc. For instance, the English auxiliary *have* selects a [+past participle] verbal projection. Similarly, in German, *werden* selects an infinitival verbal complement;
- arguments selected by predicative heads (nouns, verbs, adjectives);
- other syntactic or semantic features which might be relevant for syntactic processing such as [+pronominal] feature associated to certain verbs in French, Italian, German, etc., types and subtypes of adverbs, control properties of verbs selecting infinitival complements, and so on.

As shown in figure 1 above, the fundamental structures built by Fips all follow the same pattern, that is : LeftSubconstituents Head RightSubconstituents, which can be abbreviated as **L X R**, where **L** stands for the (possibly empty) list of left subconstituents, **X** for the (possibly empty) head of the phrase and **R** for the (possibly empty) list of right subconstituents. The possible values for **X** are the usual lexical categories **Adv**erb, **A**djective, **N**oun, **D**eterminer, **V**erb, **P**reposition, **C**omplementizer, **Inter**jection. To this list we add the functional category **T**ense, which is the head of a sentence (TP), as well as **F**unctional, used to represent predicative objects headed either by an adjective, an adverb, a noun or a preposition.

Compared to current mainstream Chomskyan representations, Fips constituent structures are relatively flat and make a rather parsimonious use of functional projections. They do, however, contain empty categories, either to represent empty subjects, for instance in infinitival complements, represented as sentences with a (usually lexically unrealized) subject. Empty categories are also used to represent "traces" of extraposed constituents, as in *wh*-constructions, where a chain of coindexed constituents is computed, headed by the extraposed element and footed by its "trace", an empty constituent in argument or adjunct position. An example of such chain is given in figure 1, where the noun *record* is first coindexed with the (lexically unrealized) relative pronoun in the specifier position of the CP constituent, which is itself related to the empty constituent $[_{\mathtt{DP}}\ \mathtt{e}]_i$ in the canonical direct object position of the verb form *broke*.

Although quite complex, the computation of such chains brings many benefits in terms of quality and accuracy of the analysis. One clear example is provided by the identification of collocation, as exemplified in example (1) with the collocation *break-record*. In that sentence, the two terms of the collocation do not occur in the expected order and do not even occur in the same clause, since *record* is the subject of the main clause, while *broke* is in the relative clause. However, as the structure give in fig. 1 shows, the presence of the "trace" of *record* in the direct object position of the verb form *broke* makes the identification of the collocation rather simple, and fig. 2 confirms that Fips has indeed recognized the collocation.

The grammar itself consists of both rules and processes. Rules specify the attachment of constituents, thus determining, at least for the main part, the constituent structure associated to a sentence. The grammatical processes, which roughly correspond to some of the earlier transformation rules of Generative Grammar, are primarily responsible for tasks such as:

- filling up the argument table associated with predicative elements (mostly verbs);
- chain formation, ie. establishing a link between an extraposed element, such as a *wh*-element and an empty category in an argument or adjunct canonical position;
- modifications of the argument structure of predicates (adding, deleting, modifying arguments), as is necessary to account for passive or Romance causative constructions;
- coordination or enumeration structures.

In all such cases, the claim is that a procedural account is simpler than a rule-based description, leading furthermore to a more efficient implementation.

3 Object-oriented design

The computational model adopted for the Fips project relies on object-oriented (OO) concepts (see, for instance, Mössenböck, 1995). An abstract model is assumed both for objects and for their associated procedures (usually called "methods" in OO-jargon) – roughly corresponding to the "universal" linguistic level – from which language-specific objects and procedures are derived. In other words, linguistic objects are defined as abstract data types, whose implementation can vary from language to language. Such variation is handled by the type extension feature provided by OO-models when the variation concerns data structures or by the procedure redefinition feature when variation concerns a process.

Fips relies on three main objects:

- lexical units (*LexicalItem*), which correspond to the "words" of a language, as they appear in the lexical database;
- syntactic projections (*Projection*), which are the syntactic constituents;
- items (*Item*), which correspond to an analysis (partial or complete) – since the parser uses a parallel strategy, many items are maintained throughout the parsing process.

The main procedures (methods) associated to those objects are *Project*, *Merge* and *Move*, corresponding to the operation of projection, combination and movement, respectively. The following subsections will briefly discuss them in turn.

3.1 Project

The projection mechanism creates a syntactic constituent (an object of type *Projection* in our model), either on the basis of a lexical object, or on the basis of another syntactic constituent. For instance, any lexical item, as computed and retrieved from the lexical database by the lexical analysis is projected into a syntactic constituent, with the lexical item as its head. Thus, given *lex*, a lexical item, *lex.Project(p)* creates a syntactic projection *p* headed by *lex*, as in example (2):

(2)a. chat $\longrightarrow$ [$_{\text{NP}}$ chat]

b. eine $\longrightarrow$ [$_{\text{DP}}$ eine]

c. with $\longrightarrow$ [$_{\text{PP}}$ with]

A more powerful variant of the projection mechanism, called metaprojection, can create richer syntactic constituents based either on specific lexical items or on other syntactic projections. For instance, we consider pronouns to be nominal-type lexical elements which project to a DP level. Similarly, verbs are taken as sentence heads, and will therefore give rise to richer syntactic constituents, as illustrated in the following examples:

(3)a. pronouns

[$_{\text{DP}}$ [$_{\text{NP}}$ toi]]

b. mangeras ("will-eat")

[$_{\text{TP}}$ mangeras$_i$ [$_{\text{VP}}$ e$_i$]]

c. reads

[$_{\text{TP}}$ [$_{\text{VP}}$ reads]]

d. regnet ("rains")

[$_{\text{CP}}$ regnet$_i$ [$_{\text{TP}}$ [$_{\text{VP}}$ e$_i$]]]

Notice that the position of the tensed verb is different in the the structures given in (3b,c,d). We assume that tensed verbs in French (and more generally in Romance) "move" to the head of TP, as shown in (3b), while such movement does not occur in English (3c). An even more drastic example of metaprojection occurs in German, where we assume that a whole clause structure is projected on the basis of a tensed verb (in matrix clause), as illustrated in (3d).

3.2 Merge

Merge is the fundamental combination mechanism in our parsing model. Each time the parser reads a word, it is first transformed into a syntactic constituent, a projection, as we have just seen. The projection, in turn, must now be combined (merged) with (partial or complete) constituents in its immediate left context. Two scenarios are considered, corresponding to left attachment and to right attachment. Left attachment occurs when the projection in the left context of the new projection can be attached as a left subconstituent of the new projection. Right attachment corresponds to the situation where the new projection can be attached as a right subconstituent of the projection in its left context. In fact, to be more accurate, the incoming projection can attach as a subconstituent not just of the projection in its left context, but to any active node of it, as illustrated in Figure 3 below:

Merge must be validated either by lexical properties such as selectional features or by general properties (adverbs, adjuncts, parentheticals can relatively freely modify projections).

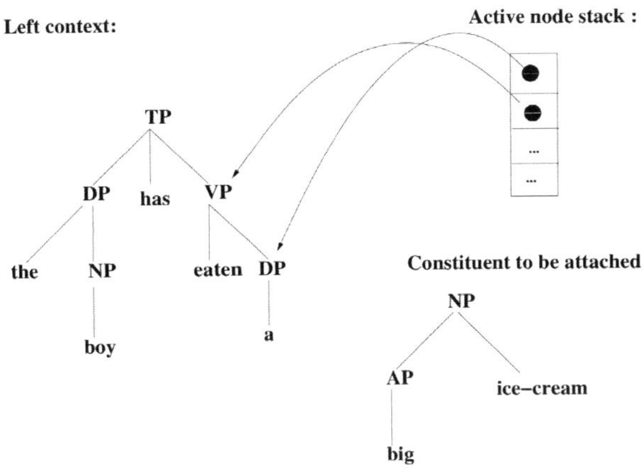

Figure 3: Active node stack

3.3 Move

Although the general architecture of surface structures results from the combination of projection and merge operations, an additional mechanism is necessary to satisfy well-formedness conditions such as thematic assignment. As mentioned earlier, such a mechanism reveals quite useful for the collocation identification process (cf. fig. 2). This mechanism handles extraposed elements and link them to empty constituents in canonical positions, thereby creating a chain between the base (canonical) position and the surface (extraposed) position of the *moved* constituent. To take another simple example, let us consider the interrogative sentence given in (4a) and the (slightly simplified) associated structure in (4b):

(4)a. who did you invite ?

b. [$_{CP}$ [$_{DP}$ who] $_i$ did$_j$ [$_{TP}$ [$_{DP}$ you] e$_j$ [$_{VP}$ invite [$_{DP}$ e] $_i$]]]

The chain mechanism functions as follows: as the parser encounters a *wh*-word in an extraposed position, it stores it in a stack associated with its governing category (typically the CP projection which dominates it). As the parse proceeds, the stack is transferred along the right edge of the structure, provided it does violate island conditions (cf. Ross, 1967). Whenever a predicative element is added to the structure, an attempt is made to complete the chain, ie. to interpret the projection on top of the stack with respect to the predicate. If successful, an empty category coindexed with the extraposed projection is inserted into the structure and the projection is removed from the stack. At the end of the parse, items containing unresolved chains are heavily penalized.

3.4 A parsing example

To illustrate the parsing procedure and the interaction of the 3 mechanisms described above, consider the following simple sentence in French.

(5)a. Paul mange une pomme.
'Paul eats an apple'

b. [$_{TP}$ [$_{DP}$ [$_{NP}$ Paul]] mange$_i$ [$_{VP}$ e $_i$ [$_{DP}$ une [$_{NP}$ pomme]]]]

Step 1 the parser reads "Paul" and metaprojects a DP structure [$_{DP}$ [$_{NP}$ Paul]].

Step 2 the parser reads "manges" and metaprojects a TP-VP structure [$_{TP}$ mange$_i$ [$_{VP}$ e$_i$]]. A merge operation is possible with the preceding DP structure, which yields [$_{TP}$ [$_{DP}$ [$_{NP}$ Paul]] mange$_i$ [$_{VP}$ e$_i$]].

Step 3 the parser reads the determiner "une" and creates a DP structure [$_{DP}$ une]. A merge operation is possible with the left-adjacent TP constituent, with DP attached as right constituent of the internal VP node [$_{TP}$ [$_{DP}$ [$_{NP}$ Paul]] mange$_i$ [$_{VP}$ e$_i$ [$_{DP}$ une]]].

Step 4 the parser reads the noun "pomme", creates an NP structure [$_{NP}$ pomme], and attach it (merge operation) as a right constituent of the DP structure in the TP structure, which yields the complete structure (5b).

3.5 The grammar

Merge operations are constrained by various mostly language-specific conditions which can be described by means of rules. Those rules are stated in a pseudo formalism which attempts to be both intuitive for linguists and relatively straightforward to code. The conditions associated to the rules take the form of boolean functions, as described in the examples (6) for left attachments and in the examples (7) for right attachments, where **a** and **b** refer, respectively, to the first and to the second constituent of a merge operation.

(6)a. AP + NP
  a.HasFeat(prenominal)
  a.AgreeWith(b, {gender, number})

b. DP + NP
  a.HasSelectionFeat(nCompl)
  a.AgreeWith(b,{gender, number, case})

Rule 6a specifies that an adjective projection structure (an AP constituent) can (left-)merge with a noun projection structure (an *NP* constituent) under the two conditions (i) that the first constituent (the adjective) bears the feature `prenominal` and (ii) that both constituents agree in number and gender. This rule, which is part of our French grammar, will allow for *petit animal* ("small animal"), but not *préhistorique animal* ("prehistorical animal"), since the adjective *préhistorique* does not bear the feature `[+prenominal]`, nor *petit animaux* ("small animals"), since *petit* is singular while *animaux* is plural and hence both do not agree in number.

Rule (6b) is taken from our German grammar. It states that a common noun can be (right-)attached to a determiner phrase, under the conditions (i) that the head of the DP bears the selectional feature `[+Ncomplement]` (ie. the determiner selects a noun), and (ii) the determiner and the noun agree in gender, number and case.

3.6 Procedural grammar

One of the original features of the Fips parser is its procedural approach to several grammatical properties. In addition to the chain mechanism described in the previous section, the procedural approach also concerns the treatment of passive and other restructuring constructions, as well as coordination. The next two paragraphs briefly sketch our treatment of passive and coordination constructions.

3.6.1 passives

Along with many linguists or various persuasions, we assume that the fundamental property of passives is the elimination (or demotion) of the subject argument of a predicate. Based on that assumption, our treatment is essentially a case of argument-structure modification: demotion of the subject argument to an optional "*by*-phrase" argument, promotion of the direct object argument to the subject argument slot. In our implementation, the treatment of passives takes the form of a grammar rule specifying the attachment of a [+past participle] verbal projection as complement of the passive auxiliary. This attachment triggers the restructuring process described above[1].

3.6.2 coordination

Coordinate structures constitute a well-known problem for both theoretical and computational linguistics. For the latter, coordination is problematic because it is a major source of non-determinism. Given the fact that such structures are extremely common in both speech and writing, it is therefore mandatory for NLP systems to handle them efficiently. Our treatment of coordination is based on the following assumptions:

- Coordination can affect any pair of like constituents;
- coordinate structures do not strictly obey the $\overline{X}$ schema. They have the following structure: $[_{XP}$ $[_{ConjP}$ XP Conj XP]], where X takes its value in the set of lexical categories augmented by T and F (see section 2 above), and CONJ is a coordination conjunction (eg. *and*, *or*, *but*, etc.).

The coordination procedure is triggered by the presence of a conjunction. All the nodes on the right edge of the constituent in its immediate left context are considered potential candidates for the coordination structure. A metaprojection creates a coordinate projection, in which the node on the right edge is the left subconstituent of the conjunction. The set of such projections is quickly filtered out by further incoming material.

To illustrate our treatment of coordinate structures, in particular the type of structure we assume (slightly simplified in the (8) sentences) as well as the potential ambiguity of coordination, consider the following simple English examples.

(7)a. the old men and women

b. $[_{DP}$ $[_{ConjP}$ $[_{DP}$ the $[_{NP}$ $[_{AP}$ old] men]] and] $[_{DP}$ $[_{NP}$ women]]]

c. $[_{DP}$ the $[_{NP}$ $[_{AP}$ old] $[_{ConjP}$ $[_{NP}$ men] and $[_{NP}$ women]]]]

[1] The same restructuring process applies to particial structures, as in John left the room, **followed** by his dog.

d. [$_{\texttt{DP}}$ the [$_{\texttt{NP}}$ [$_{\texttt{ConjP}}$ [$_{\texttt{NP}}$ [$_{\texttt{A}}$ old] men]] and] [$_{\texttt{NP}}$ women]]

(8)a. John believes Bill and Mary will be to blame.

b. John believes [$_{\texttt{TP}}$ [$_{\texttt{DP}}$ Bill and Mary] will be to blame]

c. [$_{\texttt{TP}}$ John believes Bill] and [$_{\texttt{TP}}$ Mary will be to blame]

4 Examples of cross-linguistic variation

In the Fips system, language variation occurs not only at the level of the grammar, as expected, but also at the level of the associated procedures. Consider for example, the case of the argument checking procedure. Whereas a preverbal DP can be interpreted as the subject of a verb if it agrees with it (number, person) in languages such as French or English (as well as other so-called "configurational languages"), the same criteria would not hold for case-marked languages, such as German or Modern Greek. In those languages, subjects can essentially occur anywhere in the sentence but must be marked `[+nominative]` and of course agree with the verb (number, person)[2]. Relatively similar at an abstract level, the argument checking procedure must be "tuned" for each individual language.

Our second example of cross-linguistic variation concerns clitic pronouns. The relevant data structures (objects) and interpretation procedures (methods) to handle clitics are defined at an abstract level. Specific languages (ie. Spanish, Italian, French, Greek, etc.) inherit those objects and methods, which they can further specialize according to language-specific properties and constraints. The general mechanism to handle clitics comprises two distinct steps: attachment and interpretation[3]. As a clitic is read (as an independent word or as an orthographically attached affix), it is attached to the head of the verb form which follows it (proclitic) or which precedes it (enclitic). Since this verbal head is not necessarily the one with respect to which the clitic pronoun can be interpreted (it might be an auxiliary, for instance), a temporary data structure is used to store clitics until the parser has identified the main predicate of the sentence[4]. Only then can the interpretation process start. All the clitics in the temporary data structure must be interpreted either as argument or as adjunct of the verb[5]. The examples below illustrate our analysis of clitics, applied to Italian (9), French (10) and Spanish (11). The Italian and French examples display proclitics (pre-verbal clitics), while the Spanish example is a case of enclitics (post-verbal clitics). Notice also that in Italian and Spanish we have clitic clusters (two clitics concatenated in one orthographical word), and in the Spanish example, the cluster is itself concatenated to the verb. In all three examples, the clitic pronouns have be properly analyzed, ie. interpreted as arguments of the verb. This is expressed in the resulting structures by the chains connecting a pronoun and an empty category in postverbal position. As in the *wh*-chains discussed earlier, all the elements are coindexed.

(9)a. Glielo ho dato. ("I have given it to him")

b. [$_{\texttt{TP}}$ [$_{\texttt{DP}}$ e] gli$_i$-lo$_j$ ho [$_{\texttt{VP}}$ dato [$_{\texttt{PP}}$ e$_i$] [$_{\texttt{DP}}$ e$_j$]]]

(10)a. Paul le lui a donné. ("Paul has given it to him")

b. [$_{\texttt{TP}}$ [$_{\texttt{DP}}$ Paul] le$_i$ lui$_j$ a [$_{\texttt{VP}}$ donné [$_{\texttt{DP}}$ e$_i$] [$_{\texttt{PP}}$ e$_j$]]]

(11)a. Dámmelo. ("Give it to me")

b. [$_{\texttt{TP}}$ [$_{\texttt{DP}}$ e] da$_i$-me$_j$-lo$_k$ [$_{\texttt{VP}}$ e$_i$ [$_{\texttt{PP}}$ e$_j$] [$_{\texttt{DP}}$ e$_k$]]]

Although very similar in their fundamental behavior, clitics across Romance languages are nevertheless too different to be handled by exactly the same mechanism. Furthermore, even if such mechanism could be implemented, chances are that it would prove insufficient or inadequate in some ways to handle an additional Romance language such as Romanian or Portuguese. Our approach, based on a general abstract mechanism, which can be specialized to suit the specific properties of each language seems therefore more appropriate.

[2]We assume that German (and Modern Greek) are so-called scrambling languages with an unmarked basic word order (cf. Haider and Rosengren, 1998, Hinterhölzl, 2006).

[3]From now on, the discussion will only focus on Romance clitics.

[4]This temporary structure is also used to check the well-formedness of clitic sequences.

[5]For the sake of simplicity, we will leave aside a few more complex cases, such as French clitic "en" corresponding to complements of the direct object of the main verb (*Paul* **en** *connaît la raison* "Paul knows the reason of it") or so-called "long-distance" clitics in Italian or Spanish restructuration constructions.

5 Results and evaluation

To date, the Fips multilingual parser has been developed for 6 languages (English, French, German, Italian, Spanish and Greek). Other languages have been very partially treated, such as Romanian, Russian, Polish and Romansch Sursilvan.

A significant effort has been made at the lexical level, qualitatively and quantitatively. The table in figure 4 below shows the curren approximate size of each lexicon.

language	lexemes	words	collocations
anglais	54'000	90'000	5'000
français	37'000	227'000	12'500
allemand	39'000	410'000	2'000
italien	31'000	220'000	2'500
espagnol	22'500	260'000	320
grec	12'000	90'000	225

Figure 4: Number of entries in the lexical database

At the grammar level, the coverage of the English and French grammar is quite satisfactory, Italian, Spanish and especially German still need improvements, while the Greek grammar is very partial.

Fips attempts to produce complete analyzes for input sentences. Since the parsing strategy is (pseudo-)parallel, many analyzes are produced and ranked according to preferences such as local vs. non-local attachments, argument vs. adjunct interpretation, presence vs. absence of a collocation, etc. When a complete analysis fails, the parser outputs a sequence of partial analyzes covering the whole sentence.

A comparative evaluation has been conducted to show how the various implementations of Fips compare with respect to a near identical corpus, the European Parliament corpus (cf. Koehn, 2005). We parsed approximately 1 million words in each of the six languages. The table given in figure 5 show the results:

The first line in table 5 show the size of each file in terms of symbols (word, punctuation, formatting symbol, etc.), approximately 1 million symbols for each file. The second line gives the number of unknown words, not counting words starting with an uppercase letter which are assumed to be proper nouns (given the fact that in German common nouns are capitalized, we did not leave aside capitalized unknown words for that language). The third line indicates the number of sentences approximately 40'000 for each file, slightly more for the German file. We can see that the average length of a sentence is roughly 20 to 25 symbols (slightly more for French). The fourth line shows the percentage of sentences for which Fips returned a complete analysis. The best score is obtained with English (71.95%), closely followed by French (70.01%). Greek is clearly behind with only about 31%, largely due to the fact that its grammar as well as its lexicon have received much less attention so far. We can observe a quite clear (and unsurprising) correlation between rich lexical coverage (English, French) and high number of complete analyzes.

Finally the last line shows the speed of the parser in terms of number of words per second. The mean speed of Fips is between 130 and 180 word/second. FipsGreek is somewhat faster, presumably because its grammar is less developed than the grammar of the other languages at this point. It came up as a surprise to see that FipsEnglish was clearly slower. The reason has probably to do with the high number of lexical ambiguities of the type N/V (e.g. lead, study, balance, need) which are likely to significantly increase the number of parallel (partial) analyzes.

6 Concluding remarks

Although the research described in this paper is by no means completed, it has already achieved several important goals. First of all, it has shown that "deep linguistic parsing" should not necessarily be equated with "inefficient parsing". Although clearly slower than shallow parsers, Fips is fast enough for such demanding tasks as translation or terminology extraction.

At the software level, the adopted design makes it possible to "plug" an additional language without any change or any recompilation of the system. It is sufficient to add the language-specific modules and lexical databases to have a fully functional parser for that language. Arguably the model has so far not been tested with languages belonging to widely distinct language types. In fact, it has only been applied to (a small set) of European languages. Future work will address that issue, and we are planning to extend our work towards Asian and Semitic languages.

language	German	English	Spanish	French	Greek	Italian
number of symbols	1082117	1046431	1041466	1144345	1045778	998871
unknown words	13569	879	6825	853	26529	3099
number of sentences	45880	40348	40576	38653	39812	37726
% of complete analyzes	48.04%	71.95%	56.87%	70.01%	30.99%	58.74%
speed (word/second)	138	82	127	133	243	182

Figure 5: Comparative evaluation of the parsers

Acknowledgement

Thanks to Luka Nerima, Christopher Laenzlinger, Gabriele Musillo and Antonio Leoni de León for various suggestions and comments on earlier versions of this paper. The research described here has been supported in part by a grant from the Swiss national science foundation (no 101412-103999).

7 References

Bresnan, J. (éd.), 1982. *The Mental Representation of Grammatical Relations*, Cambridge, Mass., MIT Press.

Bresnan, J., 2001. *Lexical Functional Syntax*, Oxford, Blackwell.

Chomsky, N. 1995. *The Minimalist Program*, Cambridge, Mass., MIT Press.

Chomsky, N. 2004. "Beyond Explanatory Adequacy", in A. Belletti (ed.) *The Cartography of Syntactic Structures*, Oxford, Oxford University Press.

Culicover, P. et R. Jackendoff, 2005. *Simpler Syntax*, Oxford, Oxford University Press.

Haider, H. and I. Rosengren 1998. "Scrambling" *Sprache und Pragmatik* 49, Lund University.

Hinterhölzl, R. 2006. *Scrambling, Remnant Movement and Restructuring in West Germanic*, Oxford, Oxford University Press.

Koehn, Ph., 2005. "Europarl: A Parallel Corpus for Statistical Machine Translation, MT Summit.

Mössenböck, H. 1995. *Object-Oriented Programming in Oberon-2*, New York, Springer.

Ross, .R. 1967. *Constraints on Variables in Syntax*, Ph.D. dissertation, MIT.

Seretan, V. et E. Wehrli, 2006. "Accurate collocation extraction using a multilingual parser" in *Proceedings of the 21st International Conference on Computational Linguistics and 44th Annual Meeting of the Association for Computational Linguistics (COLING/ACL 2006)*, Sydney, 952-960.

Wehrli, E. 2004. "Traduction, traduction de mots, traduction de phrases", in B. Bel et I. Marlien (eds.), *Proceedings of TALN XI*, Fes, 483-491.

Wehrli, E. 2006. "TwicPen : Hand-held Scanner and Translation Software for non-Native Readers", in *Proceedings of the 21st International Conference on Computational Linguistics and 44th Annual Meeting of the Association for Computational Linguistics (COLING/ACL 2006)*, Sydney.

Partial Parse Selection for Robust Deep Processing

Yi Zhang[†] and **Valia Kordoni**[†] and **Erin Fitzgerald**[‡]
† Dept of Computational Linguistics, Saarland University and DFKI GmbH, Germany
‡ Center for Language & Speech Processing,
Dept of Electrical & Computer Engineering, Johns Hopkins University, USA
{yzhang,kordoni}@coli.uni-sb.de
erin@clsp.jhu.edu

Abstract

This paper presents an approach to partial parse selection for robust deep processing. The work is based on a bottom-up chart parser for HPSG parsing. Following the definition of partial parses in (Kasper et al., 1999), different partial parse selection methods are presented and evaluated on the basis of multiple metrics, from both the syntactic and semantic viewpoints. The application of the partial parsing in spontaneous speech texts processing shows promising competence of the method.

1 Introduction

Linguistically deep processing is of high theoretical and application interest because of its ability to deliver fine-grained accurate analyses of natural language sentences. Unlike shallow methods which usually return analyses for any input, deep processing methods with precision grammars normally make a clear grammaticality judgment on inputs, therefore avoiding the generation of erroneous analyses for less well-formed inputs. This is a desirable feature, for it allows for a more accurate modeling of language itself.

However, this feature largely limits the robustness of deep processing, for when a sentence is judged to be ungrammatical, normally no analysis is generated. When faced with the noisy inputs in real applications (e.g., input errors introduced by speech recognizers or other pre-processors, mildly ungrammatical sentences with fragmental utterances, self-editing chunks or filler words in spoken texts, and so forth), lack of robustness means poor coverage, and makes deep processing less competitive as compared to shallow methods.

Take the English Resource Grammar (ERG; Flickinger (2000)), a large-scale accurate HPSG for English, for example. (Baldwin et al., 2004) reported coverage of 57% of the strings with full lexical span from the British National Corpus (BNC). Although recent extensions to the grammar and lexicon have improved the coverage significantly, full coverage over unseen texts by the grammar is still not anywhere in sight.

Other domains are even more likely to not fit into ERG's universe, such as transcripts of spontaneously produced speech where speaker errors and disfluencies are common. Using a recent version of the ERG, we are not able to parse 22.6% of a random sample of 500 utterances of conversational telephone speech data. 76.1% of the unparsed data was independently found to contain speaker errors and disfluencies, and the remaining data either contained filled pauses or other structures unaccounted for in the grammar. Correctly recognizing and interpreting the substrings in the utterance which have coherent deep syntax is useful both for semantic analysis and as building blocks for attempts to reconstruct the disfluent spontaneously produced utterances into well-formed sentences.

For these reasons, it is preferable to exploit the intermediate syntactic and semantic analysis even if the full analysis is not available. Various efforts have been made on the partiality of language processing. In bottom-up chart parsing, the passive parser edges licensed by the grammar can be taken as partial analyses. However, as pointed out in (Kasper et al., 1999), not all passive edges are good candidates, as not all of them provide useful syntactic/semantic information. Moreover, the huge amount of passive edges suggests the need for a technique of selecting an optimal subset of them. During recent development in statistical parse disambiguation, the use of log-linear models has been pretty much standardized. However, it remains to be explored whether the techniques can be adapted for partial parse selection.

In this paper, we adopt the same definition for partial parse as in (Kasper et al., 1999) and define the task of partial parse selection. Several dif-

Proceedings of the 5th Workshop on Important Unresolved Matters, pages 128–135,
Ann Arbor, June 2005.

ferent partial parse selection models are presented and implemented for an efficient HPSG parser – PET (Callmeier, 2001).

One of the main difficulties in the research of partial analyses is the lack of good evaluation measurements. Pure syntactic comparisons for parser evaluation are not good as they are very much specific to the annotation guidelines. Also, the deep grammars we are working with are not automatically extracted from annotated corpora. Therefore, unless there are partial treebanks built specifically for the deep grammars, there is simply no 'gold' standard for non-golden partial analyses.

Instead, in this paper, we evaluate the partial analyses results on the basis of multiple metrics, from both the syntactic and semantic point of views. Empirical evaluation has been done with the ERG on a small set of texts from the Wall Street Journal Section 22 of the Penn Treebank (Marcus et al., 1993). A pilot study of applying partial parsing in spontaneous speech text processing is also carried out.

The remainder of the paper is organized as follow. Section 2 provides background knowledge about partial analysis. Section 3 presents various partial parse selection models. Section 4 describes the evaluation setup and results. Section 5 concludes the paper.

2 Partial Parsing

2.1 HPSG Parsing

Our work on partial parsing is done with the DELPH-IN HPSG grammars. Many of these grammars can be used for both parsing and generation. In this paper, we only focus on the parsing task. For efficient parsing, we use PET.[1] The parsing module in PET is essentially a bottom-up chart parser. The parsing process is guided by the parsing tasks on an agenda. A parsing task represents the combination of a passive chart edge and an active chart edge or a rule. When the combination succeeds, new tasks are generated and put on to the agenda. The parser terminates either when the task agenda is empty or when a specific number of full analyses has been found (only in the no-packing best-first mode).

HPSG grammars use typed feature structures (TFSes) as their background formalism. The TFSes represent various linguistic objects with a set of features (attribute value pairs) and a type inheritance system. Therefore, each passive edge on the parsing chart corresponds to a TFS. A relatively small set of highly generalized rules are used to check the compatibility among smaller TFSes and build up larger ones.

[1]LKB (Copestake, 2002) has a similar chart-based parser, being less efficient mainly due to its implementation in Lisp rather than C/C++.

2.2 Partial Parses

Based on the bottom-up chart parsing, we use the term *Partial Parse* to describe a set of intermediate passive parsing edges whose spans (beginning and end positions) are non-overlapping between each other, and together they cover the entire input sequence (i.e., no skipped input tokens).

In a graph view, the intermediate results of a chart parser can be described as a directed graph, where all positions between input tokens/words are vertices, and all the passive edges derived during parsing are the directed graph arcs. Obviously such a graph is acyclic and therefore topologically sorted. A partial parse is then a path from the source vertex (the beginning position of the input) to the terminal vertex (the end position of the input).

Suppose in chart parsing, we derived the intermediate results as in Figure 1. There are in total 4 possible partial parses: $\{a, b, c, d\}$, $\{a, b, f\}$, $\{a, e, d\}$ and $\{a, g\}$.

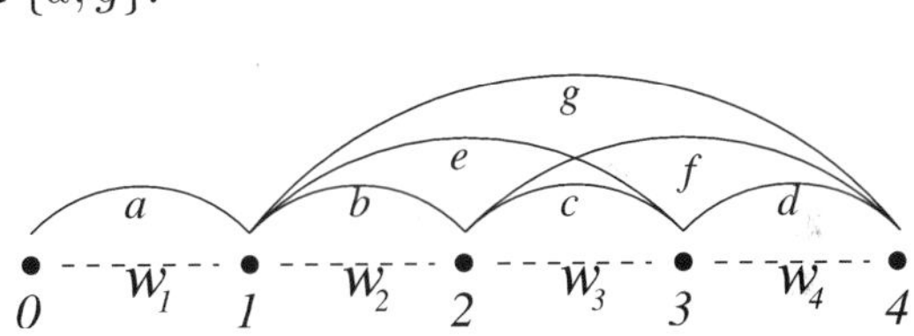

Figure 1: Graph representation of intermediate chart parsing results

Note that each passive edge is a sub-structure licensed by the grammar. A derivation tree or TFS can be reconstructed for it if required. This definition of *partial parse* is effectively the same to the view of partial analyses in (Kasper et al., 1999).

2.3 Local Ambiguity Packing

There is one more complication concerning the partial parses when the local ambiguity packing is used in the parser.

Due to the inherent ambiguity of natural language, the same sequence of input may be analyzed as the same linguistic object in different ways. Such intermediate analyses must be recorded during the processing and recovered in later stages.

Without any efficient processing technique, parsing becomes computationally intractable with the combinatory explosion of such local ambiguities. In PET, the subsumption-based ambiguity packing algorithm proposed in (Oepen and Carroll, 2000) is used. This separates the parsing into two phases: forest creation phase and read-out/unpacking phase.

In relation to the work on partial parsing in this paper, the local ambiguity packing poses an efficiency and accuracy challenge, as not all the intermediate parsing results are directly available as passive edges on the chart. Without unpacking the ambiguity readings, interesting partial analyses might be lost.[2] But exhaustively unpacking all the readings will pay back the efficiency gain by ambiguity packing, and eventually lead to computational intractable results.

To efficiently recover the ambiguous readings from packed representations, the selective unpacking algorithm has been recently implemented as an extension to the algorithm described in (Carroll and Oepen, 2005). It is able to recover the top-n best readings of a given passive parser edge based on the score assigned by a maximum entropy parse ranking model. This neat feature largely facilitates the efficient searching for best partial parses described in later sections.

3 Partial Parse Selection

A partial parse is a set of partial analyses licensed by the grammar which cover the entire input without overlapping. As shown in the previous section, there are usually more than one possible partial parses for a given input. For deep linguistic processing, a high level of local ambiguity means there are even more partial parses due to the combinatory explosion. However, not all the possible partial parses are equally good. Some partial parses partition the input into fragments that do not correspond to linguistic constituents. Even if the bracketing is correct, the different edges with the same span represent significantly different linguistic objects, and their substructures can be completely different, as well. All these indicate the need for methods that can appropriately select the best partial parses from all the possible ones.

In this section, we review some of the previous approaches to partial parse selection, as well as new partial parse ranking models.

3.1 Longest Edge

One of the simplest and most commonly used criterion in selecting the best partial parse is to prefer the partial parses which contain an edge that covers the largest fragment of the input. For example, under such a criterion, the best partial parse in Figure 1 will be $\{a, g\}$, since edge g has the largest span. The logic behind this criterion is that such largest fragments should preserve the most interesting linguistic analysis of the input. As an added incentive, finding the longest edge does not involve much search.

The limitations of such an approach are obvious. There is no guarantee that the longest edge will be significantly better than shorter edges, or that it will even correspond to a valid constituent. Moreover, when there are multiple edges with the same length (which is often the case in parsing), the criterion does not suffice for the choice of the best partial parse.

3.2 Shortest Path

(Kasper et al., 1999) proposed an alternative solution to the problem. If the preference of each edge as a part of the partial parse can be quantitatively decided as a weight of the edge (with smaller weights assigned to better candidates), then the problem of finding the best partial parse is to find the shortest path from the start vertex to the end vertex. Since the graph is completely connected (by the lexical edges spanning all the input tokens) and topologically sorted, such a path always exists. The discovery of such a path can be done in linear time ($O(|V| + |E|)$) with the DAG-shortest-path algorithm (Cormen et al., 1990). Though not explicitly pointed out by (Kasper et al., 1999), such an algorithm allows the weights of the edges to be of any real value (no assumption of positive weights) as long as the graph is a Directed Acyclic Graph (DAG).

(Kasper et al., 1999) did point out that the weights of the edges can be assigned by an estimation function. For example, the implementation of the algorithm in PET preferred phrasal edges over lexical edges. Other types of edges are not allowed in the partial parse. Suppose that we assign weight 1 to phrasal edges, 2 to lexical edges, and inf to all other edges. Then for the graph in 2, the best partial parses are $\{e, g\}$ and $\{f, g\}$, both of which have

[2] More informative analyses are subsumed by less informative ones. In subsumption-based packing, such analyses are packed and are not directly accessible.

the path length of 2. It should be noted that such an approach does not always favor the paths with the longest edges (i.e., path $\{h, d\}$ is not preferred in the given example).

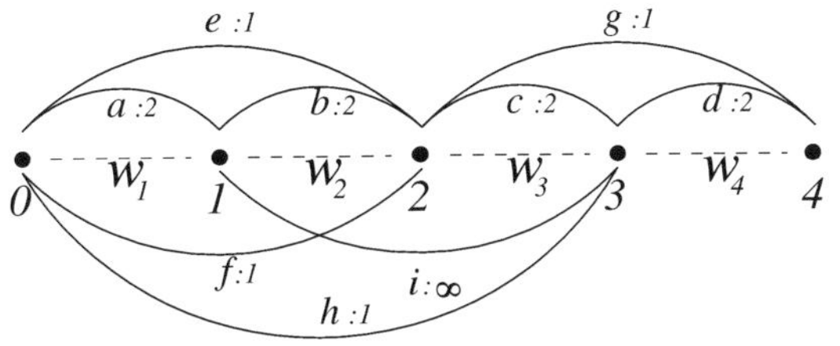

Figure 2: Shortest path partial parses with heuristically assigned edge weights

However, (Kasper et al., 1999) did not provide any sophisticated estimation functions based on the shortest path approach. Using the heuristic weight described above, usually thousands of different paths are found with the same weight. (Kasper et al., 1999) rely on another scoring function in order to re-rank the partial parses. Although different requirements for the scoring function are discussed, no further details have been defined.

It should be noted that different variations of the shortest path approach are widely in use in many robust deep parsing systems. For instance, (Riezler et al., 2002) uses the *fewest chunk* method to choose the best fragment analyses for sentences without full analysis. The well-formed chunks are preferred over token chunks. With this partial parse selection method, the grammar achieves 100% coverage on unseen data. A similar approach is also used in (van Noord et al., 1999).

3.3 Alternative Estimation Functions

Generally speaking, the weights of the edges in the shortest path approach represent the quality of the local analyses and their likelihood of appearing in the analysis of the entire input.

This is an interesting parallel to the parse selection models for the full analyses, where a goodness score is usually assigned to the full analysis. For example, the parse disambiguation model described in (Toutanova et al., 2002) uses a maximum entropy approach to model the conditional probability of a parse for a given input sequence $P(t|w)$. A similar approach has also been reported in (Johnson et al., 1999; Riezler et al., 2002; Malouf and van Noord, 2004).

For a given partial parse $\Phi = \{t_1, \ldots, t_k\}$, $\Omega = \{w_1, \ldots, w_k\}$ is a segmentation of the input sequence so that each local analysis $t_i \in \Phi$ corresponds to a substring $w_i \in \Omega$ of the input sequence w. Therefore, the probability of the partial parse Φ given an input sequence w is:

$$P(\Phi|w) = P(\Omega|w) \cdot P(\Phi|\Omega) \quad (1)$$

With the bold assumption that $P(t_i|w_i)$ are mutually independent for different i, we can derive:

$$P(\Phi|w) \approx P(\Omega|w) \cdot \prod_{i=1}^{k} P(t_i|w_i) \quad (2)$$

Therefore, the log-probability will be

$$\log P(\Phi|w) \approx \log P(\Omega|w) + \sum_{i=1}^{k} \log P(t_i|w_i) \quad (3)$$

Equation 3 indicates that the log-probability of a partial parse for a given input is the sum of the log-probability of local analyses for the sub-strings, with an additional component $-\log P(\Omega|w)$ representing the conditional log-probability of the segmentation. If we use $-\log P(t_i|w_i)$ as the weight for each local analysis, then the DAG shortest path algorithm will quickly find the partial parse that maximizes $\log P(\Phi|w) - \log P(\Omega|w)$.

The probability $P(t_i|w_i)$ can be modeled in a similar way to the maximum entropy based full parse selection models:

$$P(t_i|w_i) = \frac{\exp \sum_{j=1}^{n} \lambda_j f_j(t_i, w_i)}{\sum_{t' \in T} \exp \sum_{j=1}^{n} \lambda_j f_j(t', w_i)} \quad (4)$$

where T is the set of all possible structures that can be assigned to w_i, $f_1 \ldots f_n$ are the features and $\lambda_1 \ldots \lambda_n$ are the parameters. The parameters can be efficiently estimated from a treebank, as shown by (Malouf, 2002). The only difference from the full parse selection model is that here intermediate results are used to generate events for training the model (i.e. the intermediate nodes are used as positive events if it occurs on one of the active tree, or as negative events if not). Since there is a huge number of intermediate results availalbe, we only randomly select a part of them as training data. This is essentially similar to the approach in (Osborne, 2000), where there is an infeasibly large number of training events, only part of which is used in the estimation step. The exact features used in the log-linear model can significantly influence the disambiguation accuracy. In this experiment we used the same features as those used in the PCFG-S model in (Toutanova et al., 2002) (i.e., depth-1 derivation trees).

The estimation of $P(\Omega|w)$ is more difficult. In a sense it is similar to a segmentation or chunking model, where the task is to segment the input into fragments. However, it is difficult to collect training data to directly train such a model for the deep grammar we have. Here we take a simple rough estimation:

$$\hat{P}(\Omega|w) = \frac{|Y(\Omega)|}{|Z(w)|} \tag{5}$$

where $Y(\Omega)$ is the set of all partial parses that have the segmentation Ω; $Z(w)$ is the set of all partial parses for the input w.

Unfortunately, the shortest path algorithm is not able to directly find the maximized $P(\Phi|w)$. Fully searching all the paths is not practical, since there are usually tens of thousands of passive edges. In order to achieve a balance between accuracy and efficiency, two different approximation approaches are taken.

One way is to assume that the component $\log P(\Omega|w)$ in Equation 3 has less significant effect on the quality of the partial parse. If this is valid, then we can simply use $-\log P(t_i|w_i)$ as edge weights, and use the shortest path algorithm to obtain the best Φ. This will be referred to as *model I*.

An alternative way is to first retrieve several "good" Ω with relatively high $P(\Omega|w)$, and then select the best edges t_i that maximize $P(t_i|w_i)$ for each w_i in Ω. We call this approach the *model II*.

How well these strategies work will be evaluated in Section 4. Other strategies or more sophisticated searching algorithms (e.g., genetic algorithm) can also be used, but we will leave that to future research.

3.4 Partial Semantic Construction

For each local analysis on the partial parse derived in the above steps, a semantic fragment can be derived. The HPSG grammars we use take a compositional approach to semantic construction. Minimal Recursion Semantics (MRS; Copestake et al. (2006)) is used for semantic representation. MRS can be easily converted to (Robust) MRS (RMRS; Copestake (2006)), which allows further underspecification, and can be used for integration of deep and/or shallow processing tools.

For robust deep processing, the ability to generate partial semantics is very important. Moreover, it also provides us with a way to evaluate the partial parses which is more or less independent from the syntactic analysis.

4 Evaluation

The evaluation of partial parses is not as easy as the evaluation of full parses. For full parsers, there are generally two ways of evaluation. For parsers that are trained on a treebank using an automatically extracted grammar, an unseen set of manually annotated data is used as the test set. The parser output on the test set is compared to the gold standard annotation, either with the widely used *PARSEVAL* measurement, or with more annotation-neutral dependency relations. For parsers based on manually compiled grammars, more human judgment is involved in the evaluation. With the evolution of the grammar, the treebank as the output from the grammar changes over time (Oepen et al., 2002). The grammar writer inspects the parses generated by the grammar and either "accepts" or "rejects" the analysis.

In partial parsing for manually compiled grammars, the criterion for acceptable analyses is less evident. Most current treebanking tools are not designed for annotating partial analyses. Large-scale manually annotated treebanks do have the annotation for sentences that deep grammars are not able to fully analyze. And the annotation difference in other language resources makes the comparison less straightforward. More complication is involved with the platform and resources used in our experiment. Since the DELPH-IN grammars (ERG, JaCY, GG) use MRS for semantics representation, there is no reliable way of evaluating the output with traditional metrics, i.e., dependency relations.

In this paper, we use both manual and automatic evaluation methods on the partial parsing results. Different processing resources are used to help the evaluation from the syntactic, as well as the semantic point of view.

4.1 Syntactic Evaluation

In order to evaluate the quality of the syntactic structures of the partial parses, we implemented the partial parse models described in the previous section in the PET parser. The Nov-06 version of the ERG is used for the experiment. As test set, we used a subset of sentences from the Wall Street Journal Section 22 from the Penn Treebank. The subset contains 143 sentences which do not receive any full analysis licensed by the grammar, and do not contain lexical gaps (input tokens for which the grammar cannot create any lexical edge). The average sentence length is 24 words.

Due to the inconsistency of the tokenisation, bracketing and branching between the Penn Treebank annotation and the handling in ERG, we manually checked the partial parse derivation trees. Each output is marked as one of the three cases: **GBL** if both the bracketing and the labeling of the partial parse derivation trees are good (with no more than two brackets crossing or four false labelings); **GB** if the bracketings of the derivation trees are good (with no more than two brackets crossing), but the labeling is bad (with more than four false labelings); or **E** if otherwise.

The manual evaluation results are listed in Table 1. The test set is processed with two models presented in Section 3.3 (**M-I** for *model I*, **M-II** for *model II*). For comparison, we also evaluate for the approach using the shortest path with heuristic weights (denoted by **SP**). In case there are more than one path found with the same weight, only the first one is recorded and evaluated.

	GBL		GB		E	
	#	%	#	%	#	%
SP	55	38.5%	64	44.8%	24	16.8%
M-I	61	42.7%	46	32.2%	36	25.2%
M-II	74	51.7%	50	35.0%	19	13.3%

Table 1: Syntactic Evaluation Results

The results show that the naïve shortest path approach based on the heuristic weights works pretty well at predicting the bracketing (with 83.3% of the partial parses having less than two brackets crossing). But, when the labeling is also evaluated it is worse than *model I*, and even more significantly outperformed by *model II*.

4.2 Semantic Evaluation

Evaluation of the syntactic structure only reflects the partial parse quality from some aspects. In order to get a more thorough comparison between different selection models, we look at the semantic output generated from the partial parses.

The same set of 143 sentences from the Wall Street Journal Section 22 of the Penn Treebank is used. The RMRS semantic representations are generated from the partial parses with different selection models. To compare with, we used RASP 2 (Briscoe et al., 2006), a domain-independent robust parsing system for English. According to (Briscoe and Carroll, 2006), the parser achieves fairly good accuracy around 80%. The reasons why we choose RASP for the evaluation are: i) RASP has reasonable coverage and accuracy; ii) its output can be converted into RMRS representation with the LKB system. Since there is no large scale (R)MRS treebank with sentences not covered by the DELPH-IN precision grammars, we hope to use the RASP's RMRS output as a standalone annotation to help the evaluation of the different partial parse selection models.

To compare the RMRS from the RASP and the partial parse selection models, we used the similarity measurement proposed in (Dridan and Bond, 2006). The comparison outputs a distance value between two different RMRSes. We normalized the distance value to be between 0 and 1. For each selection model, the average RMRS distance from the RASP output is listed in Table 2.

	RMRS Dist.(ϕ)
SP	0.674
M-I	0.330
M-II	0.296

Table 2: RMRS distance to RASP outputs

Again, we see that the outputs of *model II* achieve the highest similarity when compared with the RASP output. With some manual validation, we do confirm that the different similarity does imply a significant difference in the quality of the output RMRS. The shortest path with heuristic weights yielded very poor semantic similarity. The main reason is that not every edge with the same span generates the same semantics. Therefore, although the SP receives reasonable bracketing accuracy, it has less idea of the goodness of different edges with the same span. By incorporating $P(t_i|w_i)$ in the scoring model, the model I and II can produce RMRSes with much higher quality.

4.3 Evaluating partial parses on spontaneous speech text

The above evaluation shows in a comparative way that *model II* outperforms other selection models from both syntactic and semantic points of view. In order to show its competence in real applications, we applied the best performing *model II* on spontaneous speech transcripts, which have a high level of informality and irregularity not available in newspaper texts such as the Wall Street Journal.

To evaluate the accuracy and potential interpretational value of partial parsing on spontaneous speech transcripts, we considered a 100-sentence random sample of the Fisher Conversational Telephone Speech 2004 development subcorpus (Cieri et al., 2004), used in the fall 2004 NIST Rich Transcription task.

Of these 100 sentences, six utterances received neither full nor partial parses due to lexical gaps created by words not found in the grammar's lexicon.[3] 75 utterances produced full HPSG parses. For the remaining 19 utterances, the one best partial parse is found for each using *model II*.

According to manual evaluation of the output, semantically and syntactically cohesive partial analyses were successfully assigned to 9 of the 19 partially parsed utterances. 3 of the 19 received incomplete semantics. The remaining 7 were judged to be poor due to false segmentation, the syntax and semantics within those parsed fragments, or both. In one instance, the interpretation was plausible but viewed as far less likely by the evaluator than the preferable interpretation ("... [i think you know it it 's] [court]"[4]). It is likely that n-best partial parsing could help us in most cases. This would only require a straightforward extension of the current partial parsing models.

Current partial parsing models do not use any confidence thresholds. Therefore, any input will receive some full or partial analysis (ignoring the case of unknown words), together with semantics. Semantic completeness is not checked in partial parsing. In future research, we may consider finding a sophisticated solution of assigning confidence scores to the output RMRS fragments.

Overall though, we believe that the current 50% acceptability of segmentation is reasonable performance considering the types of noise in the speech transcript input.

As a further step to show the competence of partial parsing, we briefly investigated its application in capturing disfluent regions in speech texts. The state of the art approach in identifying disfluent regions and potentially capturing meaningful text is a shallow parsing method described in (Johnson and Charniak, 2004), which searches the text string for approximately repeated constituents. We ran their system on our random sample of the Fisher data, and compared its results to the partial parse output of the nine well-segmented partial parses analyses (every utterance of which contained some speaker-induced disfluency) to see how well partial parsing could potentially fare as an approach for identifying disfluent regions of speech text.

Often the (Johnson and Charniak, 2004) method identified disfluent regions overlapped with identified fragments found in the partial parse, the removal of which would yield a fluent sentence. As we hope to learn confidence measures to determine which fragments are contentless or repetitive in the future, we identified those partial parses where whole fragments could be deleted to obtain a fluent and meaning-preserving sentence.

In three cases, simple repeated phrases caught by (Johnson and Charniak, 2004) were also caught in some form by the partial parse partitioning. In another case, the speaker interrupts one thought to say another, and both approaches identify in a single fragment the final fluent statement. Finally, of the nine well-segmented utterances, two partial parses potentially catch deeper speaker errors that cannot be caught by (Johnson and Charniak, 2004).

5 Conclusion and Future Work

In this paper, we have presented work on partial parse selection. Different selection models have been presented and evaluated from syntactic and semantic viewpoints. In the application of spontaneous speech text processing, the method shows promising competence, as well as a few problems for further study.

One thing we did not do is a systematic comparison on the efficiency of different partial parse selection models. Although it is clear that less searching is involved with the shortest path approach and *model I* comparing to *model II*, a scientific benchmarking of such difference will be helpful for the choice between efficiency and accuracy. Also, a more sophisticated estimation of $P(\Omega|w)$ can potentially help the accuracy of the selection models.

Another alternative way of evaluation would be to generate an ungrammatical corpus by randomly introducing grammar errors. The performance of the

[3]Lexical prediction was not used here to avoid obfuscating the quality of partial parsing by introducing lexical type prediction errors.

[4]The repetition error of "it" is interpreted as a topicalization.

partial parse selection models can be measured by evaluating how much of the parsing results can be recovered from original sentences.

In the study with spontaneous speech text processing, we see a need for confidence measurement for partial analyses. We also see that the conditional probability $P(t_i|w_i)$ does not serve as a good measurement, for it largely depends on the structures that can be licensed to w_i by the grammar. This should be explored in future studies, as well.

References

Timothy Baldwin, Emily M. Bender, Dan Flickinger, Ara Kim, and Stephan Oepen. 2004. Road-testing the English Resource Grammar over the British National Corpus. In *Proceedings of the Fourth International Conference on Language Resources and Evaluation (LREC 2004)*, Lisbon.

Ted Briscoe and John Carroll. 2006. Evaluating the accuracy of an unlexicalized statistical parser on the PARC DepBank. In *Proceedings of the COLING/ACL 2006 Main Conference Poster Sessions*, pages 41–48, Sydney, Australia.

Ted Briscoe, John Carroll, and Rebecca Watson. 2006. The second release of the RASP system. In *Proceedings of the COLING/ACL 2006 Interactive Presentation Sessions*, pages 77–80, Sydney, Australia.

Ulrich Callmeier. 2001. Efficient parsing with large-scale unification grammars. Master's thesis, Universität des Saarlandes, Saarbrücken, Germany.

John Carroll and Stephan Oepen. 2005. High efficiency realization for a wide-coverage unification grammar. In *Proceedings of the Second International Joint Conference on Natural Language Processing (IJCNLP05)*, pages 165–176, Jeju Island, Korea.

Christopher Cieri, Stephanie Strassel, Mohamed Maamouri, Shudong Huang, James Fiumara, David Graff, Kevin Walker, and Mark L iberman. 2004. Linguistic resource creation and distribution for EARS. In *Proceedings of the Rich Transcription Fall Workshop (RT-04F)*.

Ann Copestake, Dan Flickinger, Carl Pollard, and Ivan A. Sag. 2006. Minimal Recursion Semantics: an Introduction. *Research on Language and Computation*, 3(4):281–332.

Ann Copestake. 2002. *Implementing Typed Feature Structure Grammars*. CSLI, Stanford, CA.

Ann Copestake. 2006. Robust Minimal Recursion Semantics. Working Paper, Unpublished Draft 2004/2006, http://www.cl.cam.ac.uk/ aac10/papers.html.

Thomas H. Cormen, Charles E. Leiserson, and Ronald L. Rivest. 1990. *Introduction to Algorithms*. MIT Press, MA.

Rebecca Dridan and Francis Bond. 2006. Sentence comparison using Robust Minimal Recursion Semantics and an ontology. In *Proceedings of the ACL Workshop on Linguistic Distances*, pages 35–42, Sydney, Australia.

Dan Flickinger. 2000. On building a more efficient grammar by exploiting types. *Natural Language Engineering*, 6(1):15–28.

Mark Johnson and Eugene Charniak. 2004. A tag-based noisy-channel model of speech repairs. In *Proceedings of the 42nd Meeting of the Association for Computational Linguistics (ACL'04), Main Volume*, pages 33–39, Barcelona, Spain.

Mark Johnson, Stuart Geman, Stephen Canon, Zhiyi Chi, and Stefan Riezler. 1999. Estimators for stochastic unifcation-based grammars. In *Proceedings of the 37th Annual Meeting of the ACL*, pages 535–541, Maryland.

Walter Kasper, Bernd Kiefer, Hans-Ulrich Krieger, C.J. Rupp, and Karsten Worm. 1999. Charting the depths of robust speech processing. In *Proceedings of the 37th Meeting of the Association for Computational Linguistics (ACL'99), Main Volume*, pages 405–412, Maryland, USA, June.

Robert Malouf and Gertjan van Noord. 2004. Wide coverage parsing with stochastic attribute value grammars. In *IJCNLP-04 Workshop: Beyond shallow analyses - Formalisms and statistical modeling for deep analyses*.

Robert Malouf. 2002. A comparison of algorithms for maximum entropy parameter estimation. In *Proceedings of the Sixth Conferencde on Natural Language Learning (CoNLL-2002)*, pages 49–55.

Mitchell P. Marcus, Beatrice Santorini, and Mary Ann Marcinkiewicz. 1993. Building a large annotated corpus of English. The Penn Treebank. *Computational Linguistics*, 19:313–330.

Stephan Oepen and John Carroll. 2000. Ambiguity packing in constraint-based parsing — practical results. In *Proceedings of the 1st Conference of the North American Chapter of the ACL*, pages 162–169, Seattle, WA.

Stephan Oepen, Kristina Toutanova, Stuart Shieber, Christopher Manning, Dan Flickinger, and Thorsten Brants. 2002. The LinGO Redwoods treebank: Motivation and preliminary applications. In *Proceedings of COLING 2002: The 17th International Conference on Computational Linguistics: Project Notes*, Taipei.

Miles Osborne. 2000. Estimation of Stochastic Attribute-Value Grammars using an Informative Sample. In *The 18th International Conference on Computational Linguistics (COLING 2000)*, volume 1, pages 586–592, Saarbrücken.

Stefan Riezler, Tracy H. King, Ronald M. Kaplan, Richard Crouch, John T. III Maxwell, and Mark Johnson. 2002. Parsing the Wall Street Journal using a Lexical-Functional Grammar and Discriminative Estimation Techniques. In *Proceedings of the 40th Annual Meeting of the Association for Computational Linguistics*, pages 271–278, Philadelphia.

Kristina Toutanova, Christoper D. Manning, Stuart M. Shieber, Dan Flickinger, and Stephan Oepen. 2002. Parse ranking for a rich HPSG grammar. In *Proceedings of the First Workshop on Treebanks and Linguistic Theories (TLT2002)*, pages 253–263, Sozopol, Bulgaria.

Gertjan van Noord, Gosse Bouma, Rob Koeling, and Mark-Jan Nederhof. 1999. Robust grammatical analysis for spoken dialogue systems. *Natural language engineering*, 5(1):45–93.

Validation and Regression Testing for a Cross-linguisic Grammar Resource

Emily M. Bender, Laurie Poulson, Scott Drellishak, Chris Evans
University of Washington
Department of Linguistics
Seattle WA 98195-4340 USA
{ebender,lpoulson,sfd,chrisev@u.washington.edu}

Abstract

We present a validation methodology for a cross-linguistic grammar resource which produces output in the form of small grammars based on elicited typological descriptions. Evaluating the resource entails sampling from a very large space of language types, the type and range of which preclude the use of standard test suites development techniques. We produce a database from which gold standard test suites for these grammars can be generated on demand, including well-formed strings paired with all of their valid semantic representations as well as a sample of ill-formed strings. These string-semantics pairs are selected from a set of candidates by a system of regular-expression based filters. The filters amount to an alternative grammar building system, whose generative capacity is limited compared to the actual grammars. We perform error analysis of the discrepancies between the test suites and grammars for a range of language types, and update both systems appropriately. The resulting resource serves as a point of comparison for regression testing in future development.

1 Introduction

The development and maintenance of test suites is integral to the process of writing deep linguistic grammars (Oepen and Flickinger, 1998; Butt and King, 2003). Such test suites typically contain hand-constructed examples illustrating the grammatical phenomena treated by the grammar as well as representative examples taken from texts from the target domain. In combination with test suite management software such as [incr tsdb()] (Oepen, 2002), they are used for validation and regression testing of precision (deep linguistic) grammars as well as the exploration of potential changes to the grammar.

In this paper, we consider what happens when the precision grammar resource being developed isn't a grammar of a particular language, but rather a cross-linguistic grammar resource. In particular, we consider the LinGO Grammar Matrix (Bender et al., 2002; Bender and Flickinger, 2005). There are several (related) obstacles to making effective use of test suites in this scenario: (1) The Matrix core grammar isn't itself a grammar, and therefore can't parse any strings. (2) There is no single language modeled by the cross-linguistic resource from which to draw test strings. (3) The space of possible grammars (alternatively, language types) modeled by the resource is enormous, well beyond the scope of what can be thoroughly explored.

We present a methodology for the validation and regression testing of the Grammar Matrix that addresses these obstacles, developing the ideas originally proposed in (Poulson, 2006). In its broad outlines, our methodology looks like this:

- Define an abstract vocabulary to be used for test suite purposes.
- Define an initial small set of string-semantics pairs.
- Construct a large set of variations on the string-semantics pairs.

Proceedings of the 5th Workshop on Important Unresolved Matters, pages 136–143,
Ann Arbor, June 2005.

- Define a set of filters that can delineate the legitimate string-semantics pairs for a particular language type

The filters in effect constitute a parallel grammar definition system, albeit one that creates 'grammars' of very limited generative capacity. As such, the output of the filters cannot be taken as ground truth. Rather, it serves as a point of comparison that allows us to find discrepancies between the filters and the Grammar Matrix which in turn can lead us to errors in the Grammar Matrix.

2 Background

The Grammar Matrix is an open-source starter kit designed to jump-start the development of broad-coverage precision grammars, capable of both parsing and generation and suitable for use in a variety of NLP applications. The Grammar Matrix is written within the HPSG framework (Pollard and Sag, 1994), using Minimal Recursion Semantics (Copestake et al., 2005) for the semantic representations. The particular formalism we use is TDL (type description language) as interpreted by the LKB (Copestake, 2002) grammar development environment. Initial work on the Matrix (Bender et al., 2002; Flickinger and Bender, 2003) focused on the development of a cross-linguistic core grammar. The core grammar provides a solid foundation for sustained development of linguistically-motivated yet computationally tractable grammars (e.g., (Hellan and Haugereid, 2003; Kordoni and Neu, 2005)).

However, the core grammar alone cannot parse and generate sentences: it needs to be specialized with language-specific information such as the order of daughters in its rules (e.g., head-subject or subject-head), and it needs a lexicon. Although word order and many other phenomena vary across languages, there are still recurring patterns. To allow reuse of grammar code across languages and to increase the size of the jump-start provided by the Matrix, in more recent work (Bender and Flickinger, 2005; Drellishak and Bender, 2005), we have been developing 'libraries' implementing realizations of various linguistic phenomena. Through a web interface, grammar developers can configure an initial starter grammar by filling out a typological questionnaire about their language, which in turn calls a CGI script to 'compile' a grammar (including language-specific rule types, lexical entry types, rule entries, and lexical entries) by making appropriate selections from the libraries. These little grammars describe very small fragments of the languages they model, but they are not toys. Their purpose is to be good starting points for further development.

The initial set of libraries includes: basic word order of major constituents in matrix clauses (SOV et al), optionality/obligatoriness of determiners, noun-determiner order, NP v. PP arguments of intransitive and transitive verbs, strategies for expressing sentential negation and yes-no questions, and strategies for constituent coordination. Even with this small set of phenomena covered (and limiting ourselves for testing purposes to maximally two coordination strategies per language), we have already defined a space of hundreds of thousands of possible grammars.[1]

3 The Non-modularity of Linguistic Phenomena

In this section we discuss our findings so far about the non-modularity of linguistic phenomena, and argue that this makes the testing of a broad sample of grammars even more pressing.

The Grammar Matrix customization system reads in the user's language specification and then outputs language-specific definitions of types (rule types, lexical entry types and ancillary structures) that inherit from types defined in the crosslinguistic core of the Matrix but add constraints appropriate for the language at hand. Usability considerations put two important constraints on this system: (1) The questions must be ones that are sensible to linguists, who tend to consider phenomena one at a time. (2) The output grammar code must be both readable and maintainable. To achieve readable grammar code in the output TDL, among other things, we follow the guideline that any given constraint is stated only once. If multiple types require the same constraint, they should all inherit from some supertype bearing that constraint. In addition, all constraints pertaining to a particular type are stated in one place.

In light of the these usability considerations, we

[1] If all of the choices in the customization system were independent, we would have more than 2 x 10^{27} grammars. In actuality, constraints on possible combinations of choices limit this space considerably.

```
comp-head-phrase := basic-head-1st-comp-phrase & head-final.
subj-head-phrase := basic-head-subj-phrase & head-final &
  [ HEAD-DTR.SYNSEM.LOCAL.CAT.VAL.COMPS < > ].
```

Figure 1: Specialized phrase structure rule types for SOV language

have found that it is not possible to treat the libraries as black-box modules with respect to each other. The libraries are interdependent, and the portions of the script that interpret one part of the input questionnaire frequently need to make reference to information elicited by other parts of the questionnaire. For example, the customization system implements major constituent word order by specializing the head-complement and head-subject rule types provided in the core grammar. In an SOV language, these would both be cross-classified with the type head-final, and the head-subject rule would further be constrained to take only complement-saturated phrases as its head daughter. The TDL encoding of these constraints is shown in Figure 1.

Following standard practice in HPSG, we use the head-complement phrase not only for ordinary VPs, but also for PPs, CPs, and auxiliary-headed VPs, etc. Consider Polish, a free word order language that nonetheless has prepositions. To allow complements on either side of the head, we instantiate both head-comp and comp-head rules, inheriting from head-initial and head-final respectively. Yet the prepositions must be barred from the head-final version lest the grammar license *post*positional phrases by mistake. We do this by constraining the HEAD value of the comp-head phrase. Similarly, question particles (such as *est-ce que* in French or *ma* in Mandarin) are treated as complementizers: heads that select for an S complement. Since these, too, may differ in their word order properties from verbs (and prepositions), we need information about the question particles (elicited with the rest of the information about yes-no questions) before we have complete information about the head-complement rule. Furthermore, it is not simply a question of adding constraints to existing types. Consider the case of an SOV language with prepositions and sentence-initial question particles. This language would need a head-initial head-comp rule that can take only prepositions and complementizers as its head. To express the disjunction, we must use the supertype to *prep* and *comp*. This, in turn, means that we can't decide what constraint to put on the head value of the head-comp rule until we've considered questions as well as the basic word order facts.

We expect to study the issue of (non-)modularity as we add additional libraries to the resource and to investigate whether the grammar code can be refactored in such a way as to make the libraries into true modules. We suspect it might be possible to reduce the degree of interdependence, but not to achieve completely independent libraries, because syntactic phenomena are inherently interdependent. Agreement in NP coordination provides an example. In English and many other languages, coordinated NPs are always plural and the person of the coordinated NP is the minimal person value of the coordinands.

(1) a. A cat and a dog are/*is chasing a mouse.
    b. Kim and I should handle this ourselves.
    c. You and Kim should handle this yourselves.

Gender systems often display a similar hierarchy of values, as with French coordinated NPs, where the whole NP is feminine iff all coordinands are feminine and masculine otherwise. Thus it appears that it is not possible to define all of the necessary constraints on the coordination rules without having access to information about the agreement system.

Even if we were able to make our analyses of different linguistic phenomena completely modular, however, we would still need to test their interaction in the analysis of particular sentences. Any sentence that illustrates sentential negation, a matrix yes-no question, or coordination also necessarily illustrates at least some aspects of word order, the presence v. absence of determiners and case-marking adpositions, and the subcategorization of the verb that heads the sentence. Furthermore, broad-coverage grammars need to allow negation, questions, coordination etc. all to appear in the same sentence.

Given this non-modularity, we would ideally like to be able to validate (and do regression testing on) the full set of grammars generable by the customiza-

Form	Description	Options
det	determiner	
n1, n2	nouns	det is optional, obligatory, impossible
iv, tv	intransitive, transitive verb	subj, obj are NP or PP
p-nom, p-acc	case-marking adpositions	preposition or postposition
neg	negative element	adverb, prefix, suffix
co1, co2	coordination marks	word, prefix, suffix
qpart	question particle	

Table 1: Standardized lexicon

tion system. To approximate such thoroughness, we instead sample from the grammar space.

4 Methodology

This section describes in some detail our methodology for creating test suites on the basis of language-type descriptions. A *language type* is a collection of feature-value pairs representing a possible set of answers to the Matrix customization questionnaire. We refer to these as language types rather than languages, because the grammars produced by the customization system are underspecified with respect to actual languages, i.e., one and the same starter grammar might be extended into multiple models corresponding to multiple actual human languages. Accordingly, when we talk about the predicted (well)formedness, or (un)grammaticality, of a candidate string, we are referring to its predicted status with respect to a language type definition, not its grammaticality in any particular (human) language.

4.1 Implementation: Python and MySQL

The test suite generation system includes a MySQL database, a collection of Python scripts that interact with the database, and some stored SQL queries. As the set of items we are manipulating is quite large (and will grow as new items are added to test additional libraries), using a database is essential for rapid retrieval of relevant items. Furthermore, the database facilitates the separation of procedural and declarative knowledge in the definition of the filters.

4.2 Abstract vocabulary for abstract strings

A grammar needs not just syntactic constructions and lexical types, but also an actual lexicon. Since we are working at the level of language types, we are free to define this lexicon in whatever way is most convenient. Much of the idiosyncrasy in language resides in the lexicon, both in the form of morphemes and in the particular grammatical and collocational constraints associated with them. Of these three, only the grammatical constraints are manipulated in any interesting way within the Grammar Matrix customization system. Therefore, for the test suite, we define all of the language types to draw the *forms* of their lexical items from a shared, standardized vocabulary. Table 1 illustrates the vocabulary along with the options that are currently available for varying the grammatical constraints on the lexical entries. Using the same word forms for each grammar contributes substantially to building a single resource that can be adapted for the testing of each language type.

4.3 Constructing master item set

We use *string* to refer to a sequence of words to be input to a grammar and *result* as the (expected) semantic representation. An *item* is a particular pair of string and result. Among strings, we have *seed strings* provided by the Matrix developers to seed the test suite, and *constructed strings* derived from those seed strings. The *constructor function* is the algorithm for deriving new strings from the seed strings. Seed strings are arranged into semantic equivalence classes, from which one representative is designated the *harvester string*. We parse the harvester string with some appropriate grammar (derived from the Matrix customization system) to extract the semantic representation (*result*) to be paired with each member of the equivalence class.

The seed strings, when looked at as bags of words, should cover all possible realizations of the phenomenon treated by the library. For example, the negation library allows both inflectional and adverbial negation, as well as negation expressed through both inflection and an adverb together. To illustrate negation of transitive sentences (allowing for languages with and without determiners[2]), we require the seed strings in (2):

(2)

Semtag: neg1	Semtag: neg2
n1 n2 neg tv	det n1 det n2 neg tv
n1 n2 neg-tv	det n1 det n2 neg-tv
n1 n2 tv-neg	det n1 det n2 tv-neg
n1 n2 neg neg-tv	det n1 det n2 neg neg-tv
n1 n2 neg tv-neg	det n1 det n2 neg tv-neg

Sentential negation has the same semantic reflex across all of its realizations, but the presence v. absence of overt determiners does have a semantic effect. Accordingly, the seed strings shown in (2) can be grouped into two semantic equivalence classes, shown as the first and second columns in the table, and associated with the semantic tags 'neg1' and 'neg2', respectively. The two strings in the first row could be designated as the harvester strings, associated with a grammar for an SOV language with optional determiners preceding the noun and sentential negation expressed as a pre-head modifier of V.

We use the LKB in conjunction with [incr tsdb()] to parse the harvester strings from all of the equivalence classes with the appropriate grammars. Then the seed strings and the parsing results from the harvester strings, as well as their semantic tags, are stored and linked in our relational database. We use the constructor function to create new strings from these seed strings. This produces the master item set that provides the basis for the test suites.

Currently, we have only one constructor function ('permute') which takes in a seed string and returns all unique permutations of the morphemes in that seed string.[3] This constructor function is effective in producing test items that cover the range of word order variations currently permitted by the Grammar Matrix customization system. Currently, most of the other kinds of variation countenanced (e.g., adverbial v. inflectional negation or presence v. absence of determiners) is handled through the initial seed string construction. As the range of phenomena handled by the customization system expands, we will develop more sophisticated constructor functions to handle, for example, the addition of all possible case suffixes to each noun in the sentence.

[2]We require additional seed strings to account for languages with and without case-marking adpositions

[3]'permute' strips off any affi xes, permutes the stems, and then attaches the affi xes to the stems in all possible ways.

4.4 Filters

The master item set provides us with an inventory from which we can find positive (grammatical) examples for any language type generated by the system as well as interesting negative examples for any language type. To do so, we filter the master item set, in two steps.

4.4.1 Universal Filters

The first step is the application of 'universal' filters, which mark any item known to be ungrammatical across all language types currently produced by the system. For example, the word order library does not currently provide an analysis of radically non-configurational languages with discontinuous NPs (e.g., Warlpiri (Hale, 1981)). Accordingly, (3) will be ungrammatical across all language types:

(3) det det n1 n2 tv

The universal filter definitions (provided by the developers) each comprise one or more regular expressions, a filter type that specifies how the regular expressions are to be applied, and a list of semantic tags specifying which equivalence classes they apply to. For example, the filter that would catch example (3) above is defined as in (4):

(4)

Filter Type:	reject-unless-match
Regexp:	(det (n1|n2).*det (n1|n2))| (det (n1|n2).*(n1|n2) det)| ((n1|n2) det.*det (n1|n2))| ((n1|n2) det.*(n1|n2) det)
Sem-class:	[semantic classes for all transitive sentences with two determiners.]

We apply each filter to every item in the database. For each filter whose semantic-class value includes the semantic class of the item at hand, we store the result (pass or fail) of the filter on that item. We can then query the database to produce a list of all of the potentially well-formed items.

4.4.2 Specific Filters

The next step is to run the filters that find the grammatical examples for a particular language type. In order to facilitate sampling of the entire language space, we define these filters to be sensitive not to complete language type definitions, but rather to particular features (or small sets of features) of a language type. Thus in addition to the filter type, regular expression, and semantic class fields, the language-specific filters also encode partial descriptions of the language types to which they apply, in the form of feature-value declarations. For example, the filter in (5) plays a role in selecting the correct form of negated sentences for language types with both inflectional and adverbial negation in complementary distribution (like English *n't* and sentential *not*). The first regular expression checks for *neg* surrounded by white space (i.e., the negative adverb) and the second for the negative affixes.

(5)	Filter Type:	reject-if-both-match
	Regexp1:	(\s|^)neg(\s|$)
	Regexp2:	-neg|neg-
	Sem-class:	[sem. classes for all neg. sent.]
	Lg-feat:	and(infl_neg:on,adv_neg:on, multineg:comp)

This filter uses a conjunctive language feature specification (three feature-value pairs that must apply), but disjunctions are also possible. These specifications are converted to disjunctive normal form before further processing.

As with the universal filters, the results of the specific filters are stored in the database. We process each item that passed all of the universal filters with each specific filter. Whenever a filter's semantic-class value matches the semantic-class of the item at hand, we store the value assigned by the filter (pass or fail). We also store the feature-value pairs required by each filter, so that we can look up the relevant filters for a language-type definition.

4.4.3 Recursive Linguistic Phenomena

Making the filters relative to particular semantic classes allows us to use information about the lexical items in the sentences in the definition of the filters. This makes it easier to write regular-expression based filters that can work across many different complete language types. Complications arise, however, in examples illustrating recursive phenomena To handle such phenomena with our finite-state system, we do multiple passes with the filters. All items with coordination are first processed with the coordination filters, and then rewritten to replace any well-formed coordinations with single constituents. These rewritten strings are then processed with the rest of the filters, and we store the results as the results for those filters on the *original* strings.

4.5 Language types

The final kind of information we store in the database is definitions of language types. Even though our system allows us to create test suites for new language types on demand, we still store the language-type definitions of language types we have tested, for future regression testing purposes. When a language type is read in, the list of feature-value pairs defining it is compared to the list of feature-groups declared by the filters. For each group of feature-value pairs present in the language-type definition, we find all of the filters that use that group. We then query the database for all items that pass the filters relevant to the language type. This list of items represents all those in the master item set predicted to be well-formed for this language type. From the complement of this set, we also take a random selection of items to test for overgeneration.

4.6 Validation of grammars

Once we have created the test suite for a particular language type, the developer runs the Matrix customization system to get a starter grammar for the same language type. The test suite is loaded into [incr tsdb()] and processed with the grammar. [incr tsdb()] allows the developer to compare the grammar's output with the test suite at varying levels of detail: Do all and only the items predicted to be well-formed parse? Do they get the same number of readings as predicted? Do they get the semantic representations predicted? A discrepancy at any of these levels points to an error in either the Grammar Matrix or the test suite generation system. The developer can query the database to find which filters passed or failed a particular example as well as to discover the provenance of the example and which phenomena it is meant to test.

This methodology provides the ability to generate test suites for any arbitrary language type on demand. Although this appears to eliminate the need to store the test suites we do, in fact, store information about previous test suites. This allows us to track the evolution of the Grammar Matrix in relation to those particular language types over time.

4.7 Investment and Return

The input required from the developer in order to test any new library is as follows: (1) Seed strings illustrating the range of expressions handled by the new library, organized into equivalence classes. (2) Designated harvester strings for each equivalence class and a grammar or grammars that can parse them to get the target semantic representation. (3) Universal filters specific to the phenomenon and seed strings. (4) Specific filters picking out the right items for each language type. (5) Analysis of discrepancies between the test suite and the generated grammars. This is a substantial investment on the part of the developer but we believe the investment is worth it for the return of being able to validate a library addition and test for any loss of coverage going forward.

Arnold et al. (1994) note that writing grammars to generate test suites is impractical if the test suite generating grammars aren't substantially simpler to write than the 'actual' grammars being tested. Even though this system requires some effort to maintain, we believe the methodology remains practical for two reasons. First, the input required from the developer enumerated above is closely related to the knowledge discovered in the course of building the libraries in the first place. Second, the fact that the filters are sensitive to only particular features of language types means that a relatively small number of filters can create test suites for a very large number of language types.

5 Related Work

Kinyon and Rambow (2003) present an approach to generating test suites on the basis of descriptions of languages. The language descriptions are Meta-Grammar (MG) hierarchies. Their approach appears to be more flexible than the one presented here in some ways, and more constrained in others. It does not need any input strings, but rather produces test items from the language description. In addition, it annotates the output in multiple ways, including phrase structure, dependency structure, and LFG F-structure. On the other hand, there is no apparent provision for creating negative (ungrammatical) test data and it is does not appear possible to compose new MG descriptions on the fly. Furthermore, the focus of the MG test suite work appears to be the generation of test suites for other grammar development projects, but the MGs themselves are crosslinguistic resources in need of validation and testing. An interesting area for future work would be the comparison between the test suites generated by the system described here and the MG test suites.

The key to the test-suite development process proposed here is to leverage the work already being done by the Matrix developers into a largely automated process for creating test-suite items. The information required from the developers is essentially a structured and systematic version of the knowledge that is required for the creation of libraries in the first place. This basic approach, is also the basis for the approach taken in (Bröker, 2000); the specific forms of knowledge leveraged, and the test-suite development strategies used, however, are quite different.

6 Future Work

The addition of the next library to the Grammar Matrix will provide us with an opportunity to try to quantify the effect of this methodology. With the Grammar Matrix and the filters stabilized, the validation of a new library can be carefully tracked. We can try to quantify the number of errors obtained and the source of the errors, e.g., library or filters.

In addition to this kind of quantification and error analysis as a means of validating this methodology, we also intend to undertake a comparison of the test suites created from our database to hand built created for Matrix-derived grammars by students in the multilingual grammar engineering course at the University of Washington.[4] Students in this class each develop grammars for a different language, and create test suites of positive and negative examples as part of their development process. We plan to use the lexical types in the grammars to define a mapping from the surface lexical items used in the test suites to our abstract vocabulary. We can then compare the hand built and autogenerated test suites in order to gauge the thoroughness of the system presented here.

7 Conclusion

The methodology outlined in this paper addresses the three obstacles noted in the introduction: Al-

[4]http://courses.washington.edu/ling567

though the Grammar Matrix core itself isn't a grammar (1), we test it by deriving grammars from it. Since we are testing the derived grammars, we are simultaneously testing both the Matrix core grammar, the libraries, and the customization script. Although there is no single language being modeled from which to draw strings (2), we can nonetheless find a relevant set of strings and associate these strings with annotations of expected well-formedness. The lexical formatives of the strings are drawn from a standardized set of abstract forms. The well-formedness predictions are made on the basis of the system of filters. The system of filters doesn't represent ground truth, but rather a second pathway to the judgments in addition to the direct use of the Matrix-derived starter grammars. These pathways are independent enough that the one can serve as an error check on the other. The space of possible language types remains too large for thorough testing (3). However, since our system allows for the efficient derivation of a test suite for any arbitrary language type, it is inexpensive to sample that language-type space in many different ways.

Acknowledgments

This work has been supported by NSF grant BCS-0644097.

References

Doug Arnold, Martin Rondell, and Frederik Fouvry. 1994. Design and implementation of test suite tools. Technical Report LRE 62-089 D-WP5, University of Essex, UK.

Emily M. Bender and Dan Flickinger. 2005. Rapid prototyping of scalable grammars: Towards modularity in extensions to a language-independent core. In *Proc. IJCNLP-05 (Posters/Demos)*.

Emily M. Bender, Dan Flickinger, and Stephan Oepen. 2002. The grammar matrix: An open-source starter-kit for the rapid development of cross-linguistically consistent broad-coverage precision grammars. In *Proc. the Workshop on Grammar Engineering and Evaluation COLING 2002*, pages 8–14.

Norbert Bröker. 2000. The use of instrumentation in grammar engineering. In *Proc. COLING 2000*, pages 118–124.

Miriam Butt and Tracy Holloway King. 2003. Grammar writing, testing, and evaluation. In *Handbook for Language Engineers*, pages 129–179. CSLI.

Ann Copestake, Dan Flickinger, Carl Pollard, and Ivan A. Sag. 2005. Minimal recursion semantics: An introduction. *Research on Language & Computation*, 3(2–3):281–332.

Ann Copestake. 2002. *Implementing Typed Feature Structure Grammars*. CSLI.

Scott Drellishak and Emily M. Bender. 2005. A coordination module for a crosslinguistic grammar resource. In Stefan Müller, editor, *The Proc. HPSG 2005*, pages 108–128. CSLI.

Dan Flickinger and Emily M. Bender. 2003. Compositional semantics in a multilingual grammar resource. In *Proc. the Workshop on Ideas and Strategies for Multilingual Grammar Development, ESSLLI 2003*, pages 33–42.

Kenneth Hale. 1981. On the position of Warlpiri in the typology of the base. Distributed by Indiana University Linguistics Club, Bloomington.

Lars Hellan and Petter Haugereid. 2003. NorSource: An exercise in Matrix grammar-building design. In *Proc. the Workshop on Ideas and Strategies for Multilingual Grammar Development, ESSLLI 2003*, pages 41–48.

Alexandra Kinyon and Owen Rambow. 2003. The metagrammar: A cross-framework and cross-language test-suite generation tool. In *Proc. 4th International Workshop on Linguistically Interpreted Corpora*.

Valia Kordoni and Julia Neu. 2005. Deep analysis of Modern Greek. In Keh-Yih Su, Jun'ichi Tsujii, and Jong-Hyeok Lee, editors, *Lecture Notes in Computer Science*, volume 3248, pages 674–683. Springer-Verlag.

Stephan Oepen and Daniel P. Flickinger. 1998. Towards systematic grammar profi ling. Test suite technology ten years after. *Journal of Computer Speech and Language*, 12 (4) (Special Issue on Evaluation):411 – 436.

Stephan Oepen. 2002. *Competence and Performance Profiling for Constraint-based Grammars: A New Methodology, Toolkit, and Applications*. Ph.D. thesis, Universität des Saarlandes.

Carl Pollard and Ivan A. Sag. 1994. *Head-Driven Phrase Structure Grammar*. The University of Chicago Press.

Laurie Poulson. 2006. Evaluating a cross-linguistic grammar model: Methodology and gold-standard resource development. Master's thesis, University of Washington.

Local ambiguity packing and discontinuity in German

Berthold Crysmann
DFKI GmbH & Saarland University
Stuhlsatzenhausweg 3
D-66123 Saarbrücken
crysmann@dfki.de

Abstract

We report on recent advances in HPSG parsing of German with local ambiguity packing (Oepen and Carroll, 2000), achieving a speed-up factor of 2 on a balanced test-suite. In contrast to earlier studies carried out for English using the same packing algorithm, we show that restricting semantic features only is insufficient for achieving acceptable runtime performance with a German HPSG grammar. In a series of experiments relating to the three different types of discontinuities in German (head movement, extraction, extraposition), we examine the effects of restrictor choice, ultimately showing that extraction and head movement require partial restriction of the respective features encoding the dependency, whereas full restriction gives best results for extraposition.

1 Introduction

It is a well-known fact that chart parsing without techniques for local ambiguity packing (Earley, 1970) faces a combinatorial explosion of the search space, owing to the (structural) ambiguity imminent to natural language. Thus, identical edges with different internal derivation history can be packed into a single representative for further processing, thereby effectively solving the complexity issue. In context-free grammars augmented with a unification formalism, packing based on the CF symbol equality has been complemented by subsumption- or disjunction-based packing of the associated feature structures (Moore and Alshawi, 1992; Maxwell and Kaplan, 1995). For parsing with constraint-based grammars, such as HPSG, which do not possess an explicit context-free backbone, (Oepen and Carroll, 2000) have proposed an efficient packing algorithm based on feature structure subsumption only.

In contrast to the symbols in context-free grammars, feature structures in unification-based grammars often include information encoding (part of) the derivation history, most notably semantics. In order to achieve successful packing rates, feature restriction (Shieber, 1985) is used to remove this information during creation of the packed parse forest. During the unpacking phase, which operates only on successful parse trees, these features are unified back in again.

For their experiments with efficient subsumption-based packing, (Oepen and Carroll, 2000) experimented with different settings of the packing restrictor for the English Resource Grammar ERG (Copestake and Flickinger, 2000): they found that good packing rates, and overall good performance during forest creation and unpacking were achieved, for the ERG, with partial restriction of the semantics, e.g. keeping index features unrestricted, since they have an impact on external combinatorial potential, but restricting most of the internal MRS representation, including the list of elementary predications and scope constraints. Restriction of syntactically potent features, has thus been found both unnecessary and less efficient.

First experiments in ambiguity packing with a German HPSG grammar (GG; http://gg.dfki.de) revealed that restriction of semantics only does not give rise to any acceptible results in terms of runtime performance. It became clear quite quickly that the

Proceedings of the 5th Workshop on Important Unresolved Matters, pages 144–151,
Ann Arbor, June 2005.

bulk of failing subsumptions impeding creation of a sufficiently compact forest were related to two syntactic features, SLASH and DSL. In German, these features contain references to non-empty valence lists, which eventually wind up encoding derivation history. Using a more aggressive restrictor to eliminate these features during forest creation did not show the desired performance either: owing to massive overgeneration, the resulting forest was either not compact enough, or most of the efficiency gains were wasted on unpacking failures in the second phase.

In this paper we report on recent advances with local ambiguity packing for German, showing how partial restriction can achieve good packing rates at negligible unpacking cost, yielding an overall speedup by a factor of 2, as compared to parsing without ambiguity packing. Running a series of experiments with different restrictor setting for three different features involved with non-local dependencies we examine in detail how the choice of restrictor affects the observable performance. The paper is organised as follows: section 2 will give an overview of the relevant syntactic constructions of German, and their implementation in GG. Section 3 gives a description of the experimental setup (3.1), followed by a discussion of the main results (3.2), detailing how different settings for feature restriction affect parsing performance.

2 Discontinuity in German

Head movement German, in contrast to English is a verb-final language with a verb-second effect, that is, non-finite verbs are standardly placed sentence-finally. In clauses other than complementizer-introduced subclauses and relative clauses, the finite verb surfaces in a clause-initial position (either first or second). Any major constituent may occupy the topic position preceding the finite verb, including subject, complements or modifiers.

Owing to the V2 effect, the parts of a verb cluster are discontinuous. Since both the finite verb and the non-finite verb cluster impose constraints on constituents in the Mittelfeld, standard approaches to German syntax in HPSG assume, since (Kiss and Wesche, 1991), that the initial verb is related to the final verb cluster by means of head movement: clause-finally, a trace is inserted that combines the

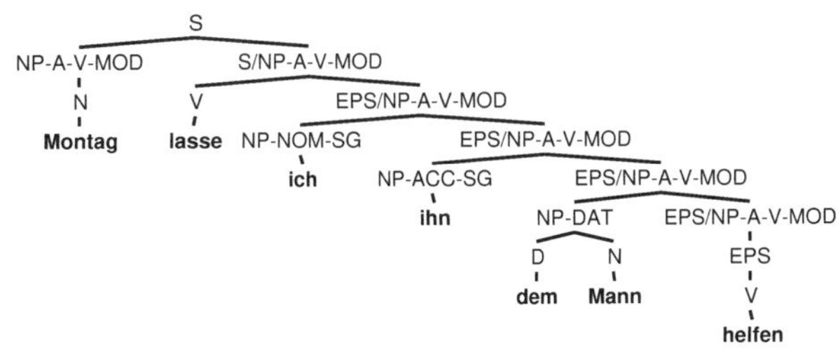

Figure 1: DSL: *Monday let he him the man help*

argument structure of the final cluster with the subcategorisation requirements percolated down from the finite verb using a special feature DSL (="double SLASH"). Arguments in the Mittelfeld are saturated as complements of the clause-final trace. The grammar used here assumes head movement for discontinuous predicates (Crysmann, 2003), following in this respect the earlier implementation by (Müller and Kasper, 2000). In order to relate the initial verb to the verb cluster and its arguments in the Mittelfeld, like the subject and direct object in figure 2, the DSL (or V1) feature must percolate subcategorisation requirements for subject and object, as well as for the verb cluster. At the gap site, the valence information percolated via DSL is inserted into the actual valence lists of the verb trace. Since the requirements are matched against actual arguments found in the Mittelfeld, the valence lists contained in DSL get instantiated to whatever argument it satisfies, thereby creating a partial representation of derivation history. While theoretically, this is just the right behaviour, it has clear repercussions for parsing with ambiguity packing.

Partial VP fronting Another aspect, in which the syntax of German differs from that of English is in the area of extraction: while in English only constituents with a saturated COMPS list can undergo wh-movement, this is not the case in German: as shown in figure 2, the verb `schenken` 'give/donate' has been fronted, leaving its two complements behind.

In HPSG, partial VP fronting is analysed by a combination of two mechanisms (Müller, 1999; Nerbonne, 1994): first, standard argument composition in the verb cluster, following (Hinrichs and Nakazawa, 1990), combined with a standard SLASH-based treatment of long-distance extraction.

Again, since argument composition is performed

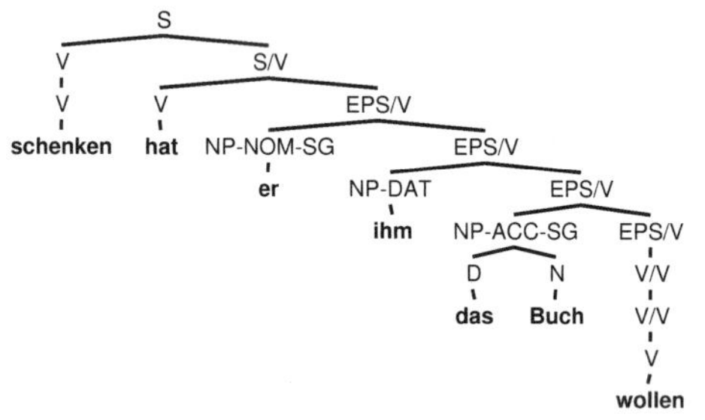

Figure 2: SLASH: *give has he him the book wanted*

by strcuture-sharing, i.e. reentrancy between the valence list of the governing predicate and the unsaturated valence list of the governed predicate, extraction of the governed predicate by means of SLASH percolation carries this reentrancy over into SLASH. From a general linguistic point of view, this is highly desirable, because valence requirements of the extracted verb must be matched against the arguments that satisfy them in the Mittelfeld. The only drawback is, that we are confronted, again, with a syntactic feature containing, among other things, records of derivation history.

3 Evaluation

3.1 Test setup

In order to systematically investigate the effect of restriction of syntactically potent features on the parsing efficiency with local ambiguity packing, we created a test field consisting of 8 different parameter settings (out of 27 logically possible settings): 1 run without packing, 1 run with optimal settings for the three features under consideration, and 2 runs with suboptimal settings for each of the three features.

All test runs were performed on a balanced test suite extracted from the Verbmobil corpus, using 100 items per input length, from sentence length 1 to 22, thus totalling 2200 test items. Although the Verbmobil corpus does contain test sentences of up to 70 words long, their number drops quite quickly from sentence length 23 on.

The parser used in the experiments is the current SVN version of Pet (Callmeier, 2000), running the March 24 version of GG (http://gg.dfki.de; (Müller and Kasper, 2000; Crysmann, 2003; Crysmann, 2005)). Tests were run on an Intel Core Duo machine using a single T2600 CPU at 2.16GHz with 2 GB main memory.

To ensure that we can study parser performance on input of increasing length, we used a rather generous upper limit of 150,000 passive edges. Taking as a guideline the average space consumption per edge of the non-packing parser, we calculated that parsing could still be done comfortably in main memory, i.e., without using swap space.

All measurements were performed using the [incr tsdb()] profiling platform (Oepen and Flickinger, 1998). Parsing times reported are total CPU times (in seconds), including *exhaustive* unpacking of the parse forest, whenever applicable.

3.2 Results

The main result of our study is that local ambiguity packing in constraint-based parsing of German can lead to performance improvements, once feature restriction is extended from purely semantic features to syntactically potent features used to model discontinuity, such as SLASH, DSL, and ANC (see below). We also found that positive performance effects could only be achieved, if SLASH and DSL features were partially restricted in such a way as to only eliminate all records of derivation history (in terms of instatiated subcategorisation lists), while retaining most of the other constraints represented in these features.

Compared to a non-packing baseline parser with feature structure unfilling, we observed an overall speed-up by a factor of 2 with local ambiguity packing on a balanced test suite. As shown by figure 3.2, local ambiguity packing with optimal restrictor settings is effective in taming the combinatorial explosition of the search observed by the non-packing parser.

Analogous to the reduction in search space, performance savings grow continuously with increasing input length: from sentence length 14 onwards (factor 0.84) relative processing time decreases continually up to a factor of 0.27 at sentence length 22. With an average CPU time of 0.69s at sentence length 22, performance is by far better than real-time behaviour. Note further, that the non-packing parser benefits here from a ceiling effect: with 25 out of 2200 test items (1%), the available resources of 150,000 passive chart edges were exhausted before the search space was fully explored. With ambiguity packing under an appropriate restrictor, by contrast, the search space was fully explored.

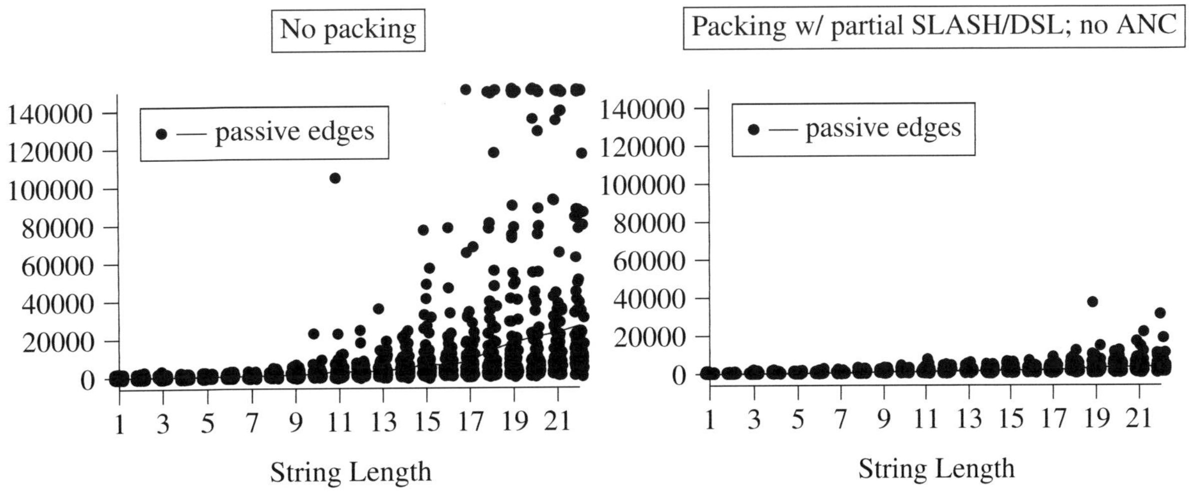

Figure 3: Comparison of chart size relative to input length

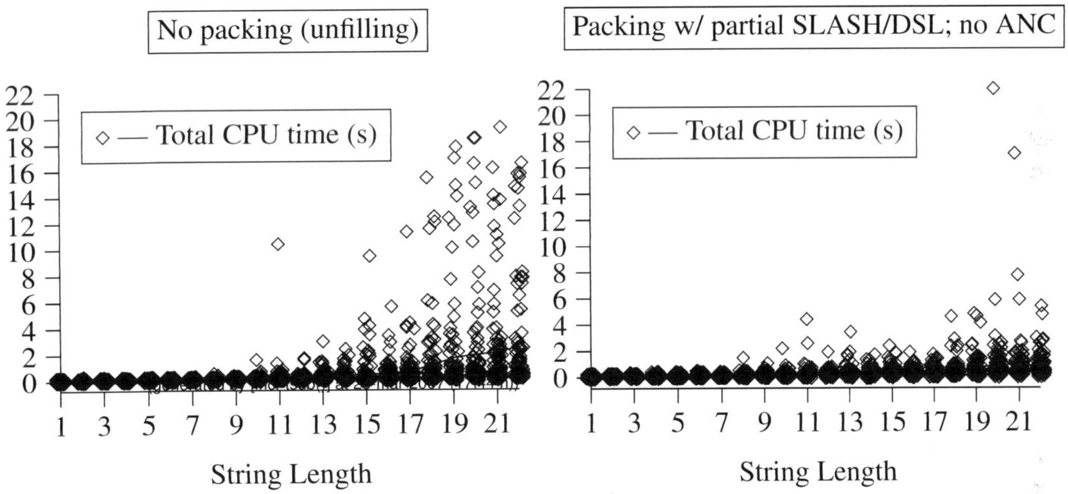

Figure 4: Comparison of processing time relative to input length

Restricting DSL The first syntactically potent feature investigated in these experiments is the feature DSL (or V1), which serves to relate, by means of simulated head movement, the finite verb in clause-second position to the clause-final verb cluster. Essentially, this feature is used to pass down the valence information from the initial verb to the clause-final verb trace, where this valence information is combined with that of the cluster. In the grammar under consideration, verb movement is restricted to discontinuous verb clusters (Crysmann, 2003), i.e., to situations where there is either an overt verb cluster, or a stranded verb particle in the right sentence bracket.

Since actual or putative arguments of the verb trace must be checked against the actual valence information of the V2 verb, derivation history must be carried along as part of the DSL feature.

Obviously, any feature that (partially) encodes derivation history is a potential threat to efficient ambiguity packing. We therefore experimented with three different settings regarding restriction of this feature: full restriction, no restriction, and a partial restriction, where only constraints pertaining to HEAD information of the final cluster were retained, such as category, or form (most crucial for stranded particles).

Results are summarised in table 1. Besides the feature studied here, the restrictor includes the se-

[1]Here, and in the following two tables $\equiv$ stands for packing under equivalence, $\sqsupset$ for proactive packing, $\sqsubset$ for retroactive packing, and $\perp$ for freezing.

	Edges	Time (s)	Unpack (s)	Subsumption	$\equiv$	$\sqsupset$	$\sqsubset$	$\bot$	Factor (time)	Subs. cost	Pack rate
Unfill	6424	0.56	0	0	0	0	0	0	1	N/A	0
Partial DSL	1494	0.28	0.01	36404.15	307.28	193.33	36.67	335.84	**0.5**	67.76	0.36
Full DSL	1832	1.96	0.01	363840.47	186.19	111.31	42.96	251.32	3.5	1068.68	0.19
No DSL	1917	0.61	0.01	106392.57	568.34	484.68	80.8	926.79	1.09	93.83	0.59

Table 1: Performance of packed parsing with different restriction of DSL[1]

mantic features like RELS and HCONS, as in (Oepen and Carroll, 2000), as well as optimal settings for SLASH and ANC.

Leaving DSL unrestricted features the lowest number of packings, amongst the three settings, both in absolute terms, and in relative packings per edge (0.19). As a consequence, average chart size is bigger than with either partially or fully restricted DSL. Another negative behaviour of packed parsing with an unrestricted DSL is the incommensurate number of subsumption tests carried out: at a ratio of 1068.68 subsumption tests per packing, this accounts chiefly for the inefficiency, in particular, when compared to the much more moderate rates of 67.76 and 93.83 achieved with partially restricted and fully restricted DSL. Thus, even though overall chart size is reduced when compared to parsing without ambiguity packing, these savings in space are not sufficient enough to pay off the overhead incurred by testing for subsumption. As a net effect, overall parsing time is 3.5 times longer compared to the non-packing baseline.[2]

Fully restricting DSL by contrast yields a very good packing rate (0.59) at moderate costs in terms of subsumption test per packing (93.83). However, with the grammar not being restrictive enough during forest creation, overall chart size is bigger (1832 passive edges) than with partially restricted DSL (1494). Best results are obtained with partially restricted DSL, where derivation history in terms of actual or putative arguments of the verb trace is removed, but reference to HEAD information of the final cluster is maintained, thereby ensuring that the initial verb only combines with appropriate verb clusters. This not only leads to the most compact chart, but also features the lowest number of subsumption tests, both absolute and relative. In sum, partial restriction of DSL was the only setting that actually beat the baseline defined by parsing without ambiguity packing.

Restricting SLASH The second experiment we carried out relates to the feature SLASH, used for long-distance dependencies. Owing to the V2 effect in German, constituents in the clause-initial preverbal position are typically placed there by means of extraction, including unmarked subjects. This differs quite clearly from English, where standard SVO order does not involve any movement at all. Another striking difference between the two languages is that German, but not English permits fronting of partial VPs: in complex predicates, as witnessed with modals and control verbs, as well as in auxiliary-participle combinations, the downstairs predicate can be fronted, leaving part (or even all) of its complements to be realised in the Mittelfeld. Since German is a non-configurational language, pretty much any combination of fronted vs. stranded complements can be found, in any order. In GG, partial VP fronting is effected by special extraction rules, which removes the valency of pertaing to the fronted verb from the subcategorisation list of the embedding predicate, and inserts it into SLASH. Simultaneously, the remaining complements of the embedding verb are composed with the locally underspecified subcategorisation list of the extracted verbal complement. In order to match the subcategorisation requirement of the extracted verb with those of its complements that are realised in the Mittelfeld, the subcategorisation list must be percolated via SLASH as well. Since elements on the subcategorisation list in SLASH are reentrant with elements on the composed subcategorisation list of the embedding predicate, the former gets specified to the complements that saturate the requirements in the Mittelfeld. As a result, we observe a massive encoding of derivation history in SLASH.

Besides the rules for partial VP fronting, the grammar recognises 3 more extraction rules, one for

[2]Edges in packed parsing are actually more costly than in parsing without ambiguity packing. Since efficient subsumption checking and feature structure unfilling are mutually exclusive, edges in general consume much more space when parsing with ambiguity packing, increasing the cost of copying in unification.

subject, one for non-subject complements, and one for adjuncts. Out of these three, only adjunct extraction rules encode reference to their extraction context in SLASH: since modifiers select the heads they adjoin to via a feature MOD, which is reentrant with the SYNSEM of that head, they inevitably carry along a good deal of that head's derivation history.

We tested three different configurations of the restrictor: one with unrestricted SLASH, one where the entire SLASH feature was removed during forest creation, and a partially restricted variant. This partially restricted variant preserves the full SLASH representation for ordinary subject and complement extraction, but uses an impoverished representation for adjunct extraction and partial VP fronting. Technically, this was achieved by using two SLASH features in parallel: an auxiliary, impoverished _SLASH to be used during forest creation, and the full SLASH feature during unpacking. For adjunct extraction and partial VP fronting, _SLASH contains type restrictions on the head value of the fronted element, together with restrictions on the saturation of valence lists, if applicable.[3] For subject and complement extraction _SLASH contains the same information as SLASH. In sum, partial restriction tries to maximise restrictiveness in those case, where no reference to the extraction context is encoded in SLASH, while at the same time it minimises encoding of derivation history in the other cases, by replacing token identity with somewhat weaker type constraints.

The results of this second experiment are summarised in table 2. Again, we have used optimal settings for DSL and ANC, as established by independent experiments.

Parallel to our observations regarding the restriction of DSL, we observe that performance is worst for packed pasring with a completely unrestricted SLASH feature: not only is the packing rate quite low (0.25 packings per edge), but also the costs for packing in terms of the number of subsumption checks carried out is highest amongst all the experiments reported on in this paper, peaking at 1355.85 subsumption tests per successful packing. The impact on chart size is slightly worse than what we observed with an unrestricted DSL feature. In sum, the suboptimal packing together with the excessive subsumption costs account for the fact that this setting performs more than 8 times as badly as the baseline.

Although packed parsing with fully restricted SLASH performs much better than having SLASH entirely unrestricted, it still falls short of the baseline by a factor of 1.36. This is due to several reasons: first, although the packing rate is good (0.59), the chart is the biggest observed with packed parsing in all the experiments carried out, being more than 2 times as big as the parse chart with optimal restrictor settings. This is mainly due to the fact that the grammar is far to unconstrained during forest creation, allowing too many inconsistent analyses to enter the chart. This is also corroborated by the fact that this is the only test run where we experienced a noticeable increase in unpacking time. Another observation, for which we cannot offer any explanation at present, pertains to the increased cost associated with retroactive packing: the amount of frezing that has to be done for edges masked by retroactive packing is far higher than any other value found in these experiments.

In a separate test run, we used simultaneous full restriction for DSL and SLASH, in order to verify whether our assumtion that the choice of one restrictor is independent from the others. By and large, our hypothesis was confirmed: having both DSL and SLASH fully restricted performed more than 2.5 times worse than full restrcition of SLASH whith partial restriction of DSL.

Still in parallel to our findings regarding DSL, partial restriction of SLASH performs best, confirming that the compromise between restrictiveness and eleimination of derivation history is effective to achieve a runtime behaviour that clearly outperforms the baseline. The packing rate achieved with partial restriction of semantics, DSL and SLASH (0.36) is actually very close to the packing rates reported in (Oepen and Carroll, 2000) for the ERG, which figures around 0.33 for input longer than 10 words. Also, the compactness of the chart with input of increasing length (cf. figure 3.2), and the low number (2) of performance outliers (cf. figure 3.2) suggest that we are indeed close to optimal feature restriction.

Decisions on which features to preserve within SLASH under partial restriction were mainly de-

[3]E.g., modifiers must have saturated valence lists, whereas fronted partial VP constituents may have open valencies relating to complements in the Mittelfeld.

	Edges	Time (s)	Unpack (s)	Subsumption	$\equiv$	$\sqsupset$	$\sqsubset$	$\perp$	Factor (time)	Subs. cost	Pack rate
Unfill	6424	0.56	0	0	0	0	0	0	1	N/A	0
Partial SLASH	1494	0.28	0.01	36404.15	307.28	193.33	36.67	335.84	**0.5**	67.76	0.36
Full SLASH	2187	4.72	0.01	728385.4	314.66	149.21	73.35	826.1	8.43	1355.85	0.25
No SLASH	3435	0.76	0.16	97965.05	883.79	994.87	145.44	2583.51	1.36	48.4	0.59

Table 2: Performance of packed parsing with different restriction of SLASH

rived in a test-debug cycle. We therefore plan to investigate different configurations of partially restricted SLASH in future work.

Restricting ANC The last experiment we carried out relates to the ANC (=ANCHOR) feature used to percolate semantic attachment anchors for relative clause extraposition in the style of (Kiss, 2005; Crysmann, 2005). Using ANC, index and handle of each and every NP are collected and passed up the tree, to be bound by an extraposed relative clause attached to the same subclause.

Again, we tested three different settings: full restriction of all 3 anchor feature (SELF, ACTIVE, INERT), no restriction, and partial retsriction, where the elements on the lists were restricted to *top*, thereby recording only the number of percolated anchors, but not their nature in terms of index features. ANC features encode derivation history in two ways: first, structurally higher anchors (NPs) are represented at the front of the list, whereas more deeply embedded anchors are found further down the list. Second, to control for spurious attachments, only anchors inherited from a left daughter are accessible for binding (ACTIVE), the others remain on the INERT list. Both the order of indices on the lists, list length and the distribution of anchors over ACTIVE and INERT lists partially encode constituent-internal structure.

Results of this experiment are summarised in table 3.

Similar to our two previous experiments, entirely unrestricted ANC behaves worst, but nowhere nearly as bad as having SLASH or DSL unrestricted. In fact, relative packing rates achieved by all three restrictor settings are by and large the same in this experiment. The main difference between unrestricted ANC concerns the overall compactness of the forest and the number of subsumption test performed.

Partial restriction already performs better than unrestricted ANC: since partially restricted ANC does not record the nature of the anchors, at least one way in which derivation history is recorded is effectively masked.

Contrary to our previous experiments, however, partial restriction does not outperform full restriction. Although this finding comes somewhat at a surprise, there is nevertheless a straightforward explanation for the difference in behaviour: while full restriction necessarily improves chart compactness, the adverse effects of full restriction do not come to bear as often as in the case of fully restricted SLASH or DSL, since attachment of extraposed relative clauses presupposes the existence of an already constructed chart edge for the relative clause. In contrast to extraction and head movement, which can be found in practically every sentence-size test item, distribution of relative clauses is comparatively low. Furthermore, constituents serving as fillers for SLASH or DSL dependencies can actually be quite small in size and different in shape, which increases the potential for overgeneration with fully restricted movement features. Relative clauses, on the other hand, are always clause-sized, and their properties depend on the information percolated in ANC only to a very little degree (namely number and gender agreement of the relative pronoun).

4 Conclusion

In this paper, we have explored the effects in the choice of restrictor for HPSG parsing of German with local ambiguity packing. Based on initial observation that a semantics-only restrictor gives suboptimal runtime performance in packed parsing, we found that three features representing discontinuities were mainly responsible for inefficiency with local ambiguity packing, namely SLASH for extraction, DSL for head movement, and ANC for relative clause extraposition, all of which may encode part of the derivation history.

We have shown that partial restriction of SLASH and DSL features, together with full restriction of ANC yields satisfactory parsing performance

	Edges	Time (s)	Unpack (s)	Subsumption	$\equiv$	$\sqsupset$	$\sqsubset$	$\perp$	Factor (time)	Subs. cost	Pack rate
Unfill	6424	0.56	0	0	0	0	0	0	1	N/A	0
Partial ANC	1586	0.37	0.01	55392.34	319.35	232.28	51.34	608.51	0.66	91.87	0.38
Full ANC	1704	0.58	0.01	104699.81	346.35	257.92	64.66	758.27	1.04	156.52	0.39
No ANC	1494	0.28	0.01	36404.15	307.28	193.33	36.67	335.84	**0.5**	67.76	0.36

Table 3: Performance of packed parsing with different restriction of ANC

with ambiguity packing, outperforming the a non-packing baseline parser with feature structure unfilling by a factor of 2. Even more importantly, combinatorial explosion at increasing input length is effectively tamed, such that performance gains improve with longer input sentences.

Acknowledgement

The research reported on in this paper has been carried out as part of the DFKI project Checkpoint, funded by the Federal State of Berlin and the EFRE programme of the European Union. I am also gratefully indepted to Bernd Kiefer for his support of the runtime parser and his expert advice. Many thanks also to Ulrich Callmeier, Dan Flickinger, Stefan Müller, Geert-Jan van Noord, and Stephan Oepen, for their comments and suggestions.

References

Ulrich Callmeier. 2000. PET — a platform for experimentation with efficient HPSG processing techniques. *Journal of Natural Language Engineering*, 6(1):99–108.

Ann Copestake and Dan Flickinger. 2000. An open-source grammar development environment and broad-coverage English grammar using HPSG. In *Proceedings of the Second conference on Language Resources and Evaluation (LREC-2000)*, Athens.

Berthold Crysmann. 2003. On the efficient implementation of German verb placement in HPSG. In *Proceedings of RANLP 2003*, pages 112–116, Borovets, Bulgaria.

Berthold Crysmann. 2005. Relative clause extraposition in German: An efficient and portable implementation. *Research on Language and Computation*, 3(1):61–82.

J. Earley. 1970. An efficient context-free parsing algorithm. *Communications of the ACM*, 13(2):94–102.

E. Hinrichs and T. Nakazawa. 1990. Subcategorization and VP structure in German. In Hughes, Shaun, and Salmons, editors, *Proceedings of the Third Symposium on Germanic Linguistics*, Amsterdam. Benjamins.

Tibor Kiss and Birgit Wesche. 1991. Verb order and head movement. In Otthein Herzog and Claus-Rolf Rollinger, editors, *Text Understanding in LILOG*, number 546 in Lecture Notes in Artificial Intelligence, pages 216–240. Springer-Verlag, Berlin.

Tibor Kiss. 2005. Semantic constraints on relative clause extraposition. *Natural Language and Linguistic Theory*, 23:281–334.

John T. Maxwell and Ronald M. Kaplan. 1995. A method for disjunctive constraint satisfaction. In Mary Dalrymple, Ronald M. Kaplan, John T. Maxwell, III, and Annie Zaenen, editors, *Formal Issues in Lexical-Functional Grammar*, pages 381–401, Stanford University. CSLI.

R. C Moore and H. Alshawi. 1992. Syntactic and semantic processing. In H. Alshawi, editor, *The Core Language Engine*, pages 129–148. The MIT Press, Cambridge, MA.

Stefan Müller and Walter Kasper. 2000. HPSG analysis of German. In Wolfgang Wahlster, editor, *Verbmobil: Foundations of Speech-to-Speech Translation*, pages 238–253. Springer, Berlin.

Stefan Müller. 1999. *Deutsche Syntax — deklarativ*. Linguistische Arbeiten. Niemeyer, Tübingen.

John Nerbonne. 1994. Partial verb phrases and spurious ambiguities. In John Nerbonne, Klaus Netter, and Carl Pollard, editors, *German in Head-Driven Phrase Structure Grammar*, number 46 in Lecture Notes, pages 109–150. CSLI Publications, Stanford University.

Stephan Oepen and John Carroll. 2000. Ambiguity packing in constraint-based parsing - practical results. In *Proceedings of the 1st Conference of the North American Chapter of the Association for Computational Linguistics*, pages 162–169, Seattle, WA.

Stephan Oepen and Dan Flickinger. 1998. Towards systematic grammar profiling. test suite technology ten years after. *Journal of Computer Speech and Language*, 12:411–436.

Stuart Shieber. 1985. Using restriction to extend parsing algorithms for complex feature-based formalisms. In *Proceedings of 23rd meeting of the Association of Computational Linguistics*, pages 145–152, Chicago, IL.

The Corpus and the Lexicon: Standardising Deep Lexical Acquisition Evaluation

Yi Zhang† and **Timothy Baldwin**‡ and **Valia Kordoni**†
† Dept of Computational Linguistics, Saarland University and DFKI GmbH, Germany
‡ Dept of Computer Science and Software Engineering, University of Melbourne, Australia
{yzhang,kordoni}@coli.uni-sb.de
tim@csse.unimelb.edu.au

Abstract

This paper is concerned with the standardisation of evaluation metrics for lexical acquisition over precision grammars, which are attuned to actual parser performance. Specifically, we investigate the impact that lexicons at varying levels of lexical item precision and recall have on the performance of pre-existing broad-coverage precision grammars in parsing, i.e., on their coverage and accuracy. The grammars used for the experiments reported here are the LinGO English Resource Grammar (ERG; Flickinger (2000)) and JACY (Siegel and Bender, 2002), precision grammars of English and Japanese, respectively. Our results show convincingly that traditional F-score-based evaluation of lexical acquisition does not correlate with actual parsing performance. What we argue for, therefore, is a recall-heavy interpretation of F-score in designing and optimising automated lexical acquisition algorithms.

1 Introduction

Deep processing is the process of applying rich linguistic resources within NLP tasks, to arrive at a detailed (=deep) syntactic and semantic analysis of the data. It is conventionally driven by deep grammars, which encode linguistically-motivated predictions of language behaviour, are usually capable of both parsing and generation, and generate a high-level semantic abstraction of the input data. While enjoying a resurgence of interest due to advances in parsing algorithms and stochastic parse pruning/ranking, deep grammars remain an underutilised resource predominantly because of their lack of coverage/robustness in parsing tasks. As noted in previous work (Baldwin et al., 2004), a significant cause of diminished coverage is the lack of lexical coverage.

Various attempts have been made to ameliorate the deficiencies of hand-crafted lexicons. More recently, there has been an explosion of interest in deep lexical acquisition (DLA; (Baldwin, 2005; Zhang and Kordoni, 2006; van de Cruys, 2006)) for broad-coverage deep grammars, either by exploiting the linguistic information encoded in the grammar itself (*in vivo*), or by using secondary language resources (*in vitro*). Such approaches provide (semi-)automatic ways of extending the lexicon with minimal (or no) human interference.

One stumbling block in DLA research has been the lack of standardisation in evaluation, with commonly-used evaluation metrics including:

- *Type precision*: the proportion of correctly hypothesised lexical entries
- *Type recall*: the proportion of gold-standard lexical entries that are correctly hypothesised
- *Type F-measure*: the harmonic mean of the type precision and type recall
- *Token Accuracy*: the accuracy of the lexical entries evaluated against their token occurrences in gold-standard corpus data

It is often the case that the different measures lead to significantly different assessments of the quality of DLA, even for a given DLA approach. Additionally, it is far from clear how the numbers generated by these evaluation metrics correlate with actual parsing performance when the output of a given DLA method is used. This makes standardised comparison among the various different approaches to DLA very difficult, if not impossible. It is far from clear which evaluation metrics are more indicative of the true "goodness" of the lexicon. The aim of this research, therefore, is to analyse how the different evaluation metrics correlate with actual parsing performance using a given lexicon, and to work towards

Proceedings of the 5th Workshop on Important Unresolved Matters, pages 152–159,
Ann Arbor, June 2005.

a standardised evaluation framework for future DLA research to ground itself in.

In this paper, we explore the utility of different evaluation metrics at predicting parse performance through a series of experiments over two broad coverage grammars: the English Resource Grammar (ERG; Flickinger (2000)) and JACY (Siegel and Bender, 2002). We simulate the results of DLA by generating lexicons at different levels of precision and recall, and test the impact of such lexicons on grammar coverage and accuracy related to gold-standard treebank data. The final outcome of this analysis is a proposed evaluation framework for future DLA research.

The remainder of the paper is organised as follows: Section 2 reviews previous work on DLA for the robust parsing task; Section 3 describes the experimental setup; Section 4 presents the experiment results; Section 5 analyses the experiment results; Section 6 concludes the paper.

2 Lexical Acquisition in Deep Parsing

Hand-crafted large-scale grammars are error-prone. An error can be roughly classified as *undergenerating* (if it prevents a grammatical sentence from being generated/parsed) or *overgenerating* (if it allows an ungrammatical sentence to be generated/parsed). Hence, errors in deep grammar lexicons can be classified into two categories: i) a lexical entry is missing for a specific lexeme; and ii) an erroneous lexical entry enters the lexicon. The former error type will cause the grammar to fail to parse/generate certain sentences (i.e. undergenerate), leading to a loss in coverage. The latter error type will allow the grammar to parse/generate inappropriate sentences (i.e. overgenerate), potentially leading to a loss in accuracy. In the first instance, we will be unable to parse sentences involving a given lexical item if it is missing from our lexicon, i.e. coverage will be affected assuming the lexical item of interest occurs in a given corpus. In the second instance, the impact is indeterminate, as certain lexical items may violate constraints in the grammar and never be licenced, whereas others may be licenced more liberally, generating competing (incorrect) parses for a given input and reducing parse accuracy. It is these two competing concerns that we seek to quantify in this research.

Traditionally, errors in the grammar are detected manually by the grammar developers. This is usually done by running the grammar over a carefully designed test suite and inspecting the outputs. This procedure becomes less reliable as the grammar gets larger. Also we can never expect to attain complete lexical coverage, due to language evolution and the effects of domain/genre. A static, manually compiled lexicon, therefore, becomes inevitably insufficient when faced with open domain text.

In recent years, some approaches have been developed to (semi-)automatically detect and/or repair the lexical errors in linguistic grammars. Such approaches can be broadly categorised as either symbolic or statistical.

Erbach (1990), Barg and Walther (1998) and Fouvry (2003) followed a unification-based symbolic approach to unknown word processing for constraint-based grammars. The basic idea is to use underspecified lexical entries, namely entries with fewer constraints, to parse whole sentences, and generate the "real" lexical entries afterwards by collecting information from the full parses. However, lexical entries generated in this way may be either too general or too specific. Underspecified lexical entries with fewer constraints allow more grammar rules to be applied while parsing, and fully-underspecified lexical entries are computationally intractable. The whole procedure gets even more complicated when two unknown words occur next to each other, potentially allowing almost any constituent to be constructed. The evaluation of these proposals has tended to be small-scale and somewhat brittle. No concrete results have been presented relating to the improvement in grammar performance, either for parsing or for generation.

Baldwin (2005) took a statistical approach to automated lexical acquisition for deep grammars. Focused on generalising the method of deriving DLA models on various secondary language resources, Baldwin used a large set of binary classifiers to predict whether a given unknown word is of a particular lexical type. This data-driven approach is grammar independent and can be scaled up for large grammars. Evaluation was via type precision, type recall, type F-measure and token accuracy, resulting in different interpretations of the data depending on the evaluation metric used.

Zhang and Kordoni (2006) tackled the robustness problem of deep processing from two aspects. They employed error mining techniques in order to semi-automatically detect errors in deep grammars. They then proposed a maximum entropy model based lexical type predictor, to generate new lexical entries on the fly. Evaluation focused on the accuracy of the lexical type predictor over unknown words, not the overall goodness of the resulting lexicon. Similarly to Baldwin (2005), the methods are applicable to other constraint-based lexicalist grammars, but no direct measurement of the impact on grammar performance was attempted.

van de Cruys (2006) took a similar approach over the Dutch Alpino grammar (cf. Bouma et al. (2001)). Specifically, he proposed a method for lexical acquisition as an extension to automatic parser error detection, based on large amounts of raw text (cf. van Noord (2004)). The method was evaluated using type precision, type recall and type F-measure. Once again, however, these numbers fail to give us any insight into the impact of lexical acquisition on parser performance.

Ideally, we hope the result of DLA to be both accurate and complete. However, in reality, there will always be a trade-off between coverage and parser accuracy. Exactly how these two concerns should be balanced up depends largely on what task the grammar is applied to (i.e. parsing or generation). In this paper, we focus exclusively on the parsing task.[1]

3 Experimental Setup

In this research, we wish to evaluate the impact of different lexicons on grammar performance. By grammar performance, we principally mean coverage and accuracy. However, it should be noted that the efficiency of the grammar—e.g. the average number of edges in the parse chart, the average time to parse a sentence and/or the average number of analyses per sentence—is also an important performance measurement which we expect the quality of the lexicon to impinge on. Here, however, we expect to be able to call on external processing optimisations[2] to dampen any loss in efficiency, in a way which we cannot with coverage and accuracy.

3.1 Resources

In order to get as representative a set of results as possible, we choose to run the experiment over two large-scale HPSGs (Pollard and Sag, 1994), based on two distinct languages.

The *LinGO English Resource Grammar* (ERG; Flickinger (2000)) is a broad-coverage, linguistically precise HPSG-based grammar of English, which represents the culmination of more than 10 person years of (largely) manual effort. We use the *jan-06* version of the grammar, which contains about 23K lexical entries and more than 800 leaf lexical types.

JACY (Siegel and Bender, 2002) is a broad-coverage linguistically precise HPSG-based grammar of Japanese. In our experiment, we use the November 2005 version of the grammar, which contains about 48K lexical entries and more than 300 leaf lexical types.

It should be noted in HPSGs, the grammar is made up of two basic components: the grammar rules/type hierarchy, and the lexicon (which interfaces with the type hierarchy via leaf lexical types). This is different to strictly lexicalised formalisms like LTAG and CCG, where essentially all linguistic description resides in individual lexical entries in the lexicon. The manually compiled grammars in our experiment are also intrinsically different to grammars automatically induced from treebanks (e.g. that used in the Charniak parser (Charniak, 2000) or the various CCG parsers (Hockenmaier, 2006)). These differences sharply differentiate our work from previous research on the interaction between lexical acquisition and parse performance.

Furthermore, to test the grammar precision and accuracy, we use two treebanks: Redwoods (Oepen et al., 2002) for English and Hinoki (Bond et al., 2004) for Japanese. These treebanks are so-called dynamic treebanks, meaning that they can be (semi-)automatically updated when the grammar is updated. This feature is especially useful when we want to evaluate the grammar performance with different lexicon configurations. With conventional treebanks, our experiment is difficult (if not impossible) to perform as the static trees in the treebank cannot be easily synchronised to the evolution of the grammar, meaning that we cannot regenerate gold-standard parse trees relative to a given lexicon (especially when for reduced recall where there is no guarantee we will be able to produce all of the parses in the 100% recall gold-standard). As a result, it is extremely difficult to faithfully update the statistical models.

The Redwoods treebank we use is the *6th growth*,

[1]In generation, we tend to have a semantic representation as input, which is linked to pre-existing lexical entries. Hence, lexical acquisition has no direct impact on generation.

[2]For example, (van Noord, 2006) shows that a HMM POS tagger trained on the parser outputs can greatly reduce the lexical ambiguity and enhance the parser efficiency, without an observable decrease in parsing accuracy.

which is synchronised with the *jan-06* version of the ERG. It contains about 41K test items in total.

The Hinoki treebank we use is updated for the November 2005 version of the JACY grammar. The *"Rei"* sections we use in our experiment contains 45K test items in total.

3.2 Lexicon Generation

To simulate the DLA results at various levels of precision and recall, a random lexicon generator is used. In order to generate a new lexicon with specific precision and recall, the generator randomly retains a portion of the gold-standard lexicon, and generates a pre-determined number of erroneous lexical entries.

More specifically, for each grammar we first extract a subset of the lexical entries from the lexicon, each of which has at least one occurrence in the treebank. This subset of lexical entries is considered to be the gold-standard lexicon (7,156 entries for the ERG, 27,308 entries for JACY).

Given the gold-standard lexicon L, the target precision P and recall R, a new lexicon L' is created, which is composed of two disjoint subsets: the retained part of the gold-standard lexicon G, and the erroneous entries E. According to the definitions of precision and recall:

$$P = \frac{|G|}{|L'|} \quad (1) \qquad R = \frac{|G|}{|L|} \quad (2)$$

and the fact that:

$$|L'| = |G| + |E| \quad (3)$$

we get:

$$|G| = |L| \cdot R \quad (4)$$

$$|E| = |L| \cdot R \cdot (\frac{1}{P} - 1) \quad (5)$$

To retain a specific number of entries from the gold-standard lexicon, we randomly select $|G|$ entries based on the combined probabilistic distribution of the corresponding lexeme and lexical types.[3] We obtain the probabilistic distribution of lexemes from large corpora (BNC for English and Mainichi Shimbun [1991-2000] for Japanese), and the distribution of lexical types from the corresponding treebanks. For each lexical entry $e(l, t)$ in the gold-standard lexicon with lexeme l and lexical type t, the combined probability is:

$$p(e(l,t)) = \frac{C_L(l) \cdot C_T(t)}{\sum_{e'(l',t') \in L} C_L(l') \cdot C_T(t')} \quad (6)$$

The erroneous entries are generated in the same way among all possible combinations of lexemes and lexical types. The difference is that only open category types and less frequent lexemes are used for generating new entries (e.g. we wouldn't expect to learn a new lexical item for the lexeme *the* or the lexical type `d_-_the_le` in English). In our experiment, we consider lexical types with more than a predefined number of lexical entries (20 for the ERG, 50 for JACY) in the gold-standard lexicon to be open-class lexical types; the upper-bound threshold on token frequency is set to 1000 for English and 537 for Japanese, i.e. lexemes which occur more frequently than this are excluded from lexical acquisition under the assumption that the grammar developers will have attained full coverage of lexical items for them.

For each grammar, we then generate 9 different lexicons at varying precision and recall levels, namely 60%, 80%, and 100%.

3.3 Parser Coverage

Coverage is an important grammar performance measurement, and indicates the proportion of inputs for which a correct parse was obtained (adjudged relative to the gold-standard parse data in the treebanks). In our experiment, we adopt a weak definition of coverage as "obtaining at least one spanning tree". The reason for this is that we want to obtain an estimate for novel data (for which we do not have gold-standard parse data) of the relative number of strings for which we can expect to be able to produce at least one spanning parse. This weak definition of coverage actually provides an upper bound estimate of coverage in the strict sense, and saves the effort to manually evaluate the correctness of the parses. Past evaluations (e.g. Baldwin et al. (2004)) have shown that the grammars we are dealing with are relatively precise. Based on this, we claim that our results for parse coverage provide a reasonable estimate indication of parse coverage in the strict sense of the word.

In principle, coverage will only decrease when the lexicon recall goes down, as adding erroneous entries should not invalidate the existing analyses. However, in practice, the introduction of erroneous entries increases lexical ambiguity dramati-

[3] For simplicity, we assume mutual independence of the lexemes and lexical types.

P \ R	0.6			0.8			1.0		
	C	E	A	C	E	A	C	E	A
0.6	4294	2862	7156	5725	3817	9542	7156	4771	11927
0.8	4294	1073	5367	5725	1431	7156	7156	1789	8945
1.0	4294	0	4294	5725	0	5725	7156	0	7156

Table 1: Different lexicon configurations for the ERG with the number of correct (C), erroneous (E) and combined (A) entries at each level of precision (P) and recall (R)

P \ R	0.6			0.8			1.0		
	C	E	A	C	E	A	C	E	A
0.6	16385	10923	27308	21846	14564	36410	27308	18205	45513
0.8	16385	4096	20481	21846	5462	27308	27308	6827	34135
1.0	16385	0	16385	21846	0	21846	27308	0	27308

Table 2: Different lexicon configurations for JACY with the number of correct (C), erroneous (E) and combined (A) entries at each level of precision (P) and recall (R)

cally, readily causing the parser to run out of memory. Moreover, some grammars use recursive unary rules which are triggered by specific lexical types. Here again, erroneous lexical entries can lead to "fail to parse" errors.

Given this, we run the coverage tests for the two grammars over the corresponding treebanks: Redwoods and Hinoki. The maximum number of passive edges is set to 10K for the parser. We used `[incr tsdb()]` (Oepen, 2001) to handle the different lexicon configurations and data sets, and `PET` (Callmeier, 2000) for parsing.

3.4 Parser Accuracy

Another important measurement of grammar performance is accuracy. Deep grammars often generate hundreds of analyses for an input, suggesting the need for some means of selecting the most probable analysis from among them. This is done with the parse disambiguation model proposed in Toutanova et al. (2002), with accuracy indicating the proportion of inputs for which we are able to accurately select the correct parse.

The disambiguation model is essentially a maximum entropy (ME) based ranking model. Given an input sentence s with possible analyses $t_1 \dots t_k$, the conditional probability for analysis t_i is given by:

$$P(t_i|s) = \frac{\exp \sum_{j=1}^{m} f_j(t_i)\lambda_j}{\sum_{i'=1}^{k} \exp \sum_{j=1}^{m} f_j(t_{i'})\lambda_j} \quad (7)$$

where $f_1 \dots f_m$ are the features and $\lambda_1 \dots \lambda_m$ are the corresponding parameters. When ranking parses, $\sum_{j=1}^{m} f_j(t_i)\lambda_j$ is the indicator of "goodness". Drawing on the discriminative nature of the ME models, various feature types can be incorporated into the model. In combination with the dynamic treebanks where the analyses are (semi-)automatically disambiguated, the models can be easily re-trained when the grammar is modified.

For each lexicon configuration, after the coverage test, we do an automatic treebank update. During the automatic treebank update, only those new parse trees which are comparable to the active trees in the gold-standard treebank are marked as correct readings. All other trees are marked as inactive and deemed as overgeneration of the grammar. The ME-based parse disambiguation models are trained/evaluated using these updated treebanks with 5-fold cross validation. Since we are only interested in the difference between different lexicon configurations, we use the simple *PCFG-S* model from (Toutanova et al., 2002), which incorporates PCFG-style features from the derivation tree of the parse. The accuracy of the disambiguation model is calculated by top analysis exact matching (i.e. a ranking is only considered correct if the top ranked analysis matches the gold standard prefered reading in the treebank).

All the Hinoki *Rei* noun sections (about 25K items) were used in the accuracy evaluation for JACY. However, due to technical limitations, only the *jh* sections (about 6K items) of the Redwoods Treebank were used for training/testing the disambiguation models for the ERG.

4 Experiment Results

The experiment consumes a considerable amount of computational resources. For each lexicon config-

P \ R	0.6	0.8	1.0
0.6	44.56%	66.88%	75.51%
0.8	42.18%	65.82%	75.86%
1.0	40.45%	66.19%	76.15%

Table 3: Parser coverage of JACY with different lexicons

P \ R	0.6	0.8	1.0
0.6	27.86%	39.17%	79.66%
0.8	27.06%	37.42%	79.57%
1.0	26.34%	37.18%	79.33%

Table 4: Parser coverage of the ERG with different lexicons

uration of a given grammar, we need to i) process (parse) all the items in the treebank, ii) compare the resulting trees with the gold-standard trees and update the treebank, and iii) retrain the disambiguation models over 5 folds of cross validation. Given the two grammars with 9 configurations each, the entire experiment takes over 1 CPU month and about 120GB of disk space.

The coverage results are shown in Table 3 and Table 4 for JACY and the ERG, respectively.[4] As expected, we see a significant increase in grammar coverage when the lexicon recall goes up. This increase is more significant for the ERG than JACY, mainly because the JACY lexicon is about twice as large as the ERG lexicon; thus, the most frequent entries are still in the lexicons even with low recall.

When the lexicon recall is fixed, the grammar coverage does not change significantly at different levels of lexicon precision. Recall that we are not evaluating the correctness of such parses at this stage.

It is clear that the increase in lexicon recall boosts the grammar coverage, as we would expect. The precision of the lexicon does not have a large influence on coverage. This result confirms that with DLA (where we hope to enhance lexical coverage relative to a given corpus/domain), the coverage of the grammar can be enhanced significantly.

The accuracy results are obtained with 5-fold cross validation, as shown in Table 5 and Table 6

[4]Note that even with the lexicons at 100% precision and recall level, there is no guarantee of 100% coverage. As the contents of the Redwoods and Hinoki treebanks were determined independently of the respective grammars, rather than the grammars being induced from the treebanks e.g., they both still contain significant numbers of strings for which the grammar cannot produce a correct analysis.

P-R	#ptree	Avg.	σ
060-060	13269	62.65%	0.89%
060-080	19800	60.57%	0.83%
060-100	22361	59.61%	0.63%
080-060	14701	63.27%	0.62%
080-080	23184	60.97%	0.48%
080-100	27111	60.04%	0.56%
100-060	15696	63.91%	0.64%
100-080	26859	61.47%	0.68%
100-100	31870	60.48%	0.71%

Table 5: Accuracy of disambiguation models for JACY with different lexicons

P-R	#ptree	Avg.	σ
060-060	737	71.11%	3.55%
060-080	1093	63.94%	2.75%
060-100	3416	60.92%	1.23%
080-060	742	70.07%	1.50%
080-080	1282	61.81%	3.60%
080-100	3842	59.05%	1.30%
100-060	778	69.76%	4.62%
100-080	1440	60.59%	2.64%
100-100	4689	57.03%	1.36%

Table 6: Accuracy of disambiguation models for the ERG with different lexicons

for JACY and the ERG, respectively. When the lexicon recall goes up, we observe a small but steady decrease in the accuracy of the disambiguation models, for both JACY and ERG. This is generally a side effect of change in coverage: as the grammar coverage goes up, the parse trees become more diverse, and are hence harder to discriminate.

When the recall is fixed and the precision of the lexicon goes up, we observe a very small accuracy gain for JACY (around 0.5% for each 20% increase in precision). This shows that the grammar accuracy gain is limited as the precision of the lexicon increases, i.e. that the disambiguation model is remarkably robust to the effects of noise.

It should be noted that for the ERG we failed to observe any accuracy gain at all with a more precise lexicon. This is partly due to the limited size of the updated treebanks. For the lexicon configuration $060-060$, we obtained only 737 preferred readings/trees to train/test the disambiguation model over. The 5-fold cross validation results vary within a margin of 10%, which means that the models are still not converging. However, the result does confirm that there is no significant gain in grammar accuracy with a higher precision lexicon.

Finally, we combine the coverage and accuracy scores into a single F-measure ($\beta = 1$) value. The results are shown in Figure 1. Again we see that the difference in lexicon recall has a more significant impact on the overall grammar performance than precision.

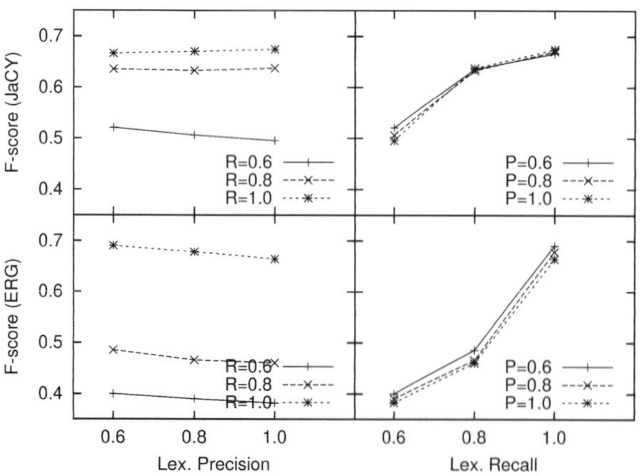

Figure 1: Grammar performance (F-score) with different lexicons

5 Discussion

5.1 Is F-measure a good metric for DLA evaluation?

As mentioned in Section 2, a number of relevant earlier works have evaluated DLA results via the unweighted F-score (relative to type precision and recall). This implicitly assumes that the precision and recall of the lexicon are equally important. However, this is clearly not the case as we can see in the results of the grammar performance. For example, the lexicon configurations 060 – 100 and 100 – 060 of JACY (i.e. 60% precision, 100% recall vs. 100% precision, 60% recall, respectively) have the same unweighted F-scores, but their corresponding overall grammar performance (parser F-score) differs by up to 17%.

5.2 Does precision matter?

The most interesting finding in our experiment is that the precision of the deep lexicon does not appear to have a significant impact on grammar accuracy. This is contrary to the earlier predominant belief that deep lexicons should be as accurate as possible. This belief is derived mainly from observation of grammars with relatively small lexicons. In such small lexicons, the closed-class lexical entries and frequent entries (which comprise the "core" of the lexicon) make up a large proportion of lexical entries. Hence, any loss in precision means a significant degradation of the "core" lexicon, which leads to performance loss of the grammar. For example, we find that the inclusion of one or two erroneous entries for frequent closed-class lexical type words (such as *the*, or *of* in English, for instance) may easily "break" the parser.

However, in state-of-the-art broad-coverage deep grammars such as JACY and ERG, the lexicons are much larger. They usually have more or less similar "cores" to the smaller lexicons, but with many more open-class lexical entries and less frequent entries, which compose the "peripheral" parts of the lexicons. In our experiment, we found that more than 95% of the lexical entries belong to the top 5% of the open-class lexical types. The bigger the lexicon is, the larger the proportion of lexical entries that belong to the "peripheral" lexicon.

In our experiment, we only change the "peripheral" lexicon by creating/removing lexical entries for less frequent lexemes and open-class lexical types, leaving the "core" lexicon intact. Therefore, a more accurate interpretation of the experimental results is that the precision of the *open type* and *less frequent* lexical entries does not have a large impact on the grammar performance, but their recall has a crucial effect on grammar coverage.

The consequence of this finding is that the balance between precision and recall in the deep lexicon should be decided by their impact on the task to which the grammar is applied. In research on automated DLA, the motivation is to enhance the robustness/coverage of the grammars. This work shows that grammar performance is very robust over the inevitable errors introduced by the DLA, and that more emphasis should be placed on recall.

Again, caution should be exercised here. We do *not* mean that by blindly adding lexical entries without worrying about their correctness, the performance of the grammar will be monotonically enhanced – there will almost certainly be a point at which noise in the lexicon swamps the parse chart and/or leads to unacceptable levels of spurious ambiguity. Also, the balance between precision and recall of the lexicon will depend on various expectations of the grammarians/lexicographers, i.e. the linguistic precision and generality, which is beyond the scope of this paper.

As a final word of warning, the absolute grammar performance change that a given level of lexicon type precision and recall brings about will obviously depend on the grammar. In looking across two grammars from two very different languages, we are confident of the robustness of our results (at least for grammars of the same ilk) and the conclusions that we have drawn from them. For any novel grammar and/or formalism, however, the performance change should ideally be quantified through a set of experiments with different lexicon configurations, based on the procedure outlined here. Based on this, it should be possible to find the optimal balance between the different lexicon evaluation metrics.

6 Conclusion

In this paper, we have investigated the relationship between evaluation metrics for deep lexical acquisition and grammar performance in parsing tasks. The results show that traditional DLA evaluation based on F-measure is not reflective of grammar performance. The precision of the lexicon appears to have minimal impact on grammar accuracy, and therefore recall should be emphasised more greatly in the design of deep lexical acquisition techniques.

References

Timothy Baldwin, Emily Bender, Dan Flickinger, Ara Kim, and Stephan Oepen. 2004. Road-testing the English Resource Grammar over the British National Corpus. In *Proc. of the fourth international conference on language resources and evaluation (LREC 2004)*, pages 2047–2050, Lisbon, Portugal.

Timothy Baldwin. 2005. Bootstrapping deep lexical resources: Resources for courses. In *Proc. of the ACL-SIGLEX 2005 workshop on deep lexical acquisition*, pages 67–76, Ann Arbor, USA.

Petra Barg and Markus Walther. 1998. Processing unknown words in HPSG. In *Proc. of the 36th Conference of the ACL and the 17th International Conference on Computational Linguistics*, pages 91–95, Montreal, Canada.

Francis Bond, Sanae Fujita, Chikara Hashimoto, Kaname Kasahara, Shigeko Nariyama, Eric Nichols, Akira Ohtani, Takaaki Tanaka, and Shigeaki Amano. 2004. The Hinoki treebank: a treebank for text understanding. In *Proc. of the first international joint conference on natural language processing (IJCNLP04)*, pages 554–562, Hainan, China.

Gosse Bouma, Gertjan van Noord, and Robert Malouf. 2001. Alpino: wide-coverage computational analysis of Dutch. In *Computational linguistics in the Netherlands 2000*, pages 45–59, Tilburg, the Netherlands.

Ulrich Callmeier. 2000. PET – a platform for experimentation with efficient HPSG processing techniques. *Natural Language Engineering*, 6(1):99–107.

Eugene Charniak. 2000. A maximum entropy-based parser. In *Proc. of the 1st Annual Meeting of the North American Chapter of Association for Computational Linguistics (NAACL2000)*, Seattle, USA.

Gregor Erbach. 1990. Syntactic processing of unknown words. IWBS Report 131, IBM, Stuttgart, Germany.

Dan Flickinger. 2000. On building a more efficient grammar by exploiting types. *Natural Language Engineering*, 6(1):15–28.

Frederik Fouvry. 2003. Lexicon acquisition with a large-coverage unification-based grammar. In *Proc. of the 10th Conference of the European Chapter of the Association for Computational Linguistics (EACL 2003)*, pages 87–90, Budapest, Hungary.

Julia Hockenmaier. 2006. Creating a CCGbank and a wide-coverage CCG lexicon for German. In *Proc. of the 21st International Conference on Computational Linguistics and 44th Annual Meeting of the Association for Computational Linguistics*, pages 505–512, Sydney, Australia.

Stephan Oepen, Kristina Toutanova, Stuart Shieber, Christopher Manning, Dan Flickinger, and Thorsten Brants. 2002. The LinGO Redwoods treebank: Motivation and preliminary applications. In *Proc. of the 17th international conference on computational linguistics (COLING 2002)*, Taipei, Taiwan.

Stephan Oepen. 2001. [incr tsdb()] — competence and performance laboratory. User manual. Technical report, Computational Linguistics, Saarland University, Saarbrücken, Germany.

Carl Pollard and Ivan Sag. 1994. *Head-Driven Phrase Structure Grammar*. University of Chicago Press, Chicago, USA.

Melanie Siegel and Emily Bender. 2002. Efficient deep processing of Japanese. In *Proc. of the 3rd Workshop on Asian Language Resources and International Standardization*, Taipei, Taiwan.

Kristina Toutanova, Christoper Manning, Stuart Shieber, Dan Flickinger, and Stephan Oepen. 2002. Parse ranking for a rich HPSG grammar. In *Proc. of the First Workshop on Treebanks and Linguistic Theories (TLT2002)*, pages 253–263, Sozopol, Bulgaria.

Tim van de Cruys. 2006. Automatically extending the lexicon for parsing. In *Proc. of the eleventh ESSLLI student session*, pages 180–191, Malaga, Spain.

Gertjan van Noord. 2004. Error mining for wide-coverage grammar engineering. In *Proc. of the 42nd Meeting of the Association for Computational Linguistics (ACL'04), Main Volume*, pages 446–453, Barcelona, Spain.

Gertjan van Noord. 2006. At Last Parsing Is Now Operational. In *Actes de la 13e conference sur le traitement automatique des langues naturelles (TALN06)*, pages 20–42, Leuven, Belgium.

Fei Xia, Chung-Hye Han, Martha Palmer, and Aravind Joshi. 2001. Automatically extracting and comparing lexicalized grammars for different languages. In *Proc. of the 17th International Joint Conference on Artificial Intelligence (IJCAI-2001)*, pages 1321–1330, Seattle, USA.

Yi Zhang and Valia Kordoni. 2006. Automated deep lexical acquisition for robust open texts processing. In *Proc. of the fifth international conference on language resources and evaluation (LREC 2006)*, pages 275–280, Genoa, Italy.

Author Index